Claude-Hélène Mayer

Artificial Walls

South African Narratives on Conflict, Difference and Identity

An Exploratory Study in Post-Apartheid South Africa

Claude-Hélène Mayer

ARTIFICIAL WALLS

South African Narratives on Conflict, Difference and Identity

An Exploratory Study in Post-Apartheid South Africa

ibidem-Verlag
Stuttgart

Bibliografische Information Der Deutschen Bibliothek

Die Deutsche Bibliothek verzeichnet diese Publikation in der Deutschen Nationalbibliografie; detaillierte bibliografische Daten sind im Internet über <http://dnb.ddb.de> abrufbar.

∞

Gedruckt auf alterungsbeständigem, säurefreien Papier
Printed on acid-free paper

ISBN: 3-89821-431-1

© *ibidem*-Verlag
Stuttgart 2005
Alle Rechte vorbehalten

Printed in Germany

Dissertation

For the Doctorate in Social Sciences
Department of Social Sciences
Georg August Universität Göttingen
Germany

Supervised by
PD Dr. Röttger-Rössler
Prof. Dr. Braukämper

2004

Translated by
Annette Braden-Rozier

The future belongs to those
who believe in the beauty of their dreams.

Eleonore Roosevelt

To
Andrew Raymond Lewin

Contents

Foreword

This book offers far-reaching insights into perceptions of conflict in South Africa. Claude-Hélène Mayer's approach is remarkable, because she imparts the recollections of numerous people from diverse ethnic and cultural backgrounds. The author captures the essence of about one-hundred interviews reflecting disparate attitudes towards social changes in the post- apartheid Republic of South Africa. Unexpected statements – for example, with respect to the continued existence of internalized apartheid – are carefully analyzed and hermeneutically understood. Thus, the reader grasps the basic premise of the philosopher, Hans Georg Gadamer, that inviting people to speak and be heard, allows space and time for the "melting of horizons" thus leading to a deeper understanding.

Her thought-provoking chapter on *identity* shows the kinds of identities people are constructing in the face of external political-social change within the social structure of the young South Africa. Surprisingly, they are cultivating *race*-related self-definitions suitable for re-interpreting and re-integrating the surroundings and personal reality. The self-images and *other-images* ("Fremdbild": literally: the image someone holds of another person or group) of different group members are mirrored in the perception and interpretation of the self and the "other."

The author also analyzes statements about the "rainbow symbol." In discussing the further development of the South African society, at least two levels of *rainbow* semantic emerge. From a critical political standpoint, the rainbow is simply a color spectrum in which the color black is missing; as a religious, spiritual symbol, the rainbow signifies the collective future vision of finally unifying all previously separated population groups in a long, peaceful process.

At the beginning of the research, presumptions might have raised expectations for the similarity between the narrative interviews. However, it becomes clear during the reading of this work that each interview was itself unique and each created a unique situation between the interviewer and the interviewee, inviting the reader to listen again and again to the spoken and analyzed words.

The thorough, months-long field stays, from September 1999 until April 2004, emphasize the researcher's exhaustive effort better to understand the perspective of the interviewees. In addition to the book's research-related merits, its data can increase the cultural competence of those readers who are interested in information on specific predominant-cultural standards in present day South Africa. Readers can more fully appreciate how the people in South Africa live a special, dynamic form of their unmatched "unity in diversity."

Dr. Christian Boness
Institute for Intercultural Practice and Conflict Management, Göttingen

Acknowledgements

Initially, I would like to thank all those without whom this project could hardly have been accomplished. From the very beginning, Dr. Birgit Röttger-Rössler and Prof. Dr. Ulrich Braukämper, *Georg-August-University Göttingen, Institute for Ethnology,* led me through the field of ethnology and helped me realize my ideas with inspiration and constructive criticism. Much thanks I also owe Prof. Dr. Hans Meliczek for his support.

Prof. Dr. M. Spiegel, *University of Cape Town,* and Dr. Johnny Maphunye, *University of Western Cape,* shared important insights with me, elucidated the scientific approach to the subject, and built my awareness of the "German perspective."

I would like to particularly thank the Cusanuswerk e.V. for its profound mentorship. The project could have never been accomplished without the spiritual, religious and financial support of the Cusanuswerk e.V.

The South Africans, Andrew Raymond Lewin, and Trevor John Edwards, assisted me extensively and continuously with their detailed feedback during my several-months stays. As my major resources of guidance and information, they stood by my side – whenever necessary – and candidly disclosed the far-reaching perspectives of individual South African thought-constructs and possible interpretations.

During the numerous discussions with Dr. Christian Boness about value discussions in African contexts, I received countless new inspirations for this project. For this I would like to thank him. For the moral and mental support and for the constructive ideas during the long process of writing in Germany, my emphatic thanks go to Peter Schmüser and Stefan Hartmann.

Also I am grateful to Dr Uta Schäfer-Richter for her feedback as a colleague, for our personal exchange on religion and church during the apartheid era, and for the important questions she raised at key moments.

I feel fortunate to have found in Annette Braden-Rozier a translator who was interested in thoroughly immersing herself in the topic of this work and its terminology, and with whom I have enjoyed fruitful cooperation.

Without technical support, technical equipment and online-assistance during the field studies, I certainly could not have worked as fast and efficiently. So my whole-hearted thanks go to Claus Schulze.

With pure pleasure, I want to thank the numerous interview partners from churches and NGOs, who, with their readiness to share their stories, supplied the foundation for my work. I am also grateful to all the persons in key positions in churches and NGOs, who drove the project forward through their release and access to personal or business resources and structures.

Last not least, I owe thanks to the *Arts for Humanity Foundation* in Durban, South Africa. The Foundation facilitated the integration of South African contemporary art into this work, allowing me to introduce additional levels of South African value orientation and perspectives of multiple realities.

Norman Kaplan
Frontispiece "South Africa's Bill of Rights" 560x295: Linocut
In: Images of Human Rights Portfolio
© Artists for Human Rights Trust

1. Introductions and Defining the Problem
1.1 Approaching the Field of Investigation

Currently, intercultural conflicts are increasing in size and complexity. Due to advancing globalization and multi-culturalization of societies - not only in the area of economic cooperation, but also in educational and political settings and in every day life - more intercultural encounters are taking place, which heighten the potential for conflict. As societies go through political, economic and cultural changes of their own, daily situations of conflict are the result.

Striving for a new multicultural identity, people meet obstacles, particularly in the area of "cultural overlapping situations" (Dadder 1987:21). Here the diversity of values, perceptions and different interpretations become apparent as they are tied contextually to personal and societal structures, as well as to historical circumstances. How do people perceive their realities? What are the values underlying the experienced conflict and its narration?

Often, individual and collective values become conscious only in conflict situations, while they otherwise may remain in the unconscious. However, the heterogeneity of a society does not necessarily imply conflict. According to Heitmeyer (1997), cultural homogeneity is not a *conditio sine qua non* for the functioning of social systems. Instead, building on the heterogeneity in thinking, feeling and being, it is possible to develop common systems of meaning, meta-cultures and national identities aimed at the design of a peaceful nation – as it is attempted through the "Rainbow Nation of South Africa."

This work, on the one hand, looks at the theoretical construction of post-apartheid South Africa through the national value-discourses (chapter 3.4ff). On the other hand, it gathers and analyzes first-hand accounts of personal experiences on the local level.[1] The original goal was to document daily situations of conflict as experienced and narrated by interviewed individuals. These conflict situations were then to be analyzed with respect to current national and further theoretical approaches. However, because this work is based on hermeneutical procedures (see 4.1), the research did not – as *initially* presumed

---

[1] The exploratory study uses the "narrative presence" as an intentional literary device throughout to bring the narrated events home to the reader.

– present us simply with straight narrations of experienced conflicts, but also with as least as many, and even a larger variety of statements concerning the Rainbow Nation. These statements concerned stereotypical images of one self and others, as well as genuine identity crises. This psychological aspect of the research material required its own consideration next to the presented conflict situations. The evaluation chapter will address them accordingly. (5.4-5.7).

1.2 Autobiographical Context

In the early1990's, the Western world received the radical political changes in South Africa with great relief. It regarded these changes as a symbol of Africa's liberation from colonialism and Western imperialism. Economic embargos ceased, and *Chiquita* – bananas appeared again on the list of "politically correct" merchandise. Schools in Germany took up South Africa's political situation and addressed it in an interdisciplinary way. Thus, already during my school years, I became familiar with Nelson Mandela, his political strive and his visions for a united and peaceful South Africa. The new "*Rainbow Nation*" had sparked my interest.

When I traveled to South Africa for the first time in 1999, I had just finished a field study in Tanzania on the subject of "value orientations at secondary schools." Target groups were members of Bantu-speaking ethnic groups, the same group I would soon encounter in South Africa, where Bantu is the most widely spread language family. South Africa - though at the time still heavily marked by the apartheid period - was on its way to becoming a new nation. Ethnic autonomy movements, land occupations, crime and the whereabouts of Nelson Mandela dominated the national news. There were reports about the president. There were speeches by politicians and former political activists who advocated a united South Africa.

Even then, I wondered what was on the average person's mind in a country so strained by historic circumstances and with such massive multiculturalism, now that their homeland was on its way to becoming a peaceful nation. How did South Africans perceive reality? What conflicts did they experience? What value orientations shaped their interpersonal relationships? These questions became the basis of this dissertation.

1.3 Thematic Approach to the Problem

This investigation belongs to the field of urban, modern ethnological studies. The approach to the problem, sample definition, selection of the field of investigation, arrangements of the field stays, points to this work's "pioneer quality", giving it an **exploratory study** status (see also 4.1). The concept is that of a "goal-oriented search for the realization of an object", which is also considered a pre-*study* or *pilot study* (Friedrich, 1990:121ff). The intent of this exploration – through the open approach described above – is to research new worlds of experience and capture "a much more concrete and vivid picture" from the perspective of the effected person (Flick, Kardoff, Steinke, 2000:7). The object of investigation in this case lends itself to the methodic-qualitative approach. First, there is no existing research on this topic, and second, this approach allows the reader to identify with the conflicts affecting the interviewee. By intent, open-ended questions prevent experiences from being immediately reduced to only partial aspects. According to this approach, there is no precise hypothesis (see 4.6), but only general expectations. The "pioneer quality" of this study is particularly evident in view of existing research and non-existent literature. There exist contemporary research essays on the subject of South African identities (Bekker, 1993/2000), value systems of the South African political elite (Katz, 1993/1997), and political "nation building" (Zartmann, 1995) in South Africa. However, missing is research on the role of value orientation in daily conflict situations and personal encounters, in the context of nation building in post–apartheid South Africa. The existing literature in this chosen field of research only marginally touches areas of this investigation. The work at hand, therefore, serves as an exploratory study for gathering and evaluating narrated conflict experiences of members of different socio-cultural groups, as well as examining their value orientation in Cape Town of the post-apartheid era.

South Africa is rapidly changing socially and culturally. This change demands new studies. Especially in a situation of radical change, the change of values along with rapid, sometimes hard to overlook social changes, leads to irritation and conflict, which show themselves within and outside socio-cultural groups. This study investigates, through momentary glimpses, how the national transformation constitutes itself on the grassroots level. My goal is to form a better understanding of differing, individual perspectives.

This study claims neither to be universally valid, nor to establish general criteria applicable to South Africa, Cape Town, or certain socio-cultural groups as a whole. Rather, its individual, qualitative data build a foundation for further in-depth studies. Additionally, the comprehensive analysis and its results may stimulate local peace work. They can encourage reflection on self-image and other-image, thus initiating changes in the perspective of different population groups. This study promotes mutual understanding and intercultural exchange through open and transparent presentation of conflict experiences and reality constructs. Therefore this work provides a useful contribution to intercultural understanding between members of different socio-cultural groups in Cape Town.

1.4 Definition of Terms

Some basic terms used in this text require clarification. The terms not defined here will be defined later in the text as necessary.

More than half a century ago, two anthropologists, A.L. Kroeber and C. Kluchhohn (1952), attempted to clarify the field of definitions for the term "culture." Even then, they encountered 164 different definitions of culture in literature. The multiplicity of definitions was due mostly to their application, but also to the fact that culture had three different meanings.[2] These three meanings still determine the large number of culture definitions today.

In order to gain a theoretically and practically applicable definition of culture, the work at hand is oriented at the modified view of Franz Boa. According to Boa, culture manifests the particularistic features of cultural diversity and simultaneously reflects universal elements. Kevin Avruch (1998:10) describes these two areas of culture as *generic culture* and *local culture* thus:

---

[2] Most definitions of culture are based on the approaches of Arnold, Tyler and Boas (see also Avruch, 1998).

The generic culture is a species-specific attribute of Homo sapiens, an adoptive feature of our kind on this planet for at least a million years or so. Local cultures are those meanings created, shared and transmitted (socially inherited) by individuals in particular social groups.

Generic culture therefore implies universal attributes of human behavior and human nature, such as basic human needs or the ability to community via language. Generic culture enables people to communicate across different cultures. All human beings are connected by virtue of "being human."[3] Thus, generic culture offers potential access to all human beings in the world.

Local culture, on the other hand, directs attention to cultural diversity, to differences and particularities. The work at hand defines the term "local culture" on the basis of "generic culture" according to Theodore Schwartz (1992):

Culture consists of the derivatives of experience, more or less organized, learned or created by the individuals of a population, including those images or encodements and their interpretations (meanings) transmitted from past generations, from contemporaries, or formed by individuals themselves.

Here the culture term is linked to *experiences,* leaving open the question of how these experiences are organized. This constructivist-oriented definition succeeds especially in showing that culture is created within and outside of individuals and groups. On an intra-personal and intra-social level, people perceive, construct, reflect, and reproduce culture, in its individual and group-specific possibilities, then pass it on accordingly. Externally, "culture" results when people learn, apply and modify images and codifications, which are specific schemes and models of preceding and contemporary

---

[3] In the data material and in the South African value discussion (see ch. 3.4), the value of "being a human being" plays an important role. The evaluation chapters will address this (ch. 5.4-5.7).

generations. Thus, culture is context-bound, flexible and ever changing, simultaneously constructed by and influencing individuals and groups. [4]

The term "individuals of a population" requires a more precise definition since individuals often belong to several different social groups at the same time. As an example, an individual can belong to the group of mothers, daughters, singers, entrepreneurs, and graduate students, whites or Germans at the same time. Within each population the individual has different experiences, which create his or her culture since the experience of situations and the definition of belonging determine thinking and behavior[5].

Therefore, each population or each group is a "potential container of culture" (Avruch, 1998:18). The following describes these groups as socio-cultural groups or as population groups. Importantly, South Africa socially constructed "race" groups, such as *Whites, Coloureds, Blacks* and *Indians,* comprise socio-cultural groups as well. *Race* was once the defining criterion for group affiliation and still is today to a certain extent (see below). However, groups have developed special socio-cultural characteristics independent from their racial affiliation.

An assumption exists that culture is not evenly spread among members of a community, because they belong to different socio-cultural groups and therefore participate in different cognitive and affective processes. A decisive factor, for example, is teaching and learning style, as well as individual acceptance and creation of culture-specific schemes. Therefore, culture is concurrently a social and an individual construction.

A person internalizes mental representations, such as symbols or schemes, in three different ways: individually, culturally and by degree. Consequently, these representations are tied to specific value orientations and emotions. The degree of

---

[4] The effect of internal and external cultural processes is clearly demonstrated in the data material in chapter 5.7.2 and 5.7.3. Here the speaker finds him/herself in the conflict between his/her individual and his/her collective, cultural construction of identity.
[5] An individual's "social reality" (see ch.4.4.2) is constituted through the cultural context, and in turn contributes to the construction of culture.

internalization is proportional to how quickly an action is triggered: the stronger the internalization, the sooner the specific action happens. This is especially true in conflict situations: the internalized schemes, values, and emotions, determine corresponding actions. In an intercultural conflict, the likelihood increases for the individual schemes, values, and emotions to surface according to the specific culture of the conflicting parties, and therefore, to exist beyond the degree of individual differences.

The definition of the term intercultural is as follows: A situation is intercultural when a person of one socio-cultural group personally interacts with a person of another socio-cultural group.[6] "Intercultural," therefore, exhibits its definition contextually and is oriented at the individual and socio-culturally created and transformed schemes. These, in turn, correspond to value orientations.

The work at hand analyses value orientations in (intercultural) conflict experiences. Therefore, it is necessary to define values. The terms value and value orientation will be used synonymously and follow Shalom Schwartz' definition (1994:21):

---

[6] In the current scientific discussion on inter-culturalism, inter-ethnicity, culture, cultural differences and intercultural relationships, scientists (see Balibar, 1990, Franchi, 2003) have repeatedly posed the following meta-theoretical question: Is it legitimate to speak of "intercultural relationships" with respect to previously segregated and still asymmetric groups, especially when – as in South Africa – we are dealing with societies, in which the legislative and executive government stands in the context of "racial categorization", ethnic inequalities" and "political asymmetry"? Franchi (2003:132) questions whether it is even ethical, epistemological pertinent, and methodically legitimate, to continue to speak of "cultural differences", "ethnicity", "interethnic and intercultural relations" when these terms are used outside their historical construction and local, socio-political context. Because they are euphemistic variations of historical and materialized terms of "racial, national and class," they risk reproducing polarization and implying inequalities.
This scientific, term-oriented discourse cannot be pursued any further here. Taking these term-critical objections under consideration, this study assumes nevertheless that it is basically legitimate to speak of "intercultural relationships," even though they are shaped and changed by asymmetric socio-economic, socio-political and psychosocial factors. This study uses these terms not in the sense of "euphemistic variations" for historically shaped terms such as "race, nation and class" and does not mean to reproduce them. Rather, the terms are understood as individual and socio-cultural constructs (see above).

Values are desirable trans-situational goals, varying in importance, which serve as guiding principle in the life of a person or other social entity. Implicit in this definition of values as goals is that

(1) they serve the interests of some social entity,

(2) they can motivate action - giving it direction and emotional intensity,

(3) they function as standards for judging and justifying action, and

(4) they are acquired both through the socialization to dominant group values and through the unique learning experience of individuals."

Here, values are defined on an individual and socio-cultural level, as well as on a level of a social unit, such as a nation. Values reflect desirable goals, which vary in importance, character and constellation, depending on situation and context. Schwartz does not explicitly distinguish between values and needs ("survival needs"). But following the African scientist, Dzobo, the work at hand equate "needs", such as food, sleep, safety, respect, love, etc. (see Maslow, 1999:62) with "survival values."[7] One reason for this choice is that "survival values," too, must be considered as goals that motivate actions, point the way and direct emotions.[8] "Survival values" also serve the interests of a person or group and vary according to context and situation. They often justify actions. How "survival values" are realized again depends on the individual and the socio-cultural conditions. Consequently, the following does not differentiate between the usage of "values" and "survival values."

This dissertation aspires to expand on the above-mentioned value definition according to Schwartz. Principally, it treats values as worthwhile, desirable goals, which lie in the interest of the socio-cultural group or individual and are considered "positive."

---

[7] Following the definitions of Dzobo (1975), values are divided up in "trans-survival-values" and "survival values". The first are, for example, recognition, solidarity, integrity, etc. "Survival values" however, are values, which direct survival and are often called "needs" These include food consumption, sleep, procreation or health (see Mayer 2001, p.58).

[8] The focus of this work is the gathering of statements about values, not the research of the connection between value orientation and behavior orientation (dependent on situation, context, culture or individual). One cannot necessarily connect certain values to certain behavior orientations. Equally limited is the possibility of correspondence between specific actions and behaviors and value orientations.

Frequently, however, conflict situations deal with different assessments, interpretations and judgments of values. Accordingly, differing value-orientations and value-priorities are a possible cause of conflict. For example, in certain ethnic groups begging is considered an expression of reciprocal behavior. This is the case, for example, for the Gogo, an ethnic group settled mostly around the Tanzanian provincial capital Dodoma, and enjoying great social esteem (Mayer/Boness/Thomas, 2003:133). Hence, when a German expert with his own cultural bias towards begging arrives in Dodoma, he is obliged to come to grips with this socially accepted reality of begging. Based on these differing moral precepts, which find expression in opposite ways of behavior, a "value – conflict" might arise. In this case, the value of reciprocal behavior is clearly different. Evidently, the judgment and assessment of value orientations can be positive as well as negative. The same values do not necessarily represent desirable goals for each person. Rather, values need to be understood as relative, individual and socio-cultural constructs, which are negotiable and changeable. In this sense, this work expands Schwartz's definition.

Therefore, to be accurate, this dissertation deals with culture and value orientations as constructed phenomenon, just like the term "race." Official governmental announcements (South African Institute of Race Relations/ (SAIRR) 2001) and current South African literature often define the population according to the traditional apartheid "race categories": *White, Coloured, Black and Indian.* Also, in everyday life individuals often define themselves through their racial affiliation (Kotzé, 1997), which – among other factors – contributes significantly to their identity development and identity management (compare chapter 3.5/5.7), as well as to their specific experiences of conflict (chapter 5).

Originally, the term *race* defined physical characteristics, such as skin color, shape of nose or hair structure, and it is still used most commonly to describe "... *(group) differences based on physical or morphological characteristics."* (Bekker, 1993:18) With this biological definition of "race," the affiliation with such a "race" is neither freely chosen nor changeable.[9]

---

[9] Biological research often defines "race" according to the frequency with which certain gene combinations occur. But in more recent studies, authors such as Lewontin, Rose and Kamin (1988),

In addition to the biological characteristics of race, common opinion is often dominated by associations of certain *race groups,* which frequently take prejudicial and stereotypical forms and are also attributed to the majority of this group.[10] According to Flohr (1994), the *race* term itself encourages the production of stereotypes and prejudices, as well as thinking and acting in an "ethnocentric" fashion.[11] The biological term of *race* attracts a socio-cultural component and becomes a socio-cultural construct. The term *race* (Rasse) has its own problems with respect to the German past. "Race categorizations" imply social stratification (see 2.2), and divide social groups into "superior" and "inferior", which purposefully creates social imbalances. Apple (1993:vii) describes the socially conditioned construction of *race* by including its chronological sequence. In doing so he shows its construction character:

> Race is not a stable category. It has changed over time. What it means, how it is used, by whom, how it is mobilized in social discourses, its role in educational and more general social policy, all of this is contingent and historical.

Looking at South Africa in history and presence, Bekker (1993:17), in accordance with Apple, determines the change of the *race* term and its meaning.[12] The meaning is

---

proved that dividing humanity into different "races" lacks any (biological-) scientific base. The authors – a zoologist, a biologist and a psychologist – conclude that about 75% of all human genes are found in all members of *Homo sapiens.* They show that the gene differences within one *"race group"* are greater than the genetic differences between different "race groups." Thus, these authors support the thesis of this work that the "race" term has to be understood as a socio-cultural rather than a biological construct.

[10] The presented data material also confirms this assumption. Here interviewees often ascribe certain stereotypes and prejudice- laden behaviors or attributes to race groups, which are expressed in self and stranger imagery and which are introduced in ch.5.

[11] The basis of ethnocentrism is the conscious and subconscious assumption on the part of individuals and collectives that their own ethnic or socio-cultural group and its own value orientations should be the measurement by which all other groups are assessed.   Accordingly, one's own group is valued positively, the other groups rather negatively.

spatial-temporal and constructed through the specific social realities of socio-cultural groups and its members. At the same time, the racial affiliations in South Africa are closely linked to power, identity, social recognition, as well as to resource distribution.[13] *"Race"* therefore has to be understood as a social and cultural construct that is (re-) constructed by the members of society.[14] Though not officially, until this day, racial assignation is part of daily life for people in South Africa and is continuously reconstructed (Franchi, 2003). This study's data (see 5) likewise reflect this tendency. Accordingly, it is necessary here to work with the given terms and categories. The terms used are to be understood as denotative terms. They do not carry connotative or pejorative intent.[15] The terms "population group", as well as "socio-cultural group" are used synonymously with the term "racial group." The reason for this is, first, that these terms presumably will trigger less negative associations among the readers. Second, the presented assumption is that racial groups, just like other groups, can be defined in socio-cultural terms. Importantly, however, the use of "race groups" as socio-cultural groups implies the special emphasis on "racial features" in contrast to other criteria of definition.

---

[12] According to Bekker (12993:17), the designation to *"race categories"* in South Africa, continues to have an identity-shaping and identity-preserving character. Bekker thinks, though, that the identity criterion of race should be replaced in the future with stronger identity definitions over socio-cultural or ethnic affiliations.

[13] This relationship between race affiliation, power, identity and social inequality means that belonging to a race often represented the context of a certain class membership and thus a certain social stratification, originating in South Africa's historic-political orientation.

[14] So "whiteness" and "blackness", according to McLaren (1994:61), are socio-cultural and politically constructed categories, which stand opposite each other and complement each other. If, for example, the construct of "whiteness" were deconstructed, it would affect the construct of "blackness". Also, "whites" often wouldn't call themselves "whites" in the first place, but primarily name their group affiliation, such as their Englishness or *Jewish ness*.

[15] Franchi (2003:126) emphasizes that "race" terms are not free from negative and pejorative associations. Despite the claim of neutrality, these terms carry unconsciously negative connotations. Therefore, only when communities using these terms do the collective work of communication, reflection and confrontation, it can free these terms from their "blind spots." Only then these terms escape their traditional definitions and emerge anew. According to the constructivist approach of this work, it is – along with the author – also up to the reader, to understand these terms in a denotative sense and thus to re-construct them.

1.5 Goals and Samples

The goal of this work is to look at the new South African nation as a reality construct and weigh its effects on everyday life. The main question is whether or to what extent daily life reflects the nation's political-value discourse, whether that discourse becomes a "reality." Examining daily conflict experiences is of special interest. The goal is to extract the here-contained value orientations and reality constructs of people in Cape Town, and to analyze them in the context of the theoretical-ideological discourse. Since people often perceive their own value orientations only when confronted with other values, they are traced in the context of conflict situations. Conflicting parties encounter their own reality in confronting the reality of others, which then can be identified and discussed.

The goals of this work are defined as follows:

- Presentation of theoretical discourses about reality constructs, nationalism and multiculturalism, and about conflict-theoretical approaches and political-ideological value discussions in South Africa
- Gathering conflict experiences
- Systematic presentation, analysis and interpretation of the gathered data
- Examination of the conflict narratives with regard to value orientation, key terms, and social reality, as well as to the theoretical discourses in chapter 3.[16]

The methods (compare 4) for achieving these goals differ on three levels:

- Planning methods for the exploratory study are those that allow a successful implementation.
- Implementation methods include methodical procedures for securing the results.
- Evaluation methods are essentially the available statistical and hermeneutical procedures for the evaluation of the collected data.

Parishioners and people from religious groups in Cape Town, as well as coworkers from NGOs who are active in peace work, comprise the study's target group. The following reasons support the selection of this sampling:

---

[16] The definition of "key terms" and "social reality" follows in ch.4.4.2.

Church organizations and NGOs in the field of peace work operate in a respected and protected context that provides open opportunities for research. Until now, churches are relatively safe, with less potential for violence than other public places.

Churches, because of their historical contributions, continue to be held in high esteem among large parts of the population. Many religious and church organizations were actively involved in the fight against apartheid and provided sanctuary for discussion and for interpersonal exchange, regardless of *race* criteria. Therefore, one assumes that church members will willingly participate in interviews.

Since the beginning of the 1990s, churches have been obliged to redefine themselves and have attempted to align their concepts with the "New South Africa" (see Mitchell, 2002:19). Hence, members of the target group are to a certain degree familiar with socio-political themes.

Today, many church groups involved in social work and conflict management are also engaged in nation building. Working at the grass root level, they represent a significant part of South Africa's "civil society."[17] Being in close touch with their communities, they attempt to collaborate with them to represent and achieve specific objectives. As places of religious and spiritual dimension, churches also offer the opportunity for closeness with God and worship. There, people from very different socio-cultural groups gather in peaceful surroundings, where they can draw strength and energy during this time of societal change, and also receive guidelines for their spiritual life. Within the churches, pastors play an important role as preachers of God's message of peace. Importantly, they often settle conflicts or function as mediators for a peaceful conflict resolution. As such, they have a broad spectrum of experiences at their disposal, which enhances the data.

Presumably, people who are active in the peace work within churches and NGOs are familiar with the topics of conflict and conflict resolution and are therefore more open

---

[17] Since the 1980s, the debate on *civil society* has sparked interest in the waves of democratization in Africa. (e.g. Comaroff & Comaroff (2000), Huntington (1991)). In South Africa the debate on "civil society" arose especially in the beginning of the 1990s. Marais (2000:199) defines "civil society" as a "...*popular movement*" *which includes grass root organizations, civics, youth groups and so on.*" Part of the citizens' initiatives is "*women's groups, trade unions, church societies and sport clubs*", who refer to the "*culture of "peoples' power*"". Because this study is particularly interested in people who work at the grass root level, churches and NGOs are ideal institutions through which to reach this target group.

and ready to talk about their conflict experiences. The assumption is that the sharing of conflict experiences in it is not necessarily unusual for many interview partners. In many traditional African societies, personal storytelling is part of the healing process after traumatic conflict situations (Hemshorn de Sanchez, 2002:47). When coping with traumatic (conflict-) events, it is important that people can describe their experiences, impressions and feelings connected to that situation. At the same time, the listener plays an important role in the healing. The interviewee opens up to the listener and entrust him/her with the story. Thus the form of "narrative interviews" is accepted as appropriate method when dealing with conflict situations (see 4.3). Also, as key people within the civil movement, people active in churches and NGOs can reach out to church members as potential interview partners. Thus, the selection of samples, on the one hand, serves as an introduction to the field in a secure and comprehendible context. On the other hand, it ensures the possibility of communicating on this specific topic.

Churches, religious associations and NGOs are locally represented in every part of town and in the former townships. This district-superceding structure is significant, because it lies in the interest of this study to reach people from different parts of town as well as from different socio-cultural and class-specific backgrounds. The network-like structure of these selected institutions of the *civic society* should be invaluable.

Also important is the assumption that churches and NGOs function in an identity-shaping way, and that they generate, maintain and/or (re-) construct value orientations. This investigation will help to filter out and analyze value orientations of members of the above-mentioned institutions.[19]

Cape Town, as the urban South African center, lends itself to the field of investigation because its inhabitants have different cultural socializations and perspectives representing a section of the multicultural South African society. At the same time, Cape Town is of special interest as capital of the Western Cape since the socio-cultural and ethnic composition of the population is 58% Coloured (see 2.5). During apartheid, it was declared as *Coloured Preferential Area*. These historical conditions still shape daily life and intercultural encounters in the big city. Furthermore, globalism impacts everyday life and interpersonal contacts. The different realities being presented and constructed here could hardly are more complex. They will be captured in some sections in the following.

Many religious and church associations as well as NGOs committed to peace work, have settled in the Western Cape in order to practice conflict management and mediation. In doing so, they have incorporated traditional African and western methods of conflict mediation, which makes them acceptable to the various population groups. Churches, religious groups and NGO's play a major role in the process of "Reconciliation", which became known in Europe thanks in large part to outreach from Anglican Bishop Desmond Tutu.

1.6 Work Design

The work design consists of the conception of the whole study, which is divided into a planning-, implementation - and evaluation phase.

The planning phase consists of the planning trip (2001), finding contact partners in South Africa, narrowing down samples, and determining investigation goals and methods. It further includes a critical look at the theoretical and methodological approaches, next to an in-depth theory and method search, in which relevant approaches in ethnology, social sciences, South African value discussion and intercultural conflict research are discussed. [20]

The phase of implementation is the execution of the exploratory study, during which interviews are conducted over several months.

The evaluation phase systematizes and analyses the data, then interprets them. The topic of this study ensues from the context of the following design:

---

[20] On African side, the project is sponsored by SAPES, the *Southern African Political Economy Series Trust*, in Harare, Zimbabwe and many different churches and NGOs in South Africa. The contact is the vice director of the regional center, which is involved in research and training in peace projects and in conflict resolution. On the German side the research project is sponsored by the Cusanuswerk e.V.

Phases	Time	Index of Content
Planning	06/2001 06/2002	• Literature inquiries • Two months planning trip to South Africa in June/July 2001 • First contacts with church organizations & NGO's • Setting up methodical tools for the investigation
Execution of Exploratory Study	06/2002 09/2002	• Four months field stay for execution of investigation
Transcription	10/2002 12/2002	• Transcription of the formally conducted interviews • First pre-evaluations
Extension Study/ Adjustment Visit	12/2002 01/2003	• Two months field stay in RSA • Consultation with interview partners about first pre-evaluations • Further informal talks with informant • Extended observations
Evaluation	02/2003 05/2004	• Presentation and analysis of the field study results • Formulating the results and their interpretation • Discussion of their application contexts • Feedback of the results to the participants in South Africa

Table 1: Phase of the Exploratory Study

This work is structured as follows:

After the introduction in Chapter 1, South Africa will be examined with respect to its socio-political and cultural background. The focus in Chapter 2 is topics on ethnic diversity and on specific regional conditions in the Western Cape. Chapter 3 contains theoretical discussions on reality constructs, nation building and multi-cultures, identity, and selected approaches in conflict theory. In addition, this chapter presents theoretical discourses and discussions on value orientation with respect to the construction of a new nation, as being conducted by South African politicians, theologians and scholars. Chapter 4 concentrates on the methods. The central significance of this chapter is the methodical processing of the forms of oral questioning, as well as the presentation and interpretation of the findings. Chapter 5 is completely dedicated to the exploration study. It includes information about pre-planning, implementation and experiences in the field, as well as the presentation, analysis and interpretation of the results. Chapter 6 contains a critical evaluation of the study, followed by the outlook in Chapter 7. The appendix includes indexes of literature, tables and graphics, as well as various documents. Included are also the transcriptions of the data material.

2. South Africa in the Post-Apartheid Era

This chapter introduces post-apartheid South Africa. Geographical, cultural and socio-political facts are presented with special attention to the country's diverse ethnic background. The main focus will be on the Western Cape, especially the city of Cape Town, since both comprise the location of our research.

Graph 1: South Africa

2.1 Geographical Data

The Republic of South Africa (RSA) presently has 44 million citizens (SAIRR, 2001:50), an area of 1,219.090 square kilometer, and an average population density of 34 inhabitants/km². In the northwest, South Africa borders on the Republic of Namibia and Botswana and in the northeast, on Zimbabwe and Mozambique. The kingdom of Swaziland is located in the east of South Africa next to Mozambique. The kingdom of Lesotho lies in the southeast and is completely enclosed by South Africa. South Africa has access to both the South Atlantic and the Southern Indian Oceans.

The country's largest cities, Johannesburg with about 5 million people and Cape Town with about 3 million people, are urban centers with fast growing populations, mostly due to new arrivals. More than half of South Africa (54%) has been urbanized. Eighty three percent of the population of European, Asian and mixed origin reside in the urban areas, while the majority of the Black population lives in the rural areas (57.3%). However, a much higher percentage of certain ethnic groups, such as the Zulus in the province of Kwa-Zulu-Natal, the Venda in the north, and the Ndeble on the inland plateau, are located in the rural areas (Naudascher-Schlag, 1994:21).

Since the end of apartheid, South Africa has -- in accordance with its new constitution-- been divided into nine newly named provinces: Free State, Gauteng, Kwa-Zula-Natal and Mpumalanga, Northern Cape, Northern Province, North-Western Province, Eastern Cape, and Western Cape.

The seat of government is in Pretoria (Gauteng), the seat of parliament in Cape Town (Western Cape), and the national court in Bloemfontain (Free State). The Western Cape is largely shaped by its provincial capital, Cape Town. It is a major economic center, which also attracts international corporations (see Mayer/Boness/Thomas, 2004). The main industries are fishing, timber, textiles, gas and oil (Mossgas). There are other industries, as well as publishing and printing companies. Agricultural products are fruits, vegetables, wine, and wheat, exclusively grown for export. Breeding of animals mainly includes sheep, ostriches and race- horses. With a regional gross national product of 53,874 billion Rand in 1994, the Western Cape provided 14.08% of the total gross inland product. The province is home to 9% of the total population (South African Embassy, 1997:13) within an area of 129,370 km^2 (10.6% of the total area of the RSA).

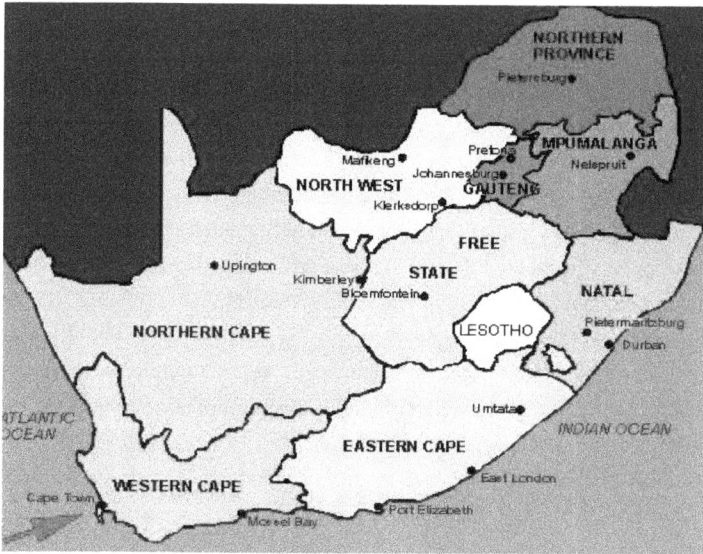

Graph 2: The South African Provinces

Since the beginning of the 1990s, South Africa has been undergoing significant changes, which are particularly reflected in the areas of education, health care, social politics, and social security. Meanwhile there are 21 universities and 15 *technicons* (vocational colleges), financed by the National Ministry of Education and attended without regard to ethnic or racial origin. The same is true for all schools, which currently work in accordance with national curricula and exams. Schooling is obligatory for children 7 to 15 years of age. A significant change in school policy has been the introduction of the predominant language of each province. These are currently integrated into the curricula, either as elective or mandatory language beside English and Afrikaans. Other main drives in educational and social policies are the reconstruction of former African family structures and dealing with the apartheid past. A nationwide endeavor is the multiculturally oriented, peaceful reconstruction of the nation with the overall goal of a democratic social system and balanced power sharing.

2.2. Socio-Political and Socio-Cultural Background

South Africa's political history and its multicultural diversity manifest themselves in every aspect of life in a complex way. The following information sheds some light on the socio-political, ethnic-cultural and religious background of this country.

For the past 100,000 years, South Africa has been inhabited almost continuously by small hunter and gatherer groups, which include the first African indigenous group, the San. According to Hirschberg (1975:389), these groups consisted of three main groups: the northern group, the middle group and the southern group - the latter living in the region of the present RSA. [1]

Not until circa 2000 years ago, the Khoikhoi [2] began to cultivate the ground for planting and cattle raising. Hirschberg (1975:396) finds four main Khoikhoi-groups: the Cape-Khoikhoi, the East-Khoikhoi, the Nama, and the Korana, each of which has sub groups. Many Khoikhoi today live in Namibia. In literature, the San and Khoikhoi are often referred to as KhoiSan . However, members of neither group use this composed name for themselves (Fadiman 200:9).

Between 500 and 1500 A.D., primarily Bantu-speaking migrants entered southern Africa. They grew crops and did metal work in river valleys and in the southeast, and are -- according to Breutz (1975:405)-- called South East Bantu. They comprise the Sotho-Tswana language group, who probably were the first Bantu-migrants to South Africa. About 200 years later, the Nguni-language groups arrived, then followed by the Tsonga-language groups from Mozambique, as well as the Venda and Lemba.

The first European immigrants to South Africa were the Portuguese in the 16th century, followed by the Dutch, the British and the French, whose descendents make up a significant portion of the White population in South Africa today. The Dutch also imported slaves from their eastern colonies and from other African countries, which greatly increased the country's ethnic diversity. The coexistence of these groups was

---

[1] The south group consists of three groups, the Xam, who reside predominantly on the Cape, the (Lesotho-San) in Basutoland, the Transvaal-San (Batwa and Twa) from former Transvaal, and the Nusan or Nuen. These ethnic groupings, which have been living in South Africa to this day, belong to the same language group, but are not united politically or socially. Accordingly, there is great political and cultural diversity between these groups, which is oriented at tribal structures.

[2] The name "Khoikhoi" originates from the self-chosen name, "Khoikhoin," which is often translated as "men of men" in U.S.-literature (Fadiman 2000:10).

characterized by competition for resources and its distribution. Especially when diamonds and gold were discovered in the Oranje Delta in the northwest, conflicts escalated between the settling British gold miners and the indigenous population (South African Embassy, 1997:16). Conflicts ensued between the colonists and Black African groups on one hand, and among Black African groups on the other hand -- such as the Ngqika-Mfengu-conflict in the Transkei (1874) or between the Rolong and the Tlhaping at the rim of the Kalahari. In the end, all African territory south of the Limpopo fell under White rule. The power struggle between the White groups resulted in the war between the Boers[3] and the British (1899-1902). The British won, but generously granted the Boers political and administrative autonomy in some areas (1906/1907). In 1909, the British and Boers parliaments together passed a constitution which secured all power exclusively in White hands and made South Africa part of the Commonwealth. Later, coalition parties of British and Afrikaans formed, and Afrikaans moved into leadership positions, such as Smuts and Botha and Hertzog as premier minister in 1926.

Whites were politically in charge from 1910 until 1960, but mainly the Afrikaners and members of the English dominated *South African Union.* 1948, the National Party (NP), the political arm of a right wing oppositional movement (*Malan,*) seized the majority of seats in parliament with a minority vote. Under changing leadership, the NP stayed in power until 1994. The party disregarded the constitution, excluded non-White voters and took South Africa out of the Commonwealth. After 1948 the apartheid ideology, which had surfaced repeatedly in less radical trends since the 17th century, became effective party policy and secured the NP's continuous power for the next decades. Blacks and Coloureds were aggregated in rural areas in so-called *homelands,* and segregated according to racial criteria. In urban areas *race* groups were resettled in so-called *townships.* Until 1996, entrance to and exit from these areas were possible only with permits and only under strict supervision. The main goal was to control the Black and Coloured educated elite in economic and political sectors, and to stratify society into *racially* defined hierarchical structures.

---

[3] They are also called *Afrikaans, Boers* or *White Tribe of Africa;* about the *Afrikaans* movement see chapter 3.1.1.

The Black resistance movement against White dominance organized itself in 1912 in the *South African Native Congress*, which later became the *African National Congress* (ANC). Until the 1970s, the ANC remained relatively powerless within society as a whole. Only after Steve Biko's death, the collapse of colonial Mozambique, and the end of the Rhodesia-war, did the resistance of the Black population gain momentum and international attention. This is reflected in the international trade and weapon boycott. In the 1980s, the ANC achieved the release of Nelson Mandela, which took place in 1990. Between 1991 and 1993, all the political parties cooperated in creating a transitional constitution. The first democratic elections were held in April 1994. Nelson Mandela became the first Black president of South Africa. In 1996, he signed the new constitution into effect.[4]

A very diverse population shapes the country's history and current politics. On different levels, the government wants to do justice to the socio-cultural heterogeneity through the process of *reconciliation*. This is, for example, reflected in the national language policy. The following eleven languages are now recognized as official languages: Xhosa, Zulu, Afrikaans, Ndebele, English, Sepedi, Sesotho, Siswasi, Setswana, Tshivenda and Xitsonga. Also, every person is entitled to an education in his/her own language, where the language is spoken by the majority of people in the province. Therefore some provinces offer regional-specific language education in their schools. In certain provinces, the dominating language group determines the regional language policy. Today in the Western Cape, English, Afrikaans, and Xhosa are officially recognized languages in administration and schools. This does not mean, however, that the policy is consistently applied in daily life in every office. The problem

---

[4] Important characteristics of the new constitution include the following: the division of the country into nine renamed provinces; the voting right for each citizen after 18 years of age; the establishment of communal administrations; the introduction of the Charta of Basic Rights, containing the right to housing, health care, food, water and social security; the building of a state-independent justice system, the introduction of eleven recognized official languages, and the provision for "traditional African leaders" who represent the population on all three government levels. A further important change in the political and economic sector is the *Affirmative Action* program. whose purpose is to promote employment of "formerly disadvantaged people" (i.e., *Blacks, Coloureds*, disabled people, women) in organizations and companies. These "racial quota" correspond to the composition of South Africa's population in percentages (see below). The goal is to make it easier for the formerly disadvantaged population groups to enter the workplace and to change the apartheid-caused inequality quickly and effectively. Whether this is the ideal approach, is still an issue of controversy in domestic policy (see 5.5.3). But this debate won't be further addressed here.

is that a person rarely speaks all languages at the same time, so communication difficulties arise easily. Thus, people often resort back to English as international language in commerce and trade.

Zulu is the most widely spoken language in South Africa (22.4 %), followed by Xhosa (17.5%), and Afrikaans (15.1%). The other languages make up less than 10% (Kotzé, 1997:2). In the Western Cape, until this day, the predominant languages in administration and public life are English and Afrikaans, since many Whites and Coloureds remain in social key positions without having any knowledge of other (Black African) languages. Therefore, there is some opposition against the official recognition of eleven languages (see 5.5.2, R6). Beside these large language groups, there are numerous smaller ethnic groups with their own languages and dialects. Additionally, the number of African immigrants is growing, many of them economic and political refugees from Southern Africa. Many South Africans are quite critical of these groups (see 3.2, table 4). The immigrants settle mostly at the margins of urban centers, in former townships or squatter camps.[5] In public life, they speak mostly English.

As already mentioned in chapter 1.4, it is common practice in the RSA to classify people in racial categories to this day. This is socially relevant because it is identity shaping. Political programs such as *Affirmative Action* show that racial assignments fundamentally determine the current socio-political restructuring measures and concrete political decisions.[6] This categorization is supposed to help accelerate the redistribution of resources and level social inequalities. Racial categorization must assist temporarily in the process of social change as orientation help for the individual and as criterion for the assessment of certain groups and their members, and in re-defining identities (see 2.5/5.). But after the official "abolishment" of the outer social structures of apartheid, socio-economic imbalances in every area of life (SAIRR, 2002:374ff), continue to exist.

---

[5] *Squattercamps* are illegal settlements made up mostly of improvised, self-made accommodations, which often lack any infrastructure. They are frequently object of heated discussions in public and government.
[6] According to Franchi (2003a:157ff), "race, racism and racialisation" continuously manifest themselves in the South-African everyday (work) life. Especially the implementation of Affirmative Action Policy places and legalizes a range of indirect manifestations of racism in post-apartheid South Africa.

To this day, racial categorizations create a certain hierarchical social structure.[7] Accordingly, Whites define themselves as "upper class," followed by Coloureds (middle class), Asians[8] (middle class) and lastly Blacks[9] (lower class). Very often, the external "apartheid structure" led to "internal apartheid," which continues to have a strong impact on self- and other-perceptions and on identity definitions (see 5.7). These intra-psychological manifestations and constructions, such as the internalized structures of inferiority and superiority based on the above-mentioned social stratification will extend age-old "racial frictions" for a long time.

On the basis of *racial* categorization, the composition of the South African population is as follows: There are 77% Blacks (of this ca. 20% Zulu), 13% Whites, 8.5% Coloureds and 2.5 Asians (predominantly of Indian descent). These numbers are, however, not representative for the Western Cape. The population structure is very different here: only 15% are Blacks (96% Xhosa), 26% Whites, 58% Coloureds and 1% Asians (Munzinger Archiv, 1994: map 2).

---

[7] It should be mentioned that the *racial* classification in South Africa is not limited to the time period from 1948 to 1994. According to Goldin (1987), the legislative and executive introduction of *racial* discrimination, segregation and oppression was already clearly visible in the 19th century. During the apartheid period the *racial* categorization was merely formalized. In this sense, it was a gradually progressing concept culminating in the apartheid policy.

[8] In literature *Asians* are also listed as *Indians*. The ethnic composition of this group consists largely of persons of Indian descent and 1% of persons of Chinese descent. The Indian community is primarily Hindu; a smaller number is Muslim. Both of these religious groups are, according to Ebr-Vally (2001:269), in themselves very heterogeneous. The original Indian population consisted mainly of people from lower casts and poor family background in India. Already at the beginning of the colonial period, European immigrants employed Indians as domestic workers or slaves. Compared to people of Black African origin, they were treated more favorably, receiving higher wages, and better social positions and therefore had a clearly higher social status. Women of Indian or sometimes Chinese descent became higher positioned maids, nurses, and seamstresses. Men of Indian or Chinese descent worked in trade (Patterson 1975:168). Even though the Asian portion of the population is relatively small today, Asians occupy leading positions in commerce and trade. In Cape Town there are only a few small Asian, respectively Indian, communities. Therefore this group is not represented in the field investigation and will not be looked at in a more detail.

[9] This hierarchical-asymmetric social structure was a system based on oppression, discrimination and segregation regarding economic, political and subjective reality, legitimized on the base of "race." According to Franchi (2003:129), the "inner" psychological effects and manifestations of apartheid well into the 21st century should not be underestimated.

Population Groups	Percentage in South Africa	Percentage on Western Cape
Blacks	77% (20% Zulu)	15% (96% Xosa)
Coloureds	8.5%	58%
Whites	13%	26%
Indians	2,5%	1%

Table 2: Population Groups

The following factors led to the special composition of the population on the Western Cape: White settlers, who initially immigrated without families, mixed with Black African women, thereby in part creating the group of Coloureds. This happened particularly in the Western Cape, since Whites were the first to permanently settle in this region (Fisch, 1991:79). This tendency was reinforced in the apartheid period, when the Western Cape was declared a *Coloured Preferencial Area* and all people designated as Coloureds were forcibly moved to the Western Cape. Compared to Blacks, they were privileged. Their living conditions were better, and they got better paying jobs.

Politically, too, the Western Cape has been always an exception. During apartheid, it was considered very liberal. Today it is the only region in South Africa that is not governed by the ANC. Instead, it is in the hands of the *Democratic Alliance* (DA), which is predominantly influenced by Whites and is elected by the majority of the Coloured and White population.[10]

The structure of the neighborhoods and settlements on the *Western Cape* and in *Cape Town* continues to be strongly determined by *race*. Former townships are divided into primarily Black, Coloured and Indian neighborhoods and show very little blending (Western, 1981:288). Langa, Cape Town's oldest *Black township,* was created 1927 through forced resettlements. Until this day, it has quite an adequate social infrastructure. The later *Black townships,* such as Nyanga and Guguletu – both built in 1960 – and Khayeliyscha (1983), have a far less developed infrastructure (Wilson

---

[10] A Coloured interview partner expresses his position on the political situation in the Western Cape. (P17:25). "That's why the ANC has the dilemma in the Western Cape. That it cannot, it will never ever outride, take hold of the Western Cape in terms of - oh yes, it will never ever be able to do that, unless it changes its attitude towards the people of the Western Cape, because it hasn't changed attitude towards the Western Cape yet. And the Western Cape people are a group that needs to be acknowledged for who they are and for the part that they played in the struggle."

1962/Wilson&Mafuje, 1993). Blacks and Coloureds continue to live in separate townships. Different religious communities, for example, Christians and Muslims, tend to separate from each other rather than mingle.

With the establishment of racially divided townships, existing social and family structures were systematically destroyed without any adequate replacement. Often, even families were divided by racial criteria and forced to live separately. High crime rates, great potential of violence, and increased organization of youth gangs are often partially attributed to the deleted family structures during apartheid. [11]

Racial integration in Cape Town's townships and districts has not taken place yet. There are only a few predominantly White districts, where today people from the rising Coloured and Black middle and upper class are moving in.[12] Some White upper class neighborhoods, which are also preferred areas for certain religious groups, such as Sea Point, Three Anchor Bay and Haut Bay, have remained almost exclusively White. In these areas, one can find more and more new gated communities, home of the economic and educational elite, protected by private security services. Our interview partners come from other districts (see 5.2), such as Rondebusch, the university quarter of the University of Cape Town (UCT), residence of the multicultural educated elite, and from the former White middle class districts: Kenilworth, Mowbray, Woodstock, University Estate and Observatory. More Coloured and Black middle class is moving into these areas. To this day, Coloureds usually live in: Sybrand Park, Mannenburg, Elsies River, Kuils River, Kraaifontain and Belgravia. Coloured Muslims mostly reside in the Bo-kaap district. Mostly Afrikaans and Coloureds inhabit the towns of Bellville and Stellenbosch, not far from Cape Town.

In the following sections, different aspects of identity of Cape Town citizens will be addressed.

2.3 Identities in the Western Cape

---

[11] One Coloured interview partner talks about this fact from his own family experience (see ch.5.6.1). He describes very touchingly the effects of segregating selected family members on his own family. His whole family situation has been one huge experience of conflict for him.

[12] The Coloured and Black middle and upper class remain relatively small. Many members of this class were in exile during apartheid, finished their education or studies abroad, and returned after the end of apartheid.

The amalgamation of a new multicultural nation comes with great challenges. One of these challenges lies in the changing identity of groups and individuals. Identity aspects such as ethnicity, race, language, regional origin, nationality, gender and social role require integration and new forms of identity development (see 3.2).

Looking at studies on multicultural identity, Kotzé (1997:7/8) finds the following: only 17.5% of the interviewed persons define themselves as "South African citizens," 35% "in terms of *race*" [13], and about 38% "in terms of culture." The term "culture" is used here synonymously with ethnic belonging. For only 6.8% of the participants, their affiliation to a religious community is of primary importance, and only 1.5% categorize themselves according to their language group. Evident here is the importance of racial and ethnic belonging. Based on survey data [14], Franchi & Swart (2003:209ff) argue that the diverse usage and meanings of "racial," "cultural" and "national self-identity" might be indicators of identity, but that they have less to do with a "substantive, authentic core of identity." Rather, these identity indicators have to be understood in the context of self- and other-concepts within space-time coordinates of material and symbolic reality. Therefore, Franci and Swart regard "race" as a social function in the sense of self- and other- understanding, rather than as an essentially identity forming one.

Bekker (2000:221) finds it problematic that the previous forms of identification over ethnic and racial affiliation persist, because they can present an obstacle to creating a new national identity. Should they dissolve, before such a national identity has been constructed, a loss of group and individual identity could occur which would generate a vacuum of adequate forms of identification. Therefore, for the sake of nation building, Bekker (2000:221) demands a conscious construction of new sub-national identities. In accordance with Erasmus (see 2.3.1), Bekker asks for an intensified perception and construction of socio-cultural identities, inviting members of all population groups to identify with criteria other than their "own *racial* affiliation." Criteria of group affiliation then, might be political, job-related, or gender- related, and dependent on region and province. On the national level, these could combine themselves in a "multi-

---

[13] The term "color" is here ascribed to the term "race."
[14] This nationwide inquiry took place during the years following the end of apartheid among secondary students from every population group.

perspective and hyper-complex way," and construct and make available new forms of identities (see 3.1.1).

In the Western Cape, Bekker (2000:224) already finds a pronounced "provincial identity." On one hand, the subgroup of politicians and politically active people shows visions of close cooperation between Afrikaans, Khoisan and Malayen/Muslim. These groups share a long tradition of good relationships and form the basis of the provincial culture and its identity. Decisive regional identity aspects are: the language, Afrikaans, predominant orthodox-religious practices, and strong ethnic diversity. On the other hand, there are remarkable value orientations such as "healthy economy," "natural beauty of the province," quality of public services, such as the educational system and the province administration. Here ethnic or socio-cultural background is not a priority. Also, the political climate of the province is marked by successful party coalitions and democratic leadership, which can be traced back to the region's opposition against apartheid. Accordingly, specific regional value orientations, such as political "loyalty," "belonging" and "pride", manifest themselves in political-economic structures of cooperation.

Since 1994, the Western Cape has experienced economic prosperity along with a new consciousness of its citizens. Political attitudes play a special role as identity forming aspects. In rural areas of the province, people tend to be "traditional-conservative," while rather "modern" in the urban areas. In Becker's study, a control group of non-politicians (2000:228) expresses its pride in the beautiful landscape and the regional traditions, such as the "old culture" of the San and Khoikoi, or such as the new South African nation with its aspiration for equality among all population groups. Compared to other provinces, the interviewees consider their own educational and administrative system "superior."

In Bekker's view (2000:225), government, provincial administration, politicians, intellectuals and theologians are shaping identities "from above," while the grassroots are working at this task "from below." In forming coalitions between oppositional political parties, the government demonstrates that it has accepted the province's identity as being heterogeneous in language, culture and religion.

In the following section, the identity shaping functions of religion and church affiliation in the Western Cape will be addressed. This aspect merits explicit consideration, given how participants of this investigation are recruited to a large part from diverse religions and churches.

2.4 Religious and Church Affiliation as Identity Shaping Elements

The religious affiliations in South Africa are just as diverse as languages, ethnicities and the socio-cultures. Officially, the majority of the population subscribes to a Christian faith. In addition there are Hindu, Muslim, Jewish and old-African [15] faith groups. Freedom of religion is guaranteed by the constitution. Numerous religious radio and television programs, as well as large religious sections in newspapers and magazines underscore the importance of religion on regional and national levels. Andersons points out (see 3.1.1) that religion contributes significantly to the construction of national, regional, local and individual identities. Therefore, this chapter pays close attention to the religious groups represented in this study.

Churches and religious communities encompass many religious identities, particularly as they combine numerous special sub-groups and religious orientations. According to Mitchell & Mullen (2002:23/27ff), "pluralistic-religious identities" arise in the field of tension among the different religious groups, such as between "African religion and African Christianity." Here African and Christian religious practices are being combined, reconstructed, and synthesized into new forms of religion and faith, thus offering great potential for the development of new identities.

---

[15] In literature, "old African" religions are often described as "indigenous" or "traditional" or "African religions" (African Traditional Religion"/ATR) see below.

Religions	Affiliation in Percent of Population (1996)	Members of this Affiliation represented in this study
No religion	12.9%	
Zion Christian	10.7%	
Dutch Reformed	9.8%	Yes
Apostolic	9.8%	Yes
Catholic	9.5%	Yes
Methodist	7.8%	Yes
Pentecostal/charismatic	6.1%	Yes
Other Zionist	6.0%	
Anglican	4.4%	Yes
Christians (not elsewhere classified)	3.5%	
Apostolic Faith Mission	3.1%	
Lutheran	2.9%	Yes
Ethiopian	2.2%	
Presbyterian	2.0%	Yes
Islam	1.5%	Yes
Hinduism	1.5%	
Bandla lama Nazaretha	1.3%	
Baptist	1.2%	Yes
Congregational	1.2%	Yes
Other reformed Christian	1.1%	Yes
Other African Independents	0.6%	Yes
Other faiths	0.6%	
Judaism	0.2%	Yes
Greek Orthodox	0.1%	

Table 3: Religious Groups

This dynamic religious-spiritual domain can counteract the vacuum of identity that often goes along with radical social change. The authors emphasize the important role faith and religion play in political processes by enhancing "imagination." They regard religion as instrumental in contributing creatively to the political change and to the vision of a "New South Africa."

According to Heuser (2002:74), the so-called *African Traditional Religions (ATR)*, and the *African Independent Churches (AIC)* are gaining ground in South Africa.[16] Both use as their core values "oral traditions" such as religious feasts, story telling, ritual shows and, as in the *AICs*, the *"setting of sacred space to re-present biblical landscape."* Of central meaning here are traditional sacrifices and ritual worship of ancestors, who are believed to remain members of the community and to actively intervene in the individual and collective life experiences (Mbiti, 1990).[17]

Related to the old-African religions are the so-called occult belief-systems. According to Kohnert (2003:1ff), occult belief-systems, such as *witchcraft*, have experienced a revival during recent years in some South African provinces and have led to increased "witchcraft violence."[18]

Many South African churches joined together in the umbrella organization of the *South African Council of Churches (SACC).*[19] Lutheran, Presbyterian and Congregational churches make up the core membership of the SACC. From the beginning, the SACC[20] advocated non-violent resistance against racism and anchored

---

[16] Almost 6 million people, ca. 13% of the South African population, officially do not belong to "formal religions." It can be assumed that a great portion of this population is part of the *ATRs*. The *ATRs* are in the process of developing adequate institutional forms. Oftentimes, Black-African church goers and Christians use old-African practices parallel to the Christian practices. The AICs, though, have for some time paved the way to an *"ecclesia africana"* and are now officially and administratively recognized.

[17] For example, for the Shona, bones represent a connection between the living and the dead and, at the same time, are an "instrument of divination" (Ephirim-Donkor, 1997:41). They are means for calling forth the ancestors and ask for help. Oftentimes old-African religious practices also stand in the context of experienced sickness and healing. According to the anthropologist Gelfand (1962:163), objects with spiritual-religious meaning, such as the bones for the Shona, are employed to sense the causes of spiritual and physical diseases. Therefore, these objects often fulfill a double purpose: they are a "divine tool" and they strengthen a person's spirituality.

[18] Similarly to end of the 1970s, the present social climate of social change with increasing gender and generation conflicts creates conditions for rising fears against witchcraft and witch-violence (Kohnert, 2002/2003). According to Delius (1997:218/219), the quickly expanding *"charismatic churches"* pick up on these fears and offer their members support against evil , which supposedly is embodied in witches.

[19] The SACC became internationally known by its former General Secretary Desmond Tutu and his position against violence in the fight against apartheid.

[20] The SACC regarded apartheid politics as an attack on the Christian faith and declared the "status confessionis", which meant that the socio-politics of apartheid were officially declared incompatible with the Christian faith. Every Christian was asked to oppose the state's politics and actions, to profess his/her faith and resist apartheid in order to remain loyal to his/her faith. Ultimately, the true Christian faith shows in "right" decisions and actions. The SACC regarded racism as idolization of *race,* which

this stance in a resolution in 1974. According to Mitchell (2002:21), since the SACCs active involvement in the liberation-struggle of the 1980s and since the overturn of the apartheid regime, the churches have played a leading role in the process of *"...nation-building, as well as in reconstruction and development."* This supposition was central for the selection of the target group in this study, since it was most likely that members and representatives of these groups were familiar with the theme of "building a peaceful nation" and with its inherent conflict potential. De Gruchys (1985) finds that especially Christian churches describe their role in the transformation process very clearly. They argue that prophetic Christianity during the struggle for liberation persistently subverted the theological legitimization of the apartheid state and created the basis for democracy in South Africa. This argument is supported particularly by the fact that the churches, like other organization building civil structures, embrace the culture of *peoples' power* and gather their strength from the grassroots (see 1.5).

The largest community of churches is the *AICs*, which have grown out of mission churches. The *AICs* have developed their own religious interpretations and draw large crowds. Even though the *AICs* during apartheid were considered "neutral," and even collaborators with the homeland governments, the Camaroffs (1993:xxiii) observe here tendencies of "ambivalent and ambiguous motives, seeking at once to contest and affirm aspects of dominant other(s)."

Generally, the role of the churches and their interpretation is diverse and controversial. According to Mitchell & Mullen (2002), churches at best are seen as supporters of their members struggling to overcome the "humiliating and inhuman" conditions of apartheid; at worst, they are seen as supporters and executers of apartheid-theological approaches. The AICs have especially demonstrated, how imperialistic influences can be deformed, scattered and transformed.[21] Literature therefore attributes

---

contradicts the first commandment. Equally, ideology and practice of apartheid contradict the central concern of the gospel. Allan Boesak shows three levels of alienation created in the process of "alienation" during apartheid:
- towards fellow human beings (distrust, hate)
- towards the self (apathy, feelings of inferiority)
- towards God (inconsistent with God's commandments)

[21] According to Chidester (1992), the "Ethopian Churches" strongly influenced "Black Theology" and the AICs, during the liberation struggle in the 1970s. They brought in new religious- cultural identity aspects and thus offered a response to the socio-political events.

the AIC s with a high degree of resilience (see Körner, 2002). The majority of the AICs belong to the Zionist and Apostolic churches, which in themselves are again very diverse (Christian Zionist, Zionist, Apostolic etc.).

The Pentecostal movement is also represented in the AICs. Of the more than 4000 independent Pentecostal churches worldwide roughly 10.8% of their members are in South Africa. Among the largest traditional Pentecostal churches are the *Apostolic Mission*, the *Assemblies of God* and the *Full Gospel Church* (SAR Embassy, 1999:36). Most of the Pentecostal/Charismatic churches and churches of the ATRs are not members of the SACC, but have their own connectional institutions. Many charismatic churches were founded only during recent years and associated with the Pentecostal churches after apartheid 1991 in the *International Fellowship of Christian Churches*, in order to form a unified front towards the challenges of social change.

The Afrikaans churches have always played a big role in South Africa's past. They belong to the family of Dutch Reformed Churches, which combines three related churches and their five million members. The *Nederduitse Gereformeerde Kerk (NGK)* with nearly 1263 congregations nationwide is the largest Afrikaans church and, at the same time, the motherchurch of the other two: the *Uniting Reformed Church of South Africa* and the *Reformed Church of South Africa*. These three churches justified "racial separation" under apartheid with religious arguments. They did not support the liberation struggle, but tried to prevent it instead (see Kuperus, 1999). Parallel to these "radical" Afrikaans churches there are the "moderate" Afrikaans churches, such as the *Nederduitschse Hervormde Kerk (NHK)* or the *Nederduitse Gerefomreede Kerk,* who welcomed Blacks and Coloureds already during apartheid.

Despite South Africa's protestant majority, the *Roman-Roman CatholicChurch (RCC)* gained influence and new members during the last years. The *RCC* today actively networks and cooperates (with other churches) in the socio-political field.[22] The church continues to follow its political-ideological concept, which it already represented publicly during apartheid: equality of all ethnic groups in church and state.

---

[22] Today many organizations are attached to the Roman Catholic church, such as *Roman Catholic Welfare* and *Development (CWD)*. They are dedicated to work on social issues, fighting poverty for example, and cooperate with other religions and confessions.

Additional churches having become established in South Africa are the Methodist church and the British liberal Anglican Church since the 19th century. These churches have always welcomed members of all groups and openly opposed race discrimination. Their probably most widely known member is the Archbishop Desmond Tutu, who has been very influential in the national construction (see 3.4.2).[23]

The largest portion of the Muslim community is of Indonesian and Malayan descent. Already in the 18th century, Indonesian and Malayan slaves and political exiles united over their religious affiliation in the Western Cape.[24] Compared to the whole society, the Muslim community is small (1.5%). However as Sicard (1989:203) points out, the Muslim community played an avant-garde role in the opposition against apartheid. During the 1990s, Muslims attempted to organize politically. They founded the *Islam Party of South Africa* in 1991, which was followed by the *African Muslim Party* before the elections in 1994, but did not win a seat on the regional or national level.

Between the Christians and Muslims, tensions have surfaced repeatedly in the Western Cape: while Christians demand separation between state and church in order to act independently against violence, Muslims want to combine the two. Latent conflict potential also exists between Muslims and Jews in the Western Cape, where both groups live in close proximity to each other. The local conflicts often are related to the events in the Middle East und therefore are impacted by global factors.

The Jewish community in South Africa is pretty small with 100,000 members. The majority are "orthodox" Jews.[25] Since Judaism has no missionary ambitions – the religion is inherited, and a conversion to the Jewish faith takes at least two years combined with strict conditions – the Jewish community consists almost exclusively of Whites. During apartheid, Jews stood in strong solidarity with the Black and Coloured community. On one hand, as a minority they had an interest to speak out for themselves.

---

[23] Additionally, there are many different *Baptist Churches*, who follow strict church traditions. Among the smaller churches there are the *Greek Orthodox* and the *Seven- Days-Adventists*. Non- Christian faith groups are the Hindus and Muslims. Two thirds of the South African Indians are Hindus, the other third consists of Muslims (20%) and Christians (12%), and 2% belonging to other faith groups. These groups, though, are not represented in the study at hand.
[24] They were supported by the British government who introduced the right for Muslims to pray in public. In 1820 the "Mohammedan Congregation in Cape Town" had ca. 1300 members, consisting of Indonesian and Malayan slaves, as well as ca. 4000 *Blacks* (Patterson 1975:195).
[25] "Orthodox" Jews originate in a specific religious-political movement in Israel.

On the other hand, Jews could identify with the situation of the Black African and Coloured population due to their own experiences and their own collective memory.

Aspects of religious identity in South Africa are closely related to socio-cultural, historic and ethnic backgrounds. As the following map shows (Floël & Haferbaum, 2002:212), religious affiliation and membership of a specific socio-cultural group often are linked. Consequently, religion and socio-culture determine the neighborhoods in Cape Town (see Chidester, 2001). Since this investigation wanted to reach persons of different religious and socio-cultural backgrounds, it conducts research in different parts of the city.

The presented graph also points to the correlation of religion and population group affiliation. Members of the Afrikaans Churches tend to be White or Coloured; Jews are almost exclusively White. Muslims are predominantly Coloured and members of the AICs and ATRs are mostly Black. In order to insure a socio-cultural mix, it will be necessary to interview people from different church groups.

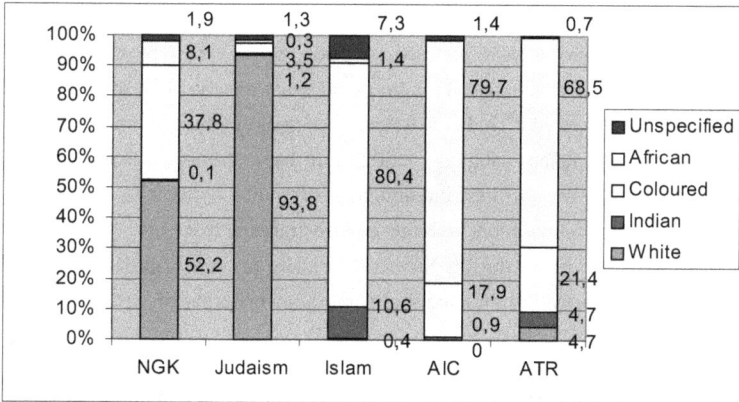

Graph 3: Religion and Population Group Affiliation

2.5 Ethnic and Socio-Cultural Affiliations as Identity Aspects

The Western Cape's population presently is made up of 58% Coloureds, 26% Whites, 15% Blacks (96% Xhosa) and 1% Asians. (Munzinger Archiv, 1994: map 2). Next to English and Afrikaans, Xhosa is the most important African language in use. Coloureds and Whites of Boers descent speak Afrikaans. English is the language spoken by Whites of British descent, used in the area of international cooperation. Locally, English often facilitates communication between people of different mother tongues. Asians are mostly of Indian descent and are only scarcely represented in this region.[26]

This chapter introduces the ethnic and cultural heterogeneity in the Western Cape, which is concealed by the categorization of population groups, and which this study assumes to be fundamental for the perception of conflict experiences on the side of the interview partners (see 1.4).

2.5.1 Coloureds

Coloureds constitute the largest population group in the Western Cape. White colonists chose this group name based on physical *race* criteria and socio-cultural standards.[27] The term Coloured [28] hides a tremendous socio-cultural, ethnic, religious and political diversity. Afrikaans language and culture have strongly influenced large parts of this group. Because Whites intentionally promoted Afrikaans as "mother tongue" for the Coloured population, a large culture transfer from the White to the Coloured population took place during the last decades, primarily in language and terminology, such as in proverbs and literature, but also in terms of culture-specific practices, such as cooking.[29]

---

[26] Because their group is hardly represented in the Western Cape, people of Indian descent by chance did not enter the sample and therefore did not participate in this study.

[27] The term "Coloured" needs to be understood as social construct which current South African literature calls "not value free" (see Martin, 2002:248). This work understands the term connotatively (see 1.4).

[28] Some authors (e.g. Grunebaum & Robins, 2001:168) regard it as extremely difficult, if not impossible, to generalize "what is means to be Coloured" because of the regional and historic specifications and the complex associations and backgrounds.

[29] One interview partner talks about the culture-specific poetry and cuisine that was part of his socialization in the Coloured community (see ch.5.7.3).

The Coloured community particularly developed in the middle of the 19th century, when this group experienced strong population growth. Until the end of the 19th century, the label *Coloureds* stood mostly for people of non-European descent, hence descendents of a blend of Asian and Black population groups. In 1904, the government reconstructed the definition. It decided that there should be three clearly defined ethnic groups in South Africa: Whites, Bantu and Coloureds. "Included in the last category were all intermediate shades between the first two." (Goldin, 1983:243) Since this new definition at beginning of the 20th century, there has been an open conversation of two main groups of Coloureds: the former so-called *Grinquas* and the *Cape Malays.*[30]

According to Goldin (1983:241), the former subgroup of Coloured, named *Grinquas,* consists of descendents of Khoi-European blending. Already in the 18th and 19th century, Europeans employed Grinquas at the Cape in their colonial fight against the Bantu. Later they became employees of the colonists and consequently were – in contrast to indigenous Africans – accepted into bourgeois society. Also, in the 18th century, Grinquas settled in Cape Town's northwest and northeast, adjacent to White areas, and oriented themselves towards Whites in language, religion, life style and attitudes: they owned horses and weapons, became landowners and gained military positions under the colonial masters. Later however, the Boers dispossessed them in the process of political changes, and their social position declined (Patterson, 1975:170).

Most members of the Grinqua subgroup are members of Christian churches. Their religious affiliation also signifies social class. This is how the Grinqua distinguish themselves from another culture-specific group of Coloureds, the so-called *Cape Malays.*

The *Malays* are descendants of Southeast Asian Muslims from Singapore, China, Indonesia and Malaya, who were imported as slaves, and merged with members of the indigenous African population. Many Cape Muslims live in segregated areas such as the Cape Muslim Quarter in the center of Cape Town, which is one of the oldest city areas - already in the 18th century Cape Malays were settled here[31] - but also in the Cape Flats, formerly townships. As slave descendents, their social status has been low from the

---

[30] The Cape Malays are also called *Cape-Muslims* or *Coloured Muslims.*
[31] Frescura (2001:99) argues that the colonial masters lay down the roots for "racial segregation" in the Southern African urban centers already in the 19th century.

beginning. Not until the 1920s, the government constituted the Cape Malays as an Afrikaans-speaking group. The change of language impacted the group culturally and also raised its social status. However, next to the Afrikaans influence, the group sustained many of their own cultural and especially Muslim traditions. In 1994, the Islamic community celebrated *"Three hundred years of Islam in South Africa."* Evidently religion is a significant identity aspect for the Cape Malays (Jeppie, 2001:82). Their religious identity draws its strength from the aggressive representation of their minority group in the South African and West Cape public. To Muslims, this identity means stability, security and orientation, to such a degree that they have been relatively independent from apartheid's identity construction through racial criteria.[32] Individual self-definition over religious and collective identity helps to overcome the degrading racial definition, which carried the trauma of historical stigmatization.

The complex history of both major Coloured groups is a continuous fight for identity, consciousness and belonging: If Coloureds tended to stand on the British side during the Anglo-Boer-War (1899-1902), they saw themselves in the following years constantly torn between the promises of the White political parties who wanted their votes, and the Black groupings.

At the beginning of the 20th century, the first political party of Coloureds formed with the purpose to promote the interests of their own group. As a result they faced growing prejudice on the side of the White working class. The national press picked up this formation of prejudice and turned it into a media campaign against Coloureds. Consequently many Coloureds lost their jobs and their respect in the White population. Increasing race discrimination eventually resulted in the exclusion of Coloured intellectuals and the Coloured bourgeoisie from the White upper class, making them lose their social status along with their class affiliation. Accordingly, this loss strengthened the solidarity between Blacks and Coloureds, even though the latter initially continued fighting for respect from the White political parties. During apartheid the educated Coloured and Black elites showed their solidarity, for example, by associating in specific political movements. They formed coalitions in founding and leading anti-racist

---

[32] Also Farie du Toit (2002) states in his investigation that "Coloured Muslims" - compared to "unemployed squatters" - find security in their "cultural identity," which they perceive as constructive. In contrast, other participants of his investigation felt rather disturbed by the idea of their "cultural identity."

and socialist organizations, and in supporting the *Black-Conscientiousness-Movement* (see 3.4.1) and its liberal Coloured fractions. During apartheid, these two political orientations led to frequent conflicts and splits within the community (Goldin, 1983:251) with lasting effects in the communities. However, these different positions also created socio-political overlap-fields for Black and Coloured intellectuals and political activists.

In the post-apartheid era, formerly labeled Coloureds are searching more than ever for an identity. As identity constructs have established hierarchical divisions of superiority and inferiority between Blacks and Whites - "They were experienced and constructed as less than White and better than Black" (Erasmus 2001:24) - the Coloured community faces a difficult phase of reconstruction. Because of political decisions, such as the *Affirmative Action Act*, Coloureds again feel themselves between the fronts, given how people are promoted based on racial characteristics. Erasmus (2001:22) expresses his feelings about the present situation as follows: "In the apartheid times we were not White enough. Today we are not Black enough to get a job." In discussing a new identity for the Coloured community and its individual members, Erasmus (2001:21) wants to discard the position that Coloureds should define themselves over "mixed race identities." Instead, people should feel that they belong to subcultures or socio-cultural groups, who define themselves over specific knowledge, cultural practices, language, memories, religion, rituals and philosophies of life (see 2.3/5.7.3). Identity formation further implies the challenge to recognize racist positions, perceptions, and practices in daily life, as well as their influence on one's own reality and personality. This can never happen while negating and denying the past, but only over the processing of injuries and discomfort during the transformation process of society and personality (2001:26). With this constructivist approach of identity formation that is particularly popular in the Coloured intellectual elite, Erasmus represents something revolutionary after decades of predominant racial definitions with the interest of setting one group apart from other groups. If this approach plays a role in the conflict perception will be examined in chapters 5.7.2 and 5.7.3.

2.5.2 Blacks

The ethnological literature (Breutz, 1975, Hirschberg, 1975, Schapera, 1934, Warmelo, 1975) on Black groups in South Africa neither agrees on migration movements, nor on ethnic divisions and unions, nor on linguistic assimilations and changes. Therefore, one constantly encounters contradictions between the names others have given to groups and how groups name themselves, depending on the given historical period and on the researcher. The ethnic names used here are, as much as possible, the ones groups use for themselves.

During apartheid, all members of the Black-African ethnic groups were combined under the title, "Black."[33] Since they mostly belonged to Bantu-speaking groups, they were also called "Bantu."[34] On the grounds of the thesis that there are cultural criteria that connect all Blacks, Breutz finds "Bantu- specific phenomena" and value orientations (1975:441).These include: community or clan affiliation rooted in the family, which acknowledges the chief as "father superior" as part of a larger advisory structure. Also, the socio-political systems in Bantu-societies share similar complex ranking systems, which are characterized by polygamous structures, ancestry worship and detailed inheritance laws. Position and status of a person are determined in the order of family, respectively clan, and age. Like Mitchell (see 2.4), Breutz states the significance of merging traditional and Christian beliefs, which play an important role in individual and collective identity.

Some interview partners belong to the Xhosa, Tswana or Shona. The following contains an introduction of these groups.

The ethnic groups living on the high plateau of the inland, between the Drakensberg and the ocean, and on the broad strip between Swaziland, Natal and the Cape Province, are summed up under the generic term *Nguni* (van Warmelo, 1975). This linguistic-geographic name is an *onomatopoeia*, since all the Nguni languages contain clucking-sounds.

---

[33] According to Bryce (1990:90), the colonial literature used for *Blacks* the prejorative term "kaffern" (Arab for "someone who lies"). Still today, this term is occasionally used in a condescending way for members of Black groups.

[34] The word "Bantu" means "Mensch" (human being) in German. This name had pejorative character during apartheid time, but will be used here in its connotative sense and original meaning.

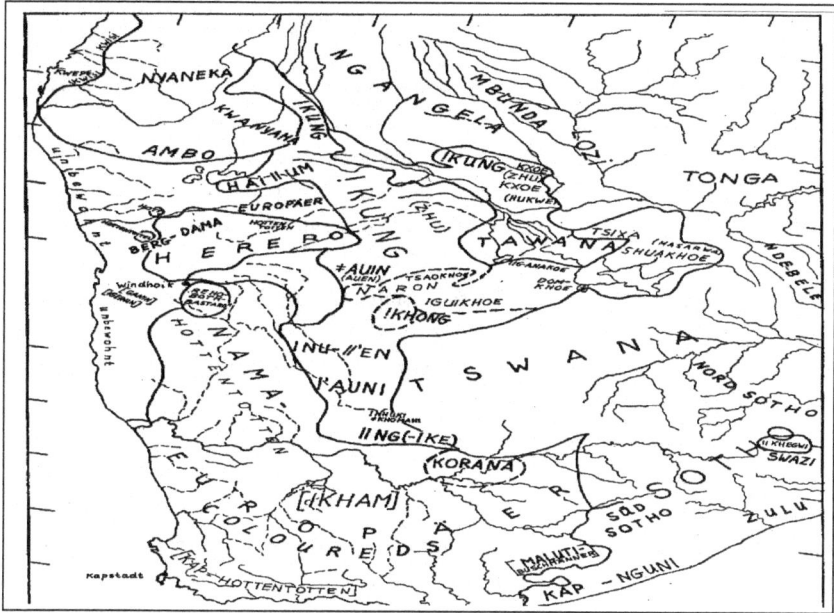

Graph 4: Ethnic groups on the Western Cape.

The Nguni-language groups are divided into Cape-Ngunies, including the Xhosa-speaking ethnic groups who originally had migrated from the East Cape to the Western Cape; the Zulu-speaking Natal-Nguni;[35] the Swazi, and the Transvaal-Ndebele. The first Nguni immigrants in South Africa were possibly Khosa and the Pondo of the Embo-group in the 13th century, who arrived at the same time as the Tsonga-language groups from Mozambique. Until this day, Xhosa settle mostly on the East Cape. Therefore, today about 96% of the Blacks on the Western Cape speak Xhosa. Because of their

---

[35] The Zulu (Natal Nguni) today represent their interests on national level through their Ithaka Freedom Party (IFP, which was founded 1991 by Mangosuthu Buthelezi and which is often considered as a counter weight to the Xhosa-dominated African National Congress (ANC). However, there are also Zulu speaking political key figures in the ANC. Naudascher-Schlag (1994:15/16) disputes as propaganda that the traditional "Zulu-Xhosa-Conflict," which already manifested itself under King Shaka in the 19th century, is today carried out on the modern, political level. Instead, the Zulus, who have about 300 subgroups, continue fighting for their political independence from the SAR.

geographical proximity to the Khoikoi, the Xhosa language today integrates different kinds of clucking sounds.[36]

In his comparative study about customs of rural Xhosa, Mayer (1994:25) observes a strong change of values regarding housekeeping, definitions of family, and leisure time. This shift manifests itself in the loosening and abolishing of patriarchal and familial structures, and the development of new connectional systems. Because of the urban conditions, urban social networks tend to be more individually structured than rural ones.

Also Naudascher-Schlag (1994:25) finds shifts of value and identity among young urban Black Africans in Cape Town (see 5.5.5, B2).[37] This is leading them away from the old-African family and hierarchy principles, such as "age before status," resulting in irritations between the different generations. According to Raum (1980:202), under urban-European influence during apartheid, the Xhosa specialized in mining, textiles, mechanics, chemical industry, and service sector in order to provide for their families left behind in the Eastern Cape. Because of a shift of values, Raum observes a great potential for conflict among the Xhosa, which is reflected in the young generation's rejection of family-and community values.[38]

Another ethnic group with great influence in South Africa are the Sotho, who primarily settled inland. They are divided roughly into South Sotho[39], North Sotho[40] and

---

[36]One Shona-speaking interview partner resents how Whites and Coloureds ridicule the clucking sounds, which he describes in his interview (see 5.7.4)

[37] In the data material, interviewees repeatedly refer to the comprehensible shift of values among urban and rural socialized *Black*.

[38] Traditionally, Xhosa solved their conflicts by enlisting ancestry cults and traditional rites, as well as the assistance of elders, whose "seniority" status gave them power to intervene in conflicts and to function as mediators (Raum, 1980:205). The heterogeneity of the Xhosa-groups caused many tensions and fights in the Western Cape. Conflicts arose not only among the Xhosa, but also between them and the other local groups, such as the Khoikhoi. They were solved by turning to third parties, through "Triangulation" (Ury, 2000:49).

[39] The South Sotho (Basotho/Basuto) live in the area around Lesotho (formerly Basuto Land). Conflicts between these subgroups historically related primarily to cattle thefts, expeditions of singular ethnic groups or internal "intrigues" (Ashton, 1952:2). Large inter-ethnic conflicts occurred mainly during the Zulu expansion under Shaka. Today many South Sotho live in the independent kingdom of Lesotho, which forms an independent "nation" (like Swaziland) with its own judicial and political system. Culturally and administratively, Lesotho divided in clans, families and villages, which again form ethnic subgroups themselves and sometimes have their own names, emblems and totems honored by their clan and family elders. Many South Sotho and Lesotho today study in Cape Town's universities.

West Sotho (Tswana) with different subgroups.[41] The West Sotho or Tswana (in older literature also called Betschuans) are the oldest representatives of the Southeast Bantu. They have integrated diverse, small ethnic groups, such as the Tlhaping, Kwena and Rolong (Schapera, 1934:4-5). The Ntwana, a subgroup of the Tswana with its ethnic origin in the West Sotho, is given special attention in literature. They are originally related to the Rolong, who define a member's status within rigid social structures. Today the Tswana are ethnically very heterogeneous, since they have combined with many other ethnic groups on their mirgation through South Africa. Seeking protection from the Ndebele, they mostly settled close to the North Sotho groups, mainly the Pedi, (Magubane, 1998:138). Originally, the Tswana lived with the Basotho in Basutoland (today Lesotho). In the middle of the 18th century, many West Sotho groups felt closer related to the Tswana groups in Bschuanaland (today Botswana) with respect to dialect, social structures and culture [42] and joined them. Therefore there are lots of cultural variables within the Tswana groups.

The last ethnic group being considered here is the Shona.[43] The majority of the Shona today reside in Zimbabwe and in the north-western region of Mozambique. Additionally, there are a number of isolated, scattered settlements in South Africa, Malawi, Botswana and Zambia. The term Shona again subsumes different groups.[44] Shona and Shona dialects of certain groups, such as the Kalanga, Kranga, Zuzure and Ndau, show cultural similarities and common traditions. In Zimbabwe, the Shona are the largest ethnic group of the country making up 80 % of the population. During the last decades, many Shona migrated from Zimbabwe to neighboring countries, where they often found employment as mine workers, so that descendents of migrant workers from

---

[40] The North Sotho (also called Transvaal-Sotho), subsuming again numerous ethnic groups and subgroups, settle in the northeastern inland plateau. The Pedi, for example, unite many subgroups (e.g. the Maroteng), whose history and language are similar. Today they settle primarily in the area around Pietersburg.

[41] The Tswana find special attention here, because one of the interview partners belongs to this group.

[42] According to Camaroff and Roberts (1983:107ff), the Tswana – similar to the Khoikoi – have a culture specific conflict management system, which regards the "triangulation" as its major tool for conflict resolution.

[43] This group is mentioned here because one interview partner defines himself over his ethnic background as Shona, among others.

[44] The South African linguist, Clemmons Doke, introduced the category *Shona* in 1931, to combine different ethnic groups with certain commonalities in language, colloquialisms, dialects and socio-political organization.

Zimbabwe live now in South Africa. The number of immigrating Shona from Zimbabwe has increased during the recent years of political change.

2.5.3 Whites

The population group of Whites consists primarily of descendents of European immigrants: beside the Dutch, respectively Boers (about 40%), and the British (about 7.5%) today there are a remarkable number of Germans (about 40%) and French (Hugenottes) (about 7.5%) in South Africa. The remaining 5% include descendants of Italians, Spanish, Portuguese and Scandinavians, who settled on the Cape during the second half of the 17th century (SAIRR, 2001).

In the last centuries, conflicts among Whites occurred repeatedly, in particular between Boers[45]and English speakers, who both wanted to maintain their political and geographical predominance (Anglo-Boers-War, 1899-1902). Until this day, there are frictions between these groups. Since the end of apartheid, a particular source of tension has been the question of guilt or responsibility for the crimes of the past. In the post-apartheid-phase, Whites – just like the other ethnic groups -- have to re-define their identity and to replace and reconstruct their position as White minority, even though they still are in positions of power and influence. Du Toit notes (2001:1) that Whites today are challenged more than ever to re-define their identity. They actually are going through an identity crisis, because of a strong sentiment of "collective guilt" based on a sense of wrongdoing in the colonial and apartheid endeavors. Because of the shifting centers of power, previously unshaken social identities are now subject of self-reflection and self-evaluation (du Toit, 2001:2).

The portion of Whites in the population has declined since the end of apartheid. Many people of Western-European descent emigrated to their countries of origin. This is legally possible up to the third generation after immigrating to South Africa. The country has experienced a great loss of Whites, often qualified professionals, as many left for fear of violent revolution, economic redistribution, political persecution of former apartheid-activists and also lack of professional perspectives. This large *brain*

---

drain presents a big problem for the nation. Only slowly a new multicultural middle and upper class is emerging, who is able to deal with the internal and external challenges.

Obviously, it is necessary to consider the topic at hand in the context of multiple identity- aspects. These offer orientation and possibilities of identity-constructions for individuals, who then combine them group-specifically. It will be necessary to include social realities and specific subgroup-cultures when looking at multiple identity-aspects. It would not be sufficient to limit one's attention to ethnic and racial aspects.

Pieta Robin
Clause 27: Arrested, detained and accused persons.
380 x 570: Linocut
In: Images of Human Rights Portfolio.
© Artists for Human Rights Trust

3. Theoretical Frame of Reference

This study is based on sociological and ethnological approaches that are dealing with the construction of social and individual realities, societal and individual value orientations, and identity aspects, and with perceptions and constructions of interpersonal conflicts. In their sociological reflections, Berger and Luckmann (2000:VI) note that society's reality is double grounded. "The individual takes possession of reality, as reality takes also possession of it." In light of Berger/Luckmann's (3.1) and Watzlawick's (2001) social theories, this work conceives the South African value discourses (3.4) as social constructions on the national level. The ensuing presentation and interpretation in chapter 5 will show how individuals on the local level construct reality with respect to their experienced (narrated) conflicts and their immanent value orientations.

In South Africa, the phenomenon of creating a peaceful, unified nation is particularly volatile: external influences, such as appeals for democratization, demands for human rights, and engagements of international corporations bring along alternative lifestyles and realities. But they also cause disorientation and irritation in a country that is already dealing with its internal ethnic and cultural diversity and looking for a synergetic way for societal and cultural change. Beside these external and internal factors, there is the ongoing struggle to deconstruct the apartheid past, which until this day determines perceptions and constructions of social and individual realities.

Anderson's (1998) theoretical approach, in part, provides the theoretical base for the discussion on "nation building," since it expounds its construction character. In accordance with Anderson's theory, "nation" here is understood in constructivist terms (see 3.1.1).

The following is a summary of the views of influential participants of the national-political value discourse (see 3.4.1/3.4.3), leading politicians, theologians and scholars. A central theme of this discourse process has been the vision of societal coexistence in post apartheid South Africa. These discussions focus on socio-cultural sectors and are an integral part of discussions of African philosophy, African knowledge, politics, cultural concepts, art and language. They offer, according to Anderson (1998), reality building blocks for the construction of the Rainbow Nation.

Naturally, the new Rainbow Nation is not harmonious and peaceful. Rather, the data gathered in this investigation point to a high conflict potential, which is confirmed by different perspectives.

As theoretical base, selected conflict-theoretical approaches (see 3.3./3.3.1/3.3.2) will assist the understanding of conflict experiences.

3.1 The Construction of Individual and Social Realities from the Viewpoint of Social Science and Ethnology

According to the sociological reflections on reality construction by Peter L. Berger and Thomas Luckmann (2000), society contains a *subjective* and an *objective* reality. It is *objective* as far as it objectifies sediments of human experience in social behavior, manifests it in social roles and materializes it in institutions and linguistic symbolic systems. Even though language is a product of human behavior, the language reality gains "quasi-autonomy." Thus, society exercises power over its members, even as these constitute its very existence. A change in the basic conditions and given knowledge of a person changes also the possibilities of perceptions and vice versa. Here begins – according to Berger/Luckmann (200:IV)- the transition to the *subjective* social reality: "The individual takes reality into possession, as it is also taken into possession by reality." The reality of daily life is a symbolically organized relationship between individual and society. Initially, this daily life appears to the individual as reality that routinely exists. However, if this routine is interrupted in the interaction of individuals, an orientation problem arises. Orientation knowledge of everyday life gives instructions on how to handle critical events in order to re-integrate them into everyday routine.

A person shares the reality of daily life with *the others* , whose perceptions of reality are different. Fundamentally important is the experience of the *other* face to face, because the *vis-à-vis situation* is the prototype of all social interactions. From here individuals derive their behavior patterns for every other interaction (Berger, 2000:31). The individual experiences the *other* primarily as subject of his daily life. The *other* participates in the process of mutual perception, as the reality of everyday life employs stereotypes or categorizations, with which it detects and treats the others. Hence, the reality of everyday life consists of a coherent and dynamic accumulation of stereotypes that become more anonymous the further one removes oneself from the *here and now*. The result is a polarization of the others, on one hand, and an anonymous abstraction of the others on the other hand, which could never arise in vis-à-vis situations.

In society, the experienced situation takes shape through the assignment of terms. A named experience is more real to the experiencing person, because it can also be potentially experienced by others through "what has been put into language." Thus, community is a construct of externalizations of individual experiences, which in personal interactions make the subjects' perceptions of the interaction comprehensible through so-called *objectivations*. Their expressions happen through language, gestures, facial expressions and vocal sign-systems, whose decoding can be learned. Social interactions and conflict experiences are communications in light of the question: "How do we experience the other?" Critical situations are becoming every day situations and normal through the daily routine, since they arise when different perceptions and expectations of reality collide with those of the others.

Berger/Luckmann's sociological theory assists in interpreting and reconstructing narrated experiences and helps to bring - through its interpretation – the narrated reality close to others. The cluster-analysis applies their theoretical approach in the following areas: perception of the Rainbow Nation (5.4), construction of self and other- images of groups (5.5), narrated conflict situations (5.6), and identity as topic of conflict (5.7). In the data material, conflicts in *vis-à-vis contacts* are identified, as well as more abstract conflict experiences in the context of self- and other-images, which mark social polarizations and anonymous-making according to Berger/Luckmann.

Of further importance for the data evaluation are some impulses from the constructivist theory approach of Paul Watzlawicks (2001a:91ff). Watzlawick interprets realities as "self-fulfilling prophecies," which "...as assumption or prediction confirm [their] own "rightness" simply by the fact that [they exist] and [expect] the assumed or expected event to become reality." For example, the person who feels despised will act overly sensitive and distrustful, causing the interacting person to respond to that distrust and confirm the first person's assumption. That is how "self-fulfilling prophecies" produce actions that form the condition for the expected events and thus become "real." Believed prophecies of events can turn into the prophesied event itself.

The phenomenon of "self-fulfilling prophecy" is not rare in (intercultural) communication situations (e.g., 5.5.3). Here the expectations of the conversation partners come to the surface and are either confirmed or not. According to Stephen (1985), people in situations of intercultural communication often experience self-confirming expectations, regardless of the other person's actual behavior. Something similar is true for the perception of group members. They are regarded as representatives of their respective groups with specific characteristics or behaviors, which - removed from a *vis-à-vis situation* – become self-fulfilling prejudices and stereotypes (see 5.5).

However, the construction of realities does not only take place in personal daily life, but also on the level of society-building theories, visions and religions. Watzlawick calls these "building blocks of ideological realities." They are highly complex and determine societies in other ways than through personal interactions (see 3.1.1). This ideological and visionary aspect of reality often brings meaning, purpose, and value to the other aspects. When one aspect of reality is acknowledged, it receives its context of meaning through the ideologies and vision linked with it. Therefore, according to Watzlawick (2001b: 219), there are two orders of reality: the *first order*, which includes facts, and the *second order,* which adds meaning through ideologies and visions. The political-ideological value-discourses (3.4) thus generate "building blocks of ideological realities" for the South African nation. These generation processes are also reflected in the data material of the interview partners (e.g., 5.4).

3.1.1 The Nation as a Construct

When examining the sociological and multicultural debates on nation building, one invariably comes across Anderson's work, *The Invention of the Nation* (1998). In anthropological terms, a nation is: "... an imagined political community – imagined as enclosed and sovereign" (ibid.,14). It is *imagined* because the members never get to know, see nor hear about most of the others, but have nevertheless the image of a shared community. Therefore all human communities are *imagined communities*, which are larger than groups in which you have exclusively *vis-à-vis contacts*. On one hand, along with Berger/Luckmann, the nation constitutes itself at its base through direct *vis-à-vis contacts.* On the other hand, according to Anderson, it constructs itself through information in literature and mass media, which create the image of a shared nation.

The nation is *enclosed* because it defines itself largely through its separation from other nations and communities. As the nation is formed through the emotional connections to the imagined, anonymous people, it is always receptive to other people and ideas, and thus to change: it forms in the memory of the past, the envisioning of the presence, the dreaming of the future, and the invention of visions. It is *sovereign,* since nations came into existence at a time when the strongest adherents of the universal religions had to come to grips with the pluralism of religions, their ontological claims, and their territorial expansion. Measure and symbol of sovereignty is the sovereign state (under God).

Finally, the nation is a *community,* since it is understood - regardless of social inequality and exploitation- as a *comrade-like union of equals,* called *brotherhood,* which guarantees the national, peaceful holding together of the people (ibid., 16). The *imagined community,* accordingly, consists of a network of symbolic values, spaces, times and religions, which can be deduced from its historical development. Basic for the development of the nation is a faith that is derived from the legitimization of political power through church and religion and can be traced back to previous dynasties. Today's nations (ibid.,19) have their roots in preceding cultural systems, such as religious communities, since these built their deeply rooted religious communities early on through signs, symbols, and literature, such as the "holy scripture." With the loss of common language in the course of changing attitudes towards religion and family, religious communities fragmented, pluralized, and territorialized. In addition, there was a radical change in the ways of perceiving the world, which made it possible "to think the nation" (ibid., 27). Newspapers and novels enabled people to think in *simultaneity.* Everybody could learn what was happening at the same time in different places of the nation. These technical means took up the rising consciousness and represented the nation. A new sense of community and a general confidence in the national unity grew as the use of language changed: a new form of imagination through language created a new base for a national consciousness (ibid., 43). The national *written languages* and the uplifting of *model characters* were made the center of ideology and politics: the nation became an intentional goal, strengthened by national literature. Today the concept of nation practically exists in every written language. The sense of "being a nation" can hardly be separated from any political awareness. However, Anderson leaves the question open whether a nation can be a nation without one common language.

Peter Fuchs (1992) goes beyond Anderson's nation definition by eliminating the community component and equating community and society. Thus, Fuchs succeeds in leaving the restrictive, nation-related perspective behind and in speaking of communities in their dynamic evolvement in post-modern times. In his theoretical discussion of construction and imagination of communities, Fuchs views societies today "as *multi-perspective*, as *hyper-complex*" (ibid., 8/9). Diverse structures emerge in postmodern societies, which no longer achieve unity among each other: various systems clash with each other, become autonomous, continue to develop, and integrate external elements according to their specific society. This phenomenon is true for every system within a society because every system carries along a certain viewpoint and its own perspective, which reconcile in the social reality (ibid., 11). Hence, every perspective, that is, every possibility of observing and evaluating, holds its own reality. One can speak of *multiplication of social realities, social multi-perspectives or poly-contextuality*. According to Fuchs, social structures parallel to these multi-perspectives imply "incompatibility" and possibly cause a central loss of meaning for society, which may imply potential for conflict.

This constructivist approach of the multi-perspectives in post-modern societies is of fundamental importance for the work at hand because of its implications for the evaluation and interpretation of the data material (e.g., 5.4). The gathering of daily conflict situations is supposed to demonstrate the "incompatibilities" of individual and society that arise due to multi-perspectives.

When comparing Anderson's definition of "nation" with the discourses on nation building in post-apartheid South Africa, one notices that the efforts of politicians, scholars and theologians (see 3.4) share an important common goal, namely to undo the more than 200 years old construct of a Boers nation and replace it.[46] Since the great

---

[46] The Boer nationalism shows up first time at the end of the 19th century, when it spread through Boers pastors and writers. These predecessors of the Afrikaans nationalism succeeded in elevating the regionally spoken Dutch *Patois* to the status of a written language, whose name *Afrikaans* did not indicate any relationship to Europe (Anderson, 1998: 69), but implied the new cultural surroundings. Hence, the idea of the *Afrikaaner nation* spread with the support of religious groups, and through

political change at the beginning of the 1990s, South Africans have been developing new concepts of reality. One of their visionary concepts is that of the *Rainbow Nation* (see 3.4.1), which they imagine, like Fuchs, as hyper-complex and containing multiple perspectives. Here, both old-African and Western-globalist influences carry weight for the construction of the nation. The recent discussions on the Rainbow Nation show how differenciated and heterogenious the elements of the future Rainbow Nation are in their constructivist conception.

This observation corresponds with the complexity of the South African society as portrayed in chapter 2, its numerous ethnic and socio-cultural groups, religious diversity, varied developments throughout history, and as it is documented in major sources.

3.1.2 Multicultural Trends in Identity Constructions

The theoretical and sociological discussions on the construction of societal and individual realities during the last decades require new approaches and further discussions on the topic of multiculturalism. Recent ethnological discussions on multiculturalism, multicultural society and nation (Anderson, 1998, Baumann, 1999; Craw, 1994; Goldberg, 1994; McLaren, 1994; Turner, 1994) push for a new understanding of culture, nation, ethnicity and religion in order to do justice to the pluralistic and multicultural understanding reality of nations.

For the creation of the justice and equality principle, according to Baumann (1999:135), three linked main branches come into play in a multicultural society: *nation* and *national identity, ethnicity* and *ethnic identity,* and *religion* and *religious identity* (see 3.2).

---

literature, magazines and newspapers. In addition, selected socio-cultural groups constructed the *new culture* through vis-à-vis contacts. The black intelligence in South Africa was of central importance for the rise of this nationalism, since they were educated in public schools to become bi-lingual and bi-cultural citizens. Even though this group had no political or economic power, which remained in the hands of the colonial masters, Indians, Arabs and Chinese, and the indigenous African elite spread the idea of the Afrikaans nation and its meaning though the *Afrikaans* language

```
┌─────────────────────────────┐         ┌──────────────────────────────┐
│ Nation and National Identity │         │ Ethnicity and Ethnic Identity │
└─────────────────────────────┘         └──────────────────────────────┘

            ┌──────────────────────────────┐
            │    Societal Main Branches     │
            │   according to Baumann, 1999  │
            └──────────────────────────────┘

                     ┌───────────────────────────────────┐
                     │ Religion and Religious Identity    │
                     └───────────────────────────────────┘
```

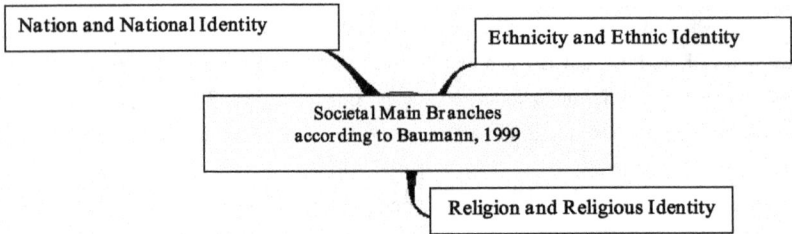

Graph 5: Main Social Branches according to Baumann

The *post-ethnic* nation is attempting to replace ethnic connections with national ones, even though it simultaneously uses pseudo-ethnic ideologies to maintain the value of Anderson's *imagined community* (see 3.1.1). Ethnicity is connected to family relationships and descent and originates independently. Religion is context-bound to position itself in its surroundings. Out of this *multicultural triangle*, problematic relationships grow between nation and ethnicity, nation and religion, as well as ethnicity and religion (Baumann, 1999:51). Religion, in this regard, plays an outstanding role in that it serves many groups in the nation as orientation and in that it simultaneously contains an objective pole, open to many directions of movements (see 2.4). In line with Berger/Luckmann's theoretical discussions on "society shaping realities" (3.1) and with regard to our data evaluation in chapter 5, it is appropriate to expand Baumann's "multicultural triangle" to include *individuality* and *individual identity*, as well as *socio-culture* and *socio-cultural identities*, which – like the religious, ethnic and national identity - make up main branches in a society. Both of these aspects of societal and individual realities have proven central for the data material.

Multiculturalism shows itself particularly complex (Baummann, 1999:82/83) in nations' big cities and capitals. This is the case in Cape Town where people may call themselves "Capetonians," but often define themselves also over their regional roots elsewhere. So they are metropolitans and "uprooted" people at the same time. Society becomes an elastic cross-over *network of multiple identif*ications and *pluralistic realities,* building society and cultural stability. The debate on multiculturalism is interdisciplinary and rich in facets. According to Craw (1994:37ff), *multiculturalism* stands for a wide range of social expressions, ideas and practices, which are reduced to a formal uniqueness by the "-ism," and at the same time cemented into an ideology of political correctness. Therefore, the term as such does not do justice to its heterogeneous character. This reduction to uniqueness has its historical origin in the monocultural obligation, to which the term, according to Goldberg (1994:3), provided a possible answer. Because of the cultural diversity in the history of the resistance, accommodation, integration and transformation developed into different trends in the interpretation of *multiculturalism.* Both trends[47], which are addressed primarily in the data evaluation chapters, are the *critical multiculturalism* and the *difference multiculturalism.* It goes without saying that these two social constructs, outlined in the following, are considered ideal types, which melt together at times within – as Baumann calls them – the "networks of pluralistic and individual realities and identifications."

Like Baumann, Turner (1994:406) sees ethnic and religious pluralism as a sign of multi-culture. *Multiculturalism* then is a conceptional framework that challenges the cultural hegemony of dominant groups by calling for equal recognition of the expressions/terms of non-hegemonial groups. Turner (1994:408) divides multiculturalism into the two forms of *critical and difference multiculturalism.* The *critical multiculturalism* starts out from the cultural diversity of different groups of a society and wants them to build an open, shared culture. Taking diversity as social base appears provocative and revisionist. It questions the basic dominating cultural norms and the principle of dominant versus minority in order to strengthen a common culture. Diversity here is the symbol of multicultural societies accompanied by complexity, new challenges and stimulations (Stiehm, 1994:140): a symbol, that moves emotions,

---

[47] The term- definitions and the descriptions of single directions of multiculturalism are equally complex as the main term itself. Some authors use different terms synonymously or with small divergences. For example, McLaren (1994:47) distinguishes between "conservative multiculturalism," liberal multiculturalism, "left-liberal multiculturalism" "critical and resistance multiculturalism." Turner (1994), on the other hand, concentrates on "difference multiculturalism." Since the discussion with the multiculturalism-debate is only part of the theoretical work, here the main focus lies on clarification and application of the two above mentioned directions (see 5) and not on the discussion of the terminology discussion.

stimulates reflection and thereby evokes positive responses. According to McLaren (1994:53), *critical multiculturalism* understands representations of race, class and gender as result of larger social struggles over signs and meanings, thereby emphasizing the transformative nature of social, cultural and institutional meanings. McLaren understands differences as product of history, culture and ideologies that arise among groups and that *critical multiculturalism* questions. A central theoretical position of this approach is the assumption that differences come about through ideological production and the reception of cultural signs and historical events. The *critical multiculturalism* therefore suggests a policy of "alliance- building," "dreaming together," and "solidarity that moves beyond condescension of, say, "race awareness week," which actually serves to keep forms of institutionalized racism intact" (McLaren, 1994:57). Thus, this form of multiculturalism wants to establish imperatives of peace, democracy and critical citizenship with the goal to build a common diverse societal base and to change the dominant systems. Differences have to be seen as political differences and have to be defined accordingly as political *difference-in-relation.* Differences are neither absolute nor unchangeable. McLaren does not want to destabilize the meaning of differences, but question and (re-) construct their historical construction. In line with this work (see 3.2), he understands the identity of a person or group in *critical multiculturalism* as "polyvalent assemblage" (contradictory and over-determined)" (1994:58).

Turner (1994:409) views *difference multiculturalism* in sharp contrast to *critical multiculturalism.* This form of multiculturalism emphasizes the differences between the cultural groups, which are reduced to *ethnic groups* in order to justify political and intellectual separatism. Turner calls this kind of multiculturalism "stereotypical," because multiculturalism here has become a homogeneous form, and a set of ideas and attitudes that encase all the different, separate groups. It focuses on the differences and the different qualities of groups, which oftentimes are seen as isolated entities, rather than in their societal-political context. A polycentric multiculturalism – like the *critical multiculturism* - demands therefore a fundamental re-conceptualization of relationships between cultural communities among nations. This should elicit dynamic, interactive cultures and overcome the idea of fixed, monolithic cultures with firmly ascribed possessions and entitlements (as in *difference multiculturalism*).

Of central importance for this work is the question what kind of multiculturalism plays a role in post-apartheid South Africa (see 5). It can be assumed that apartheid represented a form of *difference culturalism*. Now the question is which type of multiculturalism the political-ideological and visionary value discussions (see 3.4ff) propagates on the one hand, and which type is perceived and created in the minds of our interview partners on the other hand. Regarding the value discourses, the assumption is that *critical multiculturalism* is being envisioned and constructed. With respect to everyday conflicts, presumably the form of *critical multiculturalism* is ideal and desired, but *difference multiculturalism* stands in the foreground of the perception and construction of actual reality (see 5).

Vogt (1997:131) sees the recognition of different, numerous realities as an outstanding chance for national and international politics. The development of visions, discourses, and strategies of peace politics is imperative for to the reality construction of individuals, communities and nations to achieve conflict-transformation. This would be especially the case if they were translated into concrete programs. Lasting peace and future planning among nations can only be reached through repeated public discussions on positive value orientations, visions and strategies.

This work is based on Vogt's fundamental philosophy. Hence, chapter 3.4 presents selected South African discourses and visions on peace. Chapter 5 examines everyday perceptions of conflict in light of his philosophy. Everyday discourses do not – as explained above – contain only peace potentials beneficial for the construction of the South African society. Observation shows that there are individual identity constructs with problematic conflict potential. This is especially true for the construction of other-images and "supposed other-images," which are the focus of the following.

3.2   Conflict Potentials in Identity Construction

According to Layes (2001:17), the identity of a person is made up of various interests, roles, attitudes and value orientations, which he/she has to integrate and which change in their degree of importance depending on the situation.

In the post-modern discussion on identity (Keupp, 1988, 1994, 1997, Krauss, 1996), the fundamental thoughts on *post-modern identity* are based on the notion of *pluralization* of the self and consequently on the assumption of a so-called "healthy" form of *multiple identity.*[48]

For quite some time now, Erickson's identity-type (1953) [49] appears to be outdated (see Darmstädter & May, 1997). More recent voices consider this type to be inadequate and socially irrelevant because of the complex and contradictory demands of present day society, as presented in 3.1.2, which require an equally complex and flexible identity. However, the "postmodern" psychologists around Keupp, while striving to find a unifying type, end up closely to the pathological form of "multiple personality disturbance." If deprived of its pathological content, it will be weakened to a mere "multiple identity" and also turn into an adequate counterpart to societal ambiguity.

The discourse on postmodern identity will not be extended at this point. Important is only that this study – in keeping with the theoretical discussion on construction of societies, multiculturalism and conflict realities – is based on a postmodern identity type that integrates diverse elements, such as ethnic, religious, gender, cultural, provincial and racial orientations in the sense of a "patchwork-identity" (Keupp, 1988). This definition of identity seems to be most suitable for the analysis and interpretation of the presented data material, since it does justice to the various identity aspects and their social reference points that are bound to reality and create reality in post- apartheid South Africa.[50] The multiple identity depends on its „social reality" and

---

[48] This form of „multiple identity" is addressed by a Coloured pastor in chapter 5.7.3, who perceives the post-modern identity as the ideal type for Coloureds to overcome the traditional identity definitions from the past.

[49] Erickson (1953) defines the identity type, in short, as coherent whole that during adolescence has integrated "childhood patterns" and societal demands. Thus, a person is at all times and in all places the same, and accordingly develops a future oriented image of family, career and ideology.

[50] According to Keupp (1994, 1997), the understanding here is that the societal complexity is not an unreasonable demand on identity, but that it opens "creativity spaces," which the individual can grasp or counter with its multiple identity. In his definition of "patchwork identity," Keupp does not elaborate on how the particular identity aspects are connected and how role- and identity caused contradictions manifest themselves in his identity type. Relevant here is only that such contradictions do exist in the "multiple identity." They arise in the experience and construction of daily, multiple realities. Therefore, contradictory identity-aspects can cause intrapersonal and interpersonal conflicts, just like this can be the case because of complex socially constructed realities. Hence, social and identity multiplicity provides "creativity spaces," but also opens up new conflict potentials because of possible identity conflicts.

its construction. It forms itself in acceptance of and distinction from self – and other-images.

According to Layes (2003:113), identity is also an individual and socio-cultural construct (3.1), whose successful management leads to the development of one's own *self-image*. This comprises, next to the images of one's group affiliation, behavior and thought schemes, including personal wishes, goals and value orientations. Often it is difficult to identify the values and concepts that guide one's actions, since shaping one's own self-image is an effort that interprets one's own actions and fits it into a superceding context of meaning. This construction effort is not an isolated matter for the individual, but marked by his socio-cultural environment, which contributes certain socio-cultural value orientations. Thus, the formation of self–image and identity always happens in a social structure and also has the meaning of self-distinction from other people and other groups (see 5.7.4). Accordingly, people do not only construct self-images through themselves or their group, but also *other- images* through other persons and groups (5.5). These images of the *other* vary strongly from each other by degree of differentiation. Usually, the images of close people are more differentiated than the images of distant people, of whom one has only vague and scheme-like notions. Encounters between people of different socio-cultural groups can therefore easily lead to conflict when the self- and other- images clash. Additionally, according to Layes (2003:120), in intercultural encounters there are assumptions on both sides on how the other side, respectively a third side, might perceive them. Psychology calls this the "assumed other image" (see 5.6.3). Hence, a great intercultural conflict potential lies in the images people construct of members of other groups and in their associated expectations. People form other-images of groups with whose members they have never shared a vis-à-vis situation. In the same way they form images of a whole nation without ever having seen members of that nation. A study on the formation of social identities conducted in the 1990s in South Africa (Kotzé, 1997:11) shows that other-images are particularly negative when the speakers have never had contact to persons from the mentioned group, or when the group is geographically particularly far away. The following table shows implicitly how Whites, Blacks, and Coloureds classify themselves and others according to criteria of commonalities and differences with the other group.

Racegroup	People Most in Common with	People Least in Common With
Blacks	• African People (34,4%) • Zulus (15%) • Xhosas (11,1%) • People from own language (7%) • Religious or traditional belief (5%)	• White Afrikaans speakers (17,9%) • Immigrants from Africa (10%) • White people (10%) • Zulus (8,3%) • Indian People (7,5%)
Coloureds	• Coloured people (62,7%) • Religious/traditional belief (10%) • People from own language (5,6%) • Community where you live (4,9%) • Workers (4,3%)	• Zulus (29,0%) • Immigrants from Africa (12,2%) • African People (11,1%) • White People (10,1%) • Xhosa (6,8%)
Whites	• White Afrikaans People (28,8%) • White people (21,5%) • White English people (18,2%) • Religious or traditional belief (8,3%) • People from own language (5,9%)	• Members of Trade Unions (24,8%) • Immigrants from Africa (22,1%) • African People (16,1%) • Zulus (7,9%) • Xhosas (7,7%)

Table 4: Social Identities

Often, other-images reduce a certain group and their members to extremely simplified and generalized characteristics. In such case, one speaks of *stereotypes* (see 5.5),[51] whose formation actually is a basic feature of human perception. Stereotypes are unavoidable and natural. They are the result of social categorization, i.e. "pictures" of social categories, used by people to organize their environment. Stereotypes are generalizations, which come about through cognitive processes of systematizing and whose main function is to simplify. They help to simplify cognitive and behavior-

---

[51] Current studies (Lombard, 2002) on the Western Cape show that the uncertainty about "racial integration" has grown in every population group during the last 10 years. Lombard sees the causes for fear, insecurity and perception of "subtle racism" (among other things) in the strong, predominant prejudices of members of certain population groups against members of other groups. Hetero-stereotypes tend to be attached with negative, auto-stereotypes with positive opinions. Usually, the parent generation passes common prejudices on to the following generation, who accepts them and reproduces them in every day life, particularly in the schools. In the data material, too, perceptions and image construction of members of certain population groups play a big role with regard to conflict experiences (see 5.5).

relevant adaptations, which is necessary for the assimilation of complex connections and information. Gudykunst (1991) distinguishes between "stereotypes" and "social stereotypes." Some stereotypes are unique and are based on individual experiences. Others are shared with the members of one's own in-group and are therefore called "social stereotypes." When a person recalls certain stereotypical schemes for a certain group while communicating with a member of that group, the established schemes will influence the communication and the process of passing on information. This effect of hetero-stereotypes is accordingly considered in the analysis and interpretation of the data. Often the interviewee perceives his/her own expectations in the other and interprets the other's behavior in accordance with his/her own stereotype (Devine, 1989). Thus, the already existing stereotypes confirm the encountered types of communication and behavior in the sense of a self-fulfilling prophecy (3.1).

If the temporary and generalizing nature of stereotypes remain unconscious, stereotypes can turn into *prejudices*. Psychologically, prejudices are "a certain class of social attitudes whose character it is that they – just like stereotypes – contain very simple statements, which are based on personal experiences, beyond that, contain negative judgments, which can hardly be altered through differentiated, additional information" (Layes, 2003:122).[52]

According to the psychologist, Tajfel (1982), negative prejudices and stereotypes have the function to maintain a positive social identity. They are orientation help in a complex social world and provide a sense of belonging to a positively valued social group.[53] The data material reflects this stability function in statements about different population groups, where they reveal the construction of an individual, orientation-giving category system.

---

[52] The classic prejudice research understands the prejudice-term essentially from its normative moral content. Here prejudices differ from other attitudes not in specific inner qualities, but in their social undesirability. Prejudices are social judgments which rebuff accepted human and culturally determined value judgments. They come about because of hasty judgments without the effort to acquire more precise factual knowledge. Often prejudices cannot be diffused by counter- arguments. Allport (1954:10) defines prejudices towards groups as follows: "An antipathy based on a faulty and unflexible generalization. It may be felt or expressed. It may be directed toward a group as a whole, or toward an individual because he (or she) is a member of that group."

[53] Also Gudykunst (1991:69/70) states this phenomenon: prejudices are positive towards one's own group (*ingroup*), and tend to be negative towards other groups *(outgroup)*.

The mutual encounter of stereotypical perceptions in the interaction of diverse population groups entails – as can be proven – obvious and hidden conflict potentials. But it can also be assumed that, next to the conflict-prone stereotypes and prejudices, there are positive stereotypes present in the data material (see 5.5).

3.3   Contributions to Conflict Research

First approaches of conflict research date back to the advanced cultures of antiquity. Fights and conflicts were already central themes for Heraklit, the philosopher of change, Thucydides, and the Chinese philosopher Me-Ti. Ethymologically the conflict term is rooted in the Latin word "confligere." As a transitive verb the term is action-oriented and translated as "to bump together." As an intransitive verb it refers to a condition or structure and can be translated as "to have an argument," or to "be at loggerheads with somebody." These basic meanings still determine today's definitions.

In the 19th century, Social Darwinist approaches (e.g. Herbert Spencer) understood conflict as part of the natural fight for survival. Here ethnology and, later, social biology found the starting point for viewing conflict primarily as instinctive behavior. Konrad Lorenz (1993) traced human aggression back to innate behavior tendencies and cultural-historic and environmental aspects. Irenäus Eibl-Eibelsfeld (2000/2001) regards wars as consequence of anthropological features. The theoretical approaches in the fields of behavioral theory and ethnology primarily discuss the phenomenon of propensity for violence, use of force, aggression and aggressions in a wider sense, often in the context of armed conflicts and wars.[54]

Georg Simmel (1992) is regarded as the first conflict theorist.[55] He understands conflicts in a positive sense, since they contribute to socialization and change and are dealt with through interaction. Also, in conflict-theoretical approaches, such as Habermas (1981/84), Luhmann (1987), Bourdieu (1982/1992), Honneth (1994) und

---

[54] Looking at the current ethnological approaches on conflict research, one finds that they often deal with structural violence, "traditional" conflicts and mechanisms of conflict solution and with ethno-specific ways of dealing with conflicts.
[55] The so-called "conflict theories" (Daily 1991, Ricci 1980) did not arise until the 1950's. To this day, no science discipline has developed a completely comprehensive conflict-theory. Rather, theorists of different disciplines and epochs pick up conflicts as partial aspects of their own theory. The aspects relevant for this study are discussed in .3.3.2.

Lyotard (1987), conflicts are considered constructive and having positive potential in societies. In the ethnological and social science literature on conflicts in Southern Africa (Chazan, 1999; Furley, 1995; Gluckman, 1959; Horowitz, 2000; Michler, 1995; Zartmann, 1995), the main topics are national-ethnic conflicts, conflicting political structures and conflicts on the international, political level. Zartmann (1995:269ff), for example, looks at the effects of inner national power relationships and resource distribution, and at the participation of different ethnic groups in society. He (1995:268) concludes that the African civil population, in case of a national split up, would be able to fill the political vacuum with old-African authority structures (council of elders, traditional negotiation mechanisms, trade structures and community operations) on the local level, but not on the national level. This literature completely disregards the cultural dimension of conflict. Also, it is not interested in inter-personal conflicts, but instead in group-specific, socio-political and national conflicts. Often it includes the apartheid period looking at new democratic approaches and visionary scenes of racial and ethnic group conflicts: Shezi (1995:191ff) sees the solution of future conflicts mainly in securing administrative and *racial* integration in every societal sector. He finds new definitions of all social classes, patience, endurance and optimism in a process- oriented reconstruction inevitable. Similarly, Johnson (1995:47) sees apartheid as foundation for any conflict between "race groups": the high and growing readiness for violence is rooted in the practices of the former apartheid state, which has ignored the cultural aspects of community to this day. According to Johnson (1995:62ff), the main conflicts are rooted in the fight over scarce resources and imbalances in the access to resources, wealth, medical care and education. Conflicts are also caused by unemployment, population growth and unequal distribution of income due to regional industrial centers and ethnically determined living areas. Additionally, there are numerous complex conflict structures in the context of political, moral and causal dimensions.

Comaroff & Comaroff (1999:279/284) deal with conflict on the local level. They find that the apartheid factors, such as "race and class" in today's South Africa are overshadowed by the growing schisms between "different age-groups or generations, mediated by gender." Not colonialism and racism are the chief issues of conflict, but "enemies within their own ethnic, village or peer groups." Because these enemies are often intangible, people attempt to understand their actions frequently by finding explanations in "supernatural forces" (see 3.4.3). Another conflict potential, according to Johnson (1995:64), lies in the Western democratic style of debate, which places individual over collective rights (see 3.4.1), leading to violence locally and nationally. Therefore, the nation and the anti-apartheid-movement need the full support of churches in order to overcome the apartheid past and construct a peaceful South Africa.

The up to now introduced literature largely disregards cultural aspects. Four decades ago, a representative of the *Manchester-School*, Max Gluckman (1959), dealt with the phenomenon of customs and conflicts in Africa from an ethnological viewpoint. He looked at conflicts in the everyday context of family, ritual, witchcraft and authority. Gluckman (1959:137) concluded that ethnic customs and habits govern the areas of conflict, which he saw rooted in the value orientations behind those customs:

> Custom at least controls the place where quarrels take place. But custom also brings into work mechanisms which inhabit the development of the quarrels and which exert pressure for settlement. Or the conflicts are so directed by custom that there is change in their personal system, but the structure of the system persists. (Gluckman, 1959:137)

Our investigation is guided by the assumption that conflicts can arise in the encounter of different value orientations and that value orientations are particularly pronounced in conflict situations. (see 5).

Since the ethnological, Africa-specific literature deals mainly with themes of aggression, war, armed and ethno-specific conflict, and hardly looks at interpersonal and intercultural conflicts; this study reaches out to literature beyond the ethnological field. Soziologists and politologists (Augburger, 1992, Glasl 1990/1997/2000, Lederach, 1996, Moore, 1996), social- und organization-psychologists (Bond, 1998; Thomas 1996), as well as communication scientists (Gudykunst, 1985/1991), in particular, have taken a critical look at intercultural communication and intercultural conflicts. Some approaches of this literature will be incorporated into this study, thus requiring a closer look (see 3.3.2).

3.3.1 Conflicts as Reality Constructs

Conflicts are meanwhile considered as everyday, normal part of human life (see Myers et al (1992:3), Kuhn (1999:55)). A society without conflict is neither possible, and, along with Augsburger (1992:21), hardly desirable since there is an important connection between "conflict and creative, constructuve change." Conflicts entail challenge and chance for the development and improvement of mutual relationships and therefore don't need to be eliminated as such. Also, as said by Bonacker and Imbusch (1999:72), conflicts are "promoters of social change" (transl.) and, according to Habermas (1981), Luhmann (1987) und Bourdieu (1982), positive and desirable. Generally conflicts bring out different interests of the people involved and indicate that the relationships need better regulations. Thus, they open, according to Besemer (1995:24), an occasion to change societal and interpersonal relationships.

Since conflicts point out existing differences, they sensitize the "consciousness of the relativity of their own reality": "Most of the time we assume that we share a single reality with others, but we do not. We simultaneously live in multiple realities" (Augsburger 1992:17). A person who recognizes that there are multi-layered reality perceptions might easily question internalized value orientations or question his/her own identity and come to build up resistance in dealing with conflicts.

Scientists, such as Besemer (1995), Maringer & Steinweg (1997), Moore (1996) and others, see value orientations and *value conflicts* as frequent causes of conflict. Next to value conflicts, as said by Maringer & Steinweg, conflict of needs, ideology and faith, but most of all "identity conflicts on individual and collective level" (transl.) are highly important. Identity conflicts can show up especially in the context of social change, such as the re-definition of gender roles (see 5.6.3/5.7.1) (Mayer/Boness/Thomas 2003:56/57). The data material confirms this assumption on value orientation, identity and conflict (see 5.8).

The work at hand understands conflict as reality construct. Conflicts are differences in perception that communicating individuals experience as such (see also Mayer/Boness, 2004). This is further explained in the following.

3.3.2 Conflicts in Intercultural Contexts

The foremost U.S.- literature on intercultural conflicts (Augsburger, 1992; Avruch, 1998; Lederach, 1988/1995/1996) assumes that conflicts exist naturally in every culture. Like Berger/Luckmann (2000), these U.S. scholars also define conflicts as socio-culturally constructed facts resulting from interactions of the participants.

Conflicts are about the search and development of shared meaning. As said by sociologist and conflict researcher, Lederach (1996:9ff), this interactive process of finding shared meaning consists of the roots of "perceptions, interpretations, expressions and intentions," which he also calls "culture," shared knowledge and schemes (see 1.4). One constructs one's own culture out of one's "social reality" and out of networks of subjective realities with (culturally defined) collective meaning. Relating this understanding to intercultural conflicts, Lederach devises the following definition[56] (1988:39): "Conflict situations are those unique episodes when we explicitly recognize the existence of multiple realities and negotiate the creation of a common meaning." This means that in conflict situations people experience the relativity of realities (3.1)

---

[11] Lederach (1989:12) develops his theory (following Adam Curie) as a matrix, which brings together the levels of power and awareness of conflict-holding interests and needs. There are various changing levels of conflict: If there is a large imbalance of power, one conflict party might not even notice this imbalance. In that case, it is necessary to become aware of one's own interests and needs. This awareness usually leads to the desire for change and confrontation and, hence, to conflict. David W. Augsburger (1992:11) also describes conflict as a kind of crisis, which arises through the recognition of various realities. Every conflict situation, therefore, consists of mostly differing stories, which should be combined to a story with different roles and positions of all participants. In intercultural conflicts, the added difficulty lies in the fact that culture influences each possible behavior. Language, schemes of perception, techniques of analysis, value orientations, hierarchical structures, options for actions, emotions, communication-styles etc. are so culture-specific that in inter-cultural situations, one has to meta-communicate already *about* conflict negotiations. Culture here provides space, limits movements and imagination and stands always in tension between "the same and the other" (Augsburger, 1992:16). This tension can take the following forms:

- The *same* controls and reduces the *other*
- The *same* subordinates and exploits the *other*
- The *same* destroys and negates the *other*, if possible
- The *same* excludes the *other* and escapes its threat

Dealing with conflicts is connected to personal and cultural core values and the perception of "other" values. Therefore, it offers deep insight into the social reconstruction of cultural realities. Conflict situations pronounce the existing, various frames of reference and thus "multiple realities." The conflict is essentially a special type of reality, which needs to be recognized and continuously redefined.

while they simultaneously negotiate and create their shared meaning. This is true for interpersonal, but also for intrapersonal conflicts, in which a person internally works out different negotiable reality aspects. Here, an identity crisis might occur (see 5.7.3).

When looking at conflict management, such aspects as "social reality" and the ability of inter-personal communication under consideration of social and intercultural realities stand out. Therefore, in the evaluation of the investigative results, the social reality and the socio-cultural background of the interview partners will receive special attention (see 5).

According to Lederach (1996:75ff), in the intercultural perception of conflict, the understanding of language and metaphors as natural resources are especially important. By accessing language, a person can better understand cultural, socio-culturally and individually conditioned ways of thinking, talking and reacting in a conflict. Here proverbs, stories and pictures can play a special role in that they can illuminate the relationships in a conflict, the ways of handling the conflict situation and its transformation. Also, proverbs, metaphors and pictures suggest, imply and associate deep- seated cultural beliefs, thus granting insights into the cultural wisdom of people. This, too, is a fruitful approach for the data-evaluation in chapter 5.6, which analyses selected language data.

Aside from the intercultural space, there is already a wide intra-cultural spectrum of habits, personal communication styles and behavior modes that make it difficult to generalize and designate value-orientations as either culture-specific or personality-specific. The experienced social and emotional or individual limits of the spectrum are again culture-, situation- and context- bound. In conflict situations, these manifold interconnected value orientations join together in an especially complex and dynamic way, which brings the most important involved values to the surface. In order to analyze intercultural conflicts and value dimensions, Augsburger (1992:28ff) offers the following questions which are in part used in chapter 5.6 and 5.7:

- Where does the conflict take place? (Context)
- Why does it take place? (Reasons/cause)
- What is the participants' attitude towards the conflict? (Values)
- How do they deal with the conflict and its resolution? (Beliefs)
- What behavior patterns and communication styles do they use? (Behavior and feelings)

If now the conflicting parties want to overcome their own culturally and personally formed reality construction, a third person or party can be invited and bring a new perspective to the conflict. Also, the parties can leave the inside perspective of the conflict and accept the possibility of "otherness" and "hetero-thinking." This "otherness" stands for, according to Watzlawick (2001c:234), a newly constructed reality, one that represents an outside perspective and can possibly lead to the insight that the conflict does not even exist or that it can be solved quickly.

3.3.3 Ethnic Conflicts as Special Form of Intercultural Conflicts

As already mentioned in chapter 3.3, some ethnological conflict theory approaches center around the discussion of ethnic conflicts (see Horowitz, 2000).[57]

Literature often labels ethnic conflicts as "cultural conflicts," assuming that the conflict potential grows in proportion to increased cultural differences. The culture-pluralism theory sees incompatible values underlying conflicts between ethnicities, which also finds expression in the isolation and separation of groups. For the modernization-theories and the economic interest theories, conflicts are rooted in the fight for resources and other objects of common interests. There are numerous differing definitions on the term "ethnic conflict." From the ethnological viewpoint, Fisher's

---

[57] The theoretical approaches on ethnic conflicts often are connected with economic or political studies on national issues or international relationships. According to Horowitz (2000:95ff), ethnic conflict theories therefore are mostly tied up with modernization theories, economic interest theories (of classes and ethnicities) or socio-political theories, which take up cultural aspects, such as culture-pluralism-theory (Fumivall/Smith).

position (1998:15) has been particularly convincing and finds therefore entrance into the debate on ethnic conflicts in this work.:

> "...a given conflict is in fact „ethnic," with the idea that the confrontation is driven at least in part by outlooks and perceptions that have roots in a significant cultural uniqueness to which a group holds loyalty - and which are at odds with those of some other group or mainstream collectivity. But the exact role of ethnicity may be uncertain, as in many cases loyalties and identities overlap. The key task is anticipating just when people will relate to an issue on the basis of being members of their specific ethnic group..."

Horowitz (2000:18) descibes the aspect of ethnic identity in the context of ethnic conflicts as a mosaic of beliefs, religions, collective memory, emotions, mythologies and language, corresponding to their common "ethnic culture." Next to ethnic identity, the *socio-cultural identity* determines each individual's identity and self-concept (see 5.7). A person derives her socio-cultural identity from her membership to a social group, such as an ethnic group, but unlike her ethnic identity, which is limited to the latter, also from gender groups, age groups, religious communities, sportclubs etc.. To what degree an individual identifies with any group, varies depending on context and situation. But aspects of ethnic, social and personal identity influence each indivual's self-definition, often in distinction from the identity-definitions of other groups (see 3.2).

An essential characteristic of ethnic and cultural distinction is language. According to Fisher (1998:19ff), ethnic group identities are especially determined by the common language, ethical attitudes, religion and history. However, even socio-cultural groups often develop their own, singular language culture. Fisher (1998:40) finds that one's own identity consists of *"multiple identities,"* which cannot be separated easily. Overall, this multiple identity is fundamentally shaped by one's own culture and often absorbed unconsciously and passed on as such. Fisher (1998:65) calls the cultural aspect of identity *"deep culture concept."* This concept is tied to value orientations, which – though they may vary by situation and context - are so deeply rooted in a group that they can kindle a strong sense of belonging together. Fisher compares this belonging together (1998:76) with Anderson's *"imagined communities"* (see 3.1.1). According to

Anderson, ethnic groups invent their own *"social universe,"* which includes group identities, collective duties and shared interpretations of meanings. The collective history, so Fisher (1998:76), influences identity and conflict behavior accordingly. Based on Fisher's definition of ethnic conflict and ethnic identity, only those conflicts are ethnic in nature whose causes, perceptions and perspectives can be traced back explicitly to the attitudes and value orientations of ethnic groups, or whose participants draw an explicit connection between the conflict and the ethnic collective. However, to this day, researchers do not fully understand the role of ethnic conflicts (Bekker, 1993). On one hand, cultural backgrounds, such as religious beliefs, ethnic identity, naming of feelings, culture-specific sensitivities, and ethnic-collective memory are left out in many analyses of ethnic conflicts; on the other hand, the dividing line between individual and cultural attitudes is so flexible that researchers from an etic perspective often are unable to deal with the emic perspective.[58]

Therefore, this study designates as "ethnic" a conflict only if the interviewee understands it as such. Generally, though, every experienced conflict depends on ethnic, socio-cultural and individual origin of a person. A study in the urban field encounters such a complexity of historic, socio-cultural, global, individual and ethnic influences that it is impossible to distinguish explicit ethnic factors from the others. Also, there are hardly sufficient or useful accounts in Cape Town that would allow conclusions on value orientations of ethnic origin. Instead, the center of reflection here are conflicts and value-orientations in the narrator's context of socio-cultural realities and the political value discourses.

The following will examine samples of these political value discourses, as they present themselves in the arena of national discourses by prominent leaders in science, politics and theology in Southern Africa.

---

[58] "Etic" is defined as outside perspective, "emic" as inside.perspective.

3.4 South African Value-Discourse as Constructs of National Reality

Since the mid 20th century, in the course of Pan-African de-colonization movements, more intra- African discourses[59] on the construction of new African nations have come to the forefront through public discussions on value orientations, philosophies and future visions. Leading representatives (Mayer 2001) of these value discussions are people like Gbadegesin (1991, Nigeria), Mbiti (1990, Uganda), Nyerere (1997, Tanzania), Oruka (1998, Kenya) and Senghor (1961/1963, Senegal). During the last decades, South Africa has seen waves of symbol production. According to Paul Bourdieu (1992:5), the political, spiritual and intellectual leaders invested massively in "symbolic values and social capital" during the political transition period. The socio-political value discussions played an important role, given that after decades of 'difference multiculturalism," now the challenge was to build an all-encompassing umbrella in terms of 'critical multiculturalism."

The construction of new societal realities happens on the most disparate levels, be it the new constitution,[60] administration, media or interpersonal discussion. Value

---

[59] The definition of this selected term "discourse" (lat. discursus, discurrere = "(aimless) running back and forth," to hold forth at length on a subject) has already filled volumes of linguistic studies (here in connection with literature theory and discourse-analysis (e.g. Foucaults) and philosophy (e.g. Habermas). In some disciplines, the expression "discourse" has become a trendy word during recent decades. Dictionaries define discourse as
- A methodically structured treatise on a certain (scientific) topic (Metzler-Literatur-Lexikon 1990).
- "Exchange of ideas, conversation," or "intense verbal fight or exchange" (Duden 1990).
In its broadest sense, "discourse" is understood here as a treatise on the above determined subject. At the same time, it is used as a general term taken from the Anglo-American research that refers to various aspects of a text and regards discourse as coherent speech or articulated text (e.g., discourse as a text constructed by the speaker for the audience; or discourse as the result of an interactive process in a socio-cultural context). The here offered meaning of discourse is distinguished from the one in philosophical context, in which he serves a discussion aimed at finding the unique truth.

[60] The following excerpt from the current constitution (*South African Constitution* 1997) shows, how it intends to construct South Africa with respect to past, presence and future:
We, the people of South Africa, recognise the injustices of our past;
Honour those wo suffered for justice and freedom in our land;
Respect those who have worked to build and develop our country; and
Believe that South Africa belongs to all who live in it, united in our diversity.
In the forefront here stands the construction of South Africa in the sense of "critical multiculturalism" and the values such as "unity in diversity," as they appear in numerous passages of the constitution and as they are also propagated in value discussions.

discourses are conducted everywhere, thus contributing to the building of the new nation. For example, the *Department of Foreign Affairs South Africa* (2001) proclaims new visions and values: "South Africa shall strive for peace, stability, democracy and development in an African continent, which is non-racial, non-sexist, prosperous and united, contributing towards a world that is just and equitable."

The mission of the South African discourses is to combine old-African and national-Western value-orientations in order to create new realities: "In the realization of its vision and the execution of its mission, the Department will be guided by the core values of loyalty, dedication, Ubuntu, equity and professional integrity" (South African Embassy, 1999).

The value discussions are based on societal core values. A major branch of value research orients itself at the empirical value research in the scientific field, which is conducted with empirical methods[61] in comprehensive national and international comparative studies on the value topic (Kotzé, 1993). This value research remains only in the background of this study since it examines primarily the South African value discussion as they arise in the public, theological and academic arena, represented by selected scholars. This work considers emic value discussions – not Western value-questionnaires and surveys – fundamental. In its decision to concentrate on public value discourses in South Africa, it follows van Niekerk (1991:74), who assumes that African "Ethnophilosophy" and value discourses can be accessed primarily over everyday speeches and discussions, customs, traditions, proverbial sayings, everyday experiences, spirituality and faith in God. The African philosophy becomes "philosophical sagacity," which provides the African community with a space for its own philosophy. It is quite possible to change traditional philosophical value orientations by utilizing them pragmatically for democratic change. Often, the value discussions address adaptation of

---

16 This study also falls back on universalistic value theories. S. Schwartz (1994) uses instruments such as the World-Value-Survey (WVS) or the European-Value-Survey (EVS) for international comparison of his evaluated results.

religious symbols and rituals as part of political concepts and goals. This phenomenon[62] can be described as "civil religion." [63]

Along with Heuser (2002:73), especially religion provides meaning, orientation and options for the social change and the political *rites de passages* and that way establishes a balance of symbolic forces.

Selected discourse contributions serve as theoretical approach to the topic of value discourses. The representatives can be divided in[64]

- Scholars for the socio-political construction (*Rainbow Nation*, More 1998), *Ubuntu: African Humanism*(Prinsloo,1995, 1997, 1998))

- Politicians and theologians for the socio-political construction (*Black-Consciousness-Movement* (Biko 1984), *A Peaceful Nation* (Mandela, 1994), *African Renaissance* (Mbeki, 1999/2001) und *Reconciliation* (Tutu 1985))

- Scholars for the scientific discussion (*Social Theory* (Coetzee, 1998) und *Metaphysics* (Teffo & Roux 1998))

The South African value discourses have in common that they concentrate on socio-cultural areas and that they are an integral part of discussions on African philosophy, African knowledge, politics, cultural concepts, art and linguistics. References to Western philosophical or political discussions surface sometimes in the form of references or distinctions from various authors. The interest of these discourses is not to develop universalistic theories, but to find culture-specific value concepts for a particular societal context, based on the ideological attitude of each author, rooted in the local, national and Pan-African or international level (Mayer, 2001:31). Thus, the South African value discourses reflect the societal pluralism.

---

[62] Makulele (1998:37-41) believes that religious metaphors in the South African process of reconciliation and forgiveness are often tied together and misused. Especially the "Rainbow Nation metaphor" needs attention with respect to the "race-blind discourses in the New South Africa" (1998:37). In his opinion, the debate on reconciliation and forgiveness excludes the "Blacks, the poor and the marginalized - especially black women" (1998:41). Looking at comments on the "rainbow-nation" (R1-R4) in the data material, this impression is partially confirmed by some representatives of certain groups (see 5.4).

[63] This definition of the term „ civil religion" follows Mitchell (2002:24): "The discourse of civil religion is one in which competing logics of civic, ethnic and religious identity jostle for position, inventing and reinventing themselves in the effort to imagine community." (see also Anderson, .3.1.1)

[64] The division of value discourse contributions follows Mayer (2001).

The function of the following brief presentation of selected concepts on value discussion is primarily to identify particular elements of the various concepts and to prepare them for a (culture-) appropriate interpretation of the data material. For example, the evaluation chapters 5.6/5.7 look for evidence whether and to what degree concept-bound single elements of *Ubuntu*, "personhood," "collective consciousness" or "family" occur. Should these analytical examinations prove to be productive, the unfolding of South African value concepts on the theory level would have a "verifying function."

3.4.1 Scholars for the Socio-Political Construction
3.4.1.1 Magoo P. More: The Rainbow Nation

More than ten years after the radical change in South Africa, population groups continue to strive for their own identity and its re-definition (Bekker et al, 2000: 221fi) within the new "Rainbow Nation." This name pays tribute to the reality that people of different historical, ethnic, language and cultural histories live next to each other, shimmering colorful and diverse and like a rainbow (SAR Embassy, 1997:3/1998). The Old Testament image of the rainbow stands, according to Heuser (2002:73), for God's offer of reconciliation with those who survived the great catastrophe – then flood, now apartheid – and God's covenant for the future. Thus, the rainbow image accompanied especially the first transition period from apartheid to democracy when it was coined particularly by Bishop Tutu.

The phrase "Rainbow Nation South Africa" has become a slogan for the construction of a multicultural society that is simultaneously coping with the events of the past. According to Magobo P.More (1998:364), the Rainbow Nation, on one hand, is characterized by globalization, and, on the other hand, by inner cultural, ethnic and socio-cultural diversity. Globalization enters through democratization, the introduction of human rights, economic cooperation and joint ventures. The national transformation process happens in the tension field between the different socio-cultural, religious and ethnic groups and their multiple ways of dealing with the past.

M. P. More boldly attempts to tie the old-African concepts of inter-ethnic tolerance to the challenge of current globalization in order to build a suitable ideological base for South Africa's development. He mainly discusses the question of how a liberal democratic society can respond to the tension between individual and collective rights. More (1998:364) finds that the new "rainbowism" since the end of apartheid has not always been positive: on one hand, it demands a liberal democracy, based on the principles of individual autonomy, equality and freedom, and basic rights.[65] On the other hand, these democratic values collide with deep-seated, pervasive and persistent ethnic disparities. Every ethnic group wants to be acknowledged and respected in its singular identity so that it can realize, experience and live its own authenticity.

Here, value-orientations (and meanings) of diverse ethnic groups do not necessarily harmonize with democratic Western basic values and their interpretation. How can the tension between universalism and particularity work to the advantage of a newly established nation? And how can one bring together the unity, expressed in universalism, and diversity, expressed in particularity, in the political South Africa? Is that even possible? The tension between 'politics of sameness" and "politics of difference" have to be newly negotiated under the motto "unity or diversity."[66] Hence, More's concept deals with the main subject areas of "unity in diversity" versus "diversity without unity," the "Rainbow Nation" versus "competitive nation" and "universalism" versus "particularism."

More (1998:368) advocates a path between racism and anti-racism. This path implies the maintenance and support of ethnic and socio-cultural groups[67] in their uniqueness without placing them into a hierarchical order, and without exploiting or discriminating them. The goal is "unity *in* diversity," which is when all the diverse groups are concerned with the welfare of all members of society and fight for universal, generally accepted and experienced basic principles. Carrying the titles 'multi-ethnic, "

---

[65] Other authors, such as Heuser (2002:73), also associate the image of the multi-Coloured rainbow with the visualized moral consensus of the pluralistic society (consensus of plurality, equality, and tolerance). According to Heuser, however, the image of the rainbow has long been replaced by the vision of the "African Renaissance," which promotes African social values and institutional norms, in order to achieve social goals.

[66] Here the rainbow concept is closely tied to the concept of *Ubuntu*. Both concepts want to negotiate *sameness* and *otherness* in the context of discussions and dialogue. Shutte (1993:49/51) refers to the degree of the tension between proximity and distance in the discussions on equality and otherness. On one hand, the *otherness* wants to be presented and maintained in its *otherness*. On the other hand, the *other* must not become a too distant *other*. Thus, the issue of proximity and distance has become a central consideration in the shared dialogue.

[67] More uses the term „socio-cultural groups" synonymously with "races" and "ethnicities."

"multi-cultural," "multi-racial" und "multi-religious" interchangeably, the new Rainbow Nation is the counter pole to the last fifty years of apartheid.[68] But even though its name implies pluralistic features, to this day, the Rainbow Nation could not achieve a balance between liberal individualism (bourgeois) and group, or collective, rights in society. Even though the South African new constitution guaranties the universal principles of human rights for all its citizens – regardless of *race*, skin color, gender and origin - they have not been realized in every social area. Still people continue to use the *race* term and think in categories of *racial* assignments and stereotypes. Even when the educated elite today understands the term *race* as social construct, the term is symptomatic for the social reality and still rules social life.[69]

According to More (1998:370), the South African constitution guaranties predominantly universal individual interests instead of group interests. Especially in situations of conflict, the protection of the individual, which is not necessarily identical with shared, harmonious group interests, stands in the foreground. Here concepts of the individual, individuality and collectivity have to be reconsidered.[70] Harmonious group interests manifest themselves mainly when a "*balanced concept of power*" between the ethnic groups is present and when each group in theory and practice has the same entitlements to social power. The rainbow has many colors, some of which shine brighter and more radiant than others; some colors are missing altogether, which More considers to be an imbalance in the symbol: "There ain't no black in the rainbow" (see 5.4.1).

---

[68] Were there during apartheid two *civil religions* within the state - the *apartheid civil religion* and the *civil religion of the liberation movement*- these are now unified in *a civil religion of the Rainbow Nation,* according to Mitchell (2001).

[69] Many voices (such as Marais (2002) and Mitchell (2002)), claim that the issue of *race* continues to dominate the debate on the Rainbow Nation and overshadows issues like gender and class. Makulele (1998:37) points out that especially "Black thinking (Black thinkers)" have not been included in the discourse on the Rainbow Nation and its meaning. Sitas (1998:40), on the other hand, notes that the *White* population feels excluded from the national dialogue.

[70] According to Prinsloo (1997:2), individualism in Western societies frequently appears in connection with competitiveness, while in African concepts of individuality, cooperation and collective work play a highly valued role. Economic profits are considered important (Brookdryk, 1997a:4), but are not supposed to go along with exploitation of other people. Profits need to be shared evenly, since a group has the position of an extended family, its members being considered brothers and sisters of the same family. The post-apartheid society has to reflect and negotiate both Western and African concepts of group-society relationships.

Based on More's value orientations, our evaluation will present and interpret the interviewees' thoughts and feelings on the Rainbow Nation and to what degree their opinions deviate from More's concept.

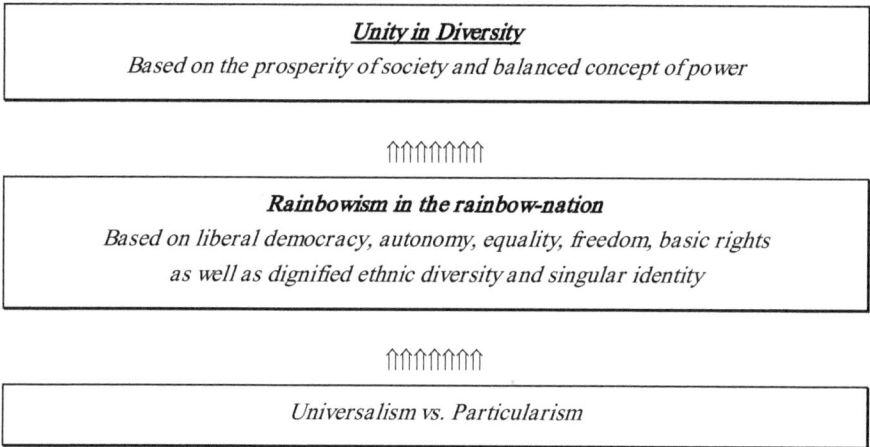

Unity in Diversity
Based on the prosperity of society and balanced concept of power

⋔⋔⋔⋔⋔⋔⋔

Rainbowism in the rainbow-nation
Based on liberal democracy, autonomy, equality, freedom, basic rights
as well as dignified ethnic diversity and singular identity

⋔⋔⋔⋔⋔⋔⋔

Universalism vs. Particularism

Graph 6: More: Rainbow Nation

3.4.1.2 Erasmus D. Prinsloo: Ubuntu: African Humanism

Erasmus D. Prinsloo approaches the topic of nation building by starting from an old-African value and life concept. In his essay "Ubuntu Culture and Participatory Management" (1998: 41ff), he relates the old-African philosophy of *Ubuntu* to the current economic challenges of the South African society. His thesis is that the integration of Ubuntu–values in African economic practices (processes) would achieve better success in business and personal management. Ubuntu is a deeply rooted concept of collectivism, which has been object of repeated and multiple discussions (Prinsloo,

1995/1998; Louw, 2003, Broodryk, 1997a, 1997b, Mbigi, 1995, Sindane, 1994, van der Merwe, 1996, van Niekerk, 1994, Teffo, 1994a/1994b).

The original Zulu-word, Ubuntu, has no directly corresponding word in Western languages. In English it is frequently translated as *personhood* (Prinsloo, 1998) or *humanness* (Louw, 2003) with the following connotation: "A person is a person because of other people" or "I am because you are," or in an extended sense of "You are because we are."[71] According to Prinsloo (1998:49), Ubuntu contains a kind of *world spirit*, which alludes to human dignity, guiding people towards harmonic and peaceful societies (1998: 49).[72] Consistent with Prinsloo, Sindane (1994:7) advocates *true Ubuntu* for South Africa's nation building. He defines it as a life concept which implies authentic respect for individual human rights, demands values related to human rights and, at the same time, recognition of differences. [73] In its view of the world, people and things, Ubuntu has often been described as the "African way of life." Its concept holds a somewhat collective consciousness, a religion and politics of its own,[74] as well as an ethnic perspective. It continues to evolve by integrating current political ideologies or by reintegrating some of their aspects.

---

[71] Following Shutte (1993:46), *"umuntu ngumuntu ngabantu":* "a person is a person through other persons."* Other authors, such as van der Merve (1096:1), translate this sentence in the sense of "a human being is a human being through (the otherness) of other human being," thus emphasizing the importance of recognizing the otherness and the diversity of citizens in post- apartheid South Africa. Here Ubuntu has become a concept that demands respect for particularity, individualism and "historicality," the latter implying the "dynamic nature or process nature" of each person (Teffo 1994a:11). A person cannot be reduced to certain characteristics. The perception of other people is never rigid and final, but adjustable and changeable. The concept of Ubuntu implies the being and becoming of a person: 'This accords with the grammar of the concept of "Ubuntu" which denotes both a state of being and one of becoming."(Broodryk, 1997a:5-7). As a process of self-realization *through others*, it includes the self-realization *of others*.

[72] But even if Ubuntu carries values of "human dignity, respect and compassion," the desire for consensus and social harmony also has its dark side, according to Mbigi (1995). The consensus orientation could demand oppressive conformity along with a high degree of group loyalty with harsh punishments for failure to comply.

[73] In this sense, Ubuntu points to the "Rainbow Nation concept," which also asks for straightforward recognition of differences, as well as unity in diversity. Therefore, it can be assumed that the concepts of Ubuntu und Rainbow Nation complement each other and are compatible.

[74] According to Louw (2003:1), the main characteristics of the Ubuntu-concept are a) 'the respect for the other as a religious other" b) "an agreement of criteria (...) which the adherents of different religious traditions may jointly judge these traditions" und c) "an inter-religious dialogue or "mutual exposure" of beliefs." By this approach, Ubuntu, as a religious-philosophical concept, invites the respect for the diverse religious currents and to bring them together in an inter-religious dialogue.

Ubuntu manifests itself in peoples' everyday behavior, in their creative expressions, in their spiritual self-fulfillment and religious attitude.[75] It emerges in a feeling of universal brotherhood, in the African way people share, and in its give and take. Ubuntu is experienced and realized through the communication with other people, and the respectful understanding and treatment of other people. Of central importance here is the human being as a social being as part of a community.

Ubuntu has also been called *African Humanism* (Prinsloo, 1998:42). According to Prinsloo (1995:4), the importance of religious faith in African Humanism sets it apart from *Western Humanism*, which minimizes or even ignores religious faith.[76] In African Humanismus, the true humanity of each person consists in open *communication*. The value of communication lies in its capacity to express empathy, understanding and consensus/ agreement.[77] *Interaction, participation, reciprocity* and *cooperation* in inter-human relationships are important ingredients of life. At the same time, *joy, fortune* and *fulfillment* are Ubuntu-values (Prinsloo 1998:43), as they are tied to the extended family concept and point to the religious component (see Ndaba, 1994). *Kindness, sympathy* and *respect* are important family values, as respect is shown not only towards the "religious other" (Louw, 2003:1-2) but also towards the older person, who has great experience and influence.

---

[75] According to Teffo (1994a:9), Ubuntu implies "a deep respect and regard for religious beliefs and practices."

[76] Van Niekerk (1994:2) points out that the religious dimension of Ubuntu shows up especially in the saying: "A person is a person through other persons." While Westeners interpret this sentence mostly in the general sense of dignity and respect for all people with no religious connotation, to Africans it means that a person becomes a person only through others, which includes the ancestors. It also means that other people carry their ancestors inside. Since ancestors are considered part of the extended family, death means "ultimate homecoming." Ndaba (1994:13/14) supports this thesis, adding that not only the living, but also the dead are connected with one another, sharing and caring for each other Thus, the key saying in Ubuntu has religious- spiritual meaning, thereby shedding its light on the entire philosophy.

[77] Louw (2003:2) finds that the concept of Ubuntu underestimates values of *consensus and agreement* compared to their traditional African role. Teffo (1994a:4), too, emphasizes the "infinite capacity for the pursuit of consensus and reconciliation" in traditional African societies. These values manifest themselves in the style of African democracy that entails long discussions, leading not necessarily to a majority decision. Broodryk (1997a:5/7/9) observes that while a hierarchy of speakers exists, each person has the same right to speak until an "agreement, consensus or group cohesion is reached." A word to express the obtaining of this goal is *simunye* ("we are one"). Hence, value concepts such as "unity is strength" correspond here with Ubuntu, as they, again, exist in the Rainbow Nation concept of *unity in diversity* (see 3.4.1).

A person finds his identity through direct interaction with family members. Here he learns to recognize prejudices, which consequently enables him to enter carefree relationships with his own self and with people from other cultures. According to Prinsloo (1998), self-identity and pride in one's own origin becomes the starting point for all other interactions (see 5.7). Another value in Ubuntu is morality, which takes the shape of *responsibility towards other people*.[78] It is a "social moral" shining through *communication, social environment, law*, and through the *protection of nature*. Humanity and nature are here seen as one. Ubuntu shows itself especially in the spirit of *equality* among people and in *solidarity*, a spontaneous readiness to fight for a fellow human being, in short: in a consciousness for collective responsibilities of each person for her immediate social environment.[79] Individual duties and virtues, which are translated into individual rights, are a central theme. Ubuntu's values are rooted in humanity and materialize in facets of old-African traditions. Among those values are the community council, social counseling, decision making, individual creativity, cooperation and collective property. Personal growth and community are always mutually related: *I am, because you are*. By offering cooperative and collective transitional forms, the Ubuntu concept shows ways to overcome hierarchical structures.

Where the South African economy orients itself at Western values, conflicts between individualistic and collectivistic basic values may easily arise. The value of the free, self-determined individual can collide with a person's understanding of being part of a social unit. Further conflict potential lies in the definition of *humanism*. While Africans (Prinsloo, 1998:46) see *Western humanism* as dictated by intellect and describe it as individualistic and aesthetic, they view *African humanism* as spiritual experience with respect to one's own emotions, expansiveness and transcendence.

---

[78] Louw (2003:6) sees the significance of this morality in connection with the values of *"caring and sharing, forgiving and reconciliation"* He attributes the peaceful transition from a totalitarian apartheid-state to a multi-party democracy to this philosophical ethos, which has yielded solidarity and commitment to a peaceful co-existence of South African population groups, despite their great socio-cultural differences.

[34] Shutte (1993:56) refers to the idea of *siriti*, an "energy, power or force which is claimed to both make us ourselves and unite us in personal interactions with others." This power allows a person to consider the self and others as moving, interconnected parts of a universal power field.

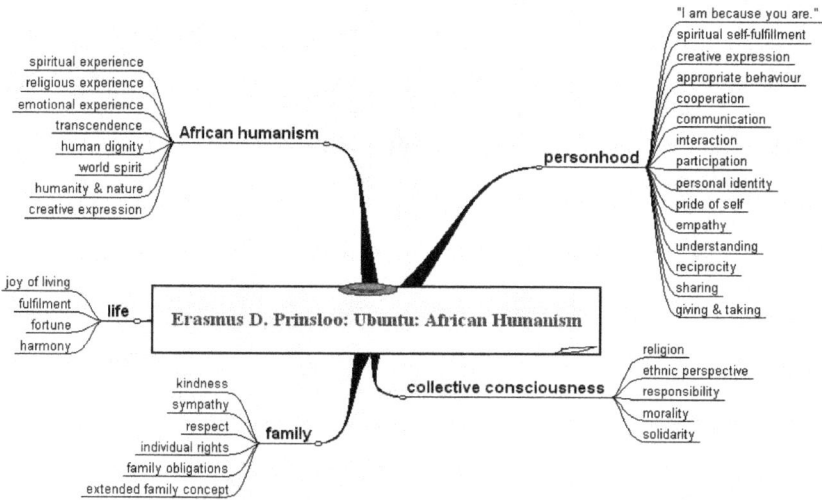

Graph 7: Prinslo: Ubuntu

3.4.2 Politicians and Theologians for the Socio-Political Construction

In the realm of South African politics and theology, Biko, Mandela, Mbeki and Tutu stand in the forefront. These representatives of value discussions have in common that they draw from the depth of the Ubuntu world of thought in its oral century-old traditions and in highlighting single elements of Ubuntu in their own socio-political context. Steve Biko interprets the elements of *man- centered society, spirituality* and *God* and relates them to his current situation. Nelson Mandela portraits *peace and human dignity* as a concept relevant to nation-building, while Tutu effectively applies the Ubuntu elements of *truth, justice and humanity* to the reconciliation process in South Africa. Finally, Thabo Mbeki attempts to lay the foundation for a macro-concept of *African Renaissance*, not only by distilling Ubuntu-elements, such as *brotherhood* and *freedom*, but also by revitalizing further Pan-African values.

3.4.2.1 Steve Biko: Black-Consciousness-Movement

Steve Biko plays a special role for the black population. As intellectual leader of the *Black-Consciousness-Movement (BC),* he still has the reputation of one of South Africa's greatest martyrs.[80] His unique appeal to all non-White groups to consciously unite against the apartheid regime continues to characterize the position and inner attitudes of many members of the Coloured and Black population groups. Biko's philosophy of political peace is based on the belief that in order for Blacks and Whites to return to themselves with dignity, Blacks have to disregard their inferiority feelings towards Whites, and that Whites have to shake off their claim of superiority over Blacks ((Biko, 1987:24/ 144): 'I am against the superior-inferior white-black stratification that makes the white a perpetual teacher and the black a perpetual pupil (and a poor one at that)." Biko asks non-Whites to unify and overcome the two forces that strongly determine their consciousness: the external forces of oppression, and the internal forces of inferiority feelings (Biko, 1987:100). Biko defines being Black in a constructivist way (Biko 1987:48):

> We have in our policy manifesto defined blacks as those who are by law or tradition politically, economically and socially discriminated against as a group in the South African society identifying themselves as a unit in the struggle towards the realization of their aspirations. This definition illustrates to us a number of things:
>
> 1. Being black is not a matter of pigmentation - being black is a reflection of a mental attitude.
>
> 2. Merely by describing yourself as black you have started on a road towards emancipation, you have committed yourself to fight against all forces that seek to use your blackness as a stamp that marks you out as a subservient being.

---

[80] Biko (1987:29) defines *BC* as follows: 'The first step therefore is to make the black man to come to himself, to pump back life into his empty shell, to infuse him with pride and dignity, to remind him of his complicity in the crime of allowing himself to be misused and therefore letting evil reign supreme in the country of his birth. This is what we mean by an inward-looking process. This is the definition of "black consciousness."''

This definition makes it possible for people to define themselves as "Black" politically and socially, and especially to dissolve the stratification among Blacks and Coloureds. Biko, in theory, creates a new consciousness and an independent 'black political identity," which constructs itself in the course of an emancipation movement. He redefines the apartheid terms from inside and converts them into something positive.[81]

According to Biko, the "Anglo-Boers culture" imposed a change of values on the black African society, which is characterized by one-sided acculturation. Biko's political manifesto, which is based on African basic values, strongly dissociates itself from Western value concepts, most of which, he suspects, are harboring superiority claims. He appeals to all Black African ethnic groups to rediscover, appreciate and respect their own culture, and create a society that promotes *human dignity*. The human being, as the base of the African society (Biko, 1994), stands in the center of everything that happens in society. Biko believes in the good inside people, in their capacity to live in a *community of brothers and sisters, to communicate, to care for other people and stand in solidarity with them. African music* und *songs* alleviate the collective hard work and are means of communication. In their lyrics and rhythms, communal songs hold the African heritage in them and play as such an important role in the fight against oppression and dominance of Western culture. The power to fight resides in the whole personality of a person, accompanied by the *spiritual energy* of a higher power. The original religious-spiritual energy restores a person's faith in his own culture and the energy for its revival. This energy finds expression in the *black consciousness movement* that wants to put a human face on humanity. The knowledge that a White person can view a Black person only from the outside protects African culture. Whites can never penetrate and analyze African culture from the inside in order to grasp the ethos of the Black community (Biko 1984a:363).

Conflict resolutions, following Biko, do not happen through analytical procedures like in Western cultures but through the ability to enter situations, experience them and confront them with one's whole personality. This process activates rational and

---

[81] In the presented interviews, some Black and Coloured interview partners also refer to the definition of "being black" following Biko (compare the interviews P5:11, P18:26).

irrational areas of the personality ((Biko 1984:26/27). Thus, conflict management consists of combining one's own experiences and personal abilities in dealing with other people.

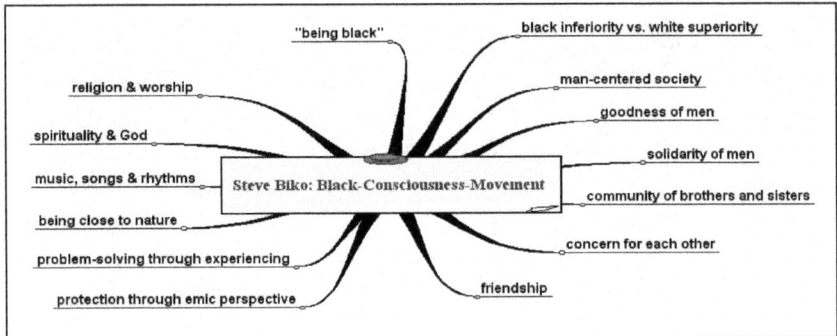

Graph 8: Biko: Black Consciousness Movement

3.4.2.2 Nelson Mandela: A Peaceful Nation

Next to Steve Biko, Nelson Mandela, as spiritual leader of the anti-apartheid movement, became one of the most important personalities and moral leaders of South Africa. After his release from prison in 1990 and later, as South Africa's first Black president and head of the *African National Congress (ANC)*, he grew to be a worldwide symbol and a driving force for the assertion of human rights and racial equality. He was supported not only by the Black majority at home but also by the international community. Values such as *peace, security, justice, racial harmony, democracy and freedom* appear persistently in his speeches (see Mandela, 1964, 1990, 1999). Whether in 1964 (Mandela, 1964) or after 27 years of captivity (Mandela, 1990), Mandela's main concern has been *equality* among people, the regaining of *human dignity* and the building of a *peaceful nation*, in which all people can live well together. Accordingly, his speeches during the recent years emphasize the desire for *unity* of the South African society. He appeals to people to strengthen their faith in themselves in order to do justice

104

to the present and future realities and to counter the violence of the apartheid ideology with *non-violent communication* (Mandela 1999). *Communication* here is the key term and the key right in human relationships and human life, through which *justice* and *equality* are realized in the world. In conflict situations it is necessary to seek "direct confrontation" by coming together to talk openly about the matter. Through thoughtful deliberation, one can work out solutions acceptable to everyone. "Thinking is the most important weapon in dealing with problems " (Mandela 2000:6). This thinking has to harmonize with faith and religion since these are the strongest powers in the world. Religions contain ethical and moral concepts of appropriate behaviors and general attitude towards life, which can unify people beyond their specific religious orientations.

Both, Biko and Mandela, worked from the center of the liberation movement during apartheid and responded to experiences with the regime in a *rational* way. Despite suffered violence, they looked for non- violent solutions.

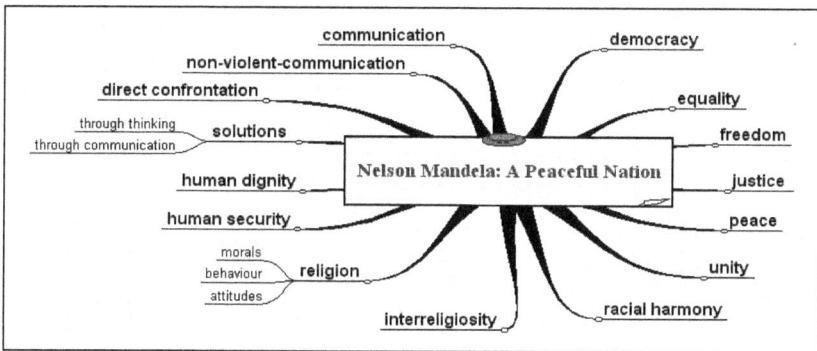

Graph 9: Mandela: A Peaceful Nation

3.4.2.3 Thabo Mbeki: African Renaissance

As Nelson Mandela's successor, South African president, Thabo Mbeki, attempts to raise public awareness for commonalities and bonds between the South African citizens. "We are a people of many colors, races, cultures, languages and ancient origins. Yet we are tied to another by a million visible and invisible threads" (Mbeki, 2001). His political appeals to South Africans are characterized by his poetic style and his narrative artistry. Central themes in all his speeches are the common *ancestors, multicultural origin, common origin of all living things* and *being a human being under God.* He calls on the *humanity of humankind* to create a society with *equality* and *dignity* for all (1996:5). In the future nation, no one should fear inequality and oppression, the denial of human rights or the power of the state. Mbeki inspires a vision of a society that refuses to make skin color, race, gender, age and geographical location discriminating factors, and that is instead based on peaceful ways of living together and solving conflicts (1996/1999:5). New individual identities should grow out of the *cultural diversity* and the *wisdom* inside each person, allowing every ego to melt together in a *We.* In a speech three years later (1999a/1999:13), Mbeki envisions not only a multicultural South Africa but also a South Africa of globalization. He advocates an ethics based on *human rights, equity* in a less torn society, *security, sustainability, development* and *inclusion* of marginalized groups in South Africa and every country in the world. Time after time (1999b: 21), Mbeki refers to the crimes of apartheid, which severely disregarded the African basic value of *humanity.* He advocates an *African Renaissance,*[82] a new flourishing of an African society that is carried especially by the *pride, wisdom* and *patriotism* of the elder members of the community.[83] He is not only talking about the rebirth and renewal of South Africa but also about the *renaissance* of the entire continent in brotherhood and revival of old-African value systems.[84] At issue is the *emancipation* of African states and actions for obtaining the *freedom* of the continent.[85]

---

[82] Sitas (1998:42) argues that the concept of *African Renaissance* as the concept of *neo-traditional Africanism* has already replaced the concept of *Rainbow Nation.* Nevertheless, this work assumes the difference between these two concepts, which continue to exist parallel in the societal discourse.

[83] Teffo (1997:19/21), too, observes that, next to the revival of Ubuntu, not only politicians but also scholars ask for an African Renaissance

[84] According to Makgoba (1999), the African Renaissance propagated in South Africa had the largest impact on the recollection of African values and indigenous knowledge.

[85] With the introduction of the African Renaissance, President Thabo Mbeki continues Africa's age-old struggle for its own identity in the quest for lasting stability, prosperity and peace. Principally, the concept of African Renaissance goes in the same direction as Ubuntu. Thus Mbeki picks up old-African concepts, which prominent leaders have publicized in other African countries.
- Kwame Nkrumah (Ghana) pursues the concept of *consciencism.*
- Kenneth Kaunda (Zambia) emphasizes the so called *humanism.*

Mbeki dedicates himself to a democratic political system, to *human rights*, to *peace* among different population groups, to *social stability* and to a *viable economic system* that plays a relevant role in the world market (1999b/1999:24/25). Mbeki presents his vision with hope and optimism. His strength and persuasive power lie in the depth of his (African) faith in the humanity and spirituality of the South African people. He urges them to fight for their long craved *peace, freedom, justice* and a better *quality of life* (1999c/1999:34), always being mindful of the apartheid era that still needs to be overcome and that necessitates a political-economic re-definition of *nation*.[86]

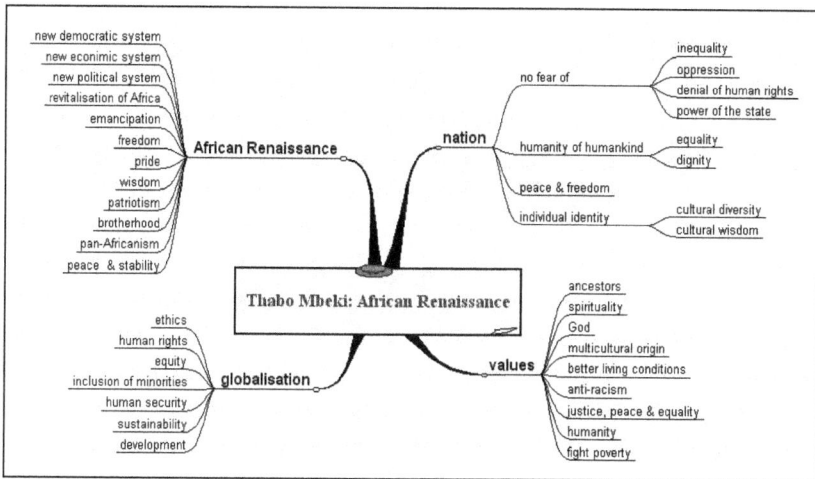

Graphic10: Mbeki: African Renaissance

- Mobuto Sese Seko (Zaire) calls his vision *authenticism*.
- Daniel Arap Moi (Kenya) formulates *nya woism*.
- Mwalimu Julius Nyerere (Tanzania) prolongs *ujamaa*.

All these concepts fall back on old African values and have a Pan-African perspective.

[86] Other voices, such as Owomoyela (1996), demand a new African concept that accelerates the "decolonization of the mind" through critical reappraising of the past and the development of new visions in the form of an African self-evaluation. Post-apartheid South Africa needs socio-cultural concepts, which depict the "diversity of Africanities in a world of hybrid cultures and identities" and present "an arena of contextualisation of meanings - a state of rationality and dissent."

3.4.2.4 Desmond Tutu: Reconciliation

Another important personality in the process of social change and reconciliation[87] is the first Black Archbishop of Cape Town, Desmond Tutu. As head and visionary if the Anglican Church, Tutu became known already during apartheid time because of his outspokenness for a free political and religious South Africa. To this day, Tutu uses his position to speak out against apartheid and in favor of *peaceful reconciliation.* Shortly after he received the Peace Nobel Price in 1984, he held a speech before the United Nations Security Council (Tutu 1985:50/52). His political manifesto, which is full of warmth, affection and solidarity for his country, names the values for South Africa's path towards a multicultural society. South Africa should be built on the basic values of *peace, harmony and contentment,* in which material and spiritual needs of the population are satisfied consistent with the Ubuntu-philosophy. He develops a *moral universe* based on *truth and justice* and realized through *Ubuntu* under the humanistic motto: "I am because you are and you are because I am" (Tutu 1998:3).

The family, so Tutu, forms the social basis for a healthy and stable society. Therefore its social structures need to be reaffirmed (Tutu, 1976). Human beings and the human community distinguish themselves in that a human being receives from others, and forms with them a network of relationships and dependencies so that all complement each other and can become one nation. Archbishop Tutu sees "the hand of God in the birth of the Rainbow Nation" (Tutu 1995:3/12).

According to Tutu, the basic concepts of apartheid are fundamentally alien to African society: injustice, pain, suffering, division, breaking apart, hostility and fear are not based on old-African value orientations. He advocates working together on abolishing the polarization between different groups. After the time of "racial prejudices" has been overcome, *reconciliation* will happen according to God's will. The major task of churches and religious groups is to work for a nation oriented at the values of *peace, harmony, happiness and gratitude* (Tutu 1985: 50).

---

[87] Current studies show (du Toit 2002) that the youth of different population groups has group-specific understandings of *reconciliation and justice in South Africa.* Whites interpret it as "seeing another's point of view," Coloureds as "coming together" and Blacks as "practical acts, not just hugs and kisses." This tendency can also be observed in the contributions to the Rainbow Nation in chapter 5.4. Tutu defines *reconciliation* in the sense of building a multicultural, democratic nation, which provides the space to deal with the past.

As part of the democratization, Tutu asks for *equality* of minorities and for the acknowledgment and unity of all groups who were deprived of dignity during apartheid time. South Africa's roots should empower all people to free themselves from the immoral and un-Christian system of apartheid. Tutu sees the task of churches to help people come to grips with their apartheid past on the basis of *justice, peace and reparations atonement* and to fulfill the vision of a true, *anti-racial society*.

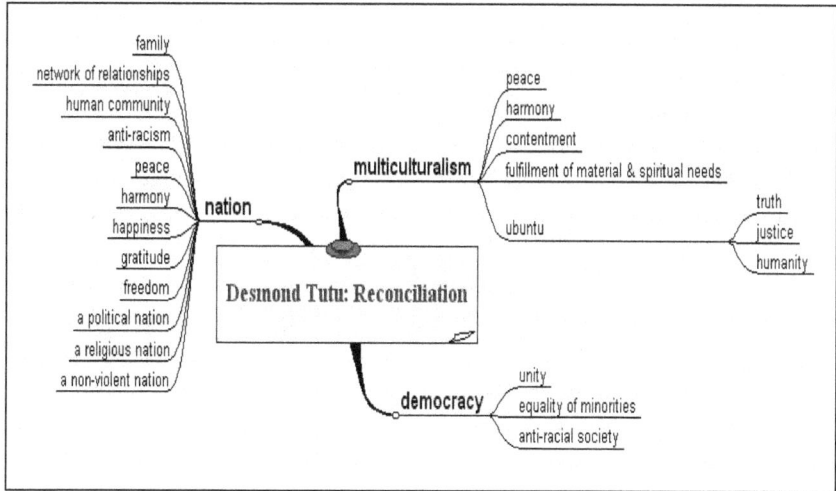

Graph 11: Tutu: Reconciliation

3.4.3 Scholars of the Scientific Discussion
3.4.3.1 Pieter H. Coetzee: Social Theory

The theoretical discourses at the universities in South Africa are essentially determined by the works of Pieter H. Coetzee, Lesiba J. Teffo und Abraham P.J. Roux. Teffo and Roux represent a metaphysically oriented approach, which takes up and develops core elements of John Mbiti's (1990) philosophy of religion. This fact in itself underlines the importance of the religion in the academic discussion.

Pieter H. Coetzee does not hold a universalistic, but a Pan-African approach, whose main focus lies in its moral philosophy (1998:275ff). According to his premise, moral questions can be solved based on the *conditio humana,* i.e., the acceptance of the common *human nature.* A fulfilled life is only possible when one's *basic needs,* such as *health, friends* and *food* are met. Securing the fulfillment of basic needs provides a cross-cultural ground for *morality.* This moral then transcends all culture-specific values.

Coetzee's particularistic approach relates to specific perspectives and is relevant to present times. He sees the African philosophy imbedded in its culture and having an innately moral nature. African ethics contains heterogeneous moral orders that are culture- and personality-bound. He defines "culture" as "an open-ended resource of social meanings upon which members of a community draw to mediate the contingencies of their everyday lives. A culture denotes the resources of a community's material and moral world.*" Community* is 'an ongoing association of men and women who have a special commitment to one another and a developed (distinct) sense of their common life. The common belief is any public discursive space which members construct through action-in-concert*"* (Coetzee, 1998:275ff). Here the communal and social *identity* of the community is the characteristic journey of the community, which is integrated into the cultural whole and with which the members stand in dialogue. Cultural identity accumulates through the *cultural capital,* reflected in traditions that manifest themselves as historically rooted and socially embedded narrations of thought systems (moral, political, epistemological, etc.) (1998:276/277).

Here, self-understanding as a logical product can only come out of a shared understanding of community. Traditions and shared collective understanding can supply the *cultural capital,* promote its social meanings, display limits of social and moral identity and integrate social processes, in which material and moral goods are produced and distributed. Coettzee develops a social theorie (1998:278ff) emphasizing four points:

- The strive for the *common good* is the predominant goal of the political community and has always priority before individual strive.
- The *common good* has the needs and goods of the individual community members in mind and consists of several single goods. It fulfills the interests of the social sphere and arises from the consensus and agreements on its values.

- The community has a common language, history and traditions (moral ones), which impact the narratives of individual lives and connect them with the ancestors.
- Society is a *community of mutuality*, in which each member stands in a dialogical relationship with the other members. The individual search for a purposeful life cannot happen with disregard for the social structures, the interest to maintaining them and the fulfillment of one's *social duties*. Hence, the meaning of life is realized in the social context and with the acknowledgement of one's *social obligations*, of which there are two kinds:

  Primary obligations: These are the duties towards immediate family and blood relatives. Here the moral obligations do not necessarily exceed the perimeter of the family structure.

  Secondary obligations: These duties apply primarily to strangers. They manifest themselves in the distribution mechanism of goods and filial relationships beyond one's biological family. For these secondary obligations, values such as *loyalty, honor and respect* are relevant, which are derived from family values.

The community is the space for the doctrine of duties (*locus of deontology*). A person attains his full status only through socialization within the community, i.e., through the continuation of *lineage*, the *kingroup* or through the provisions of the household. Once a person is integrated into the social structures, she becomes the bearer of *rights*. Her specific position within the social structure defines these rights and, accordingly, her duties. Thus, the "role-rights" of a person depend on the person's social role and position, not on the person as such (1998:280). *Justice*, which plays a special role in conflicts, is - like every other social good - part of the social structure that produces and dispenses it. *Customs* are regulations and prohibitions, attached to the following facts of life: birth and death, work and leisure, reward and punishment, and relationships between the genders and generations. They are determined by social structure, traditions and history and come about through consensus. The value of a consensus, which is supposed to produce harmony between individual and collective interests, depends on three connections:

- Priority and reflection of collective justice
- Correspondence with the claims of the common good
- Consensus in harmony with the moral identity

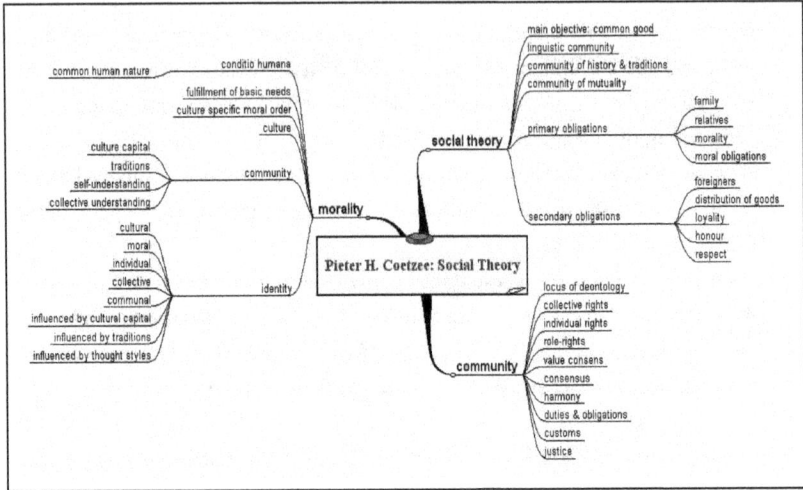

Graph 12: Coetzee: Social Theory

3.4.3.2   Lesiba J. Teffo & Abraham P. J. Roux: Metaphysics

Lesiba J. Teffo und Abraham P.J. Roux mainly discuss the topic of rationality and reality: "Why does lightning kill people?" They take up this and similar questions to demonstrate the human desire for an understanding of the world and a meaningful reality. There are two kinds of reality depending on a theological or mechanical view. The question above can be answered either with God or with an energy loaded flash of lightening.

According to Teffo and Roux, metaphysics plays a special role in life in the context of questions about existence, essence, space and time, the nature of universals, cause and effect. Distinguished from European Western philosophy, which finds its depth in the rational quest for the *one truth*, African metaphysic wants to initiate communication between different culture-specific concepts of world and life. Teffo und Roux (1998:136) note an authentic African way of approaching problems of reality with some features being more and others less important in determining reality concepts. One should not underestimate the traditional approaches, such as the belief in witch craft or in a higher being, which integrate aspects of cause, personality and responsibility (see Kohnert, 2002/2003).[88]

Central themes in African metaphysics are religious ideas: the African concepts of God and the universe and their mutual relationship. Beliefs in spirit, causality, personhood, space, time and reality play an important role in their discussion of religion, magic and ancestry worship. African metaphysics has a holistic claim. It holds that everything in reality is interconnected and that the smallest changes transform the system as a whole. African metaphysics therefore is part of principles and laws that control the so-called *vital forces*.[89] There are principles that govern the interaction of certain forces and assign them to certain hierarchies (Teffo & Roux 1998:138):[90]

Vital Frces	Chain of Being
Higher forces	God
	Ancestors
	Humankind
Lower Forces	Animals
	Plants
	Matter

Table 5: Vital Forces

---

[88] Speculations on witchcraft often go along with tensions and fears, which the charismatic and Zionist churches in South Africa (Delius, 1997:218/219, 2.4) counter in modern African anti-witchcraft movements (Kohnert 2002). According to Kohnert (2003:5), the basic attitude towards occult beliefs, which is shared by African scholars, religious teachers, philosophers and politicians, is an integral part of African culture and emic perspective, and demands consideration.

[89] The term *vital force* originally comes from Tempels (1959). According to Temples, philosophy und religion of the vital forces determine African thinking and actions and are therefore a key concepts in African philosophy and religion.

[90] The here introduced hierarchy of vital forces orients itself at Mbiti's presentation (1990:39ff).

This specific hierarchical system constitutes a connected universe of its own, in which the forces are connected with each other and change interdependently: If one person is sick, she looses life-energy, which then flows to another aspect of the vital forces; if one element of the being chain needs energy, it possibly withdraws it from another force. Special circumstances and events, such a catastrophes, sickness and death, can be ontologically and metaphysically explained at the same time. African concepts of faith cannot simply be replaced by (nature-) and science-based belief systems since they are supported by very different reality concepts. Changes can only occur when reality perceptions and sensitivities change.

Western literature often calls African metaphysics *supernatural*. But Teffo und Roux point out that in African thinking there are no dualistic reality concepts, and that one cannot distinguish between *natural* and *supernatural*. Instead, life forces stand in a holistic context and do not submit to the dualism of matter and mind (thought, soul, spirit). African metaphysics is rooted in empirical data of everyday life – not in something *supernatural*. It pays homage to the enormous complexities of the universe and the awareness of humanity's insignificance in it. The essence of metaphysics is the search for the ultimate reality in the complex relational network of the individual and its environment (1998:139).[91]

African thinking hardly distinguishes between metaphysics, social theory and morality because "philosophying," by virtue of its own communicative nature, already combines all three areas. Also, these disciplines relate to religion, i.e., the strong faith in an existing God or in a supernatural being. On one hand, African thinking regards God as the highest being, who lives and acts in harmony with the world. This faith in a "good" God does not allow for ad hoc divine interventions in the form of catastrophes.

---

[91] The key to African metaphysics lies in its causality, which differs from the Western-mechanical understanding in that it is more teleological. In African philosophy there is no coincidence, instead only the difference between a *primary* and *secondary causality*: the secondary causality often is identified with something that Western philosophy calls cause/reason, which brings about an event or change. In the statement "The petrol bomb caused the fire," the *secondary causality* is the bomb, which caused the fire. The *primary causality* is again the bomb, while the resulting fire is the expression of a goal that represents the relationship between the event (the world) and the person. The primary causality cannot be explained in physical terms, but in terms of witchcraft, magic or spirits. Immoral behavior or disturbed personal relationships can be responsible for other events.

God constitutes the spatio-temporal "totality of existence" and stands on top of the hierarchy. [92] On the other hand, God is the creator of the world, a kind of cosmic architect, who has not created the world from outside but from within. As the dichotomy of "natural and supernatural" is alien to African thinking, the same is true for the separation of matter and spirit. "The ancestors interact with mortals, and because the world of the ancestors is ontologically both analogous and contiguous to that of mortals, that is, there is no kind of difference between these worlds" (1998:141).

The African metaphysical thinking begins in the acknowledgement of social and moral facts. Immortality is a pragmatic fact; life beyond death has no personal significance. The ancestors' immortality ties the family together and guides them morally. They co-determine the ethics of group solidarity and traditions. Through rituals, the ancestors remain integrated in everyday life; through communication they are honored and asked for protection in critical situations. Only when ancestors are no longer remembered, they can enter a new dimension.

Another important facet of African philosophy represents the concept of *personhood,* which consists of *matter and mind.* There still is an ethnological debate on whether or not *thinking* has to be considered as part of the spiritual aspect (Teffo & Roux, 1998:145). While in Western philosophy, the basis of *personhood* is often of psychological or epistemological nature, African philosophy sees it in *social relations.* Hence, personality differences (especially with respect to siblings) are attributed to a personal spiritual feature, connected to God, which provide the basis for immortality. *Destiny* is an important personality aspect, since it determines the kind of choices a person has in his life and sets the boundaries in which a person individually realizes his life. A person can appeal to destiny to come to earth and exercise a positive or negative influence. It is closely related to ethics, moral and responsible behavior and, accordingly, with the *moral character of a person.* Values, such as *freedom, morality* and *responsibility* are implicitly contained: the poverty of a "lazy" person is not attributed to destiny, but to human qualities.

---

[92] People can come in contact with God through their ancestors. According to Broodryk (1997a:15), many Africans believe in a God "through the mediation of ancestors." Thus, the ancestors often have a mediator role between people and God. They also have special powers and can influence peoples' life.

The numerous African ethnicities have their own intricately developed and separate notions of destiny, personhood, witchcraft and God. Nevertheless, it can be assumed that the here introduced basic features of African philosophy are shared by many ethnic groups in Southern Africa. Under this premise, the evaluation chapter will examine some selected data with respect to concepts of Teffo's and Roux' metaphysical theory (see 5).

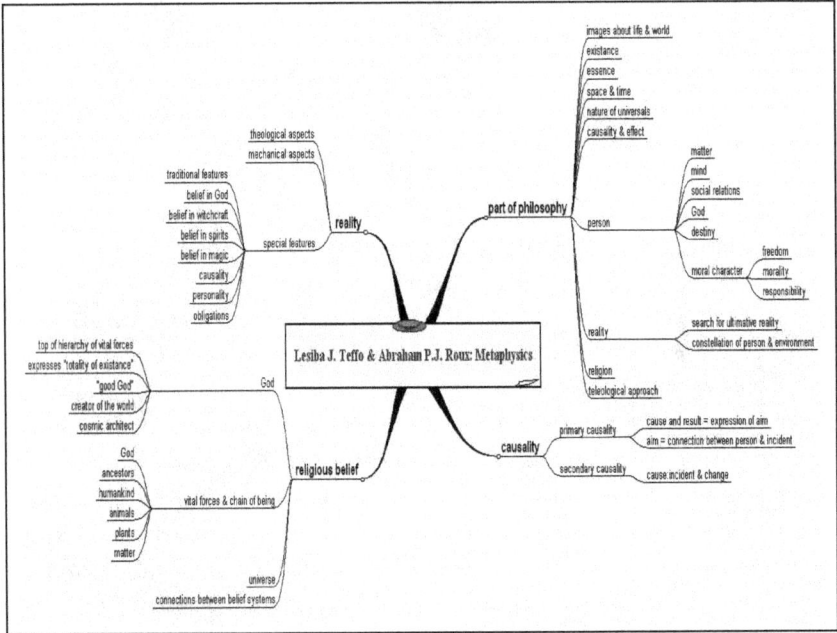

Graph 13: Teffo & Roux: Metaphysics

While it is possible to utilize the socio-political contributions of representatives of a broad South African discourse for the critical assessment of the data material, the contributions to social theory and metaphysics are less easy to handle, and therefore can be only partially "broken down" for the analysis of the data material. Nevertheless, it can be assumed that Coetzee's social theory refers to the collective experiences of

116

numerous ethnic groups in South Africa, which are implicitly reflected in the data material.

Within the whole concept of the work at hand, the theory chapter has a double function: First, the presentation and explanation of selected theoretical approaches provides insight into various theory discourses and simultaneously reflects the new state of the discussion. Secondly, the selective unfolding assists in a methodically controlled way of shedding light on the many realities in the data material and in opening a hermeneutic process of understanding

4. Methods

4.1 Methodical Approach

The exploration of the chosen theme: "Artificial Walls. South African Narratives on Conflict, Difference and Identity, A Field Study in Post-Apartheid South Africa."

- Is guided by its theoretical frame of reference
- Employs a methodical set of tools for project planning and evaluation that is oriented at the object of research and the data material and
- Refers to its level of expectation, while anticipating new insights into narrated situations of perceived conflicts.

This method chapter mainly contains a critical discussion on basic social science methodologies and on more recent ethno-methodological approaches. Representatives of diverse schools of thought in social science all agree that empirical knowledge can only be found in looking at the "derived reality" and only be secured through constructed observation and measuring tools, such as narrative interviews and controlled observation.

The interpretative orientated social science considers societal structures as being created by people and thus changeable (Kromrey, 1998:26). Therefore, it is uncommon for interpretive social science to formulate upfront hypotheses with fundamental regularities and social laws regarding the social facts to be explored. Rather, the representatives of this school attempt to find access to information through social reality: "At the outset, there are no precise hypotheses intended to be tested through confrontation with reality. Instead, one gathers as many authentic experiences as possible in the field of investigation" (transl.of Kromrey, 1998:30). In order to obtain these authentic experiences, the researcher needs to be principally open towards social and cultural phenomena while simultaneously capturing perceptions of the interacting people within the field. She needs to permit facts, themes and interpretations that are co-determined by the interacting people. To allow unexpected aspects to be considered, the study demands high flexibility from the interview partner with respect to length of interview, observation and measuring tools. This methodical approach works according to the principle of openness and communicative ascertaining of situational conditions in the social field, called "controlled subjectivity" (Kromrey, 1998:31). The study at hand is committed to this approach, understood as an approach of "qualitative social research" As explained above (1.3), it belongs to the research type of "exploratory study." From the research perspective, it orients itself at theoretical aspects from ethno-methodology and constructivism, which concentrate on the creation of social and individual realities and stand therefore in the context of the selected theoretical and methodical discourses (see 3.1). This study contributes to the content-related and methodical approach to the topic at hand in order to provide a basis for the subsequent research. The exploration of the field of thematic imagination clarifies content-dimensions so that it will be easier for future studies to specify their own concepts of investigation.

Through "inductive understanding of elements" (transl.) of the data, this work develops adequate measuring procedures and acquires valid results with respect to content analysis (Komrey, 1998:179ff), which become manifest in the building of categories. Countering the inductively obtained categories, this work conducts deductive processes in a methodical way. They function to test the elements derived from the theoretical approaches based on the data-related categories and then validate the distilled results (5). This intertwining of inductive and deductive procedures makes it possible to revise some investigative goals of this research.

Following Flick (2000:255), this study incorporates "momentary exposures" during the data gathering. The (expert-) field knowledge, revealed in the moment of the interview, i.e., is exposed through narration, coagulates as data material. The experienced and narrated perceptions of conflicts, which stand in the center of this work, are descriptions of the state of affairs at the time of the interview. The study of "momentary exposures" clearly distinguishes itself from "retrospective studies," which primarily look at biographies and the sequence events in someone's life. Instead, this exploratory study does not intend to gather data for generalizations, but rather to emphasize individual conflict experiences and their perceptions and to analyze them as such. The goal is to identify the emic perspective of the interviewees in order to present and consider it from an ethical perspective and to compile and interpret it. Thus, social events - as they exist independently from scientific processes – are recorded, analyzed and interpreted. The data gathering takes place primarily through the conduct of narrative interviews, informal everyday conversations and observations of daily life during the field research.

Ethnology defines the term *field study* from the point of view of science history. The term *field* stands for "province or department of study or activity" (Hornby, 1974:322). Commonly the ethnological research term describes the investigation in the realm of a foreign culture. In classic ethnological field research, the methodical emphasis lies on "participating observation." The researcher is required to undergo a "second socialization." She is expected to investigate the "natural life situation" as holistically as possible for at least one year (Fischer, 1992:79ff). This study differs in method and content from this classic ethnological research with respect to the length of the multiple field stays (see 5.1) and the methods used in the field (see 4.3). But it is already different from classic ethnological research in its type of research and in the choice of an urban research field.

Agnes Winifred Hoernlè is considered the pioneer of field study in South Africa. She conducted a field study among the Khoi in 1912-13 (Spiegel and Boonzaier, 1988:45) and, through her teaching, generated a following in students like Max Gluckmann, Hilda Kuper, Monica Wilson and I. Schapera in the 1920's. They gave important impulses to the ethnology of the 1930s (London School of Economics) raising international interest (Gluckman, 1975:25ff). Particularly the British colonial government supported the ethnological research in order to strengthen the "strategy of indirect rule."

According to Winkelkotte (1996), the urbanization ethnology experienced a surge in the 1960s. Ethnological research in the urban centers of South Africa oriented itself at Robert E. Park and the *Chicago School*. In the 1920s and '30s, they specialized on urban research and pointed to the importance of values and assumptions about the social world, thus diverging radically from their conservative ethnology colleagues. Park was mainly fascinated with "the mystique of the city as a dense, heterogeneous, conflictful, and very exiting place " (Kirk, 1980:39). Also Agar (1973:130), who conducted urban studies in an ethnographic way, saw the city as a new field of investigation of selected cultural groups and multicultural diversity,

Since women's literature and life stories moved to the forefront in the 1970's (Winkelkotte, 1996), South African sociology and ethnology in the 1990's have been shaped by the new political situation and the rapid social change. In this context, research on identity, African philosophy, possibilities for ethnic revitalization and socio-political issues has been conducted (Bekker, Coetzee, Kotzé). Now the perspectives of people of every cultural origin can enter the ethnological and sociological literature and bring new points of view to the discussion.

The study at hand builds on the urbanization ethnology of previous years in that it chooses an urban field of investigation and a multicultural, urban-socialized target group, and in that it identifies with Park's statement of the city as a "dense, heterogeneous, conflictful ... place."

Ethnological field research knows two basic directions in its methods. Relevant for this study is the *interpretive (hermeneutic)* ethnology, which has been led mainly by Paul Ricour and Clifford Geertz. Following the hermeneutics of the humanities, it is committed to openness, to the principal unfinishedness and ambiguity of understanding, and the notion that texts always have more levels of meaning than it appears on the first glance. On one hand, this approach is relevant for the evaluation of the data material; on the other hand, it needs to be understood in accordance with the theoretical approach outlined in chapter 3. The analysis of the interpretive nature of everyday life operates on the premise that there are no objects *per se* in the world. Rather, every object receives its reality over attributed meanings by members of society, which are formed culture-specifically, just like its perception. According to Stellrecht (1993:36), the objects of reality construct themselves only over the behavior and communication context. Thus, the world of meaningful objects becomes a world that cannot be comprehended through an externally applied measure (such as an scientific model or an objective analytical procedure). The process of interpretive data gathering in the field happens close to observation and takes place in the inter-relational context of talking, acting and understanding people. Thus, the researcher's pre-existent understanding, knowledge and interests and those of the members of the target culture determine the research results. Object and process of the research are inseparably connected. Presumably, already at the point of the data transcription (see 4.4.1) an interpretation of the research results takes place. Here the language factor is significant, since language symbols are means of reality construction. Likewise, the systematic theory of knowledge assigns language an important role in the construction of reality (Efran et al, 1992).

With this constructive role of language in mind, the role of English as the interview language has to be addressed. For the interview partners, English is neither their mother tongue nor their second language. Generally, the use of English in the investigation has not been a problem, since English is - next to Afrikaans and Xhosa – lingua franca and official language in the Western Cape and is therefore part of everyday life for the interviewed people. Nevertheless, for the people with English as a second language there might be language distortions since English terms might be filled with different semantics for people of different cultures. According to the theory of *linguistic relativity*, which Whorf and Sapir (1976) developed in the 1930s, outwardly comparable terms can assume quite different meanings for different speakers, as explained with the semantics of terms such as *race* and *Rasse* in chapter 1.4. It is based on the hypothesis that thinking, speaking and reality mutually relate and alter each other. Since they originate in different environments of application, one cannot automatically conclude from a successful communication on the surface that it also constitutes mutually agreed meaning. Indeed, the data material shows some discrepancies in this regard. Also, English is neither the mother tongue of most interview partners, nor is it the mother tongue of the interviewer, which could lead to further semantic distortions.

According to Paul Ricoeur (1979:253), hermeneutics is, on one hand, the interpretation of texts, on the other hand, the interpretation of actions in culture- specific situations. Action-situations, therefore, are texts that can be read and interpreted in different ways by the actors themselves or by the readers. There is an action-related "textuality" and a text-related "textuality," the latter being already an interpretation of the first. When the researcher, in line with Ricoeur's approach, interprets texts of other authors – in this case the narration of conflict experiences – three levels with respect to time, space and socio-cultural context come to bear:

Level 1: The South African interviewee perceives a conflict

Level 2: The interviewee remembers and, at the same time, changes the perceived conflict and gives a selective account to the researcher.

Level 3: The researcher analyzes and interprets the transcribed remembered perceptions.

In addition to the problem of producing a written text through these different levels, there is the question whether a researcher as a person from another culture is even in a position to understand hetero-cultural texts in the context of hetero-cultural possibilities of meaning. Clifford Geertz, who takes up Ricoeur's approach, states: "The culture of a people is an ensemble of texts, themselves ensembles, which the anthropologist strains to read over the shoulders of those to whom they properly belong" (Geertz, 1979:222). Geertz sees significant possibilities of interpretative ethnology in the descriptions of ethnological facts, such as cultural differences, experiences of contrasts and intercultural conflicts. In regard to the question how culture drives and shapes actions, he finds that culture might be of equal, if not overriding importance compared to other societal functional systems. Starting point of the "ethnological understanding" for Geertz is the importance of access to the counterpart and a new way to grasp and formulate "the native's point of view" (Wolff 2000:86ff). Also, by taking on cultural behavior patterns in reading them like a text, putting them into writing and interpreting them, the researcher constructs a "thick description" of the cultural behavior patterns (Geertz, 1987).

The members of the cultural community envelope the action-texts with levels of meaning, which can be understood as "subtexts." The "density" of the description is supposed to include the conceptional system in keeping with an "emic analysis." In principle, "dense descriptions" are (re-) constructions of what the participants construct as reality on the spot (Wolff, 2000:87). The problem is here that the understanding of hetero-cultural texts also includes hetero-perspective attempts of interpretation, and that this has to necessarily deviate from the intra-cultural, emic interpretation. Nevertheless, Geertz holds that the social action and its underlying meaning are public:

> Doing ethnography is like trying to read (in the sense of "construct a reading" of) a manuscript – foreign, faded, full of ellipses, incoherencies, suspicious emendations, and tendentious commentaries, but written not in conventionalized graphs of sound but in the transient examples of shaped behavior. (Geertz, 1973:10)

Since culture is public and "readable," it is possible even for a researcher from an outside culture to decode foreign text segments and to grasp their context of meaning by observing and giving attention to simple actions. This has consequences for the data gathering since the data evaluation is based on the 'relationship among the traditions of ethnography, group, and intended audience" (Agar 1986:19), and in that this is understood as core process of the negotiation of meaning and reality.

A further aspect of ethno-methodology assumes as basic fact, according to Garfinkel, the epistemological gap between societal rules and values, and the actual behavior. This can only be overcome through the interpretation of rules, values and experienced situations (Bergmann, 2000:119). Here the „objective reality" (transl.) is a product that constructs itself out of everyday activities, is produced by social interactions and finally perceived by people as "objective." Since each person creates reality in every given moment, there is in principle never a final point of time of reality construction (see 3.1). Important here are everyday knowledge, routines and interpretations by the partners of interaction since the events receive their meaning through the interaction (Bergmann, 2000:125). This also is the starting point of the *symbolic interactionism* (according to Blumer) as part of the ethno-methodology. Here the meaning that objects possess for people shapes social interaction. Self-reflecting individuals can relate these meanings symbolically through interpretation processes. Thus, they create their own world of experiences, which impacts their social interactions. Complex interpretation processes provide objects with their culture-specific meanings. There are three principles in *symbolic interactionism* that are relevant for the study at hand:

1. The basis of human behavior is the basic meaning of things.
2. The meaning of things stems from the social interactions.
3. Meanings are modified through interpretive and self-reflecting processes.

Symbolic interactionism utilizes methods such as ethnographies, interview procedures and (participating) observation. The field researcher brings her own experiences into the research in a self-reflective way in order to overcome the gap of a supposed objectivity and to establish a relationship to the "natural social reality in which the actor lives" (Coulon, 1995:7). Thus, by crossing over to another culture, these methods of observation, the conduct of interviews and the researcher's self-reflection are – also in keeping with Lederach - (1995:29) important methods to investigate "modern-day phenomena and social settings" and to overcome a postulated "objectivity." The conduct of narrative interviews and the researcher's self-reflection are decisive methodical tools in this study.

The following sub-chapters introduce the methodical procedures and tools, which are necessary for the planning of the field study, for their implementation in the field itself and for the interpretative evaluation of the data material.

4.2 Methods of Planning

An exploratory study requires method selections with respect to the following areas (Merkens, 2000:2860): case selection and case group selection, interpretation, and presentation of data material.[93]

The basic goal in choosing planning methods is to prepare and secure the access to the events and persons to be examined. For the study at hand, the selection of conversation partners and partner organizations is of special importance. Here, relative simplicity and durability of access are decisive criteria for the definition of the sample. Churches, church organizations, religious groups and NGO's in the area of peace work offer a particular suitable framework for the conduct of this investigation. Key figures in the respective organizations are consulted about possible participants in the study. The selection of the participants then orients itself at an explorative procedure, "since only during the course of the investigation can be fixated, which persons, events and activities should be included" (Merkens, 2000:295). The participating persons, therefore, are recruited in a random procedure of "networking," of accessibility and willingness to cooperate. Once somebody is ready to participate, the researcher builds a relationship with the conversation partner and facilitates an interview situation. For the access and relationship building the role of the researcher is of central importance. The researcher attempts to plant herself into the socio-cultural environment in order to be able to understand the realities and perceptions that the interviewee experiences. The role of the participants and the researcher are defined to build as much social unity as possible among them. Accordingly, the interview situation is determined by the topic-related questions and by the assignment of roles, which can be characterized – along with Denzin (1989:43) – as "a conversation, a give-and-take between two persons." While the interviewer takes on a rather active-questioning role, the interviewee has a response-

---

[93] As already mentioned in chapter 1.1, the presentation of the exploratory study and the data material uses the "narrative present tense" throughout.

giving role. Both are creating an "interpersonal drama" with certain conversation behavior, climate and role-playing, whereby the interviewer opens the "stage of the conversation" (Hermann, 2000:361/Denzin, 2000). In this way, as said by Wolff (2000a: 340), the distance between the researcher and field can be overcome, even though the interview situation as such is always artificial to a certain degree "since the interviewer and the interviewee often do not know each other very well, and the occasion for the meeting is merely the interview…" (transl. of Kromrey, 1998:337). The same is true for the study at hand.[94]

Only a few potential interview partners cannot be contacted more extensively for various reasons, such as time restraints on their side or geographical distance to their place of residence. However, the type and intensity of the relationship between the communication partners is crucial since the communication – along with Watzlawick et al (1985:56) – always entails a content and a relationship aspect, whereby the latter determines the former." The evaluation of the interviews considers these two communication aspects. Each communication carries indicators for how the communication partners define their relationship. Next to the immanent relational aspect, significant are also expectations towards the communication and its goals. The data analysis depicts content- related and relationship- oriented statements at appropriate points since in the interview situation researcher and interview partners define themselves in a special way. Frequently it happens that the conversation partners fashion their story with regard to their perception of the person sitting opposite. The assumption in this study is that the interviewees define the researcher with respect to her skin color, country of origin, gender, career, race, age and religious affiliation. Along with this classification come certain expectations towards the interviewer. Possibly the interviewees shape their responses according to what they believe the interviewer

---

[94] In this investigation, the conversation between interviewer and interviewee is principally shaped by the active-questioning mode of the interviewer. Because of the narrative approach, however, at times this active-questioning role retreats in favor of the interviewee's narration. Still, even this type of interview situation is basically directed by the questioning and enquiring manner of the interviewer. Occasionally, situations occur in which the conversation partner expects a statement or a comment from the interviewer. Naturally, communication elements such as facial expressions and gestures play a role in the conversation of give and take, which underscores the notion of an "interpersonal drama" taking place. The interviewee opens the "stage of conversation" and, at some point, takes on the active role.

expects. According to Kerlinger (1994:517), this phenomenon is called "error of leniency" and will be addressed occasionally in the data material.

Next to the interviewees, other communication partners selected are the "key informants" (Johnson, 1990:5), who play a central role. Usually they occupy a special position in the target organizations, respectively, in its social network. Here the researcher's (cultural) competence in the field is important, since the key informants are an "invaluable source of data gathering" (Johnson, 1990:9). The selection of key informants takes place over informal contacts, following Werner und Schöpfle (1987:183ff):

> After choosing anyone who cooperates, the next step is to follow the network. At first one interviews those people who are easily accessible. Then, ethnographers use the help of this first batch of people to introduce them to a widening circle of friends and relations. The "Networking" label derives from the fact that ethnographers utilize the personal networks of their earliest contacts to expand the sample.

In this study, key informants are those persons, who have an easily accessible position in the organization or its social network, thus opening up further contacts as well as deeper insights into cultural areas and the subject matter of this work.

Next to accessibility, selection of key informants and samples, quality criteria are important. The criticism of "quality research" is often directed against the lack of "solid procedures, designs and data gathering methods, which can be specified in advance and subjected to measurable, defined, operational terms" (Johnson, 1990:13). In the current literature on qualitative research, Steinke (2000:319ff) notices three basic positions concerning quality criteria: one trend orients itself at the quality criteria of quantity research. Another trend develops its own criteria for its own research A third trend approves the "postmodern rejection of criteria" (Steinke, 2000:31/321). For this exploratory study, "own criteria" are instructive in the sense that they are oriented at the data material itself and lead inductively to the building of categories (see 4.1). The two applied classic quality criteria of quality research are research-immanent validation processes by which category building has to prove itself between the data material and the theoretical frame of reference. The second quality criterion is the "inter-subjective" transparency (Steinke, 2000:324) of the research process. Central here is the documentation which allows outside observers to comprehend and evaluate the research procedure. An outside observer should be able to comprehend and assess the research object, the formulation of the questions, the methodical concept and their dynamic linking. To insure inter-subjective comprehension, the following criteria are outlined in this work:

- The researcher presents her preconception regarding explicit and implicit expectations (4.6) to compare it afterwards with the results.
- The researcher documents methods and context of the investigation (see 2;4) to increase its credibility.
- The criteria of transcription allow the review of the transcription (see 4.4.1).
- The documentation of data (see appendix) shows whether the oral forms of questioning (see 4.4.2; 4.3) were used appropriately.
- The documentation of text evaluation methods and information resources makes it possible to examine and evaluate their respective interpretations (4.4).
- In the interest of transparency, chapter 5.3 describes the experiences and difficulties in the field.

The following takes a closer look at the applied methods in the field.

4.3 Methods in the Field

The data gathering primarily takes place over narrative interviews, which – depending on situation, conversation partners and accessibility – are conducted in informal or formal settings. Additional data are gathered in informal everyday talks and everyday observations during the field stays. Informal interview situations tend to be integrated into daily life while formal interviews require scheduling time and place (setting) and therefore represent a "special situation" (Agar, 1980:90).

The "narrative interview" (Schütz, 1983) is here the obvious form of interview. While the "focused interview" provides a thread of questions along which the conversation loosely develops, the narrative interview has a more explorative function (Atteslander, 1975:94), which is preferable in an explorative study. Narrative interviews contain hardly any pre-planned guiding or controlling interventions by the interviewer. Instead, the interviewees can freely verbalize what comes to their memory. Thus, narrative interviews serve as acoustic data storage devices offering suitable material for the ensuing methods of transcription and analytic evaluation. The questioning does not intend to grasp qualities of facts, but only expose statements – in line with Kromrey (1998:337) – *about* qualities of facts.

A further characteristic of narrative interviews lies in the openness of the setting. The interviewer facilitates opportunities for speaking while adapting to the interviewee's speaking possibilities in content and style. This way, even taboo subjects can be brought up and are then at the disposal of the evaluation. The focused interview cannot offer these specific possibilities since it does not allow for direct questioning when culture-specific, critical themes come up. Often factors such as culture-specific indirect communication styles can find expression more easily in open conversation situations than in the context of fixed question catalogues. With respect to content and form, the narrating person is much more free in the narrative interview than in the focused interview. The narrative interview offers space for self-construction of personal and culture-specific elements in speech elaboration and presentation of especially important occurrences. After the self-introduction and the introduction of the project, the interviewer poses the initial question as follows: 'Can you please describe a conflict situation which you have experienced in post-apartheid South Africa? If possible, I would like to ask you to refer to an inter-personal conflict situation that you have experienced yourself." If the situation allows or demands it, the interviewer raises additional questions, which are as openly worded as possible in order to give the interviewee space to talk (Kohler Riessman, 1993:54). These questions can reflect or heighten the subject areas or aim at a more abstract level of self-interpretation. In this study, the supplemental questions mainly refer to the subject area of Rainbow Nation, as soon as the interviewees bring it up themselves. Additional extending questions relate to the area of self- and other- images.

The formal (ized) conversation situations are stored on data carriers while the informal everyday conversations are documented in writing. The same applies to everyday observations, which are saved in written observation records. These everyday observations as well as the experiences and information from informal conversation situations influence the selection and interpretation of the data. Cultural knowledge often transmits itself indirectly and culture- immanently in daily life as "tacit knowledge" (Spradley, 1979:8/9). This "tacit knowledge" stands next to the "explicit cultural knowledge," which is primarily transmitted through language and can often be sifted out of spoken words and uncovered in everyday observations.

However, the observations happen only arbitrarily without any observation criteria. In the forefront stands the "behavior observation as hetero -observation" (transl.), in which the behavior of individuals and groups is observed (Huber, 1995: 128). In the process of writing them down, field observations become "typifying, story-making, interpreting presentations ex post" (Lüders, 2000: 396). They are texts by authors who, in retrospect, present their observations and memories in a way that makes sense considering the means available to them. To this day, there are no universal rules for the production of an observation report. From the perspective of theory of knowledge, the question concerning the relationship between reality and text as a subjective reality of the recording person – as it has been continuously debated in literature – cannot be considered in this study. It must suffice to say that the written observations are subject of the author's personal perceptions and play a part in the interpretation of the data material.

4.4 Methods of Evaluation

There are two distinct steps involved in the evaluation of the data collection. First, the transcription methods need to be defined, followed by the qualitative and analytical processing of the transcribed data.

4.4.1 Transcription of Oral Survey

For the transcription procedure, only a few generally applicable standards exist, since most of the time they need to be adapted to the specific research goals and can hardly be standardized. Transcription can be defined generally as "graphic presentation of selected behavior aspects playing a role in a conversation, such as an interview " (transl.of Kowal & O'Connell, 2000:438). An appropriate transcription should be, along with Steinke (2000:327), "manageable," i.e., "simple to write, easy to read, easy to learn and to interpret (transl.)." Steinke defines transcripts as selective constructions, which reproduce aspects of the conversation behavior in a written, visual form and neglect others.

Every formal interview is recorded on mini disc in full length to insure a precise transcription. The transcribed interviews exist either in their entirety or only in segments. Due to pre-selections, some interviews have not been transcribed at all (see 5.2). The following decisions were made:

- Passages that completely digress from the topic are left out. (Indicated with ("....") Merely their themes are referred to.
- Behavior aspects of the conversation find mentioning only in so far as they play a role later in the analysis.
- The employed transcription style orients itself at the standard orthography, i.e., at the norms of written language.
- Deviations of the spoken language, such as omission of sounds or blending of sounds, are mostly ignored.
- Pauses and speech accompanying behaviors, such as laughing and throat clearing, find mentioning.
- Prosodic (e.g., tone pitch and volume) and para-linguistic characteristics (e.g., gestures and glances) are not central and only rarely mentioned.
- The non-verbal conversation aspects are indicated as follows
  –(Short) speaking pauses: "...."
  –Omission of sentences or passages: "(...)."
  –Speech accompanying behaviors, e.g., laughter: (laughs)
  –Quotations inside a quoted text passage is indicated with common quotation marks.

These decisions show that the transcription procedure mainly aims at the verbal aspects of the communication in the interest of an evaluation that is controlled by the factual words.

4.4.2 Qualitative and Analytical Methods

The narration of an event appears to be an appropriate way to convey one's own experiences and perception and make them accessible to other people. Through the narrative situation, a commonly shared reality between speaker and listener arises (see 4.1). Since the mid 1960's, social science has come to appreciate narration as a means of communication and has developed it as a research tool. Critical questions come up with regard to the quality criteria for the data gathering and analysis of narrative interviews. Narrative analysis draws attention, for example, to linguistic nuances, to the organization of a given response, the relationship between researcher and questioned person, as well as to the socio-cultural and historical contexts. For the interviewees, the systematic processing of their personal experiences and their actualized meaning stand in the forefront.

The data evaluation focuses its analysis on locating key terms and value orientations under consideration of the socio-cultural context of the interviewee (see 5). The following criteria define words as key terms:

- Key terms are those, which occupy key positions in the text extracts, i.e., a position that significantly determines text structure and conception.
- Key terms are words often emphasized in the text.
- As central text elements, key terms are repeatedly used in the text.
- Key terms can be also "high value words," such as freedom, dignity, competence, power.
- Next to value orientation terms, so-called "stigma words" can become key terms. These are words describing something or someone in a – context- and culture-bound – negative way, such as "Asylanten" (asylum seekers) in Germany or "foreigners" in the here analyzed data material.

Being of central importance in the text, the author takes up the key terms in her interpretation. Also, sporadically references are made to linguistic nuances (see 5.6), the author's self-reflection[95] (e.g., 5.5.4), and the relationship between researcher and interviewee (e.g., 5.5.4).

The overall goal of the methodical procedures is
- To de-contextualize the data material,
- To develop "clusters" (see below),
- To distill key terms and value orientations, and
- To question the developed clusters in a general and culture-specific way (see below).

The analysis itself follows Kohler Riessmann's (1993:60) method: With a main question –derived from the research topic – in mind, the interview is examined, analyzed and interpreted with respect to selected major aspects. Thus the whole data material is reduced to selected aspects. This "reduction" of the data includes the process of data extraction, the codifying and "breaking down of data to their "core elements" (transl. of Haberman & Miles, 1994). After the "de-contextualization" (Tesch, 1990), the data are clustered according to their common or similarly defined meanings, which the researcher determines. These categories serve the re-construction of information in the form of a conscious re-arrangement.

In this study, four data clusters could be identified, which the interview partners addressed particularly frequently or intensely in response to the question about their personally experienced, interpersonal conflicts: [96]

---

[95] In looking at colonialism, ethnologists coined the term "self-reflectiveness," in order to register and understand ethnographic limitations and potentials (see Alsop, 2002:1). The method of the self-reflective observation intends to realize one's own relationship to the given issues in a self-reflective way and to include these in the interpretation of the data. Thus, one's perspective with respect to the data evaluation can possibly expand, in that the self becomes aware of its social, personal and cultural context, interprets its position and brings its own background of perception and interpretation to the table in a self-reflective way (see also Reed-Damahay, 1997, Ellis und Bochner, 2000).

[96] Next to the data-supported clusters (see data clusters), the following mentions demographic-sociological clusters. They comprise collected data on the "social reality" of the interview partners, which are collected within or outside the interview.

- The "Rainbow Nation" in their daily perception (5.4)
- Self and other-images (see 5.5)
- Narrated interpersonal conflict situations in the post apartheid era (5.6)
- Identity as a subject of conflict (see 5.7)

The re-arrangement of the data in chapter 5 happens according to these four large data clusters. In line with Rosenthal & Fisher-Rosenthal (2000: 461ff), the clusters are then subjected to a detailed analysis in the following sequence:

First, all four cluster groups are scrutinized with "cluster- general questions" (CGQ), then with "cluster-specific questions" (CSQ). CGQ aim at the:

- Extraction of key terms
- Analysis, interpretation and presentation of positive and negative experienced value-orientations (see 1.4)
- Examination of key terms and value orientations in the context of socio-cultural backgrounds and the social reality of the speaker,[97] which are included according to the following criteria:

Table 6: Criteria of Social Reality

Criteria	Explanation
• Race affiliation • Ethnic, respectively socio-cultural affiliation • Language affiliation	The interviewees are classified regarding their ethnic, socio-cultural and racial origin (e.g, *Shona*, *Afrikaans-speaking White*, *Coloured*, *Black*, *Xhosa* etc.) based on the self-definitions of the interviewees within the interview.

---

[97] Literature often describes the construction of "social reality" with the phrase "social cognition" (see Thommen, 1985). "Social reality" (Thommen, 1985:37) constructs and defines itself socially and individually through the following aspects of meaning: persons, groups and institutions, profession and status, socialization and social behavior. This study designs its own main criteria for "social reality." They are those that play a major role within the context of the resear

• In-group/ out-group affiliation	This is to clarify whether or not the interviewed person feels herself to be part of the group she talks about. When, for example, a Jewish woman defines herself as Jew, she is part of the in-group of Jews. If a Roman Catholic Coloured refers to the group of Muslim coloreds, and defines himself in distinction from that group, he is likely to consider himself as an out-group member of the Muslim Coloureds, and an in-group member of the Christian Coloureds. In this case religion would determine the in-group versus out-group affiliation.
• Religious group or church affiliation	This pertains to the membership of a religious group (Jewish, Christian. Muslim) or of a certain church, such as Anglican, Dutch Reformed or Roman Catholic.
• Gender	Gender-group affiliation
• Professional, social or family position/role • Class affiliation[98] • Identification of the social milieu or lifestyle[99]	Interviewees assign themselves to a professional group, such as clergy, domestic service, skilled trade, etc., which often finds consideration in the context of class association and social background. Included here are titles appearing in the data-material, such as "working class," educational elite, etc. Also, the positions within the family, such as son, father, etc. are decisive criteria in the context of the social reality of the speaker.

Additional CGQ are:

---

[98] The concept of "social ranks" refers to the division of a society into various ranks and serves the characterization of the societal structure. The notion of social ranks is based on different criteria, mostly referring to social inequalities in a society (see below) and therefore establishing a hierarchy of groups. In contrast to "cast" and "Stand" (classes in traditional European monarchies), it is possible for people to switch in between these ranks by way of "social mobility". While the term "social rank" is merely descriptive, the "class" term has interpretive character. It primarily refers to an individual's position in the production process and is in Germany – in contrast to the Anglo-American countries – still ideologically loaded with Marxism. This study therefore prefers the use of the "social rank" concept. Even though social ranking looks different in each society, each social system has its own legitimized social inequalities. In this work, the following factors count as criteria for a person's belonging to a certain rank: power, property, social status, and social respect, and access to recourses, education, etc.

[99] The term "social milieu," first described in Durkheim's studies, comprises the environment, in which an individual grows up and lives. The milieu term assumes that peoples' life styles are not only determined by the outward circumstances, but also by inner values. Life style here is understood as the typical basic structure of peoples' everyday organization, which develops relatively independent from "objective" determining factors, but instead through biographical processes. The milieu is primarily influenced by a person's values, mentality and basic beliefs, not so much by his respective behavior. Hence, the term "social milieu "means here the sum of natural, social (socio-economic, political-administrative and socio-cultural), as well as mental environmental components that effect individuals and groups and control their thinking and actions.

- If needed, references to the interview situation and the role of the interviewer within the communication situation
- Consideration of the theoretical frame of reference of the data material with the specific orientations (see CSQ).

Regarding the individual clusters, the cluster- specific inquiries (CSQ) include the following:

- With respect to the Rainbow Nation, the clusters are related to the South African value discussion and the multiculturalism debate, i.e., difference and critical multiculturalism.
- From the data on self- and other-images, key terms of generalizing and stereotypical statements are extracted. Here the issue of the social reality of the interviewed and the in-group/ out-group- affiliation becomes important. Therefore, these statements are divided into clusters, as far as they can be filtered out of the data material: statements about "Whites, Blacks, Coloureds, Indians, Jews and Foreigners from other African countries" (see 5.6.6).
- The content related criteria, which are inductively determined from the data material, are listed in the following table:

Content- Related Text Criteria	Explanation
Perception and description of the social status of a group	This includes statements with respect to income, educational level, social and political influence, professional concentration, gender roles, and perceptions of the social positions and status of other groups, such as "They are looked down upon."
Naming, description and assignment of value-orientations to a certain group	Explicit and implicit statements about value-orientations of a group, such as "...are a peace loving community."
Mentioning of characteristics of the in/or out-group	Characteristics of a group are mentioned and specifically attributed, such as: "They stick to their own group."
Social actions of a group	Social activities of group members are emphasized and described: "They are involved in politics."

Naming, description und assignment of feelings towards a certain group, or descriptions of their emotionally marked behaviors	The emotions or emotional expressions, which an interviewee assigns to the described group, such as "They are very aggressive."

Table 7: Text Criteria

- Focal points of the data material about identity conflicts are the communication context of the interviewee, his/her social reality and the interview situation. Next to the general question, the debate on multicultural currents will find attention in the analysis and interpretation. Also, the issue of inferiority and superiority, which plays an important role in identity conflicts, will be discussed.
- The analysis of linguistic style and means augments the content analysis of the narrated interpersonal conflict situations. Here, too, the issue of inferiority and superiority, as well as the experienced forms of multiculturalism are examined, as they present themselves in the text.

The following table displays an overview of the cluster-specific questions:

Cluster / CGQ &CSQ	Rainbow Nation	Self and Other Images	Narrated Conflict Situations	Identity as Conflict Issue
CGQ	• Values and key terms through content analysis • Consideration of the social reality of the informant • Reference to the CSI	• Key terms through content analysis • Consideration of social reality of informant • Communication between interviewer & interviewee ("error of leniency") • Reference to CSQ	• Values & key terms through content analysis • Consideration of social reality of informant • Communication between interviewer & interviewee ("error of leniency") • Reference to CSQ	• Values & key terms through content analysis • Consideration of social reality of informant • Communication between interviewer & interviewee ("error of leniency") Reference to CSQ

CSQ	• Reference to South African Value Discussion (3.4) • Reference to multiculturali sm debate of "difference" & "critical multiculturali sm" (3.1.2)	• Reference to identity management through self, hetero and supposed hetero images with respect to social reality of informant and analysis of key terms	• Linguistic analysis (syntax, grammar, semantic aspects) with respect to conveyed content • Reference to South African value discourses (3.4) • Reference to multiculturalis m debate of "difference" & "critical multiculturalis m" (3.1.2)	• Definition of identity in context of social reality of the speaker • Reference to theoretical approach of "post- modern identity" (3.2) • Reference to South African value discourses (3.4) • Reference to multiculturalis m debate of "difference" & "critical multiculturalis m" (3.1.2)

Table 8: CGQ and CFQ

After outlining the analytical procedures, a portrayal of the employed methods of presentation and interpretation is in order.

4.5. Methods of Interpretation and Presentation

Following the statements in chapter 4.1 on *hermeneutic* interpretation, here the comprehending interpretation stands in the center. The interpreter of the gathered material "listens" to the intention behind the text. The text as subject begins to speak. The interpretation of the data is based on the interpreter's choice of a place, an observation, a topic to make it speak as a coincidental and casual text of everyday life

(Bude, 2000:574). The interpreter's own motives and judgment structures are implicitly present, even though she ideally allows the material to speak and merely takes on the responsibility for its interpretation. The ensuing "hermeneutic circle" conveys a story of dialogical interpretation between interpreter and speaking text, whereby the interpretation orients itself at the utilized methods and the research plan and is only as open as both allow it to be.

The interpretation and its presentation take place in the respective evaluation chapters as part of the analysis and not separate from it. In the context of interpretation, the question arises whether the data representation should happen "in a systematic (circular and linear term derivations) or in an essayistic (enlightening at certain points) (transl.)." This study generally prefers the essayistic interpretation.

In ethnology and anthropology, the problem of representation often is described as "crisis of ethnographic representation" (transl. of Matt, 2000:579). Clifford Geertz (see 4.1) attempts a re-definition of observation, interpretation and text representation. He wants to understand the text as a reality that does not represent a homogeneous creation but is characterized by ambiguity, multi-layers and contradictions. Each representation is a reality construct with a certain focus, which, moreover, is tied to a purpose and a target group. Geertz understands the presentation of reality as a new reality construct by way of certain arrangements of data, statements and results. Hence, the social-constructivist discussion emphasizes manners of (reality) construction, socio-cultural knowledge, and interpretation of situations and world with the goal to identify the societal origin of statements, and not their factual truth.

A fundamental interest of qualitative social science is the study of unique cases. Accordingly, this study in its analysis, interpretation and presentation brings to light the individuality and singularity of a case and tries to understand its specific nature. Each case is regarded in its inter-relational time-space-continuity and is not brought up to the level of generalization.

4.6 Level of Expectations

The level of expectation is the transition from the theory and method discussion to the exploratory study itself. Subject here is the conduct of the field research itself.

One assumption is that people in the multicultural metropolis of Cape Town simultaneously perceive, experience and construct conflicts. These conflicts can occur in their own socio-cultural (and ethnic) context or in a group-cross-over situation. A further assumption is that the sample selection provides interview partners who are willing to talk about their conflict experiences and to present them in a formal or informal interview situation. Nevertheless, the explosive nature of the subject demands a trusting relationship between the interview partners. Therefore, the planning allows for longer periods of building relationships.

With respect to content, the expectation is that the conflict story is individually created and does not always address the subject explicitly. For the process of evaluation, this means that the researcher will have to find and distill her points of interests from the data material and assess them individually. The data, most likely, cannot be generalized but are unique and heterogeneous. This heterogeneity of narrated conflict experiences can be reflected in the narration of personal, intercultural or social conflicts from different areas of life.

Regarding the experienced intercultural conflicts themselves, this study presumes that they are, to this day, strongly influenced by apartheid and the historical events of the last decades. Even if the Western Cape had a relatively liberal political leadership during apartheid, the historical-societal influences most likely continue to determine the perception and construction of conflicts in a specific regional way. This influence could manifest itself in that the narrated conflict experiences show symptoms of apartheid time or in that apartheid aspects shape perceptions and construction of current conflict situations.

Another basic pre-supposition is that value orientations explicitly and implicitly accompany the narration of conflict situations. Favored and disapproved value orientations will be mentioned. The expectation is that there will be statements on very heterogeneous, situation-dependent value orientations since the socio-cultural conditions of the urban environment are hyper-complex and subjected to multicultural, global and individual interests.

Regarding the South African value discourses (see 3.4), the expectation is that some segments of daily life of the interviewees will reflect the attitudes of politicians, theologians and scientists. This should be especially true for the explored stances on the Rainbow Nation. Here we are dealing with a discourse on values and a new reality design, which – even though based on African basic values -, happens far removed from the daily life of the population. Often, the so-called *survival values* (see 1.4) such as food, water and land are of higher importance on a daily basis than the so-called *trans-survival-values,* such as solidarity, commonalities or philosophy. However, a large portion of the values, which are theoretically discussed in the public value discourse, are possibly also experienced, constructed and narrated in daily life situations. The hope is that especially informal conversations and contacts will offer special insights into the topic.

It is unlikely that this exploratory study is able to clarify whether a conflict situation is primarily determined by the individual or by the culture because the layers of individuality, ethnicity and culture are rarely clear-cut. The exposed conflict situations will not result in general statements about a certain population group since in this exploratory study the personally experienced conflict situation stand in the forefront, and not the ability to transfer and generalize the results. What will happen instead is the evaluation of individually experienced conflict situation of a multicultural person who is determined by multiple identities.

With respect to the role of the interviewer the assumption is that gender, age, educational level, skin color and country of origin are factors that come to bear and possibly influence the interview situation. Moreover, it is likely that the communication is geared towards the interviewer in that the interviewee will talk about issues and stories that he believes not only to be of interest to the interviewer but also accessible to her understanding. Thus, it is possible that a black person portraits an experienced conflict with a white person more positively than he would if talking to a black person.

In conjunction with this there are more expectations concerning the methodological procedure. For the study in South Africa, the exploratory approach is preferable since there is little research material on this subject. Also, the open approach allows the interviewee to speak freely so that those selected areas of conflict that are of biographical- anamnetical significance to the narrator can come to the surface.

It will be shown to which degree these presumptions can be verified or falsified (see 5.8).

5. The Exploratory Study

The following presents the preparation, execution and evaluation of this study. The evaluation comprises analysis, presentation and interpretation of the data material. Of special significance in this context is the criterion of "inter-subjective understanding."

5.1 Preparation and Planning

During the planning phase of the exploratory study from June 2001 until June 2002, the preparations take place in Germany as well as in South Africa. The preparations in Germany are confined to the literature search, the initial building of contacts to churches and NGO's in South Africa, the theoretical and methodical narrowing down of the topic, and the preparation of the field stays.

The preparations in South Africa (June until August 2001) consist of initiating contacts with potential participants from churches and NGO's and securing access channels to the samples. Content- and method-related questions are discussed with the prospective interviewees to ensure that their needs and interests are included. Also, these discussions help to establish methods that are socio-culturally, politically, and individually adequate, as well as productive with respect to the main question.

During these first talks, people show an apparent interest in the general theme and a readiness to participate, thus confirming the assumption that the selected target group in churches and NGO's provides a favorable framework. As mentioned above (1.5), the network-like structures of these institutions enable an outsider to safely reach people of disparate origins and socializations in different areas of the city.

5.2 Execution of the Field Study

During the exploratory study (June until September 2002), 52 interviews are conducted, as well as numerous informal talks with people from diverse churches, city districts and socio-cultural backgrounds. The researcher then transcribes 43 interviews.[100] The following table shows the evaluated interviews with respect to the criteria of "social reality" (see 4.4.2) of the interview partners.[101]

I.-Nr.	Sex	Socio-Cultural/ Language Origin	Career	Organization	Part of City/ City	Excerpts from Data Material in 5
P1: 22	F	White, Afrikaans	Secretary	Dutch Reformed Church	Three Anchor Bay	F1
P2: 52	M	Black, Shona	Enterpreneur	End Times Message, Christian Fellowship, ATC	Kenilworth	W6 C12 CM3 I4 CS2 CS3
P3: 21	M	White, Afrikaans	Minister	Lutheran Church	City Bowl	-
P4: 10	M	White, English	Pastoral assistant	Anglican Church	Sea Point	-
P5: 11	M	Coloured	Priest	Roman Catholic Church	City Bowl	R7 W9
P6: 12	F	White, English	Programmer Manager	Roman Catholic Welfare & Development	Elsies River	-
	M	Black, Xhosa	Social worker			
P7: 13	M	White, English	Priest	Full Gospel Church	Three Anchor Bay	W3 WA4 B9
	F	White, English	Lecturer	Full Gospel Church		
P8: 15	M	White, English	Priest	Roman Catholic Church	Langa	W4 B12
P9: 14	M	White, English	Priest	Roman Catholic Church	Kraaifontain	CM4

---

[100] Regarding content and theme, nine interviews deviate so strongly from the starting question that they are excluded from the evaluation.
[101] For reasons of data protection, the names of the interviewees are not mentioned.

P10:16	F	Black, Xhosa	Domestic worker	Roman CatholicChurch	Langa	-
P11:17	M	Black, Xhosa	Governm. Administrator	Roman CatholicChurch	Langa	R6
P12:18	F F	Coloured Coloured	Domestic worker Domestic worker	Anglican Church	Sea Point	-
P13:19	F M	Coloured Coloured	Domestic worker Social worker	Roman CatholicWelfare & Development	Elsies River	-
P14:20	M	Coloured	Priest	Roman CatholicChurch	Belgravia	-
P15:23	F	White, English	Senior Lecturer	UWC	Bellville	-
P16:24	M	Black, Xhosa	Coordinator	Roman CatholicChurch	Kayelitsha	W7
P17:25	M	Coloured	Priest	Anglican Church	Bo-kaap	WA1
P18:26	M	Black, Tswana	Senior Lecturer	Lutheran Church	City Bowl	R8
P19:27	M	White, Afrikaans	Minister	Dutch Reformed Church	Three Anchor Bay	R4 WA2 CS5 CS6
P20:28	F	White, English	Teacher	United Congregational Presbyterian Church	Rondebosch	-
P21:29	M	White, English	Program-Coordinator	Community Peace Program	Observatory	-
P22:30	M	Coloured	Priest	Anglican Rectory	Woodstock	R1 I2 I3
P23:31	F	Coloured	Nurse	Seven Day Adventists	Three Anchor Bay	-

P24: 32	F F F M	Coloured Coloured White, English White, English	Domestic worker Domestic worker Secretary Director	YMCA	Observatory	-
P25: 33	M	White, English	Handicrafts -man	Roman CatholicChurch	Sea Point	C9 CS4
P26:3 4	M	White, English	Coordinato r	Quaker Peace Center	Mowbray	-
P27: 35	M	Coloured	Communit y worker	Quaker Peace Center	Mannenburg	-
P28:3 6	f	Coloured	Field worker	United Congregational Presbyterian Church	Rondebosch	B2 F3
P29:3 7	M	White, English	Director	UCT	Rondebosch	R13
P30: 38	F M	Coloured White, English	Domestic worker	Dutch Reformed Church	Three Anchor Bay	B4
P31: 39	M	White, Afrikaans	Director	University of Stellenbosch	Stellenbosch	-
P32:3		White, English	Reverend	Methodist Church	Sea Point	B8
P33: 40	F	Coloured	Domestic worker	Dutch Reformed Church	Three Anchor Bay	-
P34: 41	F	White, English	Administra tor, Pesion	Jewish community	Sea Point	J1
P35: 43	M	Coloured	Police Program	Center of Conflict Resolution	Rondebosch	-
P36:4 5	M	Coloured	Musician	United Congregational Presbyterian Church	Rondebosch	C1 CS1
P37: 46	M	White, English	Sociologist , Academic	Center for Spirituality	Hout Bay	I1
P38: 47	M	Coloured	Consultant, Mediator	Mediation & Transformation Practice	Kuils River	-
P39:	M	Coloured	Trustee	Institute for Healing of	Sybrand Park	R16

48				Memories		
P40: 49	F	Coloured	Senior Librarian	Center for Spirituality	Claremont	-
P41: 50	M	Black, Xhosa	Social worker, NGO	Institute for Healing of Memories	Sybrand Park	B1
P43: 51	M	White, English	Director	Interfaith Initiative	University Estate	-
P44: 9	M	White, English	Director & Program Manager	Institute for Justice and Reconciliation	Rondebosch	-
P63: p4	F	White, English, Jewish	Nanny. Crèche-owner	Jewish, orthodox	Sea Point	J2

Table 9: "Social Reality" of the Interview Partners

At the beginning of the first research stay, the already existing connections from the planning trip (June until August 2001) are re-established. The existing contacts often facilitate further contacts to potential interviewees through a *random*-procedure (see 4.2), resulting in 43 interviews of 51 persons. [102] The following table shows the gender and the diverse socio-cultural background of the interviewees (33 males, 18 females):

Conducted Interviews Total	Number of Interviewees Total	Number Of Male Participants	Number Of Female Participants	Number of the Represented Socio-Cultural Groups
43	51	33	18	White 24: English: 20, Afrikaans: 4 Black 7: Xhosa: 5, Shona: 1, Tswana: 1 Coloured: 20

Table 10: Interviewees' Gender and Socio-Cultural Background

---

[102] Five of the 43 interviews are group interviews (two to five people).

The formal conversations take place with 8 people from NGO's, 34 from churches and religious groups, and 7 from other institutions. The distribution looks as follows:

NGOs & Number	Churches and Religious Groups & Number of Participants	Other Institutions and Number of Participants
NGOs: 8	Methodist: 1, Quaker: 2, Anglican: 5, Catholic: 8 Full Gospel: 2, Lutheran: 2, Dutch Reformed: 5, Presbyterian: 3, Interfaith: 1 7-Day-Adverntist: 1, Center for Spirituality: 2 Independent African Church: 1 Jewish Community: 1	University: 3 YMCA: 4

Table 11: Number of Represented Organizations

The investigation is restricted to the Western Cape with emphasis on Cape Town. The participants come from 19 different city districts in Cape Town and two other cities in the Western Cape. The fact that to this day the residents in different districts predominantly belong to only one particular population or religious group guarantees a good mixture of interviewees with respect to their ethnic and "racial" origin and their religious affiliations. The table below shows the local distribution of the interviewees:

City Districts/ Cities	Number of Interviews
Rondebosch	6
Three Anchor Bay	6
Sea Point	5
City Bowl	3
Langa	3
Elsies River	2
Mowbray	1
Kraaifontain	1
Bo-kaap	1
Belgravia	1

Kayelitsha	1
Observatory	1
Woodstock	1
Kenilworth	1
Universtiy Estate	1
Sybrand Park	1
Hout Bay	1
Mannenburg	1
Kuils River	1
Bellville (Western Cape)	1
Stellenbosch (Western Cape)	1

Table 2: Represented City Districts

The graph below gives an overview of the included cities and city district.[103]

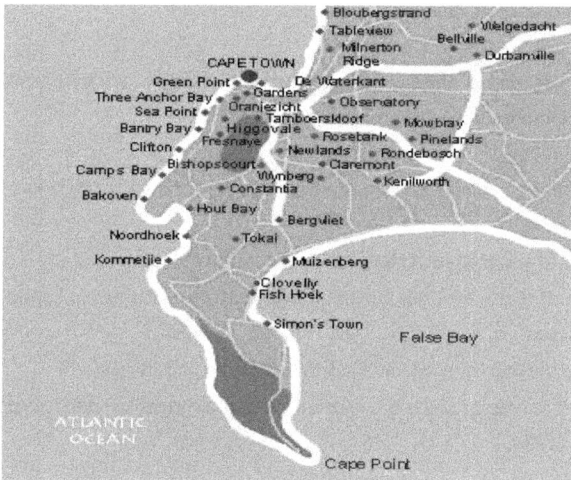

Graph 14: Districts of Cape Town

---

[103] Previous townships and some Cape Town districts are not indicated in this map: *Elsies River, Kraaifontain, Langa, Belgravia, Kayelitsha, University Estate, Sybrand Park, Mannenburg, sowie Kuils River*. Stellenbosch, located further eastward towards the Western Cape inland, is also missing on this map.

The already mentioned "informal talks" take place with partners from the "formal interviews" and with other people from the author's personal life and work context. The goal here is to enrich and expand the information from the data-material gathered in the "formal interviews."

The formal interviews contain the following sequence of introductions and explanations:

- Theme, goal and context of the research project
- Personal introduction of the interviewer
- Establishment of personal connection between interviewer and interviewee
- Assurance of anonymity of data material (data protection)
- Assurance of publication of the data in English and release of results to the participants
- Explanation of the starting question
- Clarification questions during the interview, as needed.

After the first part of the field investigation, the interviews are transcribed and pre- evaluated (October until December 2002).

A subsequent adjustment visit (December 2002 until January 2003) has the following goals:

- Consultation of selected interviewees on the initial evaluations
- Undertaking of more informal talks and everyday observations to support and expand the data material
- Extension of the experiences and findings of the exploratory study
- Expansion of the researcher's socio- cultural and political knowledge of the investigation field.

5.3   Experiences in the Field

Already during the preparation and execution phase in Cape Town, it becomes apparent that church organizations and NGO's are the appropriate partners for this investigation. It is easy to get in touch with potential interview partners, and both organizations and contacted individuals show interest and openness in their participation. Many interviewees volunteer their help in recruiting further participants, which makes this process fast and efficient. Almost without exception, the interviews take place in a pleasant atmosphere, characterized by much openness and interest on the side of the participants.[104] With one exception, all interviewees are willing to talk about the given theme of experienced conflicts and conflict perceptions.[105]

Most interviews happen at the person's work place or at a "neutral" place, such as a café or restaurant close to the work place. For the interviewer this means exposure to different parts of the city and - through more informal talks and contacts with local people – further insights into the life and living conditions in the respective district. Conducting interviews locally, however, usually entails a special logistic endeavor:

- It requires the guarantee of safe transportation, which is particularly important for the former townships.
- Visiting interview partners after work at night are – according to our key informants – advisable only in the company of a male local resident.
- The interviews require coordination between the interviewee and the accompanying persons, efficient time management [106] because of the time limit of the field stays and the planning of transportation routes to the interviews.[107]

The form of the "narrative interview" is irritating to some interview partners. Some expect to respond to a catalogue of questions with concrete definitions, rather than having to narrate freely.[108] Others, especially domestic workers, i.e., mostly women with

---

[104] The interviewees are assured that they will receive the data after the conclusion of the study.

[105] This exception pertains to a White, Afrikaans-speaking lady, who claims not ever in her life having experienced one conflict with another person, especially not with a person from a different socio-cultural group. It is interesting that this lady was recommended to me by another interview partner, who reported to have witnessed this lady at his work place involved in several conflicts with persons from the Coloured Community. When I relate her response to the interview partner, he comments that this lady might not be aware of her own conflicts or that she most likely represses her conflict experiences and therefore does not "recall" them.

[106] Frequently, interviews are spontaneously possible. In most cases, however, advance appointments are made. Short-term cancellations of appointments or postponements only happen in three cases so that an optimal schedule can be maintained.

[107] The routes are also selected according to safety criteria.

[108] Some interview partners ask for definitions of terms, such as "conflict". The interviewer then explains that the definition is up to the interviewee her/himself and is part of the evaluation.

little formal education, are very insecure in the interview situation and with respect to the questions being asked.[109]

When requesting an interview from a domestic worker, the woman expresses her wish to bring along a friend for support. After the interview she comments: "We were told that you are looking for church members who can talk about conflicts. But we didn't know what to expect. So we prayed on Monday together for us and for the meeting here and that we will have a nice time." Instead of declining and avoiding an uncomfortable situation, this woman turns to her friend for support and shared prayer.

Another domestic worker brings her employer along, explaining that she was not sure she could live up to the expectations. Accordingly, the employer assumes most of the talking, even when the questions are addressed to the woman. After the interview, in a private moment with the interviewer, the same woman says: "Hopefully we will find some time to talk together next time. So that I can tell you something about my conflicts." This shows that by the end of the interview this woman has overcome her insecurities and feels comfortable enough with the interviewer to have a conversation without a third person.

In summary, it can be said that especially women with little formal education show a high degree of insecurity at the beginning of the interview, but are able to shake it off in the course of the interview so that their statements gain narrative character. With respect to the theme, everyone is willing to talk about his or her personally experienced conflict situations and tell their story.[110]

The women with a higher degree of education and professional qualification appear very confident and reflective, showing no signs of insecurity. They quickly and directly define their conflict perceptions and even offer suggestions for analysis or interpretation.

---

[109] When an interview partner, a White pastor with Afrikaans background (P19: 27), suggests to interview some Coloured women from his bible circle, he cautions that it might not be possible to conduct an interview as freely with them as with a person with a graduate degree. He advises to be prepared for them to expect more questions. Also, he suggests that a group interview might be easier for this target group, since the possibility of taking turns would take off pressure and make the conversation easier and livelier.

[110] Whether this openness and readiness to relate conflict situations and experienced traumatic events is rooted in the "traditional African" attitudes towards coping with traumatic events, can unfortunately not be clarified here. This would require further studies on healing processes of traumas in South Africa's urban and multicultural context.

Naturally, the male and female interview partners from teaching or clergy professions have no problem with narration. They construct longer free speech passages. Often they independently report, associate and structure their thoughts on the topic and merely inquire briefly whether the interviewer is able to follow.

The conversations with women happen on a more personal level than the interviews with the male conversation partners. During the initial contact phase and at the outset of the interview, female participants frequently talk about family and children, and sometimes about common educational background and church affiliation. Often, at this point, women extend an invitation to a special event, worship service or prayer circle. The majority of the non-White interviewed women are employed in the service sector, such as domestic work. Only two of them occupy mid-level, respectively higher positions of larger institutions or companies (librarian, nurse). [111] The White interviewed women consistently have middle or higher educational degrees and matching careers.

The introductory situations with male interview partners are much more factual. Most of them are interested in the research itself and in its background, in the number and length of the field stays and the experiences of the interviewer. Also, starting topics are expectations concerning the research results, which is often the point of transition for the actual topic. Men outnumber the women in this study because they hold the majority of key positions in church and NGO's. They are very active in recruiting more participants and assist in the "networking," as well as in finding the necessary resources. Most male interview partners are highly educated with graduate degrees. Those who have opted for a vocational route are today independent entrepreneurs.

As a special aspect of the interview experience, the "error of leniency" (see 4.2) requires consideration. Often interviewees shape their responses according to what they believe the interviewer expects from them or aims at. Based on their knowledge and assessment of such factors as the interviewer's racial and national origin, gender, age, education and religion, the interviewee will construct assumptions that might influence his statements. In fact, in some cases the interviewee directly refers to the interviewer's

---

[111] The reason for this, most likely, is that many non-White women during apartheid worked in White households, i.e. in jobs that do not require formal education and training (which non-White women were unlikely to obtain during apartheid for structural and political reasons). In fact, most of the participating domestic workers have worked since several years, sometimes since decades, for the same family.

country of origin: "We Afrikaans people, we are similar to you German" (see 5.5.4). A black African interview partner keeps referring to the race of the interviewer: "You White people (...), can you understand?" (P2: 52). Already these small examples demonstrate that the participants are aware of the characteristics of racial and national origin during the interview and that their assignment of these categories defines the relationship and influences the content of the conversation. While the Afrikaans-speaking interview partner proposes an imaginary commonality between himself and the interviewer, the Shona-speaking man clearly distinguishes himself from her. He critically questions the capability of her as a "White" woman to understand what he as a black man has to say, and, above all, *means* to say. Here the interview partner addresses directly the problem of "read (ing) over the shoulder" that Geertz discusses (see 4.1).

In another interview, a Xhosa- speaking interview partner separates clearly between "White South Africans" and "White Europeans." "The Whites here in South Africa...I don't talk about the Whites up there in Europe...they are just pretending their friendliness." (see P16:24).With this differentiation, the interview partner frees himself to openly express his critical opinions of White South Africans without personally attacking the interviewer as representative of the White Europeans. In this case, the "error of leniency" facilitates an open conversation, since the interviewee expects the interviewer not to feel criticized.

The White interview partners tend to refer to the shared "in-group" of interviewer and interviewee. A White pastor remarks: "We Whites, we don't understand, you know? We don't have that in our Western culture as you know" (5.6.5; 5.6.6). The pastor includes the interviewer in this shared in-group of Whites and members of the Western culture, thus establishing a connection with the goal to continue the conversation on the same "wave length."

The non-White pastors position themselves quite the opposite way. They show themselves very reflective and critical towards the current and past socio-political events. They emphasize their own history, their fight against apartheid, their strong political-ideological opinions and their own socio-cultural background. They portray their own culture and identity – mostly grounded in the Coloured Community – very positively, and frequently in distinction from Western or White culture, whom they regard critically (see, e.g., 5.5.3, W9). In one case,[112] the criticism of the White population group is particularly pointed referring to the political history. Even though this criticism is not directed against the interviewer, she cannot help but identifying with the position of a representative of the "White, Western culture" with all its guilt. The strongly critical attitude triggers in her a pronounced feeling of "collective guilt" or "collective responsibility," the same as Whites, especially Afrikaans, in South Africa currently feel towards the other population groups.

These exemplary excerpts show the possible effects of the "error of leniency." The data distortion can have negative and positive consequences, which, in turn, can result in self-fulfilling prophesy. In conclusion, it should be noted that the "error of leniency" works in numerous communicative situations and has to be examined and interpreted case- specifically, as attempted in the following chapters.

5.4 Discourse: The Conflict Potential of the "Rainbow Nation"

The evaluation of the given data material points to the significance of the socio-political, as well as religious concept of the Rainbow Nation South Africa (see 3.4.1). Given the numerous church connections of the participants, it can be assumed that everyone is familiar with the religious and, to some degree, the political interpretation of the rainbow symbol.[113]

Religious symbolism is essential to the church's message and instrumental in the construction of religious communities (see 3.1.1). The rainbow is not only an important symbol to Christians but also to Muslims, since the texts of the Noachian branch are also part of the Muslim faith tradition. The Koran, too, refers to the rainbow symbol. Thus, Desmond Tutu, as the principal constructor of the Rainbow Nation concept, addresses different faith groups. He refers to the biblical story in order to create a covenant of reconciliation and hope:

---

[112] The same interview partner also criticizes the concept of the "Rainbow Nation", which he describes as a construct of Whites, of leaders and South Africa's elite (5.2.2, R7).

[113] Symbols are tangible signs, which stand in place of an idea. They are signs of recognition, but are also ambiguous, allowing for different interpretations. The etymological origin illustrates this primary meaning. The Greek verb, *symbállein,* refers to an ancient rite, in which clay pieces are thrown together and, when fitting together, re-establish trust among the participants.

God Yahweh wants to destroy the world, because people have revolted against him. In their God despising life-styles, they have turned away and isolated themselves from God. After the flood, God and Noah enter into a covenant, which is a reconciliatory promise in the form of an obligatory contract: The creator, God Yahweh, will preserve and accompany the world instead of leaving it to itself and to its doom. Hence the order of creation is extended to the order of preservation for the duration of its existence. The rainbow stands as the symbolic seal of the covenant, as a sign for the promised order, for the reconciliation between God and mankind.

On the second level, the rainbow is understood as a political symbol. Especially the political symbols live from being recognized by a certain collective, be it nations, parties, movements or smaller – often militant – political groups. In distinction from political metaphors, allegories and ciphers, which all exhibit "sharper semantic edges" (transl. of Wittgenstein), political symbols escape clear-cut definitions of their meaning. They want to be interpreted by association and developed in concrete contexts. Presumably, the effects of the rainbow symbol in the political field in South Africa are particularly strong because of its color aspect. The color symbolism allows people to inject new, emotionally loaded semantics into the symbol, depending on the specific political-social setting. Once the religious layers are removed from the rainbow symbol and it has been reduced to its color symbolism, it can still be used in an inclusive way. But it is also possible that the rainbow as purely political label loses its associative width of interpretation, in which case the excluding interpretive function takes effect, causing members of some population groups to question or reject the symbol since they cannot find themselves optically represented on the color scale.

Hence, the motivating power of the rainbow symbol in South Africa depends on its ability to be open for multiple interpretations in specific social and political circumstances. The greater the detachment of the political color symbolism from its basic religious meanings, the more diminished is the integrative function of the rainbow symbol.

To many interview partners, the rainbow symbol is problematic. Many only touch on the subject in response to the introductory question, address its controversy or strongly criticize it. The following will analyze and interpret some of these interview excerpts.[114] At the beginning stands the introduction of a purely political oriented interpretation by a White professor, which is followed by a mix of interpretations. Then the text excerpts are analyzed with respect to their value orientations and key terms and compared to the theoretical discourses of the South African Rainbow Nation (3.4) and the multiculturalism debate (3.1.2).

The first speaker (P29:37) is a member of the White educational elite of German-Jewish descent. His family emigrated to South Africa during the Second World War. Today he is professor of social science at the University of Cape Town. To him, the rainbow symbol has primarily political meaning. In his brief statement, he takes a critical look at the goal and effect of the symbol.

> You can play that in various ways. Ahm, it's a, it's a slogan and like all slogans it means anything and everything. Ahm, at one level the rainbow is made of 7 different colors. Ah, is it 7 or is it 9? 7, I think. Ah, and that implies that there is nice, neat boundaries and it's different pieces that kind of fit together and that's a beautiful thing. On the other hand, the rainbow is one color, it's the whole spectrum of colors and it all melts into each other. And I am not sure which people mean when they use it. Some they mean the one and the other time they mean the other. Ahm, and that's why it is a good slogan, because it's actually meaningless. (R13)

Coming from a socio-political interpretation, the speaker looks at the Rainbow Nation critically as a political "slogan," a memorable, effective phrase for the politics of national construction. He immediately gives his reasons for calling it "slogan." In his view, one has to choose between two alternative interpretations, implying two sharply contrasting political concepts:

In the first, the rainbow is made up of a certain number of colors, which are juxtaposed and can be clearly distinguished from each other. In that case, the colors exist separate from each other by their own boundaries, yet fit well together. Seen as a

---

[114] R13, R1, R16, R4, R6, R7 and R8 were selected because, first, they show tendencies and critical points also brought up by other interview partners, and, second, they complement contributions already presented in other data chapters (5.5, 5.6 and 5.7).

political-ideological concept, one can understand this in the sense of *difference multiculturalism* since the colors, symbolizing the different population groups, do not mix. Remaining basically separate, they, nevertheless, present a harmonious picture on the surface.

Or, one could say that the rainbow has one single color, in which all colors blend together. This way the rainbow symbol stands for the *critical multiculturalism*, since here boundless colors flow together into one single unity. Here the colors form one comprehensive, new whole.

However, the speaker finds himself in a (political-ideological) dilemma: he never knows when who with what intention and political ideology uses the symbol. This double meaning is irritating to him since it provides little orientation, but implies loss of orientation instead. Since the symbol can integrate both the ideology of multi-culture of apartheid and the concept and vision of the *critical multiculturalism*, it is hardly meaningful. As a slogan the symbol can be used in various ways, contexts, and situations, but it raises questions, which have not been answered so far.

His criticism holds the desire for clarity and *meaning* with respect to the nation building. The speaker wants transparency, understanding, clear positioning, and critical discussions on societal-visionary concepts and symbols. His criticism remains on a meta-level without addressing concrete aspects. He demands national symbols for support and orientation so that individuals can feel safe in knowing what kind of concept they are dealing with.[115] The rainbow symbol leaves too much room for positions that can be changed and interpreted depending on the context.[116]

As a social scientist, who analyzes and questions political, sociological and cultural phenomena and concepts, the speaker is only interested in the societal relevance and political function of the symbol, not in its religious component.

---

[115] In contrast to this speaker's opinion, the symbol definitely provides political, respectively religious orientation, according to the Coloured interview partner from R7 (5.4.2) and the Black partner from R8 (5.4.3).
[116] The interview partner R16, for example, sees in the rainbow mostly the working together of individual colors to make up the whole color spectrum. Other excerpts, such as R4 and R7 (5.4.2) emphasize the different, juxtaposed color segments (R7), which cannot simply be combined.

meaning anything & everything
therefor it's meaningless

it's a slogan

confusion about which meaning people refer to

R13: rainbow nation

7 different colours
implies nice, neet boundaries
different pieces fitting together
a beautiful thing

on the one hand

on the other hand

rainbow is 1 colour
it's the whole spectrum of coloures
melting all into each other

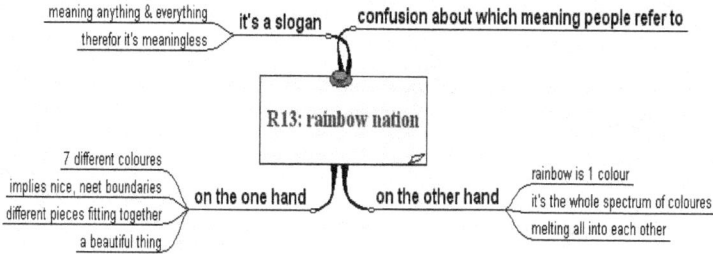

Graph 15: R13 Rainbow Nation

5.4.1. "There ain't no black...but it uses White light."

The pastor (P22:33) of an Anglican congregation in Woodstock is a member of the Coloured community.[117] He is highly educated and addresses themes going far beyond his personal field of expertise. He is well read and appears very thoughtful and reflective. Since a few months, he has been living and working as pastor in a sector of town predominated by Coloured working class, which is characterized by high unemployment and high potential for violence. Next to his work as a pastor, the speaker has the vision of a community and art center in his part of town, which he would like to realize in the near future. The center should raise the living standard of people in his congregation and offer identity-shaping elements. Themes of identity and social-ideological processes are of great importance to the speaker personally and play a big role in the construction of his own realities. When expressing his own interests, he comes to speak about the topic of the Rainbow Nation. [118]

---

[117]Compare also chapters 5.7.2 and 5.7.3. In both text excerpts about the perception of one's own identity, the author explains exactly, which groups he feels he belongs to and what role each plays for him.

[118] The atmosphere in this interview is particularly pleasant, the pastor being cordially open and friendly. In the background *Cape Town Jazz* is playing the whole time. Many times the interviewee points to the great importance of local music and poetry, especially of the Coloured community, in his life.

The new South Africa – and I am now paraphrasing – the new South Africa will be...a...synthesis of all the ghetto cultures as all great cultures have always been a synthesis. Ahm...it will not be all Black. But it will be African. And that for me is a prophetic and profound statement of recognizing the richness of diversity. And this is only when you have a sense, a profound sense of your worth and of you equality. Not your superiority or...you...ah...your lower status. But as an equal. That you can bring your culture to the tapestry of what is South Africa. Because that is something that we are still making. This is South Africa, this is New South Africa. It's there in terms of its corner stones, in our constitution, in the bill of rights, our culture and its diversity. But out of that we need to form a South Africaness. Ironically the community in which I grew up, the Coloured community, must realize that we are the first South Africans, because ...all of what is diverse is embodied in us. I didn't ever like the Rainbow Nation concept. But I worked together with Bishop Tutu. (...)

So, I, I said I have a great appreciation about, yes, the rainbow,...but, you know, there was a guy in the UK that...he wrote a book about: "There ain't no black in the union jack.." And so the question is also: There is no black in the, in the ...in the rainbow. So, it is a great symbol, but it's a symbol that I celebrate in a certain context. That breezing period from the Apartheid regime to the New South Africa. But there are other symbols that we use, you know, the symbol of the "Garip," the old Orange River. The big river that flows through the country and that's fed by many tributaries. That's one symbol that we turn to use. The river "Garip." It's a Khoisan word. And the river is a symbol for the nation that is growing. That is there. But it's a river that doesn't function on it's own. That is influenced and that is strengthened and that grows by the tributaries that flow into it. At various parts of its journey to the Atlantic. So, that is a very ideal symbol. Because it's dynamic. The river moves. Culture - when it's static - becomes reactionary, it stagnates, has all the narrowness of stagnicity. But something that is moving, there is also life in it. And it's always taking in something new, it's taking on the new youth energy of music, while we have still the old music of Cape Town Jazz.

We have that other form. So, Jazz will be another symbol, because it takes too much and while it contains the...you know, the song, the drummers, the saxophonist comes in." (R1)

This pastor primarily regards the rainbow from a political perspective. The religious level remains in the background, but shimmers through at some places. To the speaker, the rainbow symbol is a sort of transitional symbol that symbolizes South Africa's path from apartheid to post-apartheid. Even though his arguments and interpretations are political on the surface, the symbol receives here a political *and* religious component: On one hand, the speaker describes the political transition from apartheid to post-apartheid; on the other hand, he probably derives this understanding from his biblical knowledge since the biblical symbol stands for the transition of peoples' turning away from God towards reconciliation and covenant with God.

Politically the symbol stands for the synthesis of the various cultural groups in South Africa, but also for the Pan-African ideology and attitude. The rainbow asks for a future of "African-ness" that is not confined to the South African nation and which recognizes the "richness of diversity" – probably in terms of *critical multiculturalism*. These can be developed through the individual acceptance of one's own *worth* and *equality* of people, disregarding concepts of superiority and lower status. Thus, the value of *equality* stands in relationship to self-worth and appreciation of other people, independent from one's constructed status. To the speaker, the Rainbow Nation is a socio-political (re-) construction, which finds its political-ideological corner stones in the constitution, in the Bill of Rights, in the culture, and in its diversity. This new "South African-ness" he sees in particular embodied in the inner diversity of the Coloured Community. "Ironically the community in which I grew up, the Coloured Community, must realize that we are the first...all of what is diverse is embodied in us." In this statement the author expresses an attitude in line with *critical multiculturalism*. Ideally, the diversity embodied in a person and the interplay of the various identity aspects should be synthesized (see 3.2) through identity management. At the same time, it becomes clear how much the Rainbow Nation, in his view, is constructed through the consciousness and identity of each single individual. The speaker appeals to the consciousness of the Coloured Community. The Coloureds, who were previously regarded as "mixed race" and counted as less than Whites, now should be the avant-garde on the path to a multicultural society in the form of *critical multiculturalism.*[119] By assigning the group that he himself is part of and that makes up part of his social reality a spearheading role in his own social and individual construction of a multicultural society (see also 5.7.3), he also upgrades his own social and individual worth.[120] Values such as *diversity* and *equality* are prolonged and envisioned in the national value discourses, such as in More's Rainbow Nation concept (3.4.1) and discourses on Ubuntu. Hence, the author argues in line with the here introduced value discourses and their ideals, which also strive for the ideal state of the *critical multiculturalism.*

The speaker raises the critical question whether the rainbow includes the color black, which underscores his political interpretation. He sees neither himself nor his Black identity aspects integrated and represented in the symbol.[121] The color black becomes the symbol for his own person as well as his self-defined in-group, consistent with Biko (see 3.4.2).

His self-definition as "Black," and his Pan-African approach show that the author has internalized Biko's program of dismantling the social constructs of inferiority and superiority and replace them with equality and self-worth. He emphasizes the need to change the external social structures of inferiority/superiority, as well as the psychological and mental structures inside each person.[122] Values tied to the inferiority/superiority-feelings are especially *self-worth*, the value of *human dignity*,

---

[119] The author addresses this aspect of embodied diversity more thoroughly at a later point. Text excerpts on the theme of cultural diversity and identity by this speaker are closer discussed in chapters 5.7.2 and 5.7.3.

[120] In the researcher's view, this first place positioning of the Coloured Community as a group most likely to embody diversity is meant to be a daring and provocative proposal since this diversity ideal would again be associated with a hierarchy based on skin color. This shows that the speaker even with his best intentions cannot escape the constructs of *race* and *status*. At the same time, it is of course questionable whether this idea could be raised to a "national ideal" and accepted by the other population groups.

[121] The author, who points to the many aspects of his identity in 5.7.2 and 5.7.3 (including White and Black identity-elements), here only mentions black as not represented in the rainbow color scheme. He does not address his view on the color White. However, in text excerpt R16, the interview partner directly comments on the "White light" in the rainbow.

[122] Biko, too, again and again demands the change of both sides: the inner attitude and the external structures of inferiority and superiority, since they are mutually on each other (see 3.4.2).

humanity and *equality.* The feeling of inferiority often arises when these values are missing or barely present in the perspective of the effected person.

However, there is a contradiction in the author's arguments. With his emphasis of Coloureds embodying diversity, the author principally remains caught in the structures of higher and lower status. It becomes clear how his different, ambivalent identity aspects wrestle with each other and reveal contradictions[123] in his "patchwork identity." He does not succeed in breaking completely out of the political construction of social stratification, even though his visions go into another direction.

His preferred symbol for the envisioned new nation is "the old Orange River."[124] This river, which flows through South Africa and is fed on its path by many tributaries, presents his ideal metaphor. The river is dynamic, on the move, and grows through its tributaries, a symbolism ideal for *culture,* which otherwise would be static and reactionary. The river absorbs and combines old and new elements, grows with them and renews itself. Out of political consideration, he names the river with the old Khoisan word, "Garip." Instead of choosing a biblical-Christian, i.e., Western symbol, he picks one that originates in the African culture, is always visible, and can be geographically located.

In contrast to the color symbolism, the water is transparent and neutral, which avoids the controversial color-race equation. The river symbol expresses the pastor's ideal of a nation of social and individual diversity consistent with *critical multiculturalism.*

It is remarkable that - despite being a pastor – this speaker almost completely disregards a religious interpretation of the symbol. Only in the definition of the symbol as transitional symbol and, at most, with respect to the diversity of colors in the rainbow

---

[123] Similar contradictions and characteristics of inner conflict also determine his images of identity and reality construction, which stand in contrast to his everyday experiences, which trigger identity conflicts.

[124] The Orange River originates in Lesotho's Maluti Mountains and flows 2250 km to the Atlantic. It irrigates 47% of the South Africa's land. Its Khoisam name, "Garip," meaning "big river," was changed to "Orange River" in 1779 in honor of the Prince of Orange. Therefore, in using the African name from the pre-colonial time, the speaker refers to its original meaning for the Khoisan. The river symbol points to his own cultural roots of African storytelling and to that of a large part of the African population. At the same time, it implies the rejection of Western titles, Western colonialism and imperialism in Africa. The author re-conquers – so to speak – the original African river as symbol for the new nation.

a hint of religious meaning comes into play. But since he is dealing with the symbol as a national political construct, he probably wants to deal with it politically and not on a religious level. The reason for this priority most likely goes back to the speaker's highly developed political awareness through his wide-ranging engagement in former anti-apartheid politics.

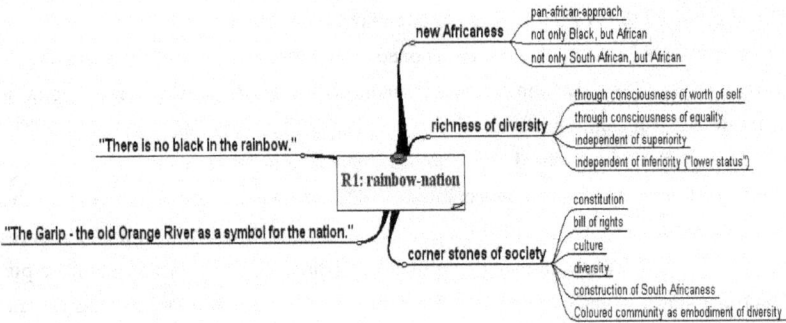

Graph 16: R1 Rainbow Nation

The following interview partner (P39:48) also uses primarily political arguments with respect to the rainbow symbol. With the key term of democracy, he explains social potentials and focal points of conflict for the Rainbow Nation. This speaker is a member of the Coloured Community and occupies several leading positions in different organizations dealing with overcoming the apartheid past. During apartheid he was active in the anti-apartheid struggle. He currently works on projects in the area of art, community life and public relations.

You know, Bishop Tutu was very foremost in the fight for democracy and, and, ah...he called us a Rainbow Nation and I think, maybe that image is a very good one, because rainbow-nation people of different colors...definitely and automatically all the colors of a rainbow - it's in there, but it uses White light, you know? And, and...that, that, that is really, as an imagery, as a metaphor to hold together what we are...ah, ah... and we obviously meet each other from a different perspective, because some people have been terribly disadvantaged against other people and, you know, we need to open up and there should be equity in terms of opportunities, that this land offers us. The equal opportunities for each and every person. That of education, that of work opportunities, that of college and all that kind of...and opportunities for houses and opportunities for...well for, for art and to express yourself. And all these others that must be given. And that's the way where our future is. We have a bright future, but there is a lot of work to do. You know, the crime is high in this country, but we must control that by bringing about the opportunities for people to realize the full potential as human beings. We don't look at the color of a persons' skin. But the, the inhaled human potential that everybody has. Everybody has dreams, everybody has aspirations, everybody has hope and, and, that is where we must focus our development of this country." (R16)

This speaker interprets the rainbow symbol entirely from a democratic-Western oriented perspective, which he already makes clear by assigning Desmond Tutu the role of a (political) fighter for democracy, instead of a church or spiritual leader. In his view, too, the Rainbow Nation embodies the cultural, colorful variety of the nation. Yet, he makes a critical point: the rainbow uses White light to unfold this variety. Again, a politically motivated argument draws a connection from the color symbolism to apartheid.[125] Over this statement, the speaker looses his train of thought. His next sentence is slightly torn apart with pauses and word repetitions. He struggles to clarify his thoughts and words, "And, and...that, that, that is really, as an imagery, as a metaphor to hold together what we are...ah, ah... and we obviously meet each other from a different perspective, because...," until he has regained control and can fill in the blanks.

To this speaker, the symbol means that the nation with its multiple identities has to stick together and consider all the different perspectives: "to hold together what we

---

[125] Here the objection from R1 is doubly explosive: while the color black has no place in the rainbow, white has a key function as foundation of the color spectrum and the color synthesis.

are." He refers to the principle of *unity in diversity* of the rainbow discourses (see 3.4.1). While again talking in political terms about ethnic diversity and different perspectives, he emphasizes especially the perspective of the "disadvantaged." He proceeds with democratic demands: "...we need to open up...[126] and "...there should be equity in terms of opportunities...," and continues with a specification: "The equal opportunities for each and every person." He names the areas in which new opportunities for individuals should be created, such as education, work, housing, art and individual expression. Mbeki, in his Western-oriented views on globalization, also mentions *equity* as an important value in peoples' living together. Tutu and Mandela, in addition, demand equality of minorities in the course of democratization. Central to this speaker's demands for equality are basic needs, as well as artistic, or individualistic value orientations, resembling western style human rights. The latter values point to the political form of open democracy.

For the author, the creation of these individual "opportunities" is the key for a bright South African "future" because they are necessary to overcome social problems. Only in "bringing about opportunities for people to realize the full potential as human beings," people can overcome their thinking in race categories. For the first time, the author brings into play a religious-philosophical viewpoint. He does not only argue politically but sees the socio-political creation of social opportunities in post-apartheid South Africa as a basis for the reactivation of African philosophies in everyday life. Only through the reconstruction of social equality and the change of the previous stratification of population groups, one can focus again on the actual human values and human potential. Finally, the speaker gives his definition of "human potential":[127]

---

[126] The pastor in R4, too, demands inner opening to innovations, change, and transformation.

[127] Compare also chapter 5.7.3. Even in the formal and informal conversations (see appendix), people again and again refer to the value of *being human*, which connects all people, regardless of race. The emphasis of this value of being recognized as human goes back to the experience of being treated as "inhuman" under Apartheid. Therefore one finds the demand to treat humans as human mostly voiced by Coloured or Black interview partners. The *being human* and the respect for all people as people is, therefore, seen as foundation for all inter-human relationships. The level, on which one can appeal to the humanity or the *being human*, is the "generic culture" (see 1.4), through which all people can connect and communicate with each other. All people have received certain human attributes and human nature, such as basic needs, which form the basis of communication and exchange over elements of "local culture" (1.4). The African concept of "being human" has to be understood as *being human* as identical with the basis of "generic culture" (1.4). In the African understanding, which is deeper and broader, *being human* not only includes the attributes of the *homo sapiens*, but at the same

"Everybody has dreams, everybody has aspirations, everybody has hope..." Human potential is determined not by physical features but by spiritual, mental and religious value orientations. Immaterial, i.e., the physicality transcending values receive a forward guiding influence in South Africa's development. The speaker constructs spiritual "trans-survival-values," as they are also propagated by African Humanism (Ubuntu, 3.4.1) and by the metaphysical value discourse of Teffo and Roux. Hence, he sees the prevalent spiritual potential of each individual to establish his/her identity and thereby build the nation.

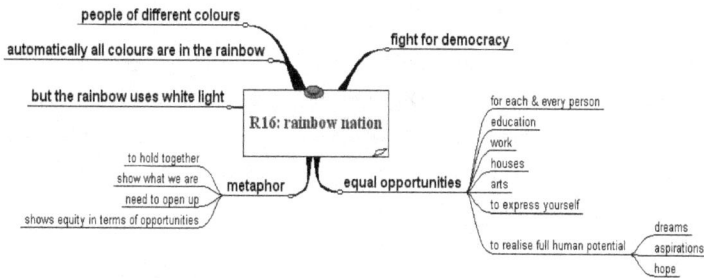

Graph 17: R16 Rainbow Nation

Consistent with Anderson and Fuchs (3.1.1), individuals' thought constructs combine into a common vision of the nation, which can become manifest on a political and religious level.

---

time the ones associated with *being human*, such as human dignity, human potential, and the respect of the person, in the sense of *personhood* according to *Ubuntu* (see 3.4.1). The concept of *being human* expands in this context the definition of "generic culture" in chapter 1.4.

5.4.2 "They are busy plugging it all over..."

The Afrikaans interview partner in this section also focuses on the political perspective of the rainbow symbol. He (P19:27) is pastor of the Dutch Reformed Church in Three Anchor Bay and has worked many years in a small, Coloured congregation in the Western Cape.[128] For some time now, he has lived and worked in an urban church, which has mostly White and a few Coloured members. He sees his mission as human being and pastor to bring church members and people of different socio-cultural groups together and get to know one another through church activities, such as prayer groups, singing and other events.

> The rainbow, I think, the rainbow is a very big rainbow, 'cause here is so many cultures in South Africa. Different in...there isn't just like Asian, White, Coloured, Black. Between the Blacks there is a lot of different cultures and so on with the Whites and Coloureds also. And we have got a lot of foreigners also in our country, so... ah, I think that's a big project if you gonna see it like one happy big community, that is living happily ever after. Ah...that, I think, it's such a, a miracle, an absolute miracle. It is actually for me a miracle that things are going so smoothly in South Africa. Ah...because of the different cultures that can misunderstand each other. Ahm...ah...the rainbow...is maybe a vision..., but...I think, the upcoming South Africans, the younger people are more open to that vision... and they are actually busy building that structure of a Rainbow Nation. I think, there can be lots, can be done more to make it...to... all the goals...to reach that vision can be implemented in this stage ...where we have got something that we can share with each other like a choir, because the Blacks like singing, you know? Like choirs and stuff...like that kind of things we can organize things like that on a more grass root level. Not on the top levels. Where people can start to know each other and know each other, ahm...the way of doing things, you know? (R4)

---

[128] In chapter 5.6.5 and 5.6.6, this interview partner describes some of the conflicts he encountered in his work with *Coloured* community members. In WA2, 5.5.4, he talks about self-image aspects of his in-group.

This interview partner views the rainbow as a symbol for the immensely heterogeneous and culturally diverse South African society. If envisioning the Rainbow Nation as a large, happy family, then its implementation is a huge project. "I think it is a big project if you gonna see it like one happy big community that is living happily ever after..." For him, the Rainbow Nation is instead a vision of diverse groups living together, whose communication is bound to be marked by misunderstandings because of their diversity. Thus, this speaker, too, differentiates between two large political trends, similarly to the author from R3.

Given the inevitable intercultural misunderstandings in this diverse society, he finds it to be a miracle that the social transformation process has been so peaceful. This is the only time that he brings the religious level into play. Just like in the Old Testament story, here the rainbow appears to be a miracle in the sky, especially after the long flood. To the speaker, the peaceful transition from apartheid to Rainbow Nation is similarly a "heavenly" miracle, something outside human grasp. By repeating the word "miracle" three times, he gives expression to his astonishment and admiration.[129]

He sees the Rainbow Nation as a vision to be realized by the new generation, who supposedly is "more open to that vision." This openness contributes to the reconstruction and new construction of the society and actually shapes the Rainbow Nation. In his opinion, this happens through encounters and actions at the grass-roots. Implicitly, the speaker asks for an even implementation of the rainbow concept on all levels of society via "bottom-up-approach." He finds the concept too theoretical-abstract when not established and realized in everyday life.[130] As an example of successful implementation of Rainbow Nation on the local level he mentions singing together in the choir. Here one can "share with each other," especially since singing is a very

---

[129] Guelke (1999:181) defines miracle as "an outcome that is both highly benign and contrary to expectations," an understanding consistent with the one in this text. In many informal conversations, especially members of White population groups have emphasized this "miracle" of peaceful transformation from apartheid to a democracy. The miracle is seen in the fact that the disadvantaged groups have not staged a violent revolution, which is particularly amazing after the events of the last decades. According to Mitchell (2003:12), many people implicitly allude to Nelson Mandela's so-called victory speech, in which he calls the birth of democracy in South Africa "a small miracle." Mitchell also notes that the expression "miracle" is generally used in the South African context of science and journalism, when the time of transition is described.

[130] Compare R6 and R7 and chapter 5.4.2

important value among Blacks.[131] This social- pragmatic approach leads to personal acquaintances and to an understanding of people from different cultural backgrounds:.... "...people can start to know each other and know each other, ahm...the way of doing things, you know?"

By aiming at the level of being and behaving and direct interactions, the speaker gives priority to the values of *sharing* of events, experiences, organization and the *getting to know* or *knowing* of other people. He acknowledges that these values are visions and so far have been only adopted by the society's "top level." But his interest is not to criticize the government or upper-class – which he himself is part of - but to use this approach in his daily work as pastor. Even though he sees the limits of this concept at this point in time, his hope and his faith in the new generation and its "openness" are unspoiled. His attitude towards the rainbow concept and its social implementation are therefore pragmatic and positive. It is interesting that this speaker, as a pastor, takes an almost exclusively political view of the rainbow symbol. Apparently, the current political situation decisively determines his construction of this symbolism.

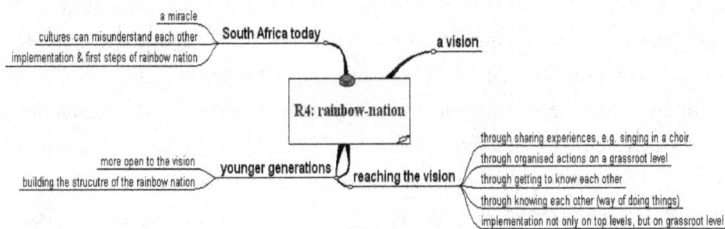

Graph 18: R4 Rainbow Nation

---

[131] It is likely that the speaker emphasizes this Black African value out of political correctness, which asks to move away from ethnocentric thinking and appreciate other cultural value orientations. In his other-image, the author picks up on the values that Biko emphasizes, such as *songs, rhythms and music* of the *Black cultures* (see 3.4.2). Here he locates a common ground not dominated by elements of White culture.

172

The following speaker (P11:17) suspects that the Rainbow Nation concept is imposed "from above." Before his retirement, back a few years already, he worked in the administration of a governmental family agency. Since a few decades, he has been living with his family in Langa. After his retirement, he increased his long time activities in the Roman Catholic Church. He is also involved in different areas and committees in his township. Being Xhosa, he speaks excellent English and is very much interested in political and social issues, which - next to his impressions from apartheid and present time[132] - determine the interview.

Ja, earlier on I have just mentioned that they are saying things on TV, they are writing things in the papers...but... we are not practicing...ah...yes...but I still say we don't feel that. We are also in the...in that rainbow. Now, there are lots of things that are still very far from here. I am sorry to go back and mention education and all that. But...but if they are talking about that. Even our language....Xhosa, very rare that you are at a place where you are asked: "Please use your language." We still go to places where we use English and Afrikaans and all that. Now, then...where does the rainbow then come in? You know? It's only in parliament where you hear...the members of parliament using Xhosa. And then it ends up there. Now, if you go to any office...okay, you go to Home Affairs you have to use English or Afrikaans, but not your language Xhosa. (...) Rainbow is there... they are busy plugging it all over, even on our flag, but they are not practicing. That is how South Africa is. Very sorry to talk like that. That is where South Africa...talking about things...but doing things is not so very good. See? We are still very...I must say we are still very, very far. And that is not good. To take us two or three years or so. It will take us ten years or so. In fact, we are not gonna benefiting for...what they gonna say....freedom, freedom as well.(R6)

This excerpt represents again a political interpretation of the rainbow symbol. Nothing points to a religious understanding. Instead, the author describes how he

---

[132] Also this interview partner's statements with respect to his other- image of Coloureds is, to this day, strongly shaped by his experiences from the apartheid period (see P11:17).

perceives the realization and construction of the Rainbow Nation, or the lack thereof, in everyday life.

In the beginning of this excerpt, the speaker informs us how the rainbow concept manifests itself in his daily life through *media realities.* He points to the "building blocks of ideological realities" (3.1) that create his daily life: governmental propaganda campaigns in newspapers and television. Consistent with Anderson, the speaker describes his perceptions of the national construction through media (3.1.1). While the media messages are reality shaping, they only have limited impact on concrete behavior in everyday life. "...but....we are not practicing...ah...yes...but I still say we don't feel it." He criticizes that the national reality constructs "from above" miss the level of concrete behavior. Especially he, as a representative of a previously discriminated group, cannot notice them.

With the example of language, the speaker demonstrates that the official language policy has only been practiced on the highest government level, such as parliament, but not in the daily routines of local government offices. To him, the unity and equality symbolized in the rainbow is barely existent on the local level. His question, "Now, then...where does the rainbow then come in?," he answers himself: "Rainbow is there...they are busy plugging it all over, even our flag, but they are not practicing." Only in parliament and in the national symbols themselves this reality is visibly constructed. His criticism is not directed against the symbol as such but against the people who propagate it in the midst of the nations daily life without practicing it. He criticizes the government policy for hardly paying attention to the grassroots. His initial "we," when talking about the concrete translation of the rainbow concept, turns into "they": "they are not practicing."[133]

He directly judges the things he perceives: "...talking about things...but doing things is not so very good." Like in R5, a communication word, "talking," becomes a key term. To this speaker, "talking" has only value when translated into concrete action. Not only is there positive value in a solution-oriented conversation but more so in the subsequent action that legitimizes the talks. Given his experiences, the population is likely to benefit from the rainbow concept only in the far future

---

[133] Here also a change occurs from the collective "we" to the "they" of a high standing in-group.

Essentially the speaker associates with the rainbow concept the values of *freedom* and *equality* and their translation into everyday life. Both values are also fundamental in the theoretical discourses on the rainbow concept (3.4.1/3.4.2), and for Mandela and Tutu in their politics of reconciliation. By demanding their practical application in daily life, the speaker shows that he does not value the discourses' function of giving orientation and identity on the ideological level as long as they fail to reach the level of practical behavior. Thus, he assigns most of the responsibility for the creation of a new nation to the leading representatives and to the government, not to the population. Only when the national avant-garde follows up their own messages with actions, the population can acknowledge, feel and own the ideas (see also 5.4.3, R8).

Graph 19: R6 Rainbow Nation

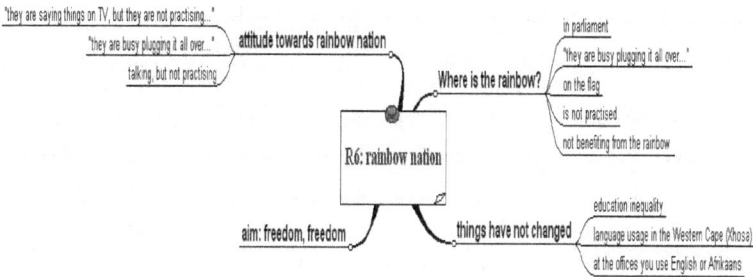

A Coloured priest (P5:11), too, is critical of the Rainbow Nation concept. He grew up in the Cape Flats, [134] where he also worked for several years after his priesthood training. At the time of the interview, he has just been transferred to a parish in Cape Town (City Bowl). Next to his work as a priest, he has been politically active. This interview is characterized by political and social criticism and, in particular, strong

---

[134] "Cape Flats" is the name for the settlements on the foothills of the Table Mountains. They consist of different townships, mostly populated by Coloureds. This area is notorious for its high crime rate, gang wars, and a generally poor milieu.

criticism of the White population.[135] He seems to speak more as a politician, than a priest.

> I think, the Rainbow Nation is a dream. I think, that is what everybody wants. Ahm...and it's an easy concept to sell, because it's romantic. You know, we all have to live together happily and...there is a pot of gold at the end of the rainbow. The colors in the rainbow don't blur. They stay where they are. They keep their position. It's fixed and that for me is a very disquieting aspect of that. Because we don't want people to be fixed. We want people to move, to find a better situation, to improve their lives, their standard of living. But a country that has had no shared social history, no cross cutting cleavages, no shared memory, no shared leaders and symbols that appeal to...but had only 300 years history of conflict and division, ahm...and pain and physical brokeness. It's an important symbol to inspire to. At least all the colors are equal. Ahm...and that is a helpful symbol for people. And so I think people believe that it's an important symbol and I think it has...uniquely ahm...guided the fact that for many people are the...the potential for racial conflict and for a melt down that could have happened and that hasn't happened and in fact at the level of thinking race, there is very little tension. Might be inscribed inside a measure to the symbol or metaphor of Rainbow Nation. And it seems it is an image that is used more by those who have then by those who don't have. I never heard people on the Cape Flat talk about it. I heard White talking about that. It's a competing thing: we are all equal now. It's a thing...the pope used it when he was in South Africa. It's a, it's a leadership thing...it's a White thing. It's not a very challenging thing or metaphor. It doesn't challenge you to change your color or place in the rainbow. Let's just cooperate nicely and be along side with one another and be happy together and have some kind of solidarity. It doesn't ask the deeper questions about how can you have solidarity when one exploits the other, when people continue to live in poverty, because the others live in wealth. Doesn't ask those...it's not the kind of metaphor or symbol that doesn't ask those kind of difficult questions. So, it's not surprising that it is a nice, comfortable symbol used by...ahm...by a certain group. And it's

---

[135] More of his critical remarks with respect to Whites are printed in W9, 5.5.3.

not only a color group. It's also where they are places in the economic and power scale: Black and White. (R7)

In calling the Rainbow Nation a "dream," the speaker right away points to the wishful, visionary character of the concept. At the same time, he declares it an image that is out of touch with reality and merely satisfies romantic desires. In a provocative way, he shares his first association with the rainbow image: a happily united family with a pot of gold at the end of the rainbow. One gets the impression that in his eyes the symbol has fairy tale character. In the following, the speaker enters his politically oriented interpretation of the symbol. At first he refers to the separate colors of the rainbow that can hardly be blurred. "The colors in the rainbow don't blur. They stay where they are. They keep their position." He is critical of the stagnancy of the color positions, notion he does not want to see transferred to society. "We don't want people to be fixed. We want people to move."[136] Movement and change[137] are priority for this speaker, and he names the goal of this change: an improvement of the social situation, of life, and the standard of living of individual and society.

But despite the image's deficit, the speaker credits the rainbow symbol with a basic peacekeeping and unifying effect. A country with "no shared social history, no cross cutting cleavages, no shared memory, no shared leaders and symbols" needs new, integrating symbols to demonstrate shared values. To a certain extent, the rainbow symbol has tempered racial conflicts. Its task is therefore to contribute to the transition from "conflict and division," from "pain and physical brokenness" of the last 300 years to a unified, peaceful nation.[138] Its symbolism is valid in that it implies the equality of colors: "At least all the colors are equal." The symbol therefore has a helpful, guiding function that qualifies social tensions and highlights the value of equality. In this sense

---

[136] Unfortunately, at this point he does not make it explicitly clear whom he means with "we." Yet, considering the parallel opinion of the interview partner in R1, we can assume that he refers to the Coloured educational elite who he feels part of. But he could also identify with the larger circle of politicians, theologians and fighters for equal opportunities and social change.

[137] Also the Coloured pastor in R1 emphasizes the importance of social change and movement essential to culture and life and symbolized in the river Garip.

[138] Again, here is a clear parallel to R1, since both authors see the rainbow symbol very critically, and allow it at best as transition symbol from apartheid to the new nation.

the author can speak of the de-escalating and peacekeeping function of the rainbow concept, as Vogt (see 3.1.2) claims it for national visions in general.

In the second part of the excerpt, the speaker looks at the promoters of the rainbow concept and the context of its use. He observes that only certain groups adopt the concept:

> And it seems it is an image that is used more by those who have, then by those who don't have. I never heard people on the Cape Flats talk about it. I heard White talking about that. It's a competing thing: we are all equal now. It's a thing...the pope used it when he was in South Africa. It's a, it's a leadership thing...it's a White thing.

Even though the concept announces *equality*, only the *haves*, the Whites and the leaders[139] use the concept, quite in contrast to the have-nots and the socially disadvantaged in the Cape Flats. The proclaimed equality cannot even manifest itself in the translation of the concept because it is constructed by and claimed only by a certain group. To the author, the *haves* are identical with the leaders and the Whites. Later he differentiates: the use of the concept cannot be ascribed to one "color group" only but to people in positions of (economic) power – Black *and* White. These people, on one hand, are in the position to publicly represent and publish these values, and, on the other hand, do not have to deal with *survival values* (see 1.4) and securing of their existence. They have the freedom and opportunity to conceive and shape ideological concepts. People on the lower end of the social scale hardly have access to education and resources, since they are occupied with daily survival. The criticism shimmering through here refers to a concept imposed "from above" without relevance for the grass roots, as expressed in R5 and R6. In this case the symbol carries its own contradiction: while symbolizing equality, it is proclaimed by people who themselves do not need equality anymore since they are already in a position of power. At this point, one can clearly sense the author's antagonism. From his social reality as someone socialized in a previously disadvantaged

---

[139] Here the speaker refers to the pope, the highest authority for a priest. To an outsider it makes sense that especially the pope in a speech in South Africa would construe the rainbow symbol in a religious rather than political way. Yet, not for a single moment does this speaker interpret the symbol in its original religious meaning.

group, who has worked himself up to a middle- or upper- class position, he criticizes the symbol as imposed from above. Despite his social ascent, he has not lost sight of the grass- roots. When he criticizes the symbol as "*not* challenging," he argues as a political, not a religious activist. The symbol is convenient for the upper class, "a nice, comfortable symbol used by...ahm...by a certain group" because it supports the status quo. They water down the message of the symbol to a platitude, a superficial idea: "Let's just cooperate nicely and be along side with one another and be happy together and have some kind of solidarity." The author may principally appreciate the values of successful cooperation, fellowship and solidarity, but sees the need for a deeper spiritual and action-oriented penetration of these values and their concrete translation, as demanded also in R5 and R6. He criticizes members of the upper class who idealize the rainbow concept verbally, but in practice remain stuck in their privileged positions. He criticizes the people in his own ranks in church and politics, possibly rejecting the rainbow concept because of his own upbringing. He knows the social realities of both the Cape Flats and the suburbs and therefore finds himself in an inner conflict. He shows solidarity with the people among whom he grew up and fights against the gap between rich and poor, continuing his fight during apartheid with the means at his disposal. Important to him are the solidarity and equality among the groups and their re-positioning in the new South Africa. The speaker takes up the values of the Rainbow Nation (3.4.1), examines them and places them in the complex social context. So far, the Rainbow Nation is still missing a common history, common leaders, common symbols and ideals, which gives it the character of *difference multiculturalism*. But he also sees the rainbow as a helpful tool on the way to realize the propagated and idealized values of *critical multiculturalism*.

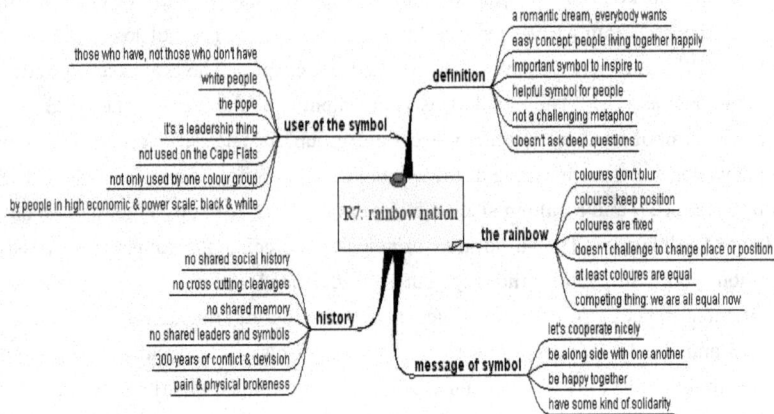

definition
- a romantic dream, everybody wants
- easy concept: people living together happily
- important symbol to inspire to
- helpful symbol for people
- not a challenging metaphor
- doesn't ask deep questions

user of the symbol
- those who have, not those who don't have
- white people
- the pope
- it's a leadership thing
- not used on the Cape Flats
- not only used by one colour group
- by people in high economic & power scale: black & white

R7: rainbow nation

the rainbow
- colours don't blur
- colours keep position
- colours are fixed
- doesn't challenge to change place or position
- at least colours are equal
- competing thing: we are all equal now

history
- no shared social history
- no cross cutting cleavages
- no shared memory
- no shared leaders and symbols
- 300 years of conflict & devision
- pain & physical brokeness

message of symbol
- let's cooperate nicely
- be along side with one another
- be happy together
- have some kind of solidarity

Graph 20: R7 Rainbow Nation

5.4.3 "They keep their artificial walls..."

The following excerpt (P18:26) comes from an interview with a South African who was, at the time of the interview, professor at the *University of Western Cape (UWC)*. The narrator, whose mother tongue is Tswana, escaped political persecution during apartheid and went into exile first in Botswana, later in Europe and in the USA, where he studied and earned his PhD. After the end of apartheid, he returned to South Africa to help with the reconstruction in the educational sector. He is very religious and actively involved in the Lutheran Church in Cape Town. In the following, he analyzes the rainbow concept first from his religious, then from his political perspective:

Ah, the Rainbow Nation concept is especially Bishop Tutu's term. I am not sure if he is the one who coined it, but he used to speak of the "rainbow people of god." It was essentially an attempt to reconcile the previously conflictual and negative racial relations in South Africa. And, and he felt that because of South Africa has got so many, ah, nationalities, cultural groups and so on. I mean, we have got Germans here, Italiens, Americans, Portuguese etc... Japanese, Chinese, you have got...the numbers might be small, but they are here,...Taiwanese, Pakistanis...Russians. The Minister of Water Affairs, he is a Jew, you see, things like that. And of course, the range of Black people that you have Zulu, Tswana and so on and from other African states, ah, they have since taken, settled here as refugees and now they take this country as theirs. So, now to Bishop Tutu and referring to him. This created a very deep and colorful range of people, okay? And I think, to be fair to him, in simple terms: Yes, we are a Rainbow Nation. We are almost like a Mini-United States of America. Right, where you find – okay, we might not have the Hispanics, but we do have a very wide range of nationalities across the globe. Right? And which makes South Africa an interesting country to stay in. And so in simple terms: Yes, we are a Rainbow Nation. And in terms of an attempt to try and reconcile the previously tense race relations in this country, there is a sudden degree of rainbow within the attempt to reconcile the races. But I am afraid, as someone who is a political analyst, observer of the political South Africa scene as far as it goes, reconciliation in South Africa, I think it has not filtered down, particularly to the White people. Many. There are few. (...)

Now, in terms of the Rainbow Nation, the reconciliation, the hand of reconciliation, some people in the truth commission where there, they have said that many Black people or at least many Black people of color, Indians or Coloureds they were former victims of the former system have extended reconciliation into the hands of their White counterparts. You know, what the White counterparts have done? They have spent the...they not even accepted the hands. Let alone reluctantly taking it. So, it's like you want to give me a very firm hand shake and I am just giving you a very lame one. So, this is why some peoples' critics of the Rainbow Nation concepts have not filtered down, particularly to the former victims of apartheid.

Reparations: you can imagine a parent who has lost a son, a woman who has lost a leg or a limb or a...some part of the body...since this thing happened in 1991 or 1987 – up to today they have not been given any reparations. That person whose house was destroyed by the apartheid forces and who is now living in the many shacks here in Kayelithsha, Gugulethu...there is no firm commitment from the state as we speak about how to at least give a compensation to this person (...). They are still sitting down with the government: how much can we give them? – But people are suffering, okay? Now, what about those who have perpetrated crimes. They are living in the Sea Points of this world. They are owning strings of chains of supermarkets, flats, and they are making money and they are driving BMWs and Mercedes Benz from Germany, you see? And it's not fair really! And in terms of justice: The legal people will tell you that justice must not only be done, but it must be seen to be done. I would argue that it was not seen to be done, okay? There is an attempt to assure that justice will be done, but it hasn't been seen to be done. It is still in the process. Ah, so that takes care of the question of the Rainbow Nation. For me, as far as I am concerned, it is very weak, if you like balance off this racial situation, because of the fact that the majority of the situation is still very, very poor, living below the red line. It's been those like me, who are said that they have made it, because I have a PhD now and presumably I can speak on the behalf of the majority, still have a lot of catching up to do, because first you never ever had any house all together. Ah...you have got all these relatives of yours who are suffering and your mother is not on pension or if the pension is there it's very minimal. (...)

And I think that is a typical example. Where you have changed the laws and, ah, there are no more exclusively White suburbs and so on, but even when people move into those suburbs or into those offices,...they keep there artificial walls. All right? Which is unfortunate for our country. And this undermines the concept of rainbow-nation. Because it renders it artificial. This is why I said earlier on: Yes, there is a rainbow, but sometimes it is very ...flimsy. Yes." (R8)

Like the speaker in R7, the interview partner describes the simple, positive religious and political aspects of the rainbow concept: the easing of racial tensions, the reconciliation and reconstruction of negative race relations. Along with Tutu, he finds that the rainbow, filled with religiosity and spirituality, symbolizes the "Rainbow People of God."

At the same time, it stands for equality of all people under God. [140] This spiritual-theological dimension as a source of reconciliation among people plays an important role for the author since it takes up the reality of the "colorful range of people" in South Africa and speaks to his Christian faith. The Rainbow Nation confirms that South Africa embodies diversity. It appeals to his vision of a society in which everyone is equal. Here appears to be a connection to the Ubuntu concept (3.4.1) with regard to the highly valued religious-spiritual dimension and *equality*. Yet, the author directly refers to Bishop Tutu as the primary creator of the rainbow concept (3.4.2), who wants to reconcile the race groups with each other and lead them towards an anti-racial society.

This speaker is the only interview partner who explicates the religious background of the symbol. He also differentiates between his religious and political analysis. In the following section of the excerpts, he moves away from his spiritual-religious dimension as a church-bound Christian to the political dimension as a professor for politics, a critical political observer and analyst. Even though the Rainbow Nation concept helped to reconcile the races to a certain extent, it has not yet penetrated society completely with the idea of reconciliation. "..reconciliation in South Africa, I think it has not filtered down, particularly to the White people." *Reconciliation* becomes now the key term as criterion for the political translations of the Rainbow Nation (with special consideration of the "victims"). He considers mainly two levels: the interpersonal relationships between White and Black South Africans and the government's compensation policy towards the victims of apartheid. He complains about the lack of commitment on the part of the government towards its citizens: "..there is no firm commitment from the state as we speak about how to at least give a compensation to this person." He then explains what he means by *commitment:* Like the speaker in R6, he resents the continuous talking ("they are still sitting down with the government"), that is not followed up by action. And like the Coloured pastor in R7, he asks that the decision makers of the state fulfil their duties and responsibilities not only in word but in deed.

In the context of state responsibilities, another (political) value emerges: *justice*. The author depicts the injustice in this situation: the victims are not compensated while

---

[140] The Coloured pastors in R1 and R7 also refer to the equality of colors and people. But unlike the speaker above, they argue from a political standpoint, not a religious one.

the perpetrators enjoy their lives in the loveliest places ("sea points of the world") without being held accountable. The value and issue of *justice* stands now next to the unrealized values of *commitment, compensation* and *reparations.* The collective experience of injustice in the past demands tangible compensation: "...justice must not only be done but it must be seen to be done." In other words, it is not enough that a person talks about justice, and not even that he acts in a just way, but *justice* has to be experienced as such by those who are supposed to benefit from it. Hence, the value of *justice* constructs itself on an interpersonal level and is principally constructivist in the context and perception of the effected people. The author finds that such a value orientation cannot be realized one-sidedly, but manifests itself only when both sides feel the impact of its realization. Like the Xhosa-speaking interview partner in R6, this speaker pleads to put the rainbow concept into concrete terms, to bring it to the level of practical, visible action. While, in his view, assurances have always been given that *justice* is happening, the indicators are still missing: "I would argue that it was not seen to be done, okay? There is an attempt to assure that justice will be done, but it hasn't been seen to be done. " The value of *justice* becomes a political key term and indicative for the fact that the rainbow concept has not been socially anchored but is still in the process of being realized. In addition, the social imbalance among the race groups can only be achieved when the economic imbalance is overcome.[141] Only then can there be a rainbow society in the political sense.

Aside from the economic imbalance, the author describes behaviors that, based on his own experiences, undermine the rainbow concept. Even though the laws have changed and everyone has the right to choose his/her place of residence, there are still certain behaviors in the suburbs which he describes in a metaphor: "...they keep their artificial walls. (...) And this undermines the rainbow-nation. Because it renders it artificial."[142] While there are recognizable structural changes in politics and law, there are also persistent inter-human barriers maintaining the separation between the different groups. These are consistent with *difference multiculturalism* and subvert the vision of

---

[141] Other speakers, too, criticize the continued social imbalance (see R6, R7, 5.4.2).

[142] At a different point in the interview, the speaker describes a conflict situation he experienced. A while ago he moved with his family to a previously White suburb. Here they live primarily among White neighbors. Some of these neighbors began greeting him and his family only after some months, others still ignore them. When talking about "artificial walls," the speaker must have situations like these in mind. This kind of everyday reality is consistent with a form of *difference multiculturalism.*

the rainbow concept as an approach of *critical multiculturalism*. Thus, the author not only demands the implementation of laws and government programs but also points to the political and inter-human responsibility of each individual in the construction of the Rainbow Nation.

In summary can be said that this author is aware of the religious and political dimension of the rainbow symbol as well as its different interpretations from both viewpoints. The values of *reconciliation, reparation* and *justice*, as the demand for economic justice, are central to him. He wants to see these values put into action on the grass-roots level by the government and by the population to abolish the still existing *artificial walls* between people. Compared to the other interview excerpts, this political scientist is the only interview partner who differentiates between the religious and the political side of the rainbow symbol. Surprisingly, not even the pastors are interested in its religious dimension (R1 and R7), which seems to indicate that they – despite their high degree of education and their strong ability to reflect – are still caught in apartheid thinking. It is particularly striking that this speaker, who lived in exile for a long time, has gained an inner distance to the social constructions and mental reproductions.

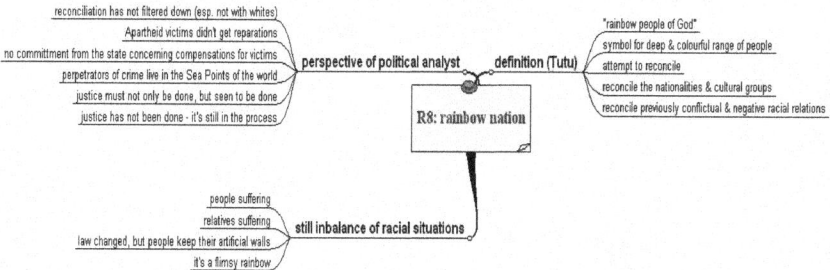

Graph 21: R8 Rainbow Nation

5.4.4 Summary

The presented data material points to a close connection between advanced education and the analysis of the rainbow symbol. Only the well educated persons discuss the Rainbow Nation concept when asked about their conflict experiences. The data support only to a certain extent the thesis from R7 that the symbol is primarily favored by the economic elite, the ruling class and Whites. Looking at the excerpts on the Rainbow Nation, one finds that the representatives of all population groups share their position on the subject equally, as long as they are educated and politically interested. Aspects of social reality penetrate the politically oriented statements (see R8, R13). Especially the Coloured and Black persons from the intellectual elite, who were often raised in townships – unlike the White interview partners, who grew up in the milieu of the educated elite – show that they have not lost touch with their places of origin and demand *equality* in their discussions of the rainbow concept. It is striking, however, that even the pastors and regular churchgoers concentrate on the political interpretation of the symbol while the original religious meaning remains in the background. Only the speaker from R8 integrates both interpretations. Possibly, from his social reality as a political scientist, a practicing Christian and as a former exile, he is more free to give credit to different perspectives.

Looking at the value orientations and key terms, the following stand out: for most interviewees the symbol stands for *diversity* of the South African society (R1, R4, R16). The speakers emphasize the *diversity* in terms of ethnic, socio-cultural (R4) and individual identity (R16). The value of *diversity* is often associated with the value of inter-ethnic "getting together," of (solution-oriented) *"communication"* [143] and the value of "sharing experiences" (R4). Furthermore, the evenness of the colors symbolizes the *equality* of people, or at least the vision of *equality*. Since none of the interview partners can detect real equality within the South African population ((R1, R6, R7, R8, R16), they demand the realization of this value for all people. They criticize the economic inequality, the imbalance of power – be it economic or political – between the

---

[143] The value of *communication* stands in the context of open communication, openness towards social change, and a commitment to democracy. The speakers want to see democratization measures taken that are practically relevant and bring along equality and freedom.

population groups (see R6 with respect to the local language policy). In demanding *equal opportunities*, particularly the Coloured interview partners of the educational elite (R7, R16) want to see basic needs met, and fundamental (Western oriented) democratic values implemented in everyday life.

The interviewees also take up the key term of *reconciliation* and interpret it in political, social, religious and economic terms. They do not only hold the government responsible for its implementations but also the people on the interpersonal level ("bottom-up approach": R6, R7, R8).

As shown above, many interviewees refer basically to the concept of *"unity in diversity"* (see 3.4.1). Most of them find the idea of the rainbow concept and its postulated values positive and desirable. Yet, it is clear that especially the partners of previously disadvantaged groups are disillusioned and frustrated with the little progress in the realization of these ideals. Next to references to More's value discourse we can identify links to Biko's value discourse and to African humanism, Ubuntu, which emphasize the central religious and social values, such as *understanding and sharing* and *worth*. Implicitly, some interview partners point to the importance of *individual* and *personal identity* (Ubuntu). Here, too, they stress the *creative expression* as entailed in Ubuntu (R16) in the context of *human dignity* and *humanism*. Also, the values mentioned by the interview partners overlap with Mandela's, Tutu's and Mbeki's value discourses, which emphasize *religion, human dignity, unity, peace, justice, equality, communication and democracy*.

Comparing the analyzed data with the multiculturalism debate introduced in chapter 3.1.2, it can be concluded that most interview partners see a form of *critical multiculturalism* as ideal for the new Rainbow Nation (R1, R4, R6, R7, R16). The rainbow symbolizes the diverse colors as being equal, complementing each other and working together to form a synthetic whole.

The speakers criticize the lasting effects of apartheid's *difference multiculturalism* (e.g., R2), which they describe as separating behaviors and influences in everyday life. They find the elements of *difference multiculturalism* desirable.

After considering these statements about the Rainbow Nation, now excerpts on self- and other- images are introduced, images that people in post-apartheid South Africa design of themselves and other people. These thought constructs contribute significantly to everyday experiences, to conflict potentials and to the vision of the Rainbow Nation.

Jonathan Comerford
Clause 10: "Freedom of Association" 395 x 295: Linocut.
In: Artists for Human Rights Portfolio
© Artists for Human Rights Trust

5.5 Self- and Other-Image as Subject of Conflict:
Perception and Construction of Socio-Cultural and Religious Groups

Next to the socio-political statements on the "Rainbow Nation," the data material comprises an especially large number of self-, other-, and supposed other-images, which are partly prejudiced or stereotypical in nature (see 3.2). The focus on self- and other-images often allows interviewees to express their experienced conflicts with people of other groups without having to go into the details of concrete experiences.[144] Instead of narrating, he/she verbalizes aspects of perceptions, feelings and impressions of his/her in-group and other groups in a general way.

The text selection of the here presented self- and other-concepts is, on one hand, linked to the material of other data evaluation chapters, 5.4, 5.6, 5.7; many excerpts show connections to the texts in other chapters and can therefore be analyzed and interpreted more thoroughly. On the other hand, the selection was made with respect to their subject- related relevance and to the frequency in which the question at hand is addressed.

Out of the total data material, the following seven categories of statements about groups can be filtered out:[145]

- Self- and other- images: Coloureds
- Other-images: Coloured Muslims
- Self- and other-images: Whites
- Self- and other-images: Afrikaners
- Self- and other-images: Jews

---

[144] This phenomenon seems particularly interesting since the first question in each interview (see 4.3) asks for a personally experienced conflict situation. Yet, a large number of interview partners tend to describe general and generalizing perceptions of people belonging to a certain group, instead of narrating concrete, experienced conflicts. In this data material, they only derive a minimal fraction of self- and other-images from concrete situations. .

[145] The here offered sequence of group statements is based on the population size of the groups in the Western Cape (see 2.2). Only one statement each, on "English-speaking Whites" and on "Indians," could be filtered out of the data material. Therefore, those statements are not represented here (see P22:30 and P8:15).

- Self- and other-images: Blacks
- Other-images: Foreigners, Refugees and People from other African countries

The data material is arranged with respect to

1) statements on certain population groups
2) categorical statements
3) concrete-situational statements on self- and other-images.

"Categorical statements" give either generalized or differentiated characteristics of one's own or another population group. "Concrete-situational statements" articulate sediments of recollected social encounters passed on by other people. These can involve either members of one's own group only or people of different population groups. The following shows the connection between categorical and concrete-situational statements, and, possibly draws a line to self-and other-stereotypes. The key terms are analyzed with the text-criteria listed in table 7, chapter 4.4.2. If necessary, the analysis takes the social reality of the author and the interview setting itself into account.

5.5.1 Self- and Other-Images: Coloureds

The statements in the data material on self-and other-images of Coloureds are very complex. Here, some of the statements of in-group and out-group members of the Coloured Community are analyzed.

A Coloured intellectual and musician relates how his family has handled the issue of identity.[146] Because of his passion for music, the speaker has left his career as computer expert and now makes his living as a pianist at jazz pubs and as a music teacher. In this interview (P36: 45), he extensively tackles the subject of identity and how it is handled in the Coloured Community. While feeling as part of this group, he also spends a lot of time with Whites, in whose company he feels quite at home.[147]

---

[146] In chapter 5.6.1, too, this interview partner describes his family's dealing with *racial* categories in past and presence, which has strongly influenced his own grappling with identity.
[147] The speaker emphasizes that he feels at home with Whites, since he himself is very light skinned, highly educated (like many Whites in South Africa) and speaks English and Afrikaans fluently, which makes it easy for him to communicate with Whites.

Accordingly, he sees some of his multiple identity aspects corresponding with either one or the other community.

> If I'd ask my father: "Who do we come from?" He'll say: "Mostly White people." Ahm...so then I said: "Oh, do we come from White people and Muslim people?" And he said: "No, no, no, no, not from Muslim people. Mostly from White people." And I said to him: "Do we come from Black people?" Then he will say: "A little." So, it is still that in the Coloured Community it is very much...if you'd speak with people...ah...ah...who are you? Where are you from? They will always tell you and try to link themselves with a...(...).
> So, normally if you speak to a Coloured person and you ask: "Who are you from?" Then, they will usually say they are from this particular White person...like for instance, you find in the Coloured community. We are all descendants from different...some of us...we are all a mix. Some of us are from India or a mix of Indian, Xhosa, Zulu, Khoisan, which is a light skin Black race here in the Cape...ah...obviously Malay and some White, a few Whites. But if you find the vast majority of us, except the Muslim people who have maintained their Malay culture. All the rest...we all have English or Afrikaans names...the British or Dutch surnames. So that was...if there was intermarriage between White and Black...they will always take the English or the Afrikaans name. (C1)

The narrator describes a concrete experience with his father in the form of a brief dialogue. Based on this dialogue, he explains his generally perceived self-image aspects as an in-group member of the Coloured Community. In this short dialogue with his father, the speaker points to the "racially" and religiously motivated notion of belonging to a certain group and to definitions of origin and identity. His father likes to underscore the White lineage of his family. He distinguishes himself from Muslims, and – as far as possible - from Blacks. Accordingly, for the father, his descent from Whites and Christians is of high value. The speaker finds that when one asks people from the Coloured Community about their origin and their identity ("Who are you?"), they try to associate with mainly one group.[148] Here the speaker interrupts his so far fluent speech, indicating inner thoughts. Also, he does not complete his sentence. Thus, he does not spell out the essential element of his statement that Coloureds like to associate their origin with Whites, thereby avoiding at first a generalizing conclusion. But this happens after a pause, after which he explicates the religious and cultural diversity within the Coloured Community. He then provides an example that shows how Coloureds assign particular value to the descent from people of Western European origin. A great number of Christian Coloureds are inclined to use English or Afrikaans names, while the Muslim Coloureds tend to keep their Malayan identity. In marriages between White and Black people, they choose the Western-European name as their family name.

Clearly, the speaker is very self-aware and articulated and wants to substantiate his general impressions. Because he derives his generalizing statement from a concrete situation and supports it with the verifiable name preferences among Coloureds, his self-image statements have only minimal stereotypical and prejudiced character.

This text supplements the narrated conflict story from chapter 5.7.1. In both cases, he describes the significance of "racial" assignment in his family with respect to each member's own identity construction and definition. His father and his aunts struggle with their social acceptance and status. Thus, the father transmits his identity constructs to the son, who, in turn, resists this type of identity construction. The fact that he is even conscious of it and that he reflects on them critically is probably due to his high degree of education and to his critical attitude as intellectual and artist. This enables him to critically question social concepts and constructs and to construct something new relatively independent from the existing order.

---

[148] Identity and the question of constructing one's own identity seem to be of particular importance for Coloured men of the educated elite (cf. 5.7). A Coloured pastor takes up the same question about his own identity and origin in his narrated identity conflicts (cf. 5.7.1 and 5.7.2) He, too, points to the group- specific, collective identity constructions in the Coloured Community and appeals to them to accept the multiplicity of their identity.

Interview-Partner	In-group	Self-Images of Coloureds
Coloured intellectual and musician P36: 45, C1	In-Group	• When you ask about origin of a Coloured: they will tell you they are from a particular White person • Muslim Coloured maintained their culture • Majority of Coloureds have all British and Afrikaans names • Coloured working class people just want to drink • During Apartheid Coloureds were complaining about the situation, but they just were just not interested in that that was provided • All Coloured people have an inferior complex

Table 13: Self-Images of Coloureds

In complete contrast to this in-group statement stands the opinion of a White handyman (P25: 33), who gives his impression of the Coloured Community. The here-introduced text is particularly interesting in comparison to the analysis and interpretation of his conflict story in chapter 5.6.4.

The speaker comes from an English farm family in Kwa-Zulu-Natal. He is a trained hotel manager. Due to *Affirmative Action* after apartheid he could not find suitable employment in his branch and has since made his living in Cape Town as a handyman. Mostly he works for White proprietors, renovating their estates and apartments. Often he employs mostly Black or Coloured day labourers. In chapter 5.6.4, he gives a vivid account of how one of these employments turns into a big conflict when a Coloured man he hires from the streets commits a theft. In other parts of the interview, such as in the following example, he expresses his opinion on the group of Coloureds very directly:

I have found that the Coloured, the Coloured Community, in my own experience are...inclined to be more devious, far more devious, calculated, clever, dishonest, clever dishonesty. But with intent. It's not by accident or...they're opportunists and they, they are devious. Ahm...and you can never take them at faith fairly, you gotta do some homework. Don't believe a word they tell. (C9)

His bluntness is striking, especially since his preceding story about the theft does hardly contain any pejorative statements about Coloureds.[149] Comparing them to Blacks, his characteristics for Coloureds here are particularly derogatory: "far more devious," "more calculated," and "more clever," "more dishonest." The only positive attribute, "clever," he links to dishonesty, and emphasizes its intentionality ("with intent," "not by accident"). He also calls this group "opportunistic" and repeatedly "devious," concluding this short section with an appeal - either directed at the interviewer or at a larger audience: "...never take them at faith fairly, you gotta do some homework. Don't believe a word they tell."

It is interesting that only *after* the conflict story, the author falls into these emotionally loaded, generalizing, pejorative statements about Coloureds. He seems to have saved up all these judgements that now burst out as a reflection of his anger. His other-image is probably not directly derived from the preceding conflict story. Instead, he has a deeply rooted, strongly negative image of Coloureds, which his story of the Coloured thief additionally confirms. Possibly, the speaker has arrived at his prejudiced other-image during years of experience of working with Coloureds. But he neglects to consider that he mostly deals with uneducated people, who live on the streets and struggle to survive. The author himself, most likely, is so occupied with his own social depravation that he has not gotten around to reflect critically on his other-images. Instead, he projects his personal despair and anger about his own social decline (see 5.6.4) onto the group of Coloureds, in whom he finds all the negative attributes combined: dishonesty, deviousness, and calculation. This group, according to author, does not fulfil his values of honesty, sincerity and mutual trust. Presumably, the speaker's image of Coloureds has turned into a self-fulfilling prophecy, which is continuously confirmed and reproduced when working with people from the Coloured lower class. Since the author hardly questions his other-image, he remains stuck in his constructs of prejudices. Thus, he assigns unchangeable characteristics to a whole group of people without differentiation. All he can do in the end is to "warn" his audience.

---

[149] This conflict experience could actually have occurred everywhere in the world. Yet, the author tells it by emphasizing that it was a *"Coloured thief,"* thereby not referring to his character or social class, but to his *race*. Here he already alludes to his negative judgment of *Coloureds* as a *race* group, which finds its full pronouncement in the above excerpt.

Interview-Partner	Out-Group	Other-Images of Coloureds	Other-Images of *Blacks*
White, catholic, handyman P25: 33, C9	Out-Group	• Coloureds are more devious, calculated, clever, dishonest, clever dishonesty, but with intent • They are opportunists, are devious • Never take them at faith fairly • Don't believe a word they tell.	• Blacks are not as devious as Coloureds • Blacks felt that

Table 14: Other-Images of Coloureds

A Shona-speaking interview partner (P2: 52), [150] too, makes rather negative comments about Coloureds. The speaker, who himself is the son of a Coloured mother and a Zimbabwean father, returned to South Africa after about 30 years of exile in Zimbabwe and Botswana. Today he lives as an independent business owner in a part of Cape Town that is mostly inhabited by White and Coloured middle class. His statements come across very generalizing and stereotyping:

> The Coloured person sees the Black person as nothing. And I don't seem to find, I mean, the Black people, I mean like having the same attitude. I find them...ah...just to be able to treat anyone as equal. Now, here, I am talking about the people I see on the streets and what I observe on the streets. You see? And which really makes me to feel, I mean, the Coloured people here in Cape Town, I mean, they, they really have a problem and I don't know how their problem is gonna be solved really. They actually say it openly they would have preferred the old situation.(...)
> "Like, I mean, the other time I was in H.[151], I mean, the place which is well known for the whales, I mean, they migrate there, ah...to that place, I mean, all the whales, as from August to October or so, I mean, I mean, you'd find a lot of White people there. It's not a question of affording, really, because there are a lot of Coloured people with cars and with a lot of money. But...they don't like going

---

[150] Further contributions by this speaker can be found in chapters 5.5.2, 5.6.2, 5.6.3 and 5.7.4.

[151] H. is a popular tourist attraction close to Cape Town.

to those places...and... I mean, I believe, I mean, they believe those things are supposed to be for White people, you see? They have got a superiority complex over the Black people, but inferiority complex over the White people. (C12)

Starting with a strongly negative other-image that Coloureds presumably hold of Blacks - "The Coloured person sees the Black person as nothing." -, the speaker immediately conveys his personal opinion about Coloureds. With an inter-racial comparison he points out that Blacks - i.e., his in-group - regard and "treat anyone as equal." At once it becomes clear that he contrasts the positive stereotype of his own group with his negative stereotype of Coloureds. [152] He then points out that he has even evidence for their racist attitudes since he heard them actually saying they preferred the old apartheid situation.[153]

Next, the speaker offers another aspect of his image of Coloureds. Even though they have the material means ("car," "a lot of money"), Coloureds do not take the opportunity to visit a great whale-watching site nearby. As interpretation for this behavior he proposes that Coloureds have an inferiority complex towards Whites, causing them to avoid places frequented by White people. Here the speaker interprets the concrete, experienced situation in H. according to the handed down apartheid-thinking pattern in a generalizing way. He does not consider the possibility that there might be other culture- or class-specific reasons keeping Coloureds from choosing H. as a destination for an outing. Instead, he reproduces a deeply rooted, racially biased prejudice or stereotype and perceives the situation in its light. The speaker's scheme of inferiority/superiority in his negative image of Coloureds plays also a decisive role in other parts of the interview. It can be assumed that for him the group of Coloureds functions as a suitable projection surface for his own negative fears and feelings. His other- image reflects his own feelings of inferiority and serves to reproduce his own

---

[152]In chapter 5.6.3 it becomes apparent that the speaker as an in-group member of *Blacks* perceives and judges the different socio-cultural groups in a very different way. His interpretation of other peoples' behavior depends largely on their group affiliation and his related prejudices and stereotypes. It is therefore likely that also the speaker's behavior options and behaviors will differ according to his differing perceptions and judgments of the respective groups.

[153] In an informal conversation, the author tells that he, during a time when he lived mostly in the Coloured Community in Cape Town, actually witnessed conversations in which Coloureds longed for the old times. It can be assumed that he generalizes singular experiences with a particular subgroup, advancing them to a stereotype of the whole group.

deeply rooted prejudices. It is problematic that the speaker assigns categories without further reflection and examination.

Interview-Partner	In-Group-Out-Group	Other-Image of Coloureds	Self-Image of Blacks
Shona-speaking, Black male, entrepreneur, handicraftsman P2: 52, C12	Out-group	• Have cars and a lot of money • Coloureds see Blacks as nothing • Coloureds would have preferred the old situation and they say it openly • Have got a superior complex over Black people, but an inferiority over White people	• Blacks treat anyone as equal

Table: Other-Images of Coloureds

The same author also comments on Coloured Muslims, thus rendering another aspect of his other-image that will be examined in the following.

5.5.2 Other-Images: Coloured Muslims

Next to the general statements on Coloureds, the data material offers also statements on Coloured Muslims made exclusively by Christians.[154] Two of these other-images are presented here, one by the Shona speaking business man already introduced in C12 and 5.5.1, the other by a White, Catholic priest (CM4).

You walk into shops...ah...apart from just an ordinary Coloured person here in the Cape, Cape Town, there is the other Coloured people, but who are of Islamic belief, that is the Muslims. Ah...it's a pity that I have to say, that those have a

---

[154] Only one interview partner (P61:p2) is a "Muslim Coloured." In an informal conversation, he talks about his experiences with "Blacks and Whites" and his memories of apartheid. He does not make statements on Muslim Coloureds, but only describes a Muslim street festival in Bo-Kaap, where people of various *races* and religions celebrate together in harmony.

distinct superiority complex. I mean, ah...I mean most of the Muslims here are Coloured or let me say the ones who are called the Malay people, who, all right, their ancestors or...ja, I mean, their ancestors are from the East, from Malaysia, ja from Malaysia, that's why they are called Malay people. Those ones, I mean, it's like you go into their shops, they are not friendly, they don't greet you, like you would expect a shop owner to welcome you because you are coming to give him business. I mean, it's like they don't want you in their place and they are such full of a very stuchy ... and very unfriendly and...ja, I mean, ja, when you try to talk to them they are not willing to compromise. Ja, they look at you with a very stony look or a cold look. And, ah...very unfriendly and it really makes one to feel like: "Those, I don't really like them." But I know I can't say that, because it's ethically very wrong to, I mean, to hate another human being. But their behavior is intolerable. Ja.(...).

Ja, but I think it's because of their religion. Ja, I don't know much about their beliefs...but...amongst the other Coloured, I mean, okay, they can talk to the other Coloureds, because I think there is another determinator here which is the language, but, I mean, to a Black person, there isn't anything. You see? Between them and the Black person, I mean, what it is with the other Coloured people who are not necessarily Muslims, here has been a lot of inter-relationships between the two. Because there is a lot of children, many children fathered by Muslims in Cape Town. Ah...with...ah...women who are Coloured but not necessarily Muslim. And now the children are born and, all right, but Muslim fathers, but maybe the mother is not Muslim, but ah, from what I have heard, those are the people who are heavily involved in drugs, actually. And someone was telling me the actual drug problem is very much Muslim-related, because they are the ones who are causing all these problems, by fathering all these children. And not looking after them. You see, they don't grow up with a proper up-bringing a child needs. And, they just grow up without a proper culture or guidance. And, they grow up with these manners of..., I mean, drug abuse, fighting, robbery, rape...that's why it's rife in the Western Cape...because Muslims, they believe in...going out with...many women, apart from, I mean, ...the one he is legally married to. There is no problem with going out with other women. You see, so they end up bearing children, a lot of them and...those are the children, I mean, who, who are...who have filled up the Western Cape, actually, or the Cape Flats, ja." (CM3)

Like the text excerpt in C12 (5.5.1), this passage is divided in two main parts: starting with a situation that he seems to experience repeatedly, he describes his own feelings and draws general conclusions. Then he depicts a social problem for which he holds Coloured Muslims responsible.

First, he illustrates his shopping experience with Coloured Muslim shopkeepers. He inserts the information that next to the "ordinary Coloured people," by which he probably means Coloured Christians, there are "other Coloured people who are of Islamic belief, that is Muslims," whose origin he further details and whom he sees afflicted with a "distinct superiority complex." He explains how he generally perceives the behavior of Coloured Muslim shopkeepers. It is interesting that he largely omits the description of the actual behaviors at such an encounter but quickly moves on to the behavior's evaluation and interpretation: they are very unfriendly, do not greet him und generally give him, the customer, the feeling of not being wanted ("They are not friendly, they don't greet you.") Further on, they are not willing to compromise and are stone faced ("stony look or a cold look"). It is striking that the speaker does not give a lot of information about these concrete, experienced situations, and yet arrives at generalizing, stereotypical statements using pejorative adjectives for Coloured Muslims. Thus, the listener cannot know what exactly happened in the concrete interaction. He is instead left with a vivid impression of the speaker's emotional state and his colorful image of Coloured Muslims.

The author's perceptions and judgements assimilated from everyday life result in a personal feeling of resentment: "Those, I don't really like them." Even though he immediately concedes that he should not "hate" other people for moral reasons, he also justifies his blunt statement with the intolerable behavior of the Coloured Muslims. Thus, he absolves himself from his own responsibility for his feelings. He surprises the listener with this fast switch from "don't really like" to "hate," since one does not expect this emotional intensity and directness.

In the second part of this section, the speaker attempts to explain why there is a lack of understanding between Coloured Muslims and Blacks. In his view, the different religions and languages present an insurmountable barrier. But between Coloured Muslims and Coloured Christians social relationships do exist because of the common language. Also, Muslim men produce many out-of-wedlock babies and thereby create - and here the author's prejudice comes in - the social conditions for Cape Towns drug problem: "And someone was telling me the actual drug problem is very much Muslim-related, because they are the ones who are causing all these problems, by fathering all these children." Here the speaker bases his other-image on somebody else's claim. Now he sees the cause of all the social evils, such as "drug abuse," "fighting," "robbery" and "rape" in the lack of supervision ("not looking after them") and guidance of Muslim children from polygynous relationships ("And, they just grow up without a proper culture or up-bringing."). Indirectly he criticises the acceptance of polygyny as part of the Muslim faith tradition by drawing a direct connection between polygyny and negligent childrearing practices. On one hand, the interviewee's other-image is based on a fellow citizen's opinion, on the other hand, on his perceptions and his scarce knowledge of Muslim religion and customs supporting polygyny. Clearly, his interpretation and negative assessment of other-image-aspects point to a personal thought construct.

As already shown in C12, our Shona speaking interview partner carries a generally negative image of Coloureds, which is now reinforced with respect to the sub-group of Coloured Muslims. His group image combines elements of "racial" and "religious" orientations, which he obviously rejects. Thus, he interprets and judges the Muslim shopkeepers' behavior negatively according to his own thought constructs and in turn reproduces his prejudices. Voices from the outside, loaded with similar negative image-constructions, fortify his prejudices and lead to highly biased allegations.

A White, Catholic priest with English family background (P9: 14) also shares his position on "Coloured Muslims." For a long time, he has worked in Coloured and Black churches in Cape Town and has experienced many conflicts during this time. He has already spent some time in Europe. At the time of the interview, he prepares for another stay in Italy, where he wants to start his dissertation on inter-religious dialogue with focus on Christianity and Islam.

So, I was living, living and working in...in, soon after I became a priest, I was living and working in the area which is called the Cape Flats. In terms of race it is Cape Coloured. Ah...and poor for the most part, very strong Muslim presence, ja, oh, very strong.[155] And the major issue in these areas was not political, but violence and crime. All centering around the drug trade and the various gangs that formed in the areas and that controlled different parts in one particularly area. So, where I was living and working, for example, there was at least 6 major gangs, all controlling sections of the community, based on the drugs, the selling of drugs and everything. Yes. Political changes in the country did not bring any dramatic or immediate fact into these areas, because the violence was between one group of people, the Coloured people and it wasn't Black, White...it was one group of people and the violence was internal and it had nothing to do with politics. It had to do with poverty and with drugs and the gangs. Even, where has been alleviation of poverty it hasn't been enough to change that situation. So, that was, that is my experience in that situation. My experience has been one of consistent violence, but, but not political violence. Violence that is based on crime.(...)

You get little movements arising, the last one spear-headed by the Muslims, but they die out, because people, people don't have the courage. They have to live in the community. They don't come in and protest against the violence and go out again. They actually have to live there. That is actually the problem that we face with the police. Got a problem, because many of the policemen lived in the area. They wouldn't dare to take all the gangsters and the drug dealers, because their lives would then be at risk. (...)

So that, that...towards the end of my time in the area, a Muslim group arose, who were very anti-gangs and it began very innocently. They were a group of educated

---

[155] At another place in the interview (P9:14), the interviewee mentions the fact that Islam in South Africa is primarily represented in the Muslim community in the Cape Flats and that Muslims make up only 2,5% of the total population. He also states that Muslims as well as non-Muslims are active in gangs and that involvement with a gang is based on poverty and social circumstances not on religious affiliation.

Muslims who said: "We have to do something. You know? We have to do something, because the police, the legal system in the country, is not." And, that was the beginning of a very famous movement in the country and I was part of it. They were seeing it from an Islamic point of view which is: "If our children, our Muslim children at school are being sold drugs, than it is an attack on Islam." That is how they understand it. That was their motivation, but it was a good start.(...)

And I still, still feel great anger, that...that gangsterism now seems to be tolerated. It's not spoken of that this radical Muslim group, they killed a gangster publicly who himself had killed so many people. And went through a long process of a long four year trial and finally was sentenced, you know? I was saying: "Well, why are the gangsters not treated in the same way?" They are constantly released from jail on a bail. You never hear of a gangster being sentenced for his murder. But these...you know, this was a part of an anti-Islamic feeling. These Muslims were immediately arrested and...now, now are in jail. Doesn't make sense. And again there is an imbalance and part of the problem is nobody knows about what to do against gangsterism. (CM4)

After describing the general situation in the Cape Flats with its difficult social problems, such as "violence, crime, gangsterism, poverty and drugs,"[156] he explains what he sees as the basic conflict, which is ingrained in the socio-economic conditions of the townships: the police, i.e., the "legal system," is not able to effectively counteract gangsters and drug traffickers in the townships because they themselves live in the same area and risk their lives by doing so. The same is true for the inhabitants. Yet, occasionally citizens' initiatives spring up to fight against violence and crime. The speaker addresses a concrete conflict experience related to the last initiative, PAGAD.[157]

---

[156] The author emphasizes that the crime is not politically, but socially motivated, and that racism does not play the large role, one might expect.

[157] PAGAD - "People against Gangsterism and Drugs" - was a citizens' initiative founded in the 1990s in the Cape Flats with the goal to stem the tide of gangsterism and drug traffic in their township. Later, radical Muslims took over the initiative. They went so far as to burn a gangster on the street. In the end, PAGAD was dismantled and outlawed, the leaders sentenced to several years of prison for murder, among other allegations.

After an "innocent" start, the radical Muslims in the organization became more aggressive and went as far as murdering a gangster. The active Muslims in PAGAD saw "gangsterism" and drug traffic as an attack on Islam itself and had therefore a strong religious motivation to fight crime. The author still feels anger over what happened. "And I still, still feel a great anger, that....that gangsterism now seems to be tolerated." While the Muslim PAGAD initiators were sentenced for murder, the criminals themselves go basically free. "You never hear of a gangster being sentenced for his murder." The priest sees the reason for this different judicial treatment in the general anti-Islamic sentiment moving through South Africa.

In this text excerpt, the narrator describes an experienced conflict situation with little judgement of the participants. Only in the end, he clarifies his own opinion based on the described events. He avoids generalizing and stereotypical statements about certain groups. Instead, he describes the activist Muslims as radicals, i.e., a sub-group, thereby distinguishing them from the whole group of Coloured Muslims. Through a change in perspective, he explains the Muslims' mostly religious motivation for their actions. His image of Coloured Muslims appears differentiated and well reflected, which is probably due to his education and his intensive dealings with the political and social situation of his surroundings, as well as with the different Islamic traditions and Christianity.

Interview-Partner	In-Group-Out-Group	Other-Images of Coloured Muslims
Shona speaking Black, entrepreneur, belonging to a Christian fellowship, AIC P2: 52, CM3	Out-Group	• Coloured Muslims have a distinct superiority complex • Their ancestors are from the East • They are not friendly, they don't greet you • They are not willing to compromise • Are very stuchy and very unfriendly • Look at you with a stony look, a cold look • Their behavior is intolerable • Are heavily involved in drugs • Drug problem is Muslim related

		• Fathering all the children, without looking after them • Are involved in drug abuse, fighting, robbery, rape • Muslims believe in going out with many women apart from the one he is married to.
White, Catholic Priest, living & working in the Cape Flats P9: 14, CM4	Out-Group	• At Cape Flats: very strong Muslim presence • Violence and Drugs and Gangsterism controlling parts of the area • Muslim and Christian Coloureds in the Cape Flats are drawn into gangsterism because of poverty

Table 16: Other-Images of Coloured Muslims

5.5.3 Self- and Other-Images: Whites

Statements on members of the White population group are divided in general statements on Whites, Afrikaners and Jews. This chapter first presents and analyzes self- and other-images of Whites and Afrikaners, then self-images of Jews.

We begin with a text excerpt of a White pastor,[158] who is pastor of the *Gospel Church* in Three Anchor Bay. In this interview (P7:13), he shares his experiences of personal interactions with different population groups. As a theologian he has been - already under apartheid - very involved in efforts to integrate his own church. Here he talks about his experiences in church politics after the end of the apartheid era and about his general impressions of White South Africans:

> There is a lot of hurt, because we...when I was in the church I declined any position in the church, in the multi-racial church, but then they turned around and said to me that: "Ah,...yes, you White people want to govern us, you governed us, you ruled us, you dominated us, you put us out off these places and into other places, now, you wanna come in the church and dominate us again." You see? So, I see it now. Let me rather withdraw, let me rather stand on the side line and watch what's gonna happen. You see? So, there was this overwhelming feeling of

---

[158] A prevalent theme in the data material is the privileged position of Whites compared to Coloureds and Blacks. This theme is often coupled with feelings and thoughts of superiority/inferiority, as the following shows.

any time a White person took a position, they would look at it or the threat that is there again...it's a domination. You know? That we are gonna dominate them now...tell them what to do. They don't wanna be told what to do. (...)

Here is a selfishness, a selfishness amongst the White and the Coloured people. As looking for themselves. But the Blacks are not like that. See, the Coloured people and I am not telling you something maybe that you don't know, but the Coloured people and the White people are very similar. In...little bit of Westernized life style. And...I, I think there are still a lot of White people who have not accepted the change that is coming into South Africa. And when you accept another human being...you are not saying you're a Xhosa, I am not saying I am a Xhosa...but when....and I can get rid of my superiority. Okay, because that is where...that might be where the whole problem came...is where the White had a superior attitude. He placed himself in a, in a...a position of saying: "I am better." And in the conveyance of the church that should not be." (W3)

There are three different aspects to this passage: first, the speaker describes his concrete-situational experiences as a White person with Coloureds in the church. Second, he compares value orientations of Whites and Coloureds. And third, he talks about the attitude of Whites towards social change.

Starting with the general acknowledgement that there is a lot of injury and pain, the speaker describes the concrete situation in which he as a White person in his church encounters the attitudes and fears of the Coloureds in the post-apartheid-era. In order to portray the perspective of non-Whites, he uses the linguistic means of quotation, which adds dynamism to the statement, underscoring its importance to the speaker. In this quote, the speaker includes past, present, and future with respect to the terminology of domination. Thus, he reflects his impression of non-White people that at no time they have perceived change, nor do they expect it. Their current other-images and their future expectations are dominated by the experiences of the past. They voice a particular resentment against a dominant leadership style. The pastor responds by retreating to an observer position. He explains that every time a White person takes up a position, Coloureds feel dominated, clearly pointing to the fears of non-White groups that are associated with the issues of White dominance, governance, ruling and dictating. In the speaker's view, the past constructions of White dominance continue to determine the other-images of Coloureds, implying solidified schemes of perception and interpretation, which - as self-fulfilling prophecies - are reproduced in everyday life (see 3.1).

In the second paragraph, the speaker directly addresses his (self-) image of Whites. He sees the White and the Coloured population-groups as "selfish" since Whites primarily care about themselves, something he associates with a "Westernized lifestyle." The same is true for Coloureds, but not at all for Blacks, whom he calls the "others" a little later in the text. Like his statement about selfishness, also this subsequent claim on Western lifestyle does not stand in a concrete-situational context but turns out to be a categorical statement. The speaker finds that "...a lot of White people [...] have not accepted the change." He adds an explanation of this assumption: they fail to perceive their fellow citizens as "human beings" and instead continue thinking in racial and ethnic categories. Acceptance of "another human being" should not require categorization.[159] To him "racial" categorization is still linked to self-worth and the feeling of superiority that he wants to discard. Especially in his position as a pastor, he pleads for the dismantling of a "superior attitude," the notion of "I am better," since constructions of superiority/inferiority have no place in the church.

While he holds White superiority responsible for conflict potential and causes, he does not substantiate this opinion with concrete-situational experiences. It appears that he expresses an uncertain feeling about his own group, producing a categorical stereotype, which continues to reproduce previous reality constructions without concrete evidence.

Another topic that in the data-material is closely related to the concepts of superiority, privilege and dominance is the *Affirmative Action*, a policy that is supposed to promote social transformation.[160]

---

[159] The author actually refers, like Avruch (see 1.4), to the "generic culture," which is the most basic level of communication between people and offers the basis for every other interaction.

[160] *Affirmative Action* is a legalized measure to help re-structure society. Employers are asked to hire applicants with the same qualification according to a quota-system in the preferred order of Blacks, Coloureds, Indians and lastly Whites. The employment quota is oriented at the percentage of each race group of the total population. Also, a business or organization should hire women preferred to men and disabled preferred to non-disabled. Yet, a recent newspaper article (Johns, April 2004:2) points out that *Affirmative Action* has not been carried through in daily life: "According to a socio-economic

A White, Catholic priest, who has worked in Langa for several years, details his impressions of Whites' reactions to the implementation of Affirmative Action. The speaker entered the ministry only a few years ago because he experienced God's calling late in his life. His new orientation has helped him to grow personally and brought him in touch with the process of the *Truth and Reconciliation Commission*. This opened his eyes to the reality of the apartheid time.

> It's called: "Affirmative Action." And it's...I am sure it causes a lot of stress on the....part of the Whites. If you hear them on the phoning radio...it's a great source of anger and it's also a kind of sarcasm, because Blacks are employed and they don't have all the experience in training. Ahm...so, anger of Blacks is expressed in things like...violence in soccer games in township, alcohol abuse, promiscuity...ahm...violence at home in the family and the anger of the Whites and the fear of the Whites afro-pessimism, is expressed in prejudices against Blacks, sarcastic comments on this is the New South Africa, ha, ha, ha, you know? (W4)

The author finds that the concept of *Affirmative Action* triggers strongly negative feelings in Whites, such as "stress," "anger" and "sarcasm."[161] They are embittered when Blacks are hired who have less experience and training than Whites. The speaker draws his impressions from radio programs where White South Africans call in to express their anger. He continues by making generalizing, categorical statements about how Black

---

review released in June: For every 100 Blacks who apply for jobs, only 3 are employed, compared to 55 out of every 100 Coloureds and 92 of every 100 White people."

[161] A White handyman P25:22), who lost his job as a hotel manager because of Affirmative Action during the radical changes in the 1990s and who - according to his own statements - cannot find new employment in his middle age (see also C9, 5.5.1, considers the whole group of Whites marginalized and degraded. "A lot of Whites have been marginalized with the "Affirmative Action Appointments" and things. Another White interview partner, who works in a top position in his community organization, also takes up the notion of the marginalization of the White population group He himself does not seem to feel effected by the law, and takes an other distance (P44:9): "Most of White people think, or a lot of White people, think there is reverse racism in "Affirmative Action", or many black people feel that the old racism hasn't disappeared. So, they....so that's the emphasis that differs." Thus, the interview partner points to two different perceptions of reality, both maintaining the continued racism in South Africa.

and White South Africans differ in their reaction to the current socio-political situation in everyday life. While Blacks express their anger in "violence," "alcohol abuse" and "promiscuity," Whites display "Afro-pessimism," "prejudices,"[162] and make "sarcastic comments." Thus, the speaker associates Blacks with physical forms of processing anger and fear while he sees Whites dealing with it on the cognitive level.[163] This association of Blacks with physical violence and Whites with cognitive violence is probably based on the fact that the media conveys physical violence in a different way than verbal violence. Also, the speaker should be more familiar with expressions of anger in his own group than with the processing mechanisms of Blacks. Therefore, his image of Blacks represents mostly what he can perceive on the surface. It is striking that he uses expressions for Blacks that must be extremely offensive to his moral and religious stance. While he portrays the angry expressions of Whites also as negative, they are less repulsive to Christian moral than those he ascribes to Blacks. These stereotypical, categorical statements reflect a deep-seated White prejudice, according to which Whites tend to prefer cognitive means to solve conflicts while Blacks tend to act in emotional and physical ways. The speaker uses categorical descriptions without linking them to concrete situations.

Interview -Partner	In- Group	Self-Images of Whites	Self-Images of Coloureds	Other-Images of Blacks
White pastor from the Gospel Church, Three Anchor Bay P7: 13,	In-group	• Whites are seen as if they want to dominate and govern • Whites are selfish • Have a Westernized life style • Many White people have not yet accepted the change • Don't accept others as human beings • Have a superiority, a superior	• Feel threatened by White domination and government when a White wants to get into a position	• Feel threatened by White domination and government when a White wants to get into a position

---

[162] In the date material, the topic of prejudices and stereotypes is again and again brought up as a cause of conflict by people who are highly educated and who belong to the middle- or upper- class (see e.g., B1, 5.5.6).

[163] Yet, a Xhosa- speaking interview partner points out that prejudices and stereotype-constructions are also common among Blacks and contribute to compensate negative feelings and experiences (see B1, 5.5.6).

W3		attitude • Put themselves in a conveyance of the church that should not be	• Coloureds have the same selfishness • Have Western life style	• Blacks are different from Whites and Coloureds
White catholic pastor, preaching in Langa P8: 15, W4	In-group	• Affirmative Action caused a lot of stress on Whites • Feel anger and sarcasm inside • Anger and fear of White people is expressed in Afro-pessimism, prejudices against Blacks, sarcastic comments on the New South Africa		• Anger of Blacks is expressed in violence in soccer games, alcohol abuse, promiscuity, violence at home and in family

Table 17: Self-Images of Whites

Also the Shona-speaking interview partner, who already made strongly pejorative statements about Coloureds and Coloured Muslims in C12 (5.5.1) and CM3 (5.5.2), talks about the group of Whites. This excerpts comes from a formal interview situation (P2: 52), which is preceded by several informal conversations.

And I really feel pity for the Coloureds, you see, because if you look up at White people nowadays, I mean, it's only the right wingers who are now very few of them, standing out there on their own and trying to side up, I mean, with something which can be turned or which would be termed as....ah....ah...human rights abuse. Or that kind of a thing. You see? The rest of the White people, I mean, they don't want to side up with anything like that. In actual fact, ah, they are siding up with the right thing. So, I mean, I believe, one has to learn in life...that there comes a time, whether you like it or not, you have to adjust, like I have seen the Whites doing here. The Blacks also. The attitude amongst the Blacks was, I mean, hatred, you see, they used to hate the Whites. You see? But it's not like that anymore. (W6)

In strong distinction from his quite negative perception of Coloureds, the speaker here shows a relatively positive opinion of Whites. He divides the Whites in "right wingers" and "the rest of the White people," thus differentiating for the first time between sub-groups, quite in contrast to his statements on Coloureds. He attributes "human rights abuse" only to a minority of radical right-wing Whites. Implicitly he blames also the negative experiences from the past on this sub-group of right wing extremists since the remaining White South Africans show an appropriate attitude: "..they are siding up with the right thing."[164] Coloureds, like the White "right wingers," are on the wrong side. Again, he demonstrates his aversion against Coloureds.

His philosophy of life includes the value of *adjustment ability* ("So, I mean, I believe, one has to learn in life...that there comes a time, whether you like it or not, you have to adjust..."), which he now applies to the different socio-cultural groups. The Whites have adjusted and stand now on the "right side." Also the Blacks, so he claims for his in-group, have adjusted in that they "used to hate" Whites, but now have overcome their hate.[165]

From the interviewer's perspective, this section of the interview heavily marked by an *error of leniency*. Aside from the "right wingers," the speaker refers to only positive attitudes and value orientations of Whites. His negative impressions are limited to the rightwing Whites. A few weeks before this interview, an informal conversation took place between the interviewer and the interviewee. When asked about her political orientation, the interviewer positioned herself - in short - on the "left." A longer, detailed conversation on political orientations and extremist right-wing tendencies in Germany ensued. The memory of this preceding conversation sheds some light on this formal interview situation and explains the *error of leniency*. Also, there were other meetings, which always took place in a pleasant, relaxed and very open atmosphere. Hence, at the point of the formal interview, one can speak of an intimate conversation atmosphere. Probably because of the preceding intensive exchanges and the intimate situation, the speaker attempts to portray the interviewer's in-group as positively as possible. Since he

---

[164] This passage stands out as the only one when a black interview partner says something positive about Whites. All other statements by Blacks about Whites are rather negative (see e.g., W7, 5.53).

[165] This claim stands in direct contrast to several self-image statements of Whites, who find that Whites have not adjusted their attitudes to the new situation (see W3/W4, 5.5.3) and instead remain stuck in old thinking patterns.

cannot disregard Blacks' negative individual and collective experiences with Whites, he chooses the option to delegate all his negative associations to a politically defined sub-group of Whites. It is likely that he picks this political sub-group since he knows from previous conversations that the interviewer does not identify with this group. He does not want to say something negative about a group that the interviewer might feel associated with. In comparing the White and Black population groups, he tries to construct a common ground for both interview partners as representatives of both groups. This commonality he finds in the value consensus of the *ability to adjust*: Whites have accepted the change, and Blacks do not hate Whites anymore. In this light, this text passage almost comes across as a personal *reconciliation*. It seems that the speaker works through his experiences and presents them to the interviewer[166] in a strongly placatory mood. The so created common ground between both interview partners affects the atmosphere of the conversation positively and constructively. Possibly he uses generalizing, stereotypical phrases to build a buffer zone for himself. By talking about a collective phenomenon, he does not have to take a position on his own personal change. It is striking that the speaker does not refer directly to negative behaviors and actions of Whites in South Africa. Instead, he talks about Blacks' feelings against Whites in the past, which they supposedly have discarded since. By naming a collective feeling of his in-group, he conveys also an I-message about the burdened past. The speaker does not accuse but uses denotations, which stand out in comparison to C12 and CM3. Here, too, the author is trying hard to conduct a harmonious, constructive conversation based on commonalities and mutual understanding. Even though he makes categorical statements about a certain sub-group and the rest of the White community, he does not reconstruct conventional, collective feelings and thinking patterns - quite in contrast to the text excerpts C12 and CM13. Instead, he is concerned with constructing new, present day and future oriented possibilities, leaving behind historically determined, collective feelings, such as guilt.

---

[166] Through these frequent informal talks, this interview partner has had his first chance - as said by himself - to get to know a European and to openly raise questions of interest to him. It is possible that in the course of these contacts he gained new impressions about Whites, which in turn influence his attitudes and feelings towards Whites in general. Parallel to his experiences with the White girlfriend (see 5.6.3), he now can expand, differentiate and reconstruct his other-image of Whites.

The next excerpt comes from a Xhosa speaking interview partner (P16: 24). Before looking at the text itself, something should be said about the unusual interview situation. The interview takes place in an open-plan office of the Roman Catholic Church. In the beginning, the interview partner hardly responds to the initial question, but gets lost in small talk, which – on the first glance– is completely unrelated to the topic. He avoids each question related to the interview topic of conflict experiences. When, after an hour, the conversation draws to its end, the interviewee asks the interviewer to stay a little longer. He continues talking about diverse topics until, a little while later, a White colleague steps out of a side room and enters the interview room. Greeting us, he crosses the room and leaves towards the stairway. Shortly after the White man has closed the door behind him, the interviewee begins talking about his conflict experiences, opening with the words: "Okay, now we can talk about conflicts...." His personal critical opinion about Whites becomes evident very soon. It is not surprising anymore that he did not want to take a position with the White man in listening- range.

> When you just pretend as if you love me and you just laugh, like for instance they act. White people, they expect us to always smile. To smile for what? (...) But not all of them, must say, some of our White brothers they just pretend when greeting you. Ha. I mean, they are not meaning that inside. Whilst, myself, I must try to tell you about myself. When I am saying, C., when I am greeting you, with a smile or whatever, I mean it deep down. I am not just superficial, you know? Some of our brothers, now... they are superficial and...they pretend as if...ah...we are brothers and sisters and we...whilst we are not." (W7)

The short excerpt refers to his perception of Whites. He believes that they merely feign ("pretend") friendliness and "love" in their laughing. At the same time, he suspects that Whites expect Blacks to always smile.[167] Here he works with a double generalization: "White people, they expect us always to smile." Without putting this categorical statement into a concrete-situational context, the speaker asks himself - as

---

[167] The speaker does not explain how he arrived at this other-image aspect and does not go back to a concrete experienced situation.

well as the listener - the rhetorical question why Whites should expect from Blacks to always smile. After a short pause, he corrects himself and differentiates putting it in more concrete terms: only some of his "White brothers" feign friendliness and interest when greeting. The author probably chooses the example of greeting because it has a particular high value in Bantu cultures. The greeting as the first contact between two parties determines the course of the conversation. For the speaker, the greeting has to come from "inside," and should not be "superficial." In Whites he cannot find sincerity. "They are not meaning it inside." He provides an illustration for how he envisions a greeting: "When I am saying, C., when I am greeting you, with a smile or whatever, I mean it *deep down*. I am not just superficial, you know?" When the outward and inward attitudes do not agree, he interprets the outward gesture as "superficial" and negative. He notices this discrepancy between outward acting and inner attitude particularly with Whites, implying that it comes to bear particularly in Black -White relationships. "Some of our brothers, now... they are superficial and...they pretend as if...ah...we are brothers and sisters and we...whilst we are not." Thus, the speaker considers the attempt of Whites to enter a brotherly/sisterly relationship with Blacks as failed because they only fake brother/sisterhood. Again, he does not give a concrete context or a criterion for lacking "brotherhood/sisterhood."[168]

Judging also from the interview situation itself, the speaker has had experiences with Whites that he now applies in a stereotyping way to the whole White population group, instead of dissolving it or changing it through reflection and feedback. His opinion is strongly marked by judgemental and categorical interpretations, lacking concrete evidence.

---

[168] It is likely that he refers to brotherliness practiced in many Bantu-societies in expressions of attachment. Brotherhood is then connected to the values of solidarity, loyalty, sympathy, but also with equality and equal rights, and concepts of giving, taking and sharing. As an employee of the Roman Catholic Church and as a Christian, he might refer to the biblical brotherhood/sisterhood, which is also related to solidarity and equality before God.

Interview -Partner	Out- Group	Other-Images of Whites	Other-Images of Coloureds	Other-Images of Blacks
Black Shona speaking, enterprene urP2: 52, W6	Out- group	• There are some few White right wingers trying to side up with human rights abuse • The rest of the White people they are siding up with the right thing • White people have learned to adjust	• Coloureds didn't adjust	• The Blacks have adjusted: they used to hate the Whites, but not anymore
Xhosa- speaking male employed by the catholic church P16: 24, W7	Out- group	• White people expect Blacks to always smile • Some of White brothers just pretend greeting you • They are not meaning the greeting inside • Some of them are superficial • Pretend as if we are brothers and sisters whilst we are not		• Blacks mean greetings deep down, are not superficial

Table 18: Other-Images of Whites

A Coloured, Catholic priest (P5: 11), who is very involved in Cape Town politics, comments on Whites and their attitudes towards Blacks. He has worked as a pastor for several years in the Cape Flats, his place of upbringing. Today he ministers to a dominantly White church in the center of Cape Town (see also R7, 5.4.2). His attitude towards Whites is strongly politically oriented:

> Especially where people think they can be critical of the new government - 'cause the government is not doing enough for the poor - without any background why social delivery is slow or why there is crime...it's generally perceived, especially by White South Africans and...middle class people generally that it is a weakness of the government...Blacks can't...Blacks can't control.... Strongly, from a different ideological position that tries to...understand and explain that there are complex social and economic factors within and beyond South Africa that

determine how a government reacts and how they politicise and why things are slow, whether it shall be in solving crimes or ahm...social delivery. That's one area that I shall find...ahm...generally White South Africans don't understand the complexity and are quick to criticise and Black South Africans haven't got understanding generally to ask why and are defensive about the government. That would be one...ahm...area where I would see conflict. (...)

I think there are economical values. I think...ahm...I think basically Whites grieve the loss of power, political power, 'cause they still have economic power. Unchallenged economic power. Ahm...and therefore any opportunity that they have...ahm...they are open to...being hypercritical about everything Blacks do. And so I think there is a...and I think part of it...a big part of it is that they feel...ahm...for one reason or another a bit emasculated. The power has been taken from them and ahm...so, anybody who feels that they had a core area of their life taken away becomes very...ahm ...hypercritical of the groups that's taken it away. So, I think...there are things like there is a deep down fear, there are prejudices, ah...there is a sense of ah...you pointed the finger at us. Now we are going to point the fingers on you. So, I think fear, prejudices, ahm ...the need to show very often that not only Whites were wrong: "Now, it is your turn to govern and now you are wrong. So, now we are all wrong together, don't kind of dump the past on us." Ahm...those would be the kinds of instincts that kind of motivate people crystallizing an idealized position. Ahm,...fear, prejudices, greed, ahm...not wanting to let go, fearing that if they concede that the government is right, they will have to concede that some of the values they lived by are wrong. Like greed and racism. You don't concede it. You'd rather point a finger and devalue the other side. In that way you don't have to concede that you might be wrong and your values that prompt to you might be wrong. None of us has to concede any shift of values or be challenged by shifting values. So, I would think that lies of the bottom of a lot of that positioning. (W9)

Despite his high degree of education and his close (working-) relationships with Whites, the speaker makes stereotypical, categorical statements. He talks in general terms about the political attitudes of Whites, their prevalent value orientations and their social position in the current situation in South Africa.

As his starting point, the author picks the topic of *social delivery.* From his perspective, the White South Africans[169] — and he specifies, after a short pause, the White middle class — are very critical of current government politics. They criticize the lack of social compensation and the scarcely existing measures against crime and poverty as "weakness of government." The narrator then defines his impression of Whites' image of Blacks: "Blacks can't...Blacks can't control."[170] The value of *political control* seems to be of enormous importance to the speaker, who himself is active in politics. In his view as clergy and politician, Whites see this value as unfulfilled, since political programs, such as social compensation, are implemented at a rather slow pace. He shows his reaction to this supposed White attitude in the following text excerpt, in which he clearly distinguishes himself from the White middle class by providing a different ideological understanding of the economic factors ("Strongly, from a different ideological position..."). In his view, Whites disregard the political and economic complexity and are therefore premature in their criticism: "...White South Africans don't understand the complexity and are quick to criticize..." Immediately following, he compares the White South Africans with the Black South Africans: "..and Black South Africans haven't got the understanding generally to ask why and are defensive about the government."

Next to Whites' difficulty of understanding complex problems, the author puts Blacks' difficulty to understand the problems' causes. He also notes a defensive attitude in Blacks, which he indirectly resents. Implicitly he rejects both groups, leaving the group of Coloureds, whom he does not mention explicitly. The strong criticism of Whites ("hypercritical") he explains with their "economic values" and their loss of political power, which they still have not come to terms with, even though they still have their economic power. "I think basically Whites grieve the loss of power, political power, 'cause they still have economic power. Unchallenged economic power." Their "hypercritical" attitude is based on their feeling of being "emasculated": "that they

---

[169] The speaker mostly uses the term "White South Africans" instead of only "Whites," possibly to avoid grouping the interviewer with this criticized category.

[170] The supposed other-image that Blacks are incapable to lead and control also occurs in other interview passages (see e.g., 5.5.3).

feel....ahm...for one reason or another a bit emasculated."[171] He intentionally picks this extremely vivid metaphor of emasculation to illustrate his view: every person who looses an essential part of his/her life ("core area of life"), such as political power in the case of Whites - will be hypercritical towards a certain group.

The speaker seems to understand this situation and the hypercritical attitude very well since he himself is very critical towards Whites in his role as interviewee. From his own experience, he probably knows what it is like having to respond to the loss of an identity shaping area of life. The fears and prejudices he senses in Whites ("there is a deep down fear, there are prejudices...") trigger their harsh criticism against the Black government and call attention to mistakes of Blacks to block out the past. For emphasis he presents the Whites' opinion in quotation. Their social criticism serves as self-protection against the past, hiding "fear, prejudices, and greed" and "not wanting to let go," and their refusal to admit their own mistakes. Actually the author wants them to be self-critical and look at their own values and behavior from multiple perspectives, instead of denigrating the other side ("You'd rather point a finger and devalue the other side."). Ironically the "advantage" in this situation is that no one is being challenged to change: "None of us has to concede any shift of values or be challenged by shifting values." Hence, the basic reason for the White criticism is their fear of value change and of the possibility of collective re-orientation, which lastly would effect the definition of their own identity. Repeatedly the speaker points out connotatively and pejoratively that Whites' value orientation is closely connected to the apartheid past. In his view, White peoples' attitudes are the same now as they were in the past, and their tendency is to maintain the traditional value system or to reconstruct it. Actually the author shares the opinion of the speaker in W3 that Whites in essence have not changed, do not see the past critically, and avoid a change of values.

Hence, he reconstructs the same perspectives and attributes that he probably already acquired in the past. Highly generalizing, he assigns categories, which - at least in this text excerpt - are not based on concrete-situational statements. The listener is left

---

[171] The speaker uses here the passive voice, maybe, to indicate that Whites did not voluntarily relinquish their power. He points to the tendency of Whites to hold on to political power.

with broad statements regarding feelings, values and behaviors of Whites without knowing their empirical origin.

It is remarkable that this speaker's church background has no bearing on his talk. While his role as a political activist, engaged public speaker and politician comes to the fore, his role as pastor and his theology seem secondary.

Interview-Partner	Out-Group	Other-Images of Whites	Other-Images of Blacks
Coloured, catholic priest, Diocese of Cape Town P5: 11, W9	Out-group	• Are critical and hypocritical of the new government • See slow changes in social delivery as weakness of the government • Think that Blacks can't control • White South Africans don't understand the complexity of politics • Are quick to criticize • Are in economical values • Grieve the loss of power, political power • Still have (unchallenged) economic power • Whites feel emasculated • Power has been taken from them • They have a deep down fear, prejudices, greed • They need to show that not only Whites are wrong • Not wanting to let go • Feat of having to concede that some of their values they live by are wrong - like greed and racism • They point a finger and devalue the other side • Don't want to concede any shift of values or be challenged by shifting values	• Haven't got the understanding generally, that's why they are defensive of the government

Table 19: Other-Images of Whites

5.5.4 Self-and Other-Images: Afrikaners

The data material contains several statements on White Afrikaners. The following examination focuses on two self-image statements and one other-image statement about this group. All three speakers have a graduate degree, are clergy or church employees, having worked for many years in various local churches. They are members of the White community and live in predominantly White neighbourhoods in Cape Town.

An Afrikaans-speaking Anglican pastor, who works in Cape Town's *City Bowl*, apparently met many Germans in South Africa. He describes Afrikaners from his in-group perspective and refers to the cultural similarities between Afrikaners and Germans (P3:21):

> You may...and I believe that you will get this tendency, where ah...Afrikaans speaking South Africans almost turn to be a little more like the German way. And I am speaking openly. This is my view, my view and my opinion. Afrikaans speaking turn to be like the German way and...so you have, when you...the people can't come very much closer...they say, that they want to see it, but, but... you know, that word but...you'll be there and you'll be there. You see? When you are more,...when your culture is more of sharing and helping, then...you are more...closer. (WA1)

This excerpt primarily contains the notion that Afrikaners are similar to Germans ("are like the German way"). He repeats this impression without linking it to a concrete situation. The area in which Germans and Afrikaners are supposedly alike is management of interpersonal closeness and distance: "...the people can't come very much closer..." It is likely that the speaker refers to this self-constructed cultural similarity between Germans and Afrikaners because of the *error of leniency*. In his comparison he alludes to the common ancestors of the Dutch and the Germans, the Germanic West- Friesians and East-Friesians, who - at the time of the great peoples' migration (ca. 300-500 A.D.) - settled in present day Lower Saxony and Holland.[172] By pointing indirectly to this common "racial," background the speaker probably wants to establish a common level of communication and solidarity between himself and the interviewer.[173]

---

[172] Probably, this statement points simply to the common ancestry.

[173] On one hand, the interviewer suspects that the interviewee - by underscoring the shared ancestry - also wants to include the interviewer in his collective guilt experience. In building a common ground of communication, he relieves himself psychologically and ask for solidarity. On the other hand, the statement has indeed the "intended" effect to trigger feelings of guilt in the interviewer, as well as a

Related to the experienced interpersonal distance in the Afrikaans culture are the little developed (Christian) values of *sharing* and mutual *help*. Even though he notices that people verbally consider inter-human closeness an ideal, he does not see its practical implementation. This is especially true for Afrikaners' interaction with other cultural groups.[174] Here the speaker stays with generalizing, categorical assertions without concrete-situational evidence. It is remarkable that the speaker's image of his in-group is rather negative, which might again be an indication for his own feelings of collective guilt.

The same Afrikaans trait that this author sees as little developed inter-human "closeness" the following interview partner (P19:27) considers as a culturally conditioned way of "being reserved." This pastor also speaks Afrikaans and works in the Dutch Reformed Church in Three Anchor Bay, a formerly White area. For several years he has lived and worked in a Coloured Community until he was transferred to his present church.[175] Here he attempts to promote the inter-cultural and inter-religious dialogue through inter-cultural prayer circles. In this excerpt, he relates his personal impressions on his in-group:

> But the Afrikaans White people...are very reserved.... I think we have got that from, maybe our German ancestors (laughing)...and our Dutch ancestors. They are very much reserved. The Afrikaans White people struggle to pray loudly in public. They don't pray, don't like to do it loudly. My communication here, the church council...we must tell them...ah...at least two or three weeks before the

---

feeling of resistance against such a share of responsibility. A very likely motivation for his similarity statements may stem from the refusal to touch on the public themes of racial belonging and acceptance of guilt. In that case, he attempts to preclude question on this topic by making the interviewer part of the *racial* in-group. Unconsciously he hopes to trigger feelings and emotions in the interviewer that will distract her from the topic of wrongdoing and guilt.

[174]At a different place in the interview, it becomes clear that the author finds in both the Afrikaans and the German culture a strong cohesive in-group behavior with respect to values of helping and sharing. But this behavior is rarely practiced - and if, then only in a distant manner - towards out-group people. A Coloured female interview partner, too, refers to Whites' reserved social style towards other groups and to their in-group oriented social values (P40:49). "They have morals and everything, but it only relates to other White people - the same values of morality." Her statement also points to a strong coherence within the group.

[175] See also chapter 5.6.5 and 5.6.6

time...actually give them...ah...a pray...plan for the month...when every Sunday an elder must pray on that Sunday, you must give him two or three weeks before the time. So that they can prepare for that prayer in the small group where the church council is gathering before church. They must know it before the time...so it's very difficult for them to do things like that. (WA2)

"Reserved behavior" ("are very reserved") obviously is a central cultural self-concept of Afrikaners, which the speaker traces back to the German - and after a short laugh and a pause - also to the Dutch ancestors. Thus, he too - like the speaker in WA1 - refers to a common *racial* and cultural concept, establishing a bond between him as an Afrikaner and the interviewer as a German. This way, he also constructs a common base of communication.

After mentioning this connection, the speaker has to laugh. Probably in this moment he becomes aware of his a-historic construction of this link and corrects himself by at least including the Dutch in the following sentence. With respect to time, place and history, the Afrikaners' connection to the Dutch is much closer than to the Germans. By laughing, the speaker might also try to cover up his insecurity and irritation about his own statement. Most likely, the author mentions the German ancestry because of the interviewer's country of origin (see above), and because of the cognitive ties he sees between Afrikaners and Germans.[176] Like the speaker in W1, he shows a collective guilt that is responsible for these ties. Both speakers implicitly point to a comparison group by using a comparative form without explicitly and concretely naming it.[177]

---

[176] In South Africa, many people see a link between apartheid and National Socialism. Overlapping areas between the two are publicly exposed (in museums, public exhibitions, etc.). It can be assumed that especially educated Afrikaners have dealt with the connection between these two historical political systems and therefore associate Afrikaans with German cultural and socio-political phenomena.

[177] While both of these interview partners use the strategy of bringing the interviewer into alliance in order to reduce the possibility of being asked questions about their historical guilt, the other two Afrikaans speaking interview partners (P1:22, P31:39) do not once mention apartheid, nor the processing of the trauma, nor the question of guilt. An Afrikaans-speaking secretary (P1:22) of a Dutch Reformed Church is the only interview partner who even denies ever in her life having experienced only one conflict with people from another socio-cultural or *racial* group. It is generally remarkable that not one interviewee of this subgroup deals explicitly with the issue of their own role in this group. They might have developed repression mechanisms that reach from including the conversation partner in their in-group, to complete denial of the whole problem (see P1:22).

Transitioning from categorical to concrete-situational statements, the author provides an example from his congregation for his claim of Afrikaners being "reserved." This Afrikaans reserved-ness expresses itself especially in their reluctance towards public prayer. "The Afrikaans White people struggle to pray loudly in public." Thus, their reserved-ness is particularly related to public performance. Several adjustments have to be made because of this reserved-ness: A speaking event needs long-term planning ("time," "plan for the month") so that the congregation has time to prepare ("they can prepare"), and discuss the event in a small, private group. Thus, the author gives us insights into the value orientation of his in-group, such as long-term planning and preparation of public performances, designed to avoid insecurity.[178]

In summary, it is remarkable that both Afrikaans speakers refer to their German ancestry. A possible reason could be found in their motivation to fend off the danger of being judged as guilty collaborators[179] by making the German interviewer an equally guilty ally. Both speakers also mention the culture-specific behaviors around closeness, distance, reserved-ness within the in-group and towards out-groups, and in the private and public arena. Contrary to the analyzed self-images of members of other groups, these Afrikaans self-image statements are critical and negative and also attempt to explain culturally conditioned behaviors. At the same time, the experience of collective guilt is such an important factor in the self-image construction that the interview partners restrict themselves to *racially* justify cultural phenomena.

---

[178] He also elaborates on the role of public performance and public apologies in chapters 5.6.5/ 5.6.6.

[179] The thinking in dualistic perpetrator/victim structures is not uncommon. Often, the "previously disadvantaged groups" - as this title implies - are seen as the victims of apartheid, or describe themselves as such. Hence it is possible that both interview partners - by referring to their German ancestry - include the interviewer in the group of socially constructed "culprits," thereby preventing *her* from accusing *them* as such. Suddenly the interviewer finds herself in the role of the "co-defendant," who - by virtue of her descent - sits "in the same boat." Her being German makes her especially suitable for such a role because of the long discussed link between apartheid and Nazi past. Thus, the interviewees address two levels of solidarity: the collective guilt with respect to apartheid, and the collective guilt of the German "Volk" regarding the "Third Reich". By loading this constructed double burden on the interviewer, the Afrikaans pastors may want to evade a possible discussion of the guilt-issue in this interview situation

Interview Partner	In-Group	Self-Images of Afrikaner
White, Afrikaner, Priest in the Anglican Church, P17:25, WA1	In-group Afrikaner	• The Afrikaner are more the German way • They don't come very close together • Not having a culture of sharing an helping, then they would be closer
White, Afrikaner priest from Dutch Reformed Church, P19: 27, WA2	In-group Afrikaner	• Afrikaner are reserved because of their German and Dutch ancestors • It's a shame for them to stand up in public • Afrikaner people struggle to pray loudly in public • Need time to prepare themselves to pray in public • Need to prepare themselves in small groups before praying in public

Table 20: Self-Images of Afrikaners

A White, Christian woman of British origin, who served on the board of the Presbyterian church, and still is an active volunteer in her congregation, talks about her conflict experience with Afrikaans-speaking people in her church. Already during apartheid she fought for integration in the church. Here she picks the topic of integration in order to illustrate her experience with Afrikaners in a concrete experienced situation (P7:13).

The White section, when I spoke to them, especially the Afrikaner ladies...this is fact, I can't help it, but it's true. They would speak to me: "Well, we don't have a problem. I drink tea out of their cups." You see? That...and I realised that the mentality of my colleagues of understanding...of our Whites colleagues, understanding as being integrated as one, as I would say incrust...if you have Christian values, your brotherhood goes above your color. Your brotherhood is from within. It's not from what you are without. But they, they were missing the boat as I would call it. (WA4)

This short passage deals with differing understandings of integration ("understanding as being integrated as one") and the implementation of integration measures for the sake of creating one single unit. From her Christian perspective, the English speaking narrator describes the attitude of her Afrikaans speaking colleagues: "They would speak to me: "Well, we don't have a problem. I drink tea out of their cups." The speaker finds this statement problematic since integration of different socio-cultural groups to her is not about superficial acts - such as the drinking out of the same cup - but about the internalization and practicing of "Christian values." When people have internalized these values, they apply the Christian value of "brotherhood" to everyone and not only to a selected group based on outside characteristics such as skin color. They then accept people as people, not as bearers of certain racial features. While acknowledging her Afrikaans colleagues' efforts to approach the subject, she finds that they have not integrated these values, and do not understand that "brotherhood" is an inner value. Unconsciously they are stuck on the superficial level and in their conventional value orientations. She expresses this with a metaphor: "But they, they were missing the boat, as I would call it."

Looking at the entire data collection, it is striking that – with the exception of the speaker in W6 – only Whites make statements on a White sub-groups, as in the case of self- and other images of Jews (see 5.5.5). The members of the other population groups do not differentiate within the category of Whites. Self-images through in-group perceptions are much more differentiated and probably pursue the purpose to make distinctions in one's own "race category," maybe to enhance the status of one's own sub-group.

Interview-Partner	Out-Group	Other-Images of Afrikaners
White, English socialized Christian, Gospel Church P7:13, WA 4	Out-group English	• Afrikaans ladies have a different understanding of integration • Don't see Christian values and brotherhood from within • Have missed the boat

Table 21: Other-Images of Afrikaners

5.5.5 Self-Images: Jews

In the whole data material, three interviewees talk about self- and other-images of South African Jews, partially viewing them as conflicted, partially as very positive.[180] The first interview partner (P34: I 41) calls herself Jewish. She lives in a sector of Cape Town that has a strongly Jewish character. She does not consider herself very religious, meaning that she only partially practices her faith and has adopted only a few selected religious customs. Previously, she worked for the government; now she is retired and manages a real estate business together with her husband. During the interview on experienced conflict experiences, she refers to her in-group:

> The Jewish community generally are, here, are a peace loving community. They just wanted to get on with their own lives. I mean, they get involved in politics as they do anywhere. But it's generally...ahm...they are a non-violent community. I would say, they are a totally White community. Ja. I think in this kind of country where the Black people have been the underdogs they certainly wouldn't convert to another group that is also looked down upon. (J1)

Using wholly categorical statements, the interview partner (P34: 41) talks in a generally positive way about the Jewish community. To her, the Jewish community in South Africa is a "peace loving community," who is primarily interested in pursuing their own happiness and to live in peace. "They just wanted to get on with their own lives." She then specifies this "getting on" with respect to socially relevant actions such as political involvement: "...they get involved in politics." Almost apologetically she ads "as they do anywhere," thus integrating them into the world- wide Jewish community. Again strongly generalizing, she sees Jews universally involved in politics. In this

---

[180] Jews in South Africa are 93.8% White, 3,5% Coloured, 1,3% unspecified, 1,2% Blacks, and 0,3% Indians. The data material contains only one stereotypical other-image of Jews, provided by an English speaking, Anglican Church assistant, who gives mostly categorical personal impressions about Jews from the apartheid era (see P4: 10). This perspective is not included here because it refers to the apartheid period and is therefore less relevant for our purposes.

context, she adds that Jews on the whole are a "non-violent community," stressing the notion of non-violence.[181]

Suddenly there is a switch of direction in the monologue. The speaker turns to the racial composition of the Jewish community, stating that they are a totally White community. The explanation follows immediately: Blacks, who were the "underdogs" in South Africa, are not willing to convert to a religious group that enjoys little respect in society. Here the interviewee describes the social status of the Jews as very low and equates it with Blacks' "underdog" status in the racial hierarchy. Not only does she give a reason for the racial composition of the Jewish community but she also provides a self-image that focuses on the marginal position of her in-group. Her perception of her own group as "looked down upon" could either be based on the collective experience and history of Jews worldwide or it could be based on specific experiences during the recent apartheid past. Under apartheid, the Jewish community - despite their affiliation with the "White race" - had a lower status than other Whites. Its comparison with the Black population group with respect to social non-acceptance is notable because many Jews aligned themselves with Blacks against apartheid to the point that one could speak of solidarity between Jews and Blacks. But now the interviewee claims that it would not make sense for Blacks to join a non-respected group. It is likely that, on one hand, the speaker wants to show that Blacks are independent and self-responsible when they decide not to join the Jewish community, leaving out the question how ready the community would be to welcome conversion-ready Blacks. On the other hand, the narrator assigns Blacks with an other-image of Jews: she implies that Blacks, whom she refers to as "underdogs," see Jews as an inferior marginal group. She completely disregards the conflicting religious and culture-specific attitudes between the Black African and the Jewish population, which could indicate a quite ethnocentric basic philosophy. However, the interviewee might not want to emphasize cultural differences, but instead rather imply the tolerance of the Jewish community towards converts and emphasize the newly acquired chance of self-determination and equal opportunities for

---

[181] This is little surprising, since at the time of the interview (2002/2003) the Israeli-Palestinian conflict had erupted in full force, as one could see daily in the South African media. Therefore, the speaker seems to feel the need to justify and excuse the violent proceedings of the Israeli government. Possibly her statements on non-violence can also be seen in the context of the latent tensions between Jewish and Muslim South Africans, which are repeatedly addressed in conversations with other interview partners (e.g., P63:p4, P43:51)

all race groups. In no way does she want to communicate the impression that certain race groups are excluded from the Jewish community. Therefore she argues through a projected other-image, which integrates an attempt to change perspectives. Yet, this change of perspective is strongly determined by her ethnocentric experience.[182] Her in-group statements are auto-stereotypical, exclusively positive and not self-critical.

Another Jewish interviewee (P63:P4) looks at her in-group in a much more differentiated and reflected manner. She is a Kindergarten teacher and educator, who - at the time of the interview - manages her own childcare center in a previously Jewish dominated sector of Cape Town. In responding to the question of conflict experiences, she talks about the value orientations of her own group. The narrator describes herself as a very faithful Jew, who belongs to the group of Orthodox Jews and is active in the Jewish community. A few years ago, she lived and worked in Israel for about ten years. Now she is back in Cape Town, where her family of origin lives.

> But I can just highlight some of our values: you have to be a good person. You know, being a good person means living like it is in the Seven A's: don't lie, don't murder...etc.. Being a good person also means in the first case being kindly and living a life with God. Looking to the good things in life.
> We Jews are sticking together very much, because we are very spread all over the world and we are very close to each other. That's also important. The Jews are mostly Whites here in South Africa. There are some who are Black, but converted to our religion. But these are only a few. Because we Jewish are not a religion which acts like a mission.
> We, the Jewish and the Muslims, are trying to get along with each other, you know? Until now, there is no open conflict. But there is a tension, because of the media propaganda and the history. But not in our daily lives. But I could imagine there would be a problem, you know? We all have the same roots and we share somehow the same culture of eating. But the Muslims they send their children to

---

[182] Aside from the speaker's argument, there are many other possible reasons for Blacks' unwillingness to convert to Judaism. First of all, the Jewish faith is passed on through the generations and not through missionary efforts. Also, there are many areas of incompatibility with Christian and traditional African belief systems. Furthermore, there is the requirement of a two-year novitiate.

die, they send them to be martyrs and that makes me angry and fearful, and that makes me also sad. Yeah, I have a very big fear when I think about that fact when we as Westerners can't really understand and imagine that they send their children to die and commit suicide.

There are sometimes conflicts in the Jewish community. Mostly here in South Africa between the "Reformed Jewish" and the Orthodox. The Reformed, they don't believe in the Old Testament, as we do. The Orthodox call themselves like this, even if they are not strictly Orthodox and not following the strict rules. But this is singular in the world. You won't find it anywhere else. So, the Orthodox feel closer to the Christians than to the Reformed, because we believe in the Old Testament. But in the whole community there is a high sense of belonging. (J2)

At the beginning, the speaker provides general information on the value orientations of her own community, which are strongly influenced by religion. She points to the "seven A's," the seven basic ethical principles in Judaism. Without being prompted, this speaker, too, explains why there are so few Black Jews, indicating an urgent desire to justify her community's racial composition.[183] The reason for its being predominantly White she sees in its non-existent mission concept.

The other group- specific value that she addresses is the strong cohesion and closeness in her group. In categorical statements she also refers to the Jewish world community, like the narrator in J1: "We Jews are sticking together very much, because we are very spread all over the world and we are very close to each other."

At the top of the list of their important social and collective-oriented values, the speaker mentions "being a good person" as the encompassing core value for the community and the individual. Accordingly, she describes its meaning:

...being a good person means living like it is in the Seven A's: don't lie, don't murder... etc. Being a good person also means in the first case being kindly and living a life with God. Looking to the good things in life.

---

[183] This is not surprising, since in South Africa companies and other organizations have to officially justify their racial composition in line with *Affirmative Action* (see 5.5.3). Accordingly, the interview partners, particularly Whites, feel again and again that they have to comment on this issue.

Religious values, the same as in Christianity, characterize a "good person." He/she practices the seven commandments and makes God and good neighbourly relations a priority. In the continuing excerpt, the speaker turns to the relationship between the different religious groups in South Africa. In the center stand again general statements - here with respect to Muslims and Jews - that are not grounded in a concrete situation. Latent tensions exist between both groups. While they want to live peacefully with each other, the conflict potential lies in the history- and media- created realities. The speaker has not experienced conflicts in her own (inter-personal) vis-à-vis contacts, which explains why she remains on the level of generalization. Recognizing many commonalities between Jews and Muslims ("roots," "culture of eating"), she sees their main difference in their dealing with martyrdom. In her view, Muslims make their children martyrs in the name of their religion. This thought causes her to feel anger, sadness and fear. Her fear is especially great when she sees that Westerners have no understanding and no way of imagining ("can't really understand and imagine") how Muslims leave it up to their children to commit suicide.

By classifying herself and the interviewer as members of one group ("we as Westerners") with the same value orientations, the speaker draws a direct connection to the interviewer. She picks a super-ordinate category for her in-group construction, neither religious nor racial, to create a common ground of communication. Suddenly, the attempt of Jews and Muslims to live together peacefully is raised to a global level, where we find "Western Culture" versus the "Others." Thus, the speaker creates a meta-culture, transcending the beliefs of a White, South African Jewish woman and the interviewer as a White, Roman Catholic European woman. On this level the problematic history of Jews and Germans is not important since it represents solidarity and "Western sentiment," based on the "Western perspective" and the "Western value system." The speaker does not condemn the Muslim behavior. Instead, she refers in a denotative, thoughtful way to her own feelings and to her incompetence to understand Muslims due to her conditioning in the Western culture, which she sees true for other Westerners too. She even appears to despair over her lack of understanding, especially since there are important commonalities between Jews and Muslims beside their differences.

In the last section of the excerpt, the speaker talks about the conflict potential in her own group. She breaks up the harmonious, auto-stereotypical portrayal of her own group and its values and brings out the intra-religious differences in the Jewish community. She shows the different religious movements within the community, dissembling the image of a homogeneous Jewish community. She considers herself an "Orthodox Jew."[184] The Orthodox believe in the Old Testament, follow relatively strict rules, and, at the same time, strongly distinguish themselves from the "Reformed Jews." [185] With the statement that the Orthodox Jews are closer to Christianity than to the Reformed Jews, the speaker again links up with the interviewer. Finally, she brings up the point again that, despite their differences, there is a strong feeling of solidarity in the Jewish community.

Especially her in-group perspective might enable this interviewee to differentiate between the groups within the Jewish community. This text excerpt (J2) shows her (diverse) multiple identity aspects, the most important being Jewish, Jewish-Orthodox, and Western.

Both Jewish interview partners describe their own group in a very positive way, emphasizing their (religious) values. They strongly define themselves and their Jewish group over global membership and over their religious values, as well as over areas of involvement, such as politics. Both speakers make little references to apartheid. Yet, both feel compelled to justify the scarcity of Black Jews in South Africa. This desire to explain the racial composition of their religious group might have been generated by the historical events and social politics.

Interview-Partner	In-Group	Self-Images of Jews	Other-Images of Muslims	Other-Images of Blacks
A White Jewish	Ingroup	• Pace-loving community • Just getting on with own lives		• have been "under-

---

[184] The Orthodox Jews in South Africa have developed a different religious-cultural character than the Orthodox Jews in Israel or elsewhere. The speaker refers to this uniqueness.
[185] The movement of the "Reformed Jews" originated in Germany. The Reformed Jews have their own religious customs and rituals and differ in many other aspects from the Orthodox Jews.

woman, owner of apartments and hotels P34:41, (J1)		• Ivolved in politics • Non-violent • Only Whites • Community is looked down upon by others		dogs" during Apartheid
A White Jewish woman, owning and running a Jewish creche P63:p4, (J2)	In-group	• Values: being a good person (living like it is in the 7 A's, being kind, living with God, seeing good things in life) • Sticking together, networking, close to each other, high sense of belonging • Spread of all over the world • Mostly Whites • Not acting like a mission • Have high respect on different religious groups • Conflicts between reformed and orthodox Jews • Orthodox Jews feel closer to Christians than to reformed Jews	• have the same roots and culture of eating • send children to die and make them martyrs by committing suicide	

Table 22: Jews

5.5.6 Self- and Other-Images: Blacks

The following selections provide statements on self- and other-images of Black South Africans by people of diverse socio-cultural origins. Some themes return in many statements about people from Black African ethnic groups, such as modern, young Black people, feelings of inferiority perceived in Blacks, traditions, ceremonies, rituals and religious practices.

The data material contains only one single self-image statement about Blacks. The interviewee (P41:50) speaks Xhosa and grew up in the Western Cape. He works at an NGO that specializes on the area of dream processing and collective healing processes:

There are a lot of positive things in the Coloured communities and with the same in the Black community, you know? We are not all criminals. Yes, there are people who are involved in criminal activities, you know, selling drugs and whatever, but not everybody is supporting that. But I think it's more stereotyping and prejudices that causes a lot of conflicts within the two communities.(...).

And Black people are still facing with a lot of issues like unemployment, poverty, and trying to make the ends meet on a daily bases. People who still feel they haven't managed to be part of the new dispensation. You know, people would feel that yes, certain Black people would feel kind of benefiting from this new democracy. But they feel that they are not benefiting. They are not part of it. You know, the anger grows and grows and you know, a number of issues are happening in South Africa. (B1)

Central to this passage is the speaker's assumption that many conflicts between the different population groups arise because of the upholding and passing on of "stereotypes" and "prejudices."

Whites, for example, carry the prejudice that all Blacks and Coloureds are "criminals." The speaker tries to break up this stereotype by making categorical statements without giving a concrete-situational example. He continues in this categorical and generalizing mode when describing the problem of Blacks' unfulfilled expectations: The problem is that Blacks do not feel that they are included in the new social re-distribution ("new dispensation"), nor that they benefit from it. Instead, Blacks continue to struggle with basic problems, such as unemployment, poverty and "trying to make ends meet on a daily basis." This feeling of being excluded from the new democracy triggers anger in Blacks. "You know, the anger grows and grows..." [186]

At this point, the speaker chooses the third person plural, indicating that he does not refer to himself in these statements, and that he might even want to distance himself from them in this interview situation. Clearly, from his social reality as a social worker and counsellor, he does not have to deal with the same issues he just mentioned and can look at them from afar. While detailing his perception of his in-group, he can personally

---

[186] Also a White pastor (see B9, 5.5.6) notes negative feelings among Blacks in a generalizing way. He says: "Most Blacks are bitter in their hearts." Another speaker stresses that among Blacks there is a lot of "anger, rage and fear" (P8:15)

distinguish himself. It seems to be very important to him to pinpoint Blacks' anger not in the past but in the present societal situation of failed re-distribution arrangements.

Despite his in-group affiliation, he stays with categorical statements about his own group, their attitudes and feelings without adding concrete-situational elements. Thus, he reconfirms his own criticism that most problems are created by stereotypes, prejudices and corresponding categorical statements.

Interview-Partner	In-Group	Self-Images of Blacks	Other-Images of Whites	Other-Images of Coloureds
Xhosa-speaking, NGO, social-worker P41:50, B1	Ingroup	• Are not all criminals • Conflicts through stereotyping and prejudices • Blacks facing a lot of issues like unemployment and poverty • Make ends meet on a daily bases • Blacks feel they haven't been part of the new dispensation • Are not benefiting/ not part of new dispensation • Only some Black people are benefiting from the new democracy • The anger grows and grows in the Black community	• Whites believe that Blacks can't rule a state demo-cratically • See Blacks as inferior	• Coloureds believe that Blacks can't rule a state demo-cratically • See Blacks as inferior

Table 23: Self-Images of Blacks

The next interviewee is a Coloured woman, a member of the Presbyterian church in Rondebosch. She comments on "modern Blacks," who she feels display materialistic attitudes especially in the urban setting. [187] The speaker, who is very active in her church, works in an NGO, which is a refuge for immigrants in Cape Town's

---

[187] See also the excerpt F3, chapter 5.5.7 and chapter 2.5.2, which also deal with the topic of value change in Blacks.

Greenmarket district. She moved to this university district a few months ago in order to raise her children in a safe environment and give them a good education (P28:36).

> The modern Black persons are into material things and that's, that's a sad part, this materialism. The old tradition has faded out. Unless you go to the people who still live in the villages and outside. There you still find the warmth. (...) The warmth, the connection that was amongst them, they didn't even feel the difficulties. And this is what happened: If you have got a good vipe and environment, you don't feel the pressures of life. Believe me or not. (...) This is where you find the real people. The old connection of people. But not in the cities. (B2)

This interview partner distinguishes between "modern Blacks" in urban centers and "traditional Blacks" in villages and rural areas. She feels that the urban Blacks are undergoing a change of values away from their traditions and inter-human "warmth," towards "materialism" ("they are in material things"). She finds the strength of the Black communities in their inter-human warmth and connections and in their positive community climate ("good vipe and environment"). When these basic values are intact, people do not feel the "difficulties" and "pressures of life" so much. She clearly values the "traditional" values in Black African ethnic groups over the materialistic ones. Probably, to the speaker materialism is symptomatic for the entry of Western, colonialist or imperialistic influences since she does not locate them in traditional, Black African communities. Clearly she does not find the transformation of values in modern Black African societies to be a good thing. She confirms this in her concluding statement that the "real people," the "old connection of people," i.e., the relationships characterized by warmth, only exist in the rural areas in South Africa. Implicitly she holds a very pessimistic view of modern influences in that they destroy humanity and neighbourly care. She idealizes the old African value orientations, contrasting them with the negative current changes in cities, without using concrete-situational statements or giving examples. Consequently, she does not clarify the meaning of values, such as materialism and inter-human warmth nor how they manifest themselves in daily life. Accordingly, her statements on other-images are determined by generalizations, idealization, positive and negative stereotypes.

The next speaker, another Coloured woman (P30:38), is a domestic worker for a White family in Sea Point, for whom she has worked for several years. As a member of the Anglican Church, she participates in a prayer circle at the Dutch Reformed Church in Sea Point. During the interview, her employer is present, who strongly dominates the conversation (see 5.3). But when the interview partner has a chance to speak, she comments on her personal impressions on Blacks:

> There is a vast difference between the Black culture and....the culture of the other groups. For the simple reason...if we take the culture of...ahm...of circumcision, number one. It's something they do not want to pull away from. And, ah...it has taken many young lives that have been circumcised. You see a lot of them on the N1. They live in the bush. Ahm, so we look at that section. There is nothing. They can continue doing it. But they were asked that: can it be done in such a way where they are trained to that whatever they chose it gets sterilised. That even is not accepted. They still do it the way it must be. So, one look at that side, this is difficult to understand. (...) Well, I would say not from...there is a small majority of Blacks...that can adjust to any of the other groupings, but the majority did not receive the...let me say...the occasion to get educated properly. That is really a problem and that is such a big...lack of understanding. (B4)

The speaker begins with the generalizing remark that the Black culture distinguishes itself from all the other groups. She verifies this statement with the example of circumcision,[188] a custom that is still maintained despite its often deadly consequences. In her opinion, Blacks should not abandon their tradition, but modify it. She cannot understand ("it's difficult to understand") that they insist on their traditions and do not accept suggestions for improvement from outside. The image she communicates is one in which Blacks are very tradition-conscious and even fixated on

---

[188] The topic of circumcision also plays an important role in the view of a White church employee (see 5.5.6, B14) - even though her arguments are based on different motives.

their customs. The speaker finds that circumcision as an initiation rite is inconsistent with her own and current social values and norms in general.

She might have picked the example of circumcision for several reasons. For once, circumcision is not practiced in the Coloured Community. Thus, she gives to understand that she feels as part of a community that is connected less with Black traditions than with Western-modern attitudes. That way she enhances her status as a person and group member. Or she might have chosen this example because of the relationship-constellation in the interview situation with the White interviewer and the White employer. She creates a common base for communication with the interviewer through her identification with Western value orientations and her dissociation from Blacks.

In her opinion, there is only a small group of Blacks that is able to adjust to other population groups since this ability is related to their degree of education. The majority of Blacks lack education and "understanding." It is clear to the speaker that Blacks have to adjust to the others groups and not vice versa. These statements mirror the old mindset of hierarchical social stratification, unbalanced distribution of power and preferred Western values. Basically she asks Blacks to be more willing to understand the objections of other groups.

Her statements on Blacks are merely categorical without concrete-situational connections. They are generalizing and stereotyping and most likely based on the *error of leniency* in the conversation situation. With the topic of circumcision, the speaker tries to illustrate her general impressions without reflecting on them. Accordingly her statements are mostly undifferentiated.

Interview Partner	Out-Group	Other-Images of Blacks
Coloured woman, Presbyterian Church, NGO-immigrant worker P28:36, B2	Out-group	• Modern Black person is in materialism • Black tradition has faded out • Traditional Black people live in the villages • Traditional value: warmth and connection amongst the people • Value: a good vipe and environment

Coloured maid, belongs to the Dutch Reformed Church P30:38, B4	Out-group	• They don't want to pull away from circumcision • Don't accept new influences on their circumcision (like using sterilized materials) • Only a small group of Blacks can adjust • Most didn't get educated properly • There is a big lack of understanding

Table 24: Blacks

A White pastor, who works at the *Gospel Church* in Three Anchor Bay, now describes phenomena that he found positively striking in the Black community. Already under apartheid, he worked actively for a "multicultural church" and tries to realize this in everyday life. In one interview (P7:13), he comments on his current perceptions of the emotional state and the value orientations of Blacks:

> You know,...the Black people did not show the hurt as much as the Coloured folks. Ah, Mister Mandela, who came out off jail after 27 years, he came out with a beautiful attitude. Nobody expected this, but the man came out with such a wonderful, kind, soft, gentle attitude. He came out with no bitterness, no hatred or anything. Ah...and, and, and he is unique. To me, he is a very unique man. (...)
> I think, there are most of the Black people and Coloured people which is most probably the biggest problem at the moment. I think they are very, very bitter in their hearts. (...) The Black people to me, I find...are...are far more forgiving. That...and I am talking in the conveyance of church. They, they are far more forgiving. And they are ready to get on and to do things." (B9)

The interviewee begins with a generalizing statement in a comparison between Blacks and Coloureds. "The Black people did not show the hurt as much as the Coloured folks." Beginning with this categorical generalization regarding the feelings of Blacks, he chooses the concrete, yet exceptional, example of Nelson Mandela as a representative of the Black community. He admires in Mandela that he - despite his prison experience of many years - showed "a wonderful kind, soft, gentle attitude." Because he is amazed that Mandela does not carry any "bitterness" nor "hatred," he calls him "unique," contradicting his attempt to offer him as an example of the generally forgiving Black nature.

Then he makes the generalizing claim that most Blacks and Coloureds today are embittered, ("they are very bitter in their hearts"), which he considers as one of the biggest problems. Hence, the statement about Mandela compares and contrasts two categorical generalizations about the Black and Coloured population group and breaks up the generalization a little bit. But as a whole the speaker stays with his stereotypical generalizations without deriving them from examples or situational contexts. After mentioning these rather negative perceptions of sentiments in Blacks *and* Coloureds, the speaker now repeats the previous claim that at least Blacks are more "forgiving" ("..they are ready to get on and do things.").

The same is true for the excerpt B8. A White Afrikaans-speaking pastor from the *Free State*, who has worked for some time at the Methodist church in Sea Point, also expresses his amazement over the behavior and attitude of Blacks (P32:3):

> Because they have much...to take revenge if they wanted, because of the way they have been treated. And it has always amazed me how Black people can be so forgiving and it seems to be in their nature to be forgiving. (...) It, it will appear if it would be a White nation and it had turned the other way around...it would never have gone 300 years and this is my own opinion that there seems to be something in the Black psyche that is long suffering and forgiving. And that amazes me that they have forgiven all these things that have been done to them and they are prepared to reach out and take a White and say: "Let's move forward together."
> (B8)

In view of the oppression of Black Africans during the last 300 years by Whites, the speaker empathizes with Blacks. He is impressed that Blacks do not "take revenge," but are forgiving in the face of all the suffered injustices. "... it has always amazed me how Black people can be so forgiving and it seems to be in their nature to be forgiving." He chooses a deterministic explanation in the (God given?) "nature" of the Black race. Later he specifies this "nature" with respect to the psyche. The pastor credits Black people with the daily practice of Christian basic values, forgiveness and "long suffering." He interprets the relinquishing of immediate revenge positively in terms of forgiveness and "long suffering" and does not consider that anger - which the speaker in B1 as an in-group member seems to clearly notice - in Black African cultures possibly expresses itself in other ways than in acts of revenge or direct confrontation. He confines himself to his own patterns of behavior interpretation, not taking into account possible culture-specific explanations. His simplistic reduction of their motives to the two values indicate that he subconsciously uses his own Christian value orientation to interpret and understand the behavior of Blacks.

Remarkable here is the emphasis on the Christian value of *forgiveness* tied to action, the walking ahead together, as it is also stressed in B8. However, both speakers (B8 and B9) stay put in stereotypical, categorical statements - separated from a concrete-situational context. Even though the speaker in B9 acknowledges both the negative attitude of bitterness and hatred and the positive attitude of *forgiveness* and *endurance*, he does not provide a concrete-situational background, which would allow differentiation. Therefore, we are left with his stereotypical, categorical statements.

A Catholic, English speaking pastor, who has worked since a few years in Langa in a Xhosa- speaking congregation, also shares his perceptions of Blacks. [189] In this excerpt, he refers to the "wounds" from the past, and to the culture-specific value orientations and African traditions (P8:15):

> And, you know, there are wounds... there is anger, fear and rage...as you put it. There is certainly anger amongst the Blacks. So, I picked it up for about 2,5 years. There is anger because of what happened to them and many, there were...a lot of anger and many were hurt and killed and bullshit, but the majority was just put up to the bottom of the pack. In terms of...inferior education, inferior job opportunities.(...)
> So, there is this hurt feelings and this feeling of wanting to assert themselves and saying that, you know: "I have achieved something and a desire to achieve and ah ...to get somewhere and to be recognized and to pass a degree. " Ahm...so I picked

---

[189] The same pastor talks in W4, chapter 5.5.3 commenting mostly on Affirmative Action.

up a sort of...sometimes I feel I am sort of looked up a bit too much, because they know, you are priest and you have training and education and all that...so I feel a bit of a distance because of that ahm...and because of the experiences they have had with the White people. Ahm...as I said wounded dignity...feelings of inferiority, lack of empowerment, a great lack of empowerment compared to other parishes...like....ahm...I can't really get anyone you can do my books for me, you know?" (B12)

Like the interview partner in B9, this pastor, too, acknowledges "hurts" and strongly negative feelings. "There are wounds...there is anger, fear and rage." In specifying the reasons for these lingering resentments, the pastor underlines the "inferior education, inferior job opportunities," Blacks had to put up with in the past. While he sees their negative feelings rooted in the socio-political and socio-historic contexts, he does not link his perceptions of current Black sentiments to concrete situations.

In general terms he explains that the hurts of the past have triggered in Blacks the "feeling of wanting to assert themselves" through achievements. This desire to succeed the author even expresses in quotation for emphasis when he connects self-assertion and (achievement -oriented) goal setting ("desire to achieve something"). Accordingly, the goal's achievement depends on the desire to get ahead and be respected ("to get somewhere and be recognized."). By skillfully rewording the perceived negative feelings and experienced deficits, the speaker puts a positive spin on them and now focuses on Blacks' aspirations and values related to socially acceptable pursuits, such as a graduate degree. In his view, a graduate degree has something like a compensatory function for Blacks, which is supposed to make up for past hurts and provide social recognition beyond categories of *race* and socio-cultural origin.

Subsequently, the narrator describes his personal feelings towards Blacks. Because of his social class and educational degree and because of Blacks' (collective) experiences with Whites in the past, he senses a gap ("distance") between himself and his congregation. He assumes that Blacks come from an experience of "wounded dignity." This, together with "feelings of inferiority" and the "lack of empowerment" he regards as especially pronounced in his own church.

His descriptions are very general. He interprets all his perceptions from a historical perspective, leaving no room for other interpretive options. But by comparing his congregation with others, he makes it clear that he primarily refers to his own congregation.

Interview-Partner	Out-Group	Other-Images of Blacks	Other-Images of Coloureds
Afrikaaner, pastor, Methodist, Sea Point, P32:3, B8	Out-group	• Black people are forgiving • It is in their nature to be forgiving • Something in the Black psyche is long suffering and forgiving • Are prepared to take a White and move forward together	
A White priest, Gospel Church, Three Anchor Bay P7:13, B9	Out-group	• Blacks don't show hurt as much as Coloureds • Mandela has a wonderful, kind, soft, gentle attitude - he is unique • Most of the Blacks and Coloureds are bitter in their hearts • Black people are far more forgiving • Ready to get on	• Are bitter in their hearts
White Catholic pastor in Langa, P8:15, B12	Out-group	• Anger, fear, range and hurt amongst Blacks • Have got inferior education and job opportunities • Want to achieve something, have a desire to achieve something, want to be recognized and pass a degree • Blacks have a wounded dignity, feelings of inferiority, lack of empowerment	

Table 25: Other Images of Blacks

5.5.7 Other-images: Foreigners, Refugees and People from Other African Countries

Next to the statements on self-and other-images of Black South Africans, the data material contains special statements on "refugees," "immigrants from Africa," "foreigners" or "people from other African countries."[190] The label "Blacks" stands here for people with their origin in other African countries.[191] In the context of these references, Nigerians ("the Nigerians") often play a special role, as the following excerpt shows.

A female White Afrikaner and employee of the Dutch Reformed Church in Three Anchor Bay, who stresses throughout the interview that she has *never* experienced a conflict with people of different cultural origin (see 5.5.4), comments especially on the behavior of Nigerians that she observes in Sea Point ((P1:22):

> Well, they all come to look for work. But, they don't find. And if they don't find... ahm... or if they do find our people living here, they can't find jobs. Then they say: "Look, people from outside they find jobs, but why can't we?" Then, you know, there is conflict out there, so, also...but most of them don't work and then in the long run they turn to drugs, selling drugs, and drinking and all that sort of things, make money to live. I think that's the bottom line. (...)
> Sometimes these Nigerian people will come here and they, they ask for money, 'cause they haven't got work. They come here to ask for money, but, they don't belong to our church and they only come when they are in need. They want money, they want food, food we don't keep here to give them, money we don't give. Then they, they get aggressive, you know, they get cross, verbally. Aggression, I would say, say: "Ja, you're the church and why can't you help us and bla bla bla?" No, that's the only thing really that, that I have experienced and people coming here to beg, you know?(...).
> So, they live in flats, one person comes and applies, maybe not necessarily a Nigerian, but maybe a European person or Coloured or whatever come in and apply for a flat to live. And in the end there is a whole lot of them living in one

---

[190] As chapter 3.2 shows,: "Immigrants from Africa" stand in the second place of groups with whom South Africans can least identify, with Blacks (10%), Coloureds (12,2%) und Whites (22,1%). This assessment is confirmed in the presented data material, which shows mostly negative attributions to "foreigners" by native South Africans.

[191] Often, the statements on Blacks from other African countries refer to people with refugee status or to migrant workers, who come from the entire Southern Africa. The migrant workers usually have little education and financial means and are typically not part of the African elite. Since none of the interview partners belongs to this group, only other-images exist in this data material.

flat and, and, there is a bloc of flats in Green Point. I believe their behavior is so bad that the European people who live in there...are moving out. Because they cannot stand it, you know, they just feel that these people are so badly, they behave so badly. That they feel, they can't live like that. And then they move out and eventually it will only be Nigerians living there." (F1)

The speaker describes the problems that, in her view, go along with the African immigrants: if they find work in South Africa, South Africans complain that they cannot get a job. Work becomes a much contested "survival value." If the immigrants do not find work, they - according to the speaker - turn to drugs and alcohol ("selling drugs, drinking").[192] Thus, the speaker experiences the immigrants basically as a problem. She concludes her categorical statement by saying that she finds this to be a basic problem. She frames her statement in a matter-of-fact, neutral way and distances herself from it by saying: "There is conflict out there." Actually she holds back her personal opinion. She dissociates herself from her generalizations and remains in a shelter of self-protection.

In the next passage, she turns specifically to those Nigerians,[193] with whom she has had concrete conflict experiences. She describes in a concrete-situational way with interspersed quotations how Nigerians occasionally come by the church to ask for food and money. The narrator makes the point that the Nigerians only come when they need something, even though they are not members of the church. The values that seem to be important to the speaker are *religious affiliation, reciprocal behavior, asking and giving (requests and fulfilment of requests).* She cannot recognize these values in the begging Nigerians. Their reaction to her refusal she experiences as "aggressive" and angry ("get cross"). She even portrays their verbal aggression in citation for added emphasis and

---

[192]Also a White English speaking Catholic priest (P9:14) comments on the Nigerians in Sea Point: "And this area here, Sea Point, is the heart of the drug trade, you know? It's...it just is. You will find that many Nigerians have moved into that area. Now, some Nigerians are unfortunately involved in drugs. Not all of them, but some are. And they have a reputation for this, unfortunately." The speaker mentions that the Nigerians are known for their drug trafficking ("have a reputation"). But he dissolves the prevailing other- image of all Nigerians selling drugs. He makes it clear that there are *some* Nigerians in the drug business and that these are responsible for that reputation.

[193] Today many Nigerians live in *Sea Point* and *Three Anchor Bay.* Since the speaker lives and works in both districts, she must be particularly aware of the existing social problems with respect to the Nigerians. Yet, many immigrants live in the townships or in the squatter camps outside the city.

liveliness: "Aggression, I would say, say: "Ja, you're the church and why can't you help us and bla bla bla?" She does not complete the quote, instead ends it with a "bla bla bla," which she accentuates in the interview with a repelling gesture. Her words and body language express her strong inner rejection and her disdain for the Nigerians. Their statements are not even worth repeating. Her already existing prejudices and stereotypical assumptions towards foreigners seem to support her rejection and negative judgement in this concrete situation. At the end of the passage, she points out that this conflict with beggars has been the only one she has ever experienced.[194]

Subsequently, she confirms her disregard for the Nigerians by describing their conduct in housing areas in a generalizing way.[195] The first renter soon lets other Nigerians move in. She repeats in strongly pejorative terms that the Nigerians "behave so badly" that the European [196] renters move out. It is remarkable that the speaker now refers to Europeans who are disturbed by the Nigerians. In this way, she not only builds a bridge to the interviewer, but makes it also possible to project the tensions between the different groups in South Africa into the relationship between Nigerians and Europeans and distract from the country's apartheid history. Also, her criticism is not directed against a specific South African group. Instead, she uses the Europeans as antagonists in her rendition of the conflict. In her other-image, the Nigerians take on the role of the misbehaved people while the Europeans, on the other side, are the ones with the "good behavior" and, at the same time, the "victims." In the end, only Nigerians remain in the housing area. This conflict experience is almost a mirror of the larger reality: where Blacks move into the spaces of Whites, Whites retreat from the neighbourhoods. The interviewer might unconsciously select two groups that do not belong to the South

---

[194] Her repeated insistence that she has not experienced any conflicts in her life - especially not with people from other socio-cultural groups - can be seen as a repression in the context of a collective guilt experience, respectively of the tremendous fear to be accused, which is noticeable among Afrikaners and other Whites.

[195] It is clear that she speaks about Nigerians, but she introduces the subject of bad conduct seemingly neutral: if "a person" - never mind his/her origin - wants to rent an apartment: "Maybe not necessarily Nigerian, but maybe a European person, a Coloured or whatever come in and apply for a flat...." Even though she says that the reprehensible conduct is not tied to a certain socio-cultural group, she does not follow through. Instead, from now on she talks exclusively about Nigerians. Presumably, she tries to be "politically correct" by not falling into blatant stereotypes, but in this regard she is not very successful in her monologue.

[196] It seems as if the speaker uses "Europeans" here synonymously for White South Africans, or Afrikaners. She might want to reconstruct the apartheid patterns of thinking, speaking and categorizing.

244

African nation. She tries to project her personal involvement and her continued negative other-images – most likely towards South African Blacks – into a group from the outside since it would not be "politically correct" to publicly express negative attitudes towards other native socio-cultural groups. Non-South African groups come in handy as ideal entities for her own projections of impressions, perceptions, and feelings, which actually have their origin somewhere else.

Likewise, a Coloured interview partner (P28:36) talks about "foreigners." She works in an NGO that offers integration assistance for refugees and immigrants[197] so that she is constantly in touch with people from other African countries. Hence, she distinguishes far more between people from various national origins and compares their behavior to that of South African Blacks:

> But a lot of this people are actually skilled. Like people from the West. You find a lot of them being doctors. Ja, and they come back. They take the opportunity of studying in South Africa. But the difference is: the people from the West, they are very...ambitious. They look for opportunities. They look: "What can we do to make money?"
>
> But people coming...from Tanzania. This is actually a group that is more backwards. They are not so moving forward too much. Those are the real strugglers. The Tanzanians, when I look at them, with my own way of looking. I looked at them as very much like the South African Black people.....they don't see beyond. They don't look hoping for the best for the future. It's like things are just ending here.
>
> And that I have learned from the West African guys...to have keep hope alive and you have to move on. And that's, that's the one thing: You have to keep hope alive. Doesn't matter what it is. But tomorrow will be a better day. And this is how I live." (F3)

---

[197] Vgl. auch Textauszug B2, Kapitel 5.5.6, in dem sich die Sprecherin zu den "Blacks" äußert.

Making mostly categorical statements about the "foreigners," the narrator nevertheless differentiates between immigrants from West-Africa ("people from the West") and Tanzanians, who remind her of South African Blacks. She characterizes the West Africans in a very positive way, crediting them with positive qualities: They have abilities and skills ("are skilled"), are doctors and students, have ambitions to seize opportunities to get ahead and secure their survival ("What can we do to make money?"). In contrast, the Tanzanians are "more backwards:" "They are not moving forward too much. These are the real strugglers." In her assessment it is doubtful that the Tanzanians are able to establish themselves successfully.

In the following sentence, the speaker - strongly emphasizing that this is her personal view - relates her impression that the Tanzanians resemble the South African Blacks. Both groups are not far-sighted ("they don't see beyond"), are not optimistic and future-oriented ("don't look hoping for the best for the future. It's like things are just ending here"). Apparently, imagination and ambition are of great personal significance to the author. She cannot see these values embodied in the Tanzanians nor in the South African Blacks in everyday life.

In the following passage, she points out that she herself has adopted certain value orientations from the West-Africans, such as their positive outlook: "...keep hope and move on." The speaker credits her experience of the value of *hope* and her positive attitude towards the future to her interaction with West Africans, making it a motto of her life: "And this is how I live." As a Coloured woman she (definitely) equates her own value orientations with those she previously ascribed to West Africans and then contrasts them with Tanzanians and Black South Africans.

The speaker constructs categories of "foreigners" with positive and negative value orientations, for which she then finds corresponding South African groups. Here, like in F1, the speaker seems to avoid criticizing South African groups directly. Instead she uses the description and assessment of selected immigrant groups to render her attitudes and values with respect to Coloureds and Black South Africans. Probably the speaker chooses this method subconsciously because of post-apartheid South Africa's high sensitivity towards racist comments. Hence, it is easier for the interviewee to express her criticism against foreigners and then in analogy to national population groups (see also F1).

While the interviewee in F1 judges "foreigners" as negative, the latter distinguishes between positive West Africans and negative Tanzanians. In both cases, the described collective other-images have the function to project one's perception of current social and group phenomena on an outside group. This stereotyping also functions as an outlet for repressed negative feelings towards South African population groups, which are not permitted in a public climate of "political correctness." [198] Whether and to what degree there is truth to these other-images and how much of it is merely projection, cannot be clarified at this point.

Interview-Partner	Out-Group	Other-Image of Blacks	Other-Image of Foreigners	Other-Image of Nigerians
A White, afrikaans-speaking woman, secretary in Dutch Reformed Church P1:22, F1	Out-group			• Ask for money and food • Look for work and don't find • Find work and take it • Come to church when being in need • Are aggressive • Behave badly, are bad • Drug selling, drinking • Making money to live • Overwhelming living areas
Coloured woman, Immigration - NGO, Presbyt., P28:36, F3	Out-group	• Tanzanians are like Black South Africans	• People from the West are skilled and ambitious • Look for opportunities • Keep hope & move on	

---

[198] In his study of some immigrant groups in South Africa, Kotzé (1997:12) also finds that there are certain tendencies on the part of the native South Africans to be judgemental towards the foreigners. He, too, feels that negative and stereotypical judgements and evaluations of foreigners often take on an outlet function. "Foreigners" are ascribed negative behaviors that equally apply to South African groups. For many South Africans in the post-apartheid era it is easier to speak negatively about immigrants than about South African groups since any judgements of native groups have a historically loaded dimension.

			• Supply South Africans with drugs • Tanzanians: are more backwards, not moving forward, don't see beyond, don't look hoping for the best of the future, it's like things are just ending here	

Table 26: Other-Image of Foreigners

5.5.8 Summary

Looking at the data on self- and other-images, we find that people still operate with apartheid-related race categories. For example, in-group and out-group members both speak of "Coloureds." They often fill these race categories[199] with generalizing and categorical statements, characterized by stereotypes and prejudices. Categorical statements recur especially in connection with other-image statements. This confirms the assumption of chapter 3.2 that other-images are presented less differentiated than self-images and that the former tend to be closer to stereotypes than the latter. The lack of differentiation leaves much room for (mis-) interpretation and judgement of behaviors and value orientations, which the interview partners often exercise out of their own cultural, political and individual perspective without changing the (cultural) perspective.

The self-image aspects of Afrikaners are an exception at this point (WA1/WA2, 5.5.4). Compared to the other interviewees' auto-stereotypical statements, both Afrikaans participants are remarkably critical towards their in-group's value orientations.

---

[199] Next to the race categories, religious categories play an important role (e.g., Jews, "Coloured Muslims"), as well as sub-group categories within the race categories (e.g. Afrikaner). Here it is remarkable that sub-group divisions among Whites into Afrikaners and Jews are undertaken exclusively by in-group members of Whites. This might point to the fact that the ability to differentiate is stronger in one's own "race group." Yet, in contrast, the subgroup of Coloureds, the "Coloured Muslims," is also distinguished as such by members of an out-group.

In contrast, the in-group descriptions of both Jewish females are positive (J1/ J2, 5.5.5). Both emphasize the positive aspects of their self-image while their remaining self-image statements are more denotative, and not so much judgmental or interpretive (C1, W4, B1).

It is interesting that even self-image statements often include categorical statements and that concrete-situational self-image statements are often connected with categorical ones. Furthermore, it can be concluded that mostly people with a higher education, a graduate degree, or foreign country experience prefer the narration of concrete situational experience (see W3, WA2, C1, CM4, WA4) to categorical statements. The participants with little formal education exclusively stick to categorical statements.

In a table, the presented excerpts are assigned to categories as follows:

	Categorical Statements	Concrete-situational Statements	Combined: categorical & concrete-situational statements
Self-Images	W4 WA1 J1, J2 B1	W3 WA2 C1	W3 WA2
Other-Images	C9, C12, CM3 W6, W7, W9 B2, B4, B8, B9, B12 F1, F3	CM4 WA4	F1

Table 27: Text excerpts on Self- and Other-Images

Regarding key terms and value orientations, the interviewees focus on the areas of racial origin, religion, and religious practices. They address Christian, Jewish and Muslim values, but also largely economic and political value orientations. They often are concerned with adding specific content to value orientations, such as *brotherhood, forgiveness, justice, equality,* and *adjustment,* according to their own value hierarchies in the context of other- and self-image evaluations and interpretations. Occasionally, they describe perceptions of feelings and emotional expressions (eg., anger, rage), as well as characteristic behaviors and behavior orientations in their own group.

On the whole, it is impossible to draw general conclusions from the interviewees' attributions to specific groups since these strongly depend on each person's social reality, his/her specific sub-group perspective and individual situation. Therefore the data material holds such a variety of viewpoints that the selected material can merely indicate tendencies. In order to generalize group specific tendencies with respect to self- and other-images, it would be necessary to target a much larger number of people in each sub-group.

Also, the *error of leniency* plays a significant role in the data material (see e.g., WA1, WA2 und W6), an impact that could possibly be reduced by having a multicultural interview team.

In conclusion can be said that the data material points to a great conflict potential in the perception, judgement and interpretation of group-specific self- and other-images, rooted mostly in the apartheid past. Probably it will take a long time of (national) coming to terms with conventional stereotypes and prejudices to diminish this conflict potential. This can be accomplished through self-reflection, open communication and discussions in intercultural relationships and vis-à-vis contacts, special training workshops for coping with past trauma, and workshops for developing intercultural competence.

5.6 Narrated Conflict Situations in Post-Apartheid Cape Town

After considering statements on the Rainbow Nation, self-, and other-images, now concrete conflict stories stand in the center of analysis and interpretation.[200] The selection of the following stories by four different interview partners[201] is based on two criteria: first, they portray inter-personal conflicts, not intra-personal conflicts, which are targeted at a later point, e.g., in chapter 5.7.3; second, they demonstrate the kind of depth that allows their analysis with respect to value orientations. Having the character of *short stories*, these narrations will also be studied on the level of formal syntax. The limited analysis of linguistic means has only the auxiliary function to support the analysis of content.

Analysis and interpretation of the data in this chapter appear in the following sequence:

- Analysis of key terms and value orientations, including aspects of linguistic means, which center on grammar and semantic aspects. Also, thought-forms and thought-figurations are considered, and, on occasion, speech and writing styles and speech acts. Phonetics and phonology remain mostly unaddressed.
- Deliberation of value orientations and key terms in relation to the
  a) social reality of the author
  b) national value discourses (see 3.4)
  c) multiculturalism debate (see 3.1.2)

5.6.1 Apartheid in My Family

The narrator of the first story (P36: 45) is a man socialized in the Coloured Community. He is a faithful Christian, regularly attending the *United Congregational and* Presbyterian church in the university district, Rondebosch. He is a trained computer

---

[200] The original intention (see 1.1), to analyze and evaluate narrated conflict situations, changed in favor of a hermeneutical approach that has shifted and extended the focus of this work (see 5.4-5.8). However, chapter 5.6. addresses the original intention.
[201] The excerpts CS2/CS3, and CS5/CS6 are by the same speaker. This is interesting, because the points of analysis and interpretation can be compared in two stories.

expert, but gave up his previous job to become a freelance jazz musician and music teacher.[202]

A repeatedly recurring theme in this interview is the speaker's feeling that he does not fully belong to the group in which he was socialized. On one hand, he does not feel accepted in his community of origin because of his relatively light skin, his very good language skills in English and Afrikaans, and his high degree of education as an intellectual. On the other hand, even if the White community offers a partial alternative for him, he does not feel fully belonging there either. He tries to illustrate his inner dilemma in search of his own individual identity with a story about a conflict situation in his family:

There is all Apartheid in my family. Ah...this is an interesting story. My grandparents, they were Afrikaans speaking. And what would often happen was that there was a family where the father was Coloured and the mother was, was Coloured, but maybe fair, then they would classify the father Coloured and the mother White and they would classify one of the children White and some Coloured and then they actually break up the family. And they would say...if it was a grown up family, then they would say: "Okay, now the non-White family members must get out of this area, ahm, and ...so, you must split up and not speak to each other anymore." And it did happen. And with my aunts. The second child was classified Coloured and all the children after that, including my mother were Coloured. And then the last child was born and the last child was really dark...my youngest aunt. And then, when my mother and two sisters went to the graveside or walked in public...what the oldest sister, the White sister, would do...she would make the two Coloured sisters walk in a distance behind, let's say with the flowers...so and the dark sister. And then the White people would greet her, but they would not make a connection of these two are her sister. So, they would greet the White sister. And they would just walk pass the Coloured sisters, 'cause they would just have a different status. Ahm...and so, there was that thing between the oldest sister and the youngest sister and even now, the oldest sister and the

[202] Another text excerpt by the same speaker about self-image aspects of Coloureds appears in chapter .5.5.1, C1.

youngest sister are living together in the grandparents house and they are 75 and 65 and they are still fighting, like for, over who is better. I, I wonder, I will go to their home after church and they are having such a fight. They don't speak to each other - very sad. If it is the ones birthday, the other one will sit there and the other one will give out, hand out cakes, but the other one will not. If the other one comes and says: "Here is a cake for you", then she will say: "No." ...or she will go into her room. So, and this is still today and this is 2002 and this is Apartheid in the family. So, ja, that's quite a sad thing. Yes. The system worked very effectively. But there is quite some change in the families. (CS1)

Already in the beginning sentence, the narrator touches on the theme of this spontaneously remembered conflict: "apartheid in my family." Starting with his grandparents, who spoke Afrikaans, he finds the system of classification over language, skin colors, and origin problematic in the way they effected his family. He is mystified by how the different shades of skin color in his parents' generation came about and what classification criteria the South African government applied:

I don't know exactly how it works, but they were classified as White, but at any rate, ahm...their first child, they have had their first child, ah...now the government was classifying everybody from that point onwards. So, my eldest aunt, she was classified as White. But then the second child was born and the second child was dark. So, that child was classified Coloured. So, you had the parents and the first child classified as White...and the second child...and that happened. The next child classified as Coloured.

The story begins with short, paratactic constructions, which are occasionally interrupted by structuring interjections: "This is an interesting story...", "Ahm...their first child", "Ahm...now the government was classifying...". Thus, the author's current identity conflict is clearly connected to the central theme of racial affiliation within his family, as well as to apartheid and its consequences. Two levels of conflict coincide here: the structural conflict imposed by the government and the relational conflict between family members as a result of classification.

The interviewee begins the story about his family by assigning his grandparents to the categories of White and Afrikaans speaking, consistent with apartheid policy. After noting that his grandparents' children were classified either as White or as Coloured, he shifts from his personal family history to explain the policy of the apartheid government.[203] At this point, it is remarkable that he switches to citation, letting the government declare its race ideology. Grammatically this is a statement: 'Okay, now the non-White family members must get out of this area, ahm, and...." In its meaning, however, this is an order. On a third analytical level, it has the character of a declaration because the order to leave the area addresses and confirms the societal status of the family members. Behind this, of course, stands the government's intention to separate the *races*, which consequently separates family members and forbids them to communicate with each other. By using quotation, the informant dramatizes his family's conflict and emphasizes its importance to him. The text is repeatedly interrupted by quotes, especially in the middle and towards the end.

The narrator then describes the long-term effect of the government policy on his family. He links the present lack of communication between his aunts to its political cause ("to split up and not talk to each other anymore"). Again, his use of citation expresses his concern for the virulent and lasting consequences of this policy. When using citation for his aunts' dialogue, the narrator draws, on the linguistic level, a connection between governmental classification and its consequences in his family. Again, the first part of this dialogue is formally a statement, but semantically a demand. The response part of the dialogue ("No...") defies this demand, but the sisters' communication runs out without explication.

To illustrate the direct consequences of the government policy, the narrator relates a short family episode from the past about his mother and her sisters walking in public. His mother, the oldest, White sister, would walk ahead and make her Coloured sisters walk behind her, so that she could be greeted by other White people. Here he emphasizes the value of communication, which in public is symbolically expressed in "greet [ing] each other." At the same time, the speaker stresses the Whites' in-group

---

[203] The motivation for this informative insert about the conditions during apartheid might be the "error of leniency." Possibly, the speaker wants to provide history related information that the listener is not necessarily familiar with. But is it also possible that the speaker wants to recall these events for himself to clarify his present situation and put it in context.

behavior: they share the value of communication only with their own racially defined group. He offers this explanation: "they would just walk past the Coloured sisters, 'cause they would just have a different status." Hence, the value of equal communication depends on the value of status, which, in turn, is based on racial qualifications. The speaker describes this status diplomatically as "different" without expressing concrete judgements. That Whites enjoy a higher status can be concluded from the fact that they do not greet the Coloured girls. Apparently, they have the power to determine the greeting patterns derived from their superior social position. Accordingly, the White sister walks *ahead*, which symbolizes her "forerunner" position. When the speaker describes the White people "walk[ing] past" the Coloured sisters, he again illustrates the break in communication. Implied is that the White people intentionally ignore the Coloured girls.

The speaker then moves to the present time. Interrupted by two short thinking and speaking pauses, he summarizes the situation of the past and connects the past and present situation of his family in one sentence. "Ahm...and so, there was that thing between the oldest sister and the youngest sister and even now, the oldest sister and the youngest sister are living together in the grandparents' house and they are 75 and 65 and they are still fighting." The notion of "fight" is of explosive nature in this statement, especially in the context of presenting the age of the two sisters, which highlights the permanence of the conflict. The consecutive interpretation immediately shows the purpose of the fight: "they are still fighting, like, for over who is better." This statement does not only reflect the conflicted sibling relationship but also points to the origin of the apartheid ideology and its lasting social conflict: the issue of superiority or inferiority of persons based on their racial characteristics and, thus, the lasting inequality between population groups. The narrator does not explicitly articulate his personal opinion about this mentality of inferiority and superiority, but, with the laconic assertion, "They are still fighting," he merely points to the current nature and indefiniteness of the fight. He shows how deeply ingrained the apartheid system is in the life of individuals and groups, not only on the level of social structure but also on an intra-personal level, and how it has taken on a dynamic of its own.

In his consecutive announcement that he would not be surprised today if he would find his aunts fighting when visiting them, he emphasizes the persistence of this family conflict in its daily, certain presence. At the same time, he shows the rigidity and the heaviness of the situation and the lack of alternative options for the speaker to deal with the situation. The troubled communication between the aunts has now become the recurring element and overriding key term of this conflict story. It points to stagnating structures, passivity and lack of joy. The aunts' conflict exemplifies the inherited conflict potential of the society as a whole.

Before conveying the small dialogue towards the end of the excerpt, the author calls the silence between the sisters "very sad." He indicates his distress over this situation also by an incomplete sentence, an *ellipsis*. The missing predicate implies that there is no information about the subject nor the verb. Instead, with this emotional phrase, the informant expresses an uncertain feeling of dejection without offering further data about his own personal involvement. He moves beyond the level of pure narration to the level of his own feelings to comment on the situation of non-existing communication. Yet, he de-personalizes the feeling of mourning or sadness and puts it out as a fact, so that it comes across as definitive and unchangeable. Through this self-distancing form, he expresses his being effected, without becoming too emotionally involved. One could almost think that the phrase "very sad" carries the speaker's resignation, making him put up with the status quo. Thus, his sadness is closely related to the unfulfilled need for an unconditional communication between the population groups and particularly in his own family. Family seems to be of high value for the author. He shows how apartheid destabilized families, reflected until this day in disturbed communication patterns during typical family occasions, such as walks to the cemetery, greeting rituals, and birthday celebrations. While on such occasions, the family is normally united, this is not the case in his family. Choosing one aunt's birthday as an example, the speaker illustrates the gravity of the intra-familial conflict: When the birthday sister offers the other a piece of cake, the latter declines with a rude "No," or – and here the speaker pauses briefly – leaves the room. The narrator is dealing here with an intensified form of rejection in word and gestures. The sister not only responds negatively but even leaves the room, thereby denying any chance for communication.

In the last but one line, the interviewee makes a comment on his mood. "So, and this is still today and this is 2002 and this is Apartheid in the family. So, ja, that's quite a sad thing. Yes." An interjecting "ja," which points to an act of self-reflection, "so" follows the consecutive. The self-reflecting expression concludes with a supporting "Yes." Here, once again, the informant confirms the appropriateness and importance of his emotional reaction to this situation. It appears as if he himself can hardly believe that this situation is still playing out in 2002, ten years after apartheid. He continues by stating again the emotional side: "So, ja, that's quite a sad thing. Yes. The system worked very effectively." Again the speaker expresses his personal feelings matter-of-factly and depersonalized. He emphasizes the feeling with a repeated affirmation: "Ja," respectively "Yes." Grammatically the sadness refers ambiguously to the personal situation or the effectiveness of the system. The repeated mentioning of sadness gives the ending of his story a sense of gravity, which he tries to overcome in the final sentence: "But there is quite some change in the families." Here the speaker, attempting to be future oriented and positive, claims that there is change in families after all. However, his wording is quite cautious and vague. After his poignant description of a stuck situation, he now refers abstractly to visible social change. The notion of change sounds positive in this context and has to be understood in the context of apartheid's dismantling. The social, respectively, familial change represents change towards something positive and hope for the future.[204] According to the speaker, the families as the smallest social units of society fundamentally initiate change. Most likely this concluding sentence – which is so contrary to the described situation – is strongly determined by the interview situation and that the *error of leniency* plays a special role here. Being faced with a foreign interviewer, who is a guest in his country, the speaker might not want to end his narrative on a negative note without a glimmer of hope. At the same time, the speaker is aware that his story could be publicized, a knowledge that might compel him to navigate towards a "happy ending."

It is remarkable that the speaker's statements generally do not contain explicit judgements with respect to the presented situation. He merely indicates under what conditions what actions and behaviors most likely occur. These findings are also validated by the realization that, despite his emotional involvement in the portrayed the

---

[204] According to Mitchell (2002:2), the concept of "change" in South Africa has, since the 1980's, often been defined as *"positive sense to describe moves away from Apartheid."* While this depicts its general use, literature employs the term mostly in an imprecise way and often in the context of related categories, such as "transition" and transformation." In the presented data material, the notion of "change" occurs frequently in the context of "transition," "transformation," "personal and social change," "change of Apartheid," "structural change," political change and democracy."

conflict-ridden family events, the author refrains from judging statements for the most part. Even when describing his feelings, the narrator uses denotative words and does not succumb to the temptation to apply derogatory terms, which might put down his family members, government agencies or other groups. His self- restraint here is probably based on his high degree of self- reflection and education, his working experiences outside and inside the country, which help him to look at experienced situations analytically and interpret them without premature judgements.[205]

In summary, it can be said that the classification according to race criteria to this day plays an important, if undesired, role in his close family circle. The author highly values *family* and describes its destruction under apartheid. He repeatedly emphasizes that the events trigger in him feelings of mourning and sadness. To illustrate the effectiveness of the apartheid system, he picks family events that exemplify the continuing divisions within his family. In the example of communication, he depicts the split up of the family into persons with different, race-based status. The greeting as a form of communication becomes an important gesture for equality or inequality, just as the mere act of "speaking with each other." Finally, he describes the intra-familial fights as driven by concepts of superiority and inferiority. He closely relates this ongoing struggle for one's own positioning and identity within the family to the former official assignment to a superior or inferior group. In antithesis, however, he points to hopeful changes taking place in other families.

Looking at this conflict story and its implied value orientations in view of the South African value discourses, the following can be concluded: values, as proclaimed, for example, by Steve Biko (*solidarity; concern for each other; community of brothers and sisters; goodness of men)* or by Mandela *(non-violent-communication; communication; equality; unity; racial harmony; peace)* are not explicitly articulated. Instead, they are only present in their glaring absence in that they are clearly not represented by the actors of the story. The value of *communication*, for example, is repeatedly shown in its absence and brokenness. The same is true for *non-violent*

---

[205] Like his self-image portrayal (see C1, 5.5.1), this whole interview (P36:45) is characterized by denotative word usage, pointing to the speaker's high degree of reflection and thus supporting the presented supposition.

communication. Psychologically the communication in the described conflicts appears more violent than non-violent. Also, the value of *taking care of one another*, of *brother- and sisterhood* and of *racial harmony* are not existent in this story. Yet, these values, which Tutu proclaims as ideal for daily life in the nation, are actually the underlying standards for the conflict story. It becomes clear that the author attaches a high value to *family* and to *social and familial relationships (network of relationships)*, and that he is pained by the fact that they are not lived in everyday life. For his story he selects situations that highlight the diversity of his family, but also show its lack of unity. Another often addressed value in the public debate is the value of *multiculturalism* (Mbeki, Tutu), which is reflected in this family in the sense of *critical multiculturalism*. The author describes a pronounced *difference multiculturalism* that in no way strives for an intra-familial synthesis of cultural influences or common dreams. If Tutu aims for a *multiculturalism,* characterized by *peace, harmony and contentment,* it must be said that these values are certainly not represented by the sisters. The *diversity* in this family lacks the *unity* that the Rainbow Nation is supposed to have (More). The same is true for *equality,* the *balanced concept of power* and the acceptance of *ethnic, singular identity,* which the author indirectly declares absent in his family. Not even in his close family he can see signs of the concept of the Rainbow Nation taking hold. The same is true for the values of *brotherhood* and *humanity of humankind* which should be characterized by *dignity* and *equality.* Neither does the concept of *personhood,* which plays a special role in Ubuntu (Prinsloo) and is typified by *spiritual self-fulfillment, communication, creative self-expression, pride of self and own identity,* as well as *sharing, empathy and understanding,* find any attention in his family. Given the narrated situations, there is no indication that *communication* and mutual *sharing, empathy and understanding* have found acknowledgement in this family. With respect to the topic of "personhood and environment," he sees the relationships between the introduced people poorly developed. Even though "family values and social relationships," as emphasized by Teffo and Roux and in Coetzee's social theory, are central to the conflict story, they are in a "sad" state. The racial classifications within the family run so deep that the desired values for the national construction are not being integrated in this family life – at least not in the described every day situations. The rip in the family has torn so far that the family members and the author can not even fall back on the value of the shared *conditio humana* as a common ground that runs deeper than the constructs of race and culture.

In conclusion, it can be said that the values spread by the South African national discourses in this conflict story are present for the author only as desirable goals, not as living, positively expressed attitudes in every day situations. Thus, his conflict example underlines the hypothesis that the theoretical value discourses, which are supposed to contribute to the "nation building," remain only worthwhile goals and values. They find little regard in everyday life, and their absence is cause of conflict.

Generally the here described multiculturalism shows many elements of *difference multiculturalism*. The author repeatedly highlights the differences the parties perceive and produce. In fact, he portrays these differences as being more pronounced than their common family background. They have yet to rediscover their commonalities. For the author's family, co-existence in the spirit of *critical multiculturalism* remains only a vision. However, it seems that for himself its values are advisable goals in every day life.

5.6.2 My Mother had a Dog

The following conflict story (P2: 52) is told by a Shona-speaking South African man. At the age of three, his father took him from his birthplace in South Africa to Zimbabwe, where he grew up and was socialized in a Shona group.[206] In Zimbabwe he was very active in a religious group of the *Independent African Churches*, who named itself *Christian Fellowship* and belonged to the *AIC*. After 30 years of exile in Zimbabwe and Botswana, the speaker returned to Cape Town, his birthplace, after the end of apartheid. There he met his mother again, whom he had not seen for 30 years. During apartheid, his mother was classified as Coloured. Accordingly, she spoke Afrikaans as her mother language and went through the socialization and enculturation of the Coloured Community. The professional background of the interview partner is in business. He is an independent small entrepreneur in the production sector of interior

---

[206] The interview partner gives a very detailed description in I4, chapter 5.7.4, of his identity conflict and definition. Further contributions of this speaker can be found in W6, C12, and in CM3 in chapter 5.5.

design. He lives in a district dominated by White middle class (see 5.7.4) and speaks English and Shona fluently.

The interviews and many informal talks with this participant contain several narrations of smaller and larger conflicts of recent years in Cape Town. The following presents two of these stories. The first conflict story is about an encounter he had with his mother, and her dog, "Honey":

> My mother had a dog. Ja. A dog. Ja, and that dog was called "Honey", (laughing). And that dog was very attached to my mother as well and very jealous (laughing). I remember one time, you know, I was just teasing it like I wanted to get ah....get off part of its food from its plate. I don't know whether it was a bone or a piece of meat. And my mother was warning me that: "You have to be very careful, because the way it's snarling and going on like that... in actual fact you may think, I mean, you are playing, but it doesn't see it that way. It's very serious about it ...(laughing)...and, I mean, it's...getting very offended.." ... And I should be very careful, because it will soon bite me (laughing). And no sooner than she had finished talking, it had bitten me already (laughing). So, I was, I was quite offended, you see? And...well I didn't grew up with a dog, but at times I would go to the rural areas, I mean, these rural boys, like, their dogs, I mean, they were quite disciplined (laughing)...and this one actually I had thought this was very bad disciplined (laughing). You see, ... ja, in actual fact it's like, I mean, when I would buy, like some take-away food...I would expect that she would give like the dog some left-overs, but in fact she would go like...(laughing) ...I mean, to me it was like she is sharing equally with the dog (laughing)... and I wouldn't understand it. I would get offended by it. And I would confront her by saying: "I mean, how can you share ah...ah...the food I mean ...with the dog?", (laughing). "I mean, how can a dog be treated on the same level with human beings?" I wouldn't understand that. You see? And this is something, actually, you wouldn't find in the African culture or in that culture...ah...in which I grew up in Zimbabwe. I mean, it's like dogs would be given left-overs at the end of the meal after people have finished eating. Then the dogs would be given something to eat. You see? All right, there will be also some part for the dogs, not only bones, but they would not be almost

equated as human beings. So, that was something I wouldn't really understand, but as time went on, you see, I learnt to live with it (laughing), because my mother valued her dog very much and she was saying why this dog ... is important to her...or was so important to her...was that, I mean, she was almost like the door-bell for her. I mean, anyone who would come to the house, just a slight scratch outside, before they even tapped on the door, you see, it would be sounding the alarm already – the dog. You see? So, being an old woman, sickly woman, she was ah...okay, with my old step-father who was alcoholic, you see, ja, then got to understand how important that dog was to her. Okay, that was one thing about the dog (laughing). And well, and that was about my mother. (CS2)

In this short story, the author depicts the triangular relationship between his mother, her dog and himself. He introduces the topic artfully with the simple statement: "My mother had a dog.", followed by an assertive "Yes," a word repetition, "dog," and, again, a confirming "Yes." This short introduction makes it clear right away that the story is about the relationship between the author, his mother and her dog. He places the dog into the center of the narrative events, which he confirms by his statement in the last line of the story: "Okay, that was the thing about the dog (laughing). And well, and that was about my mother."

The crucial issue of the conflict is how to deal with a dog, or, with animals and nature in general. The narrator thoroughly describes the point of dissent between him and his mother, from both his own and his mother's perspective. Primarily this story deals with value orientations that are weighed differently by the two. The author names values important to himself, such as "discipline," and attitudes towards "sharing" of food in the context of people-animal- relationship. Explicitly he refers to the "African culture" in contrast to the Coloured Community, where his mother was brought up.

The issue is basically a familial relationship between two people from different socio-cultural backgrounds and their attitude towards animal nature. It is remarkable that the author himself is part of the story and, at the same time, repeatedly inserts reflections about himself. His tension between his personal involvement and simultaneous distancing comes across in his repeated laughs. Already in the first 14 lines in the first half of the story there are 10 interjections.[207] The last emphatic interruptions occur in the remaining interview excerpt, in which the speaker concludes his (core) story mostly with comments.

The author starts the story by introducing his mother, who had a dog. Right from the beginning, he mentions the name of the dog, "Honey," which he seems to find very funny since he has to laugh. He also laughs often at his subsequent descriptions of the dog, whom he gives anthropomorphic attributes: "And that dog was very attached to my mother as well, and very jealous (laughing)." Again he laughs, probably at the thought of personifying the dog, which he might find inappropriate.

The speaker remembers a small episode with this dog, in which he teasingly wants to take away a bone from it. As if his mother's warning rings still in his ear, he lively quotes her word by word: "You have to be very careful, because the way it's snarling and going on like that... in actual fact you may think, I mean, you are playing, but it doesn't see it that way. It's very serious about it...(laughing)...and I mean, it's...getting very offended..." The mother advises her son to be careful, explaining the dog's perspective, who understands the son's behavior as a serious threat to his food. The speaker reverts back to indirect speech by repeating his mother's warning and showing the biting as the consequence of his behavior. At these two important junctures of the story, he creates a narrative scenery for the listener. He switches back and forth between I-narrator and citation, showing the mother giving an extensive warning to the son, to which he turns a deaf ear. Adding to the comical nature of the situation, he portrays himself happily playing with the dog when the animal suddenly changes into a "biting beast." With the consecutive sentence, "And no sooner than she had finished, it had bitten me already (laughing)," he illustrates the dynamic of the situation and the quick chain of events, which he had miscalculated and which amuses him in retrospect. The tables have turned now: not the dog is "offended," by the bitten author. He inserts here an *anamnestic* passage: "And...well I didn't grew up with a dog, but..." In this reflective passage, the author provides the reasons for his attitude towards dogs. First, he remembers dogs as "disciplined" from his home country. Second, he does not place

---

[207] The emphasis, the emotional expression through gestures and language, show a lively and talented way of delivering a story. The listener can hardly resist the invitation to actively participate in the dog story. Additionally, this interactive way of narration is supported by the repeatedly rhetorical questions: "You know," "You see?", "You see?".

them on the same level with people, which corresponds with the value and life hierarchies in numerous Bantu-groups.[208] Thus, his reflection culminates in the rhetorical question towards the listener: "I mean, how can you share ah...ah...the food, I mean...with the dog?" (laughing). "I mean, how can a dog be treated on the same level with human beings?" These rhetorical questions are in their syntax splintered and express irritation. The author wrestles with the notion of people sharing their food equally with a dog. The splintering shows up in a repeated "I mean", in two thought pauses, and, finally, in two interjections "...ah...ah." Here, too, the author struggles for words when asking the rhetorical question. The author's immediate laugh marks the end of this lively story.

The value of "discipline" is of special meaning in this excerpt. The speaker explains that the boys in rural areas raise their dogs – contrary to his mother – to be more disciplined. In Bantu groups, the value of discipline is conveyed through the head of the family, usually the father, i.e., a male figure. Being a Shona male, the speaker probably associates the ability to discipline with boys, rather than with females. Again, he makes contact with the listener ("You see...") in order to present, after a short pause, another point he finds difficult.

> Ja, in actual fact it's like, I mean, when I would buy, like some take-away food...I would expect that she would give like the dog some left-overs, but in fact she would go like...(laughing) ...I mean to me it was like she is sharing equally with the dog (laughing)... and I wouldn't understand it. I would get offended by it.

The speaker explains his expectation for a dog to receive the leftovers of a meal. Instead, his mother engages in "sharing [the food] equally" with the dog, treating him – in the eyes of the author – as an equal. Again, this thought makes him laugh. He adds that he cannot understand his own mother, and that he feels offended by her behavior. This equal sharing of food between person and animal seems to trigger a value conflict in the author, which he verbalizes:

---

[208] Compare also John Mbiti (1990), "hierarchy of vital forces."

And I would confront her by saying: "I mean, how can you share ah...ah...the food I mean ...with the dog?" (laughing). "I mean, how can a dog be treated on the same level with human beings?" I wouldn't understand that. You see?

Here he expresses his strong irritation about his mother's behavior in a threefold way: First, he chooses the word "confront." In Bantu cultures it is rather uncommon that children – regardless of age – confront their parents verbally, since this is considered a lack of respect and good manners. When the speaker decides, nevertheless, to confront his mother, he shows that he finds his deeply seated values challenged so much that he cannot contain himself. Second, in quoting his mother, which again focuses on the dynamic and importance of her statement, he also names the central topic: the important value of sharing equally. Third, to him meal sharing is an exclusively human affair. Again, he emphasizes his disbelief over human values being transferred to a dog. This, to him, offends human dignity.

The second half of the excerpt (L14-26) contains culture-specific information on the author's Shona background with respect to the treatment of dogs. He then confronts his own cultural script for "dog" with the one of his mother, whose cultural background obviously has remained foreign to him to this day. This becomes particularly clear when he indicates that he needed to adjust: "I learned to live with it.". Even though he has come to terms with his mother's relationship to her dog, he has not accepted it. He reflects on his own cultural perceptions, and - maybe influenced by the *error of leniency* – provides an explanation for his own attitudes and behaviors. Moreover, he expounds - in contrast to his mother's behavior - the script for food and dogs in his socialization culture, according to which people eat first and let dogs then feed on the leftovers. Through this sequence of food consumption, the ranking order of the "vital forces" is stated and followed. The importance of this statement on sharing with dogs equally is expressed in the doubling-up of the content. He wants to emphasize that, while dogs are appreciated in the African culture, this appreciation has to be distinguished from inter-human relationships.

Apparent here is the influence of the different socializations of mother and son and --compounded by thirty years of separation -- their moment of strongly felt estrangement, (see also C1, 5.5.1). However, the speaker declares that while he cannot accept such dealings with a dog, he has come to grips with it over time. The implied values in this statement, which are highly important to the author, are the capabilities of *adjustment* and *learning* (see 5.5.3, W6). The speaker shows that a person can adapt even when his values are deeply offended. By laughing he subsequently lightens up the situation. He takes the heaviness and seriousness off this deeply rooted value conflict by pointing to his ability to adjust and "survive." He also explains why the dog is so important to his mother:

> So that was something I wouldn't really understand, but as time went on, you see, I learned to live with it (laughing), because my mother valued her dog very much and she was saying why this dog ... is important to her...or was so important to her, was that, I mean, she was almost like the door-bell for her. I mean, anyone who would come to the house, just a slight scratch outside, before they even tapped on the door, you see, it would be sounding the alarm already – the dog. You see?

The speaker points out that the dog is such an important companion for his mother because of safety reasons, and that she values him therefore so much. Now his own appreciation of the dog is tied to his mother's appreciation for the animal. He can appreciate the dog because he respects and values his mother. He recognizes that it is the dog's function as a guardian that makes him valuable. He uses for him the metaphor "door bell," which rings whenever a person approaches the house. Through this metaphor he does not elevate the dog to the level of a human being, rather assigns him the nature of a technical-functional device. Symbolically, he again expresses his attitude that the dog is closer to "un-animated things" than to people. To him, the argument for having a dog in the house is only valid with respect to its practical-functional side. Before this background, he can understand and accept his mother's affection for the dog.

His persistent use of "it" as the personal pronoun for the dog supports the assumption that the author regards the dog, first and foremost, as a "thing." There is only one exception to this: "She was almost like the door-bell for her." This is the only time he uses the third person singular feminine for the dog, thus personalizing the otherwise object-like animal. The dog receives personal character and is portrayed as a companion functioning as a personal guard. For the first and only time, the author takes his mother's perspective, seeing "Honey" as an equal companion, maybe even as the substitute for the "loss" of the stepfather as her protector, whom he describes as old and alcoholic. Also, he characterizes his mother as an old, sickly woman, who is in need of help and protection. Next to the incapacitated stepfather, now the dog occupies not only the role of an "undisciplined child," but also of the protector of the home. Then the author inquires whether the interviewer can understand ("You see?") and reconfirms for himself that his mother's attitude is based on his own interpretation of the dog's functionality.

In summary it can be said that in this triangular relationship it is of fundamental importance that the mother grew up in the community of Coloureds, the son in the community of Shona, and that both have different values concerning attitude and behavior towards dogs. For the author, the dog is an object that should not be treated on the same level with human beings, and should also be disciplined. The value conflict arises where his mother values her dog almost like a human companion. The speaker concedes that the dog functions as a competent "security guard," especially since his mother is old and sickly and no one else can guarantee her safety. This understanding allows him to accept the dog and to adjust to the situation.

This story dealing with the relationship between humans and animals (*nature*) is now examined with respect to the theoretical value discussion. Biko's values, such as *close to nature, concern for each other*, and *problem-solving through experiencing* are also important in this narrative. Human closeness to nature is evident in the relationship between mother and dog. But even if mother and son have different opinions on the nature and the motivating factors of the relationship, this value as such is relevant to both. The author describes how he handles the differences. On one hand, he solves the conflict by actually going through the experience and coming to grips with it ("I learned to live with it"). On the other hand, he reacts to the tension between him and his mother by communicating: he "confronts" his mother with his own opinions. Thus, like Mandela in his speeches, he assigns *communication* a highly positive value as part of his conflict resolution. At stake here is the communication between two individuals and their personhood, as developed in Ubuntu. Mother and son communicate and thereby interact in order to exchange ideas and to understand each other. The author repeatedly underlines his desire to be sensitive to his mother's thoughts and feelings towards the dog. This way he indirectly conveys that he places a high value on *empathy*, consistent again with the teaching of Ubuntu. In conjunction with the value of *sharing*, the speaker refers to the *conditio humana*, an essential ingredient in Coetzee's social theory and in Mbeki's philosophy. He thereby claims *humanity* as a value clearly set apart from and above animals. Interwoven with humanity are Mbeki's values of *dignity and equality*, which in this story are true for the position of mother and son with respect to sharing of food. To the narrator, equality should only exist among people, while the dog – according to the *hierarchy of vital forces* (Teffo & Roux) – should be excluded from it. In contrast, by sharing equally with the dog, the mother disregards the *hierarchy of vital forces* and lifts the dog to the level of *human being* He himself then provides the reasons for their differing attitudes towards the dog. He orients himself at values of the *African culture*, while his mother goes by other values, whom he does not further illuminate nor assign. All we know is that his mother was socialized in the Coloured Community. By pointing to these cultural differences, he expresses his own awareness of *ethnic diversity* and *ethnic culture* (Ubuntu), and demonstrates that the value of diversity has to be constantly negotiated among people. Diversity also includes, according to Coetzee's social theory, *self- and collective understanding* with respect to one's own group and the inter-group relationships. Here, traditions, group values, and the *common good* play an important role. Likewise, the author justifies his attitude with his rootedness in *African culture*, its traditions and shared values. Indirectly the author conveys in this conflict story that the relationship to his mother, i.e., family relationships, (*family and network of relationships*/Tutu) are very important to him. He negotiates this area of conflict in the long-term and seems to find an appropriate solution. The argument between mother and son is carried by the high value of *family* and *harmonious family relationships*, which compels them to finish with a *consensus* on the issue. In this case, the consensus consists in the author's realization that the dog is a security factor and as such important for his mother. Because he has gained this understanding, his mother is now free to treat her dog as usual. By applying his own values *(communication, interaction, empathy, understanding, family, human relationships, etc.)*, which are consistent with those proclaimed in the South African value discourses, he is able to solve the value conflict.

Looking at this story in light of the Rainbow Nation concept, we can conclude that both conflict partners successfully apply its values and ideas here in everyday life. While the author pronounces their differences in attitude, cultural and personal background, by way of discussion mother and son find their way back to familial unity. The conflict does not drive them apart, since both respect each other's *singular identity*, which is associated with different value orientations. Likewise, they accept the ethnically determined differences (*ethnic diversity*) of the other so that a familial unity, dog including, can be achieved. This also implies a *balance concept of power*, where no one tries to dominate the other. The visionary value orientations of the Rainbow Nation have become a living reality in this family: diversities are recognized, negotiated and unity is constructed. This conflict story exemplifies how the whole nation should negotiate shared and diverging values. The issue in this story is not interfamilial belonging to a race category – as in CS1 – but the negotiation of different values rooted in different cultures of socialization. Not once does the speaker directly mention his mother's racial classification as Coloured. [209]

In addition, it can be concluded that the author in this narrative and in his opinions represents a kind of *critical multiculturalism*. His conflict example is based on his awareness of the cultural differences between him and his mother and describes a lively negotiation of their conflicting value orientations. At no time does he indicate that he finds racial categories insurmountable or fixed. Instead, he shows ways of problem solving through the creation of a new shared culture of communication and mutual understanding. These then lead to reflection of the self and the other and contribute to the preservation of mutual respect of the conflicting parties. At this point, however, the author's openness towards negotiating differences could very well be related to the mother-son- relationship.

---

[209] This phenomenon is striking because the author, in other excerpts, talks about the group of Coloureds in strongly pejorative way (see 5.5.1, C 12 and .5.5.2, CM 3), while yet at other places, he refers to Whites in a very differentiated way (see W 6, .5.5.3). It is remarkable that the speaker begins to differentiate at a point, when he has personal contact to and enters a relationship with a member of another group. In such case, he is able to break up his stranger image, expand it, or revise it. In his White girlfriend (see CS 3) and in the interviewer (see W 6, 5.5.3) he encounters a reference for the group of Whites, which allows him to differentiate. Through his mother, he has a closer relationship to the group of Coloureds,. But instead of falling into race categories when explaining his

In the following conflict story by the same author, the negotiation of the elements of *critical and difference multiculturalism* looks completely different.

5.6.3 The Mixed Couple

At a different point in the same interview (P2: 52), the interview partner relates another situation in which he experiences a strong conflict. The focus here is his relationship to a woman from the White community. In the following excerpt, the interviewee articulates his experiences and feelings when the mixed couple appears in public in the Western Cape. Important here is the speaker's perception of members of the Coloured Community and their assumed attitudes towards his relationship with a White woman:

One of the experiences I had...ah...was after I befriended someone who was White and we had a close friendship or relationship one would call it and we would drive out a lot. Many times and it's like...ah...(laughing)...on the way whilst we were driving...okay, I would be driving most of the time and she would be sitting next to me and it so happened, she was White. And, ah...it wasn't just the two of us, ah...there was a baby also. Ah, a White baby, her baby and ah...I noticed that most motorists, like, okay, this would be in the Western Cape, and most of them are Coloured people....I mean, they would stare at us...in a way that would make me feel quite uncomfortable or very uncomfortable, because I would sense, I mean, they would be poking their nose into our business. I would say, they would be surprised...to see a Black person, that is myself, driving around with a White lady. I mean,... there is still,...I mean,...can not come to terms, I mean, a Black person can't go out, I mean, with, I mean with a White girl. You see, they would look at you with piercing eyes and...I mean, they'll be so curious to want to understand or know what it is that is happening. For them, I mean, it's...abnormal (laughing). You understand? Ja, really. Ja, it's especially the Coloured people. Ja, but, I mean, so...I mean, that's where the irony is. I mean, it's something, which, I mean, they actually should understand, but they don't seem to. I mean...for example we went to a certain place, we drove to a certain place, ahm...in F., ah...it is an estate, ah...or a manor, you know, these old farm houses. It is a farmhouse that has since been turned into a, a, a sort of restaurant or museum where, I mean, you can go and view how a manor used to be in its old days, I mean, the furniture and the people who occupied it and the way how these used to live. It so happens that there is a restaurant there and it's a very beautiful restaurant which is visited by a lot of tourists, okay, mostly White people. Some local and some, I mean, overseas people. And, the workers there or the waitresses, ja, I have noticed they are all waitresses, I mean, I haven't seen a waiter there...when we got there and we helped ourselves to a table, we sat, we sat there for, I mean, quite a long time, and no one came to serve us or to meet us, to ask us what our needs were...they could see us, I mean, from a distance of about 30 meters or so...and they would look at us, I mean, such curiosity...and they would be standing there in a cluster and...ah...I mean, the picture I got from them was: "Oh, now, what is this Black boy doing or trying to do, I mean, sitting there, I mean, with a White woman. And the rest of the people that are here, they are all White couples or ...White families. But, I mean, this odd pair now, can't, I mean, can't they see that this is not quite acceptable?" Why I am saying so, because, I mean, no one came as you would expect with a smile: "Good afternoon, what can I help you with?" 'Till, I mean, there was a waitress who was going to serve another table and on her way back, ah...I stopped her or interrupted her, by asking her: "Ah, can we ask for help please?" But anyway, what I was expecting to get from them they didn't have. (...) But this is, I mean, that kind of a thing, I mean, in South Africa, I mean, generally...you know, if you are a Black person and also Black male and...you happen to be going out with a White female, it will raise a lot of eye brows. But as I say ...from the White people, they will just glance at it, but from the Coloured people it is as they would almost pass remarks, you know, by the way how they look and...really pierce, I mean, their eyes, I mean, into, I mean, into whatever you're doing or your presence. You see? I find it, I mean, difficult still, to deal with..... (CS3)

Clearly the fundamental basis of the here presented conflict (like in CS1, 5.6.1) is again the construction of race. The whole conflict experienced by the speaker is almost exclusively defined through his view of different racial groups. Again, like in CS1 and CS2, the issue is race, familial or relational structures, and dealing with them in public. The speaker perceives and interprets certain situations in terms of group affiliation of the participants. This starts right at the beginning, when he introduces his friendship with a White person. Initially, he describes their relationship as of that kind that they take fieldtrips in the car together. He clearly defines his male role in that he portrays himself as the driver and the woman as the passenger. Metaphorically speaking, the speaker and his friend are on the same level in the car, but the man holds the steering wheel: "okay, I would be driving most of the time and she would be sitting next to me and it so happened, she was White." As if he can hardly believe it himself, the speaker stresses again that his girlfriend is White. While the listener at this point expects a continuing narration of events, the speaker surprises him by the repeated referral to the race of the friend. His underlining of the inter-racial relationship might indicate that the author thinks of this relationship as something special and unusual.[210]

He continues by introducing another person, namely, a White baby. With this racially underscored description, the speaker now distances himself from the woman, on one hand, and the baby, on the other hand. After a small pause, he emphasizes that people in public stare at the couple and the baby. This shows that the speaker himself finds this *patchwork* relationship constellation unusual. He refers to his own irritation and possibly projects his own feelings - described in the rhetorical figure of *correctio*[211] - into the perception of his social surroundings, especially the Coloureds: "I mean, they would stare at us...in a way that would make me feel quite uncomfortable or very uncomfortable." Whether the environment produces his feelings of discomfort or, vice versa, whether he projects these feelings onto the environment, cannot be clarified. Most likely both are the case.

---

[210] In other informal conversations, the author says directly that he found it a „miracle" to have a White girlfriend, since he never expected this to be possible for him as a Black person. He also experienced this relationship as great enrichment and as personal and social enhancement.
[211] He uses the correctio in line 2 and line 5. *There was a baby also. Ah, a White baby, her baby and ah....*This double correctio implies an escalation of meaning: first the baby is introduced, so the audience knows that the couple is not alone. Then the baby is classified as White indicating that it is not their common baby. Then he says: *her baby,* which means that the speaker completely distances himself from the child and biological fatherhood.

Because of the staring, the narrator is overcome by a feeling of indignation that the onlookers intrude into his private affairs: "They would be poking their nose into our business", an idiomatic expression that underlines his deep resentment against that kind of curiosity. However, this metaphor also carries pejorative features. Looking at his use of self-referencing verbs, one notices neutral terms of feeling and observing: "I noticed...", "I mean", "I would sense", "I would say". Yet, the verbs attached to Coloureds have a clearly degrading effect: "they stare" means that someone feels uncomfortable; "they are poking their nose into our business" implies they are ill-mannered by overstepping such boundaries. Then he comments on the reasons for their behavior: "I would say, they would be surprised...to see a Black person, that is myself, driving around with a White lady." Here, the public's general astonishment at the sight of a mixed couple serves in itself as a reason for their behavior. At the same time, the speaker positions himself for the first time – also in terms of racial belonging – as "Black." The listener and reader are likely to detect in his wording not so much a positive surprise, but feelings of indignation. The speaker's culture-specific style of communication, which appears rather indirect, might forbid him to use direct attributes for the Coloured people. Instead he chooses words with a moderately negative undertone. Furthermore, their body language is upsetting to him. He talks about "piercing eyes" or "raise a lot of eye brows," and even about "pass(ing) remarks." Again, we can observe an escalation from non-verbal to verbal means of communication. In reviewing his verb usage, it is notable that he talks about the others in a distancing condescending way.

The author repeats his sense of the public's astonishment about the couple in the form of strongly torn apart statements, an *anacoluthon*: "I mean...there is still,...I mean,...can not come to terms, I mean, a Black person can go out, I mean, with, I mean, with a White girl." In tearing apart the inner structure of the sentence: "I mean...," he indicates deeper experiences and irritations. Only in the third attempt – "I mean, a Black person can go out, I mean, with, I mean with a White girl" – he succeeds in making his point. The fact that he pauses three times within this *anacoluthon* leads to the conclusion that he has not been able to order his thoughts in a way that he could articulate them on the level of syntactical and grammatical flowing speech. Characteristics of the sentence structure of an *anacoluthon* are asyndetical word compositions, which – interrupted by thought pauses - show that the speaker listens deeply to his inner self. Here, it becomes as evident as never before that the author himself is insecure and torn apart: not only the public's amazement plays a role here but also his own disbelief and his own insecurity about the mixed couple regarding their embodiment of moral and social judgements. Another reason for his interrupted flow of speech might have to do with the interview situation itself, which he might associate with a cultural scheme of conversation situation, gender roles, public nature of the interview, and race affiliation. So he struggles with words in order to adequately articulate himself in the face of a young, academically educated, White interviewer.

It is also remarkable that he titles the White woman in his story first as "lady," later as "girl." This change could be an indication of the author's gender bias, or it could say something about the relationship of the couple. But this question needs to remain open here.

Again, the speaker is irritated about the "piercing" glances of the Coloured onlookers. The motive behind these glances he believes is the curiosity of those who cannot understand. They want to understand what is happening. He adds laughing: "For them, I mean, it's...abnormal (laughing)." On one hand, his laughing appears almost arrogant since he gives the reader the impression that the Coloureds cannot comprehend the relationship constellation because of their narrow view. Thus, he places them in the position of those who have not overcome the categorization of apartheid. On the other hand, his wording might as well be interpreted as the author's own projection, which transfers his own bewilderment on the Coloureds. He underlines his statement by his subsequent statement: "...you understand?" and a self-confirming "Ja, really. Ja." Then he points out that especially Coloureds should understand this kind of relationship constellation since they are a product of such a connection: "...it's something which I mean they actually should understand."

How different is this informant's word use and description with respect to the White people he encounters (see also 5.5.3, W6)! In the narration of the restaurant visit, he talks about them as equals. He notices that Whites look at the mixed couple in a certain way. "They will just glance at it." This elevated or even precise choice of words of "(casual) glances" indicates a positive judgement or perception of the White population group in this situation. In the following antithetical wording, he tells us that the Coloureds make almost condescending remarks ("passing remarks"). It is evident here that the speaker strongly distinguishes himself from both groups, Whites and Coloureds. His elevated word use with respect to Whites either betrays a close affiliation to this group or shows his felt obligation towards his White interviewer to make more friendly references. In that case, we would be dealing with a pronounced *error of leniency.*[212]

In switching scenes to an outing in the countryside, the speaker gives a conflict example, to which he provides a rather detailed introduction. The couple and the baby are taking a sightseeing trip in the Western Cape. He describes the surroundings and the general situation so that the listener suddenly gets the feeling of dealing with a completely new conversation situation. The introductory description brings a sense of calm to the monologue – especially after the preceding statements. In contrast to the negative connotations with respect to the Coloureds, the interviewee now describes a recreational place that is mainly frequented by White people. He divides the group of Whites in overseas tourists and natives. There are also the restaurant's waitresses. He tells us that the couple has to wait a long time without being served: "...we helped ourselves to a table, we sat, we sat there for, I mean, quite a long time and no one came to serve us or to meet us, to ask us what our needs were." He underlines the length of the wait with the double use of the verb "sat" and the adverbial phrase "quite a long time." The narrator puts himself into the perspective of the waitresses and explains:."..they could see us, I mean, from a distance of about 30 metres or so...and they would look at us, I mean, such curiosity...and they would be standing there in a cluster and...ah..." The initially described general behavior of Coloureds is now also observed in this concrete situation, which suggests that the waitresses who gaze at the couple are Coloured, too. Here again, he associates Coloureds with the term curiosity. The listener gets the impression of an imbalanced situation, with the group of Coloureds on one side, the group of Whites on the other, and the couple in between.

The peak of the narration follows in the inserted supposed other- image in the form of quotation:

---

[212] The interpretation that the speaker has a rather positive attitude towards Whites is supported in excerpt W6 in chapter 5.5.3. But it cannot be elucidated at this point whether this represents his basic opinion or whether he gives this impression because of the *error of leniency* towards the interviewer or because of his close relationship to his White girlfriend.

I mean, the picture I got from them was: Oh, now, what is this Black boy doing or trying to do? I mean, sitting there, I mean, with a White woman. And the rest of the people that are here, they are all White couples or ...White families. But, I mean, this odd pair now, can't, I mean, can't they see that this is not quite acceptable?

Here the author seems to project his own anxiety about social acceptance onto the waiters. It is exciting that he, at this time, refers to himself as "boy" and to his friend as "woman," while their roles were exactly reversed in the above mentioned car situation. Then he was the "man" behind the wheel and she the "girl" on the passenger seat. This change in the supposed other- image may point to the author's inner feeling of inferiority. He reproduces the old apartheid stratifications, which are partly brought on by the fact that he finds himself in the position of the Black minority in this situation, especially since this location was inaccessible to him only a few years ago. The position of his friend is, in his view, strengthened by the White-dominated surroundings. He senses an imbalance between himself and his friend, which finds its corresponding expression in the change of titles for himself and his friend as mirrored in the public eye. While as driver the author can position himself in public with the status symbol of the car and therefore as member of the middle class, here at the restaurant table he is not the steering man anymore, but only the "Black boy" next to a "White woman" with her child. He has no position that he could find socially acceptable in any way, neither as a "Black man" at the side of a "White woman" nor as the non-biological father of the child. At this point, the value of *family* comes to the fore next to the value of *racial* affiliation (minority versus majority). The mixed couple with the White child does not even embody – conservatively speaking – a family unit since the child is obviously not their biological child. This "family" resembles a "patchwork" in its composition. But it is difficult to draw any conclusions from this observation to the author's feelings regarding his role as a man and partner in public (last not least for a female researcher). However, in the supposed other- image, the speaker himself describes the couple as "odd pair." He introduces this descriptive phrase in quotation as the dramatic climax in the flow of his story. He concludes this *oratio directa* with an expression of moral indignation: "Can't they see that this is not quite acceptable?" As the man in this "odd" relationship constellation, the author wrestles with the issue of social acceptance. He projects his own lack of self-confidence into the other-image Coloureds presumably hold of him.[213] He as a Black entrepreneur experiences an – however motivated - feeling of inferiority towards Coloureds as well as towards the constructed status and role of his White girlfriend.[214] In another talk he comments that it is socially more acceptable when Black women date White men than vice versa (see P2:52). The speaker's opinion is probably related to African gender role concepts in the private and public spheres. Since the African man in many African cultures holds a superior status in public while the woman is sovereign and responsible in the domestic sector (see also Mayer et al 2003: 56/57), he, as an African man and narrator, may experience a status and role dilemma here. In the company of the White woman, he no longer self-evidently occupies the typical male role of decision maker and status bearer for the family. In public, his male status, which normally is simply determined by gender roles, is no longer clear. Moreover, the status of race-affiliation determines the status of gender affiliation and dominates it.[215] Hence, the male narrator finds himself in a situation where he has to re-negotiate his identity components of gender and race, which is irritating and unsettling to him – especially in public. At the side of his White girlfriend, the speaker enters an

---

[213] In an informal talk, the speaker declares that Blacks respond differently to relationships between Black men and White women than Coloureds. In his view, they show solidarity and are much more accepting towards an interracial friendship.

[214] A Xhosa-speaking male interview partner (P11:17/ 5.4.2,R6) when talking about workplace, states that, to this day, skin color is a decisive factor in career advancement, and that Whites still regard Blacks as inferior. "But he won't reach that senior position, because of his color. Our color is still looked down as inferior...by Whites, yes." This supposed other-image is not an isolated case. Instead, he claims that Blacks again and again make similar statements in casual talks. Therefore, this seems to be a group-specific assumption carried over from apartheid which is still valid for both speakers.

However, a White interview partner and employee of a Christian organization (P24:32) sees it the other way around. In her view, Whites do not think of Blacks as inferior, but that Blacks themselves have developed an inner attitude of feeling inferior, which they then package it in the form of supposed White other-images: "It is basically a cultural thing. They think that...ah... that they are not good enough, because their skin is black. Which is rubbish." The interviewee refers here to Biko, who insisted that Blacks disregard their "inner inferiority" (see 3.4.2).

[215] During informal talks, the speaker repeatedly speculates that the "public" might them of him as the "bodyguard", when he shows up with his White girlfriend. This repeated statement also points to his insecurity and inferiority feelings regarding his role as a male and partner at the side of a White woman.

"identity crisis," since he remains in the conceptual framework of race and gender-role definitions.

Immediately following, the narrator explains his assumptions on the thoughts of the waitresses. Unexpectedly, no one approaches the couple to serve them. He has to make an effort to receive the desired attention: "I stopped her or interrupted her by asking her: "Ah...can we ask for help please?" This *correctio* in his story peaks in the quotation of his polite request whether he could ask for help. This statement reflects an extreme role reversal of the accepted communication between personnel and customer, and simultaneously points to his increased insecurity causing him stress, especially since he is in the company of his White girlfriend.

He concludes his short story with a generalizing remark: "But this is, I mean, that kind of a thing, I mean, in South Africa, I mean, generally...if you are a Black person and you are also Black male and...you happen to be going out with a White female, it will raise a lot of eye brows." This statement indicates the social bewilderment and lack of acceptance surrounding mixed couples. At the same time, it also shows the author's inferiority complex now with respect to his race and masculinity. Evidently, he is not capable to overcome the social constructions of race, gender, inferiority/superiority and step out of them. Instead of resisting the reproduction of previous concepts, he falls into severe self- doubts and negative feelings. His insecurity, caused by the perceived lack of acceptance and his poorly developed self-confidence and sense of self-worth, points to a deeply rooted, persistent inferiority complex.[216] In his concluding explicit statement, he goes back to the group-titles:

> But as I say....from the White people, they will just glance at it, but from the Coloured people it is as they would almost pass remarks, you know, by the way

---

[216] This interpretation is strengthened by many informal conversations with the narrator, in which he himself frequently brings up his "inferiority complex" as an issue that troubles him.

how they look and...really pierce, I mean, their eyes, I mean, into, I mean, into whatever you're doing or your presence. You see?

This final passage of the interview ends with a thought-movement that again underlines his Black-White perception in a generalizing way. Coloureds seems to be threatening to him in that they stereotypically could determine his personal, or even social position between the population groups.[217] Consequently he admits: "I find, I mean, difficult still, to deal with..."

In summary, it can be said, that the author here tells a story that is strongly characterized by his out-group assessment. In the center stands the close friendship or relationship to a White woman. This relationship and every perception, expression and intention regarding his surroundings are completely penetrated by the criterion of racial affiliation. Unlike CS2, 5.6.2, this story is not about cultural differences but exclusively about racial definition of people, which is the underlying fact of everything that happens.

The author's theme circles around his experience of the "others," mostly Whites and Coloureds in this story. At the same time, his feelings are linked to private and public spheres. He calls the interest of the Coloured public "curiosity," which he understands in a negative sense as transgression into the private sphere. In the second part of the interview, the value of *family* plays an important role. The focus is on the composition of a family. The author contrasts his "patchwork family" with the "White families," who are not multi-racial and, therefore, do not appear "odd." In the portrayal of presumed other-images, the author signifies his own inferiority complex in view of the groups of Coloureds, Whites, and his girlfriend.

Looking at the theoretical value discourses, we can find here agreements as well, either in the sense that the speaker exhibits some ideal values as desirable, not yet achieved goals, or in the sense that he recognizes the importance of these values for this concrete situation. For the moment, it can be said that -- especially in comparison to the previous conflict example-- the entire conflict narration is in form and content

---

[217] Considering the generally negative comments on Coloureds throughout his interview, it is remarkable that his mother– even though socialized as Coloured (see CS2) – is the only person he exempts from this negative view. With regard to his mother, the speaker strongly differentiates: he recognizes her as a person, and not merely as a member of this particular group.

characterized by elements of *difference multiculturalism*. Contrary to the preceding example, the author continuously stresses the separateness of the groups and simultaneously reduces persons in his personal surroundings to representatives of these groups ("White lady," "Coloured waitresses"). Throughout the narration, the listeners are not given the impression that they are dealing with group members who have overcome their socio-cultural differences and have melted together in unity, as it would be the case in *critical multiculturalism*. Instead, the described group members are separated and reduced and not positively acknowledged as different individuals. Even though the author recognizes that, from his perspective, Whites react rather positive and Coloureds rather negative to the mixed couple, at no point in the story he constructs new categories for groups of people. Rather, he remains in the separation of racial categories and traditional patterns of assessment and interpretation. This is especially striking since the author in the context of his own family (CS2) is able to positively change the given cultural differences and create a unity in the sense of *critical multiculturalism*. But in this situation of public anonymity, he emphasizes the group differences instead of bridging them. Given the speaker's consistent negative perceptions and interpretations particularly of the Coloureds' behavior, a coming together and creation of a common culture appears almost unthinkable. He does not permit the chance to negotiate perceptions, nor does he allow positive self- and other-images.

As mentioned above, the author displays values that are also part of the theoretical value debate. He calls the relationship to his White girlfriend *close friendship* or *relationship,* consistent with Biko, who, in his speeches, advocates friendship between the population groups. In the friendship between the author and his girlfriend, values such as *racial harmony, unity, equality, freedom, communication,* and *non-violent communication,* as Mandela proclaims them, come to bear. Values, such as *inter-human unity,* surely exists but seem to be unstable even in this close relationship because of the racial assignments and the constructions of race and social status. On one hand, a kind of *racial harmony* and *communication* exist; on the other hand, both are of a special kind and broken in the social context. Regarding the relationship constellation, values such as *family and relationship networks, anti-racism und multiculturalism* (Tutu) are important and present for the author. He and his friend practice a kind of *unity in diversiy,* as described in the Rainbow Nation concept, and acknowledge each other's *ethnic and singular identity.* While the basic trend in this story is *difference multiculturalism*, there are also elements of *critical multiculturalism*. Like in CS2, these emerge exclusively with respect to one closely related person: was it in CS2 the author's mother with whom he created a new culture of communication and unity beyond their differences, here it is the girlfriend with whom he represents a unit, even if he continuously puts the racial characteristics upfront. The question whether the power of that unity is the result of his familial connection to his girlfriend or rather their close inter-human ties, cannot be answered here. It is, nevertheless, evident that the narrator does not create a (narrative) unity with the population group of Coloureds and with respect to personal relationships to members of that group – with the exception of his mother.

Thus, he describes the communication between him and the Coloureds as existent, but not at all as *non-violent* (Mandela). He completely disregards the value of *non-violence* and portrays a rather violent communication instead. Also values, such as *community of brothers and sisters* and *concern for each other* (Biko) appear to be unrealized in the view of the author. On the contrary: nothing indicates a *brotherly community* among Blacks (Biko).[218] Even though he gives the gawking Coloureds credit for being interested in the couple and trying to "understand" the situation, their craving to understand remains the only positive aspect in his other- image. In this positive sense, it corresponds with the desire for *understanding* and *empathy* in Ubuntu. But aside from this hint of positive quality, the narrated situation does not allow for values such as *inclusion of minorities, no fear of inequality,* acceptance of *cultural diversity* and the shared *humanity of humankind* (Mbeki).

In the restaurant, he has the uncomfortable feeling of being in the minority position, neither being accepted nor shown enough consideration. There is also the underlying fear of being violated in his basic rights, a sense of unequal, even unjust treatment by the Coloureds, especially compared to the White guests in the restaurant. There is no trace of multiculturalism in the spirit of *peace, harmony and contentment* as envisioned by Tutu. While the author is fully aware of the multicultural nature of the restaurant situation, he does not enjoy a sense of peace, harmony and satisfaction. He

---

[218] According to Biko, "Black" are all those who feel „oppressed." In South Africa, mostly Coloureds and Blacks counted themselves as part of that group (see 3.4).

disregards the value of the *conditio humana*, of *being a human being* (Coetzee), as a connecting bond between him and the others or as a positive basis for the creation of a new culture. He sees his social environment split into members of different race groups and approaches his self-reflection and reflection of others with respect to their assumed other-images in a negative way. Here, the relationship to his girlfriend is important to him in that it represents to him, to some degree, his value of familial togetherness, even though it is diminished on the level of race, and on the level of family definition.

These two interview excerpts show that the prominence or significance of the participant's value orientations depend on the context of the situation and on the author's perception of social reality. In CS3 his social reality is characterized predominantly by racial assignments, as well as gender role concepts. Yet, in CS2 the aspects of socialization, culture of origin, and position within the family are at stake, such as mother and son relationship. Evidently, in different conflict situation different concepts of social reality come into play. Each time different aspects of the "multiple personality" (see 3.2) are addressed and emerge.

5.6.4 The Coloured Thief

The following conflict story is of a special kind. The narrator is a White South African, who grew up in the province of Kwa-Zulu-Natal as one of nine children and as son of a South African farmer of English origin. His religious background is Roman Catholic, but he does neither attend church nor can he identify with the Roman Catholic faith.

The interviewee has been living in Cape Town for a long time. He is a trained hotel expert, but has throughout his life worked in various other fields. After the end of apartheid, in the course of socio-political and socio-economic restructuring (*Affirmative Action*), he lost his leading position in a pretty large company. Since then he has made his living as an independent handyman. Often, he employs workers on a short-term basis for certain projects. The following conflict story, which resembles a crime story, is clearly distinct from the other statements in the same interview (P25:33). [219]

Yes, I employed...a young Coloured man, ahm...who approached me on the street one evening when I was on my way to buy cigarettes. And he asked, he said, that he had noticed that I had, had, was most often packing, ah, paint and building materials into my car or taking them out. Ahm...and he asked me if I didn't have work for him. So, I said: „Yes." I did have work at that time and it was just painting and it was painting and staining, a pretty arbitrary work and we discussed a daily rate which he accepted. Now, he had been living in the street and so, firstly, I gave him some old clothes and a pillow and a blanket and I said I would be quite willing to give him...a night shelter. There is a shelter here in Green Point. Except there are rules there and you have to be in at six in the evening and in return for that you get a hot plate of soup and some bread and you can take a shower. So, anyway, to cut a long story short, he worked for me, ach, for quite ten days and then after that...I paid him on a daily basis. Ahm, and then after that we had another client who asked us to work in a separate apartment in Mouille Point, near the Waterfront. And it's a very luxurious apartment. They own it and they live in it and they let it out to, you know, fairly upper-class, 'cause they charge a high rental, fully furnished and it has a TV and an M-net-decoder and a CD-player etc., etc., video recorder and what have you. So, we had worked together on that project also...and we had worked there a few days...there was, ah... various things that we had to...and we finished there on a Friday afternoon and on the Saturday morning he came to me...asking if we were working today. It was a Saturday. We had coffee first and I said: "No." I didn't need him on that Saturday, 'cause there were a few things that I had to do, that had to be done, but I didn't need his assistance. Then he asked, if he could leave some things in my room. And I said: "Yes, fine." And I was out on the balcony, 'cause we have been out drinking coffee and smoking outside. And...he obviously went into my room and

---

[219] Parallel to the „mystery story"(CS4) this interview contains multiple generalizations, critical and negative comments about Coloureds. An excerpt of this side of the interview is presented in .5.5.1, C9). This conflict story (CS4) differs from the rest of the interview in that it hardly shows any elements of judgment.

without my knowing took the keys to the apartment. And I said to him I was first going out to the airport and then pop in the apartment and get the last of my tools and things. So, he obviously thought, going to the airport I'd be gone at least an hour or two, 'cause I had to go and get a quote there and that would give him the change to go and get into the apartment and to take whatever he wanted. And when I left here about half an hour after he had I couldn't find the keys for the apartment. I looked in my toolbox, I searched my car, came back to my room, I looked everywhere, thought that's very obvious. There were only two of us who know I had the keys: that's the owner and the chap who was working with me. And then I just got a funny feeling. So I phoned the owner and I said: "Look, I seem to have mislayed the keys to your apartment. Do you have another set?" And he said: "Yes, of course." And I said: "Would you be kind enough to meet me there?" And he must have sensed the sort of concern in my voice and so I drove from here straight there, as he did. So did he. But on the way, on his way there, he saw J. coming the opposite direction carrying two refuse bags. And he stopped and he said: "Are you not working today?" And J. said: "No, T. said, he doesn't need me." And the owner then thought: "Well, that's strange." Anyway he drove off. He said, J. was very nervous and didn't want to chat and seemed to be in a terrible hurry. As he drove off, he thought: "Now, hang on...if we are not working together why is he coming from the direction of the flat and carrying two Black bags?" So, he quickly turned around to try and pursue him and of course he had disappeared. So, by the time he got to the flat he knew what he expected. I got there minutes later. And he said, he said: "We are both too late. He has taken the electric draw, he has taken the video recorder and he has taken the CD-player." And the CD-player was brand new. It still had the plastic on it. So, his concern was that now, someone has access to the building. It was a smart building and he went on to the chairman of the body cooperate and to report what had happened and the chairman of the body cooperate said: "You are going to have to replace not only the front door lock, but the locks of...you gonna have to replace every, every residence front door key as well." We phoned the lock smith and the lock smith said: "Yes, I know the building very well." He said: "You are looking at about 4000 or 4500 Rand to do all that." He said: "I am too busy. I won't go there to do it during the next four days." Now, that was on a Saturday and that meant the whole weekend, gonna go through a whole weekend with, with a security risk. And the owner of that flat was, was obviously very concerned and I was feeling very bad. Ahm, and I said to him: "Can we just, can we just hang on a minute? Before you go mad and start over-reacting let's just wait an hour. Would you?" And he said: "I can't. I am going away for the weekend and we must solve out all these things before we go." So, I said: "All right. If I had stolen good that I wanted to sell *quickly for money, I'd go to Cash* Cruisaders who would deal with second hand goods and there is another one called Cash Converters." Ahm, I'd contact a few of the better known pound-shops, I will contact the police and I'd contact that neighborhood watch for that area. Which is what we did. We were able to even give a description of the CD-player and the serial number, 'cause it had been brand new. And then, the owner asked me to wait there, in case anyone should phone and he was contacting his co-owner who also owned an apartment there and...ah...in case the partner phoned there to know what was going on. So, I waited at the flat and within an hour the phone rang and it was the local neighbourhood watch, saying that they apprehended someone, ahm...could I come and identify them. By this time the owner came back to the flat. So, I said: !I am going off to identify him." Sure enough it was J., that youngster, who had firstly lied about his name, about his age, ah...I don't think he was even 18. Ahm, and he told me that sad story that he had been robbed and assaulted and his ID-documents had been stolen. And he was, in the time we worked together, assaulted a couple of times, I didn't realize from being big mouthed and he has had a few beers, you see? So, he was apprehended and when I got to him I said: "I want only three things from you and I certainly will consider dropping charges and will speak to the owners about doing the same. I want the owners belongings back and I would like my drill back." It was a brand new drill and a very expensive one. So, he said: "I can give you the owners things back, but I can't give you the drill." He had offered my drill as a bribe to the construction foreman of a new block of flats that have been built. So he had gone there and said: "Please hide this for me. You can get that as a gift – if you do that." So, the foreman had brought him onto the side and dressed him up with an overall and a helmet. So he looked like one of the casual staff. But fortunately the local neighborhood watch had seen him gone up. Anyway, ah, they took him to the police station and we retrieved all the goods. And, he was kept over the weekend in the police station and it took about 3 or 4 days to get the owners stuff back. And then, about 3 weeks later, we appeared in court. And then came the lies. He told me, ah, that...he told the court that his mother was widowed and unemployed and destitute and if he was imprisoned she would be starved to death. Meanwhile his mother had thrown him out of the house, 'cause he was so bad. Ahm...and that he lived on the streets in Sea Point, because there was just nowhere else he could go. And his family had all said that he was welcomed to stay with them, but he prechoses not to. Ahm, later when I had time to speak to the court I said: "I had offered to pay for his shelter at the shelter in advance, it didn't seem to...he preferred to do the drugs and the prostitution and everything on the streets. And it was very lucrative for him. He liked the lifestyle and he was willing to put up with the discomfort. Ahm, then he said, the reason why he had stolen these goods was I had expected him to do very dangerous work, extremely dangerous work which I wasn't willing to do myself. It was a lie. And secondly he said I never paid him. So, he had to have money to eat and to survive and that's why he took these things. He said, then I...he had a chance to speak to the court first, then I, it was my turn, and also the owner of the flats talked also. He said, he was paid on a daily basis, ahm, so that he could eat and survive and get transport. He accepted the daily rate, I can't remember how much it was, but it was what I am paying my other guys. I had given him clothes, I had given him food, ahm...I mean blankets and what have you and... so, at the end of all this – and the owner had also been very kind to him – ahm...he got a suspended sentence of...an 18 month suspended sentence...ja. So which means that he would have to have gone 6 month in jail for house breaking, but given (me) all the extenuate circumstances and long stories the court lenient with him. So, he was released, ahm...and I said to him as we left the courtroom. I said: "Don't ever come near me again. And don't ask me for a single thing." So, I don't know where he is whether he has been rehabilitated or maybe he saw the fault of his ways. I don't know. He was very street smart. He is an intelligent kid.

And he could really do something with his life. But I mean - already committing crime at that age - what hope is there? (CS4)

This story represents one of the longest, joint narratives in the data material. The underlying conflict is one of the most prevalently discussed in the literature on political and economic conflicts in South Africa: the distribution of resources among the population groups.[220]

An employee of the author steals a key in order to rob the apartment in which he has worked. The object of contention is his appropriation of resources and material goods and his relationship to his employer, the author, whom he has repeatedly given false information about himself.

In order to gain a broader and deeper understanding of the text at hand, it seems appropriate to examine it in the context of the entire interview since there are apparent differences between this conflict story and the rest of the interview. The speaker's statements following the story (see P25:33), making up twice the length of the conflict story itself, are formally much less structured and contain primarily judgmental statements about Coloureds. The author characterizes Coloureds as "devious, calculated, clever and dishonest" (see 5.5.2, C9). These pejorative characteristics shed a certain light on the remarkably neutral wording of the above presented conflict story.

With respect to the biographical background of the author and aspects of its social reality, it should be emphasized that he comes from a rural family from the north west of the country, but has mostly worked in the urban areas on his professional journey. In other conversations, [221] he mentions having positive childhood memories of his relationship with the Zulus, who lived and worked in his surroundings.[222] This is

---

[220] See Johnson (1995), chap. 3.3

[221] In the course of different field stays, many "informal interviews" (P25:33) and numerous informal talks took place with this author.

[222] Comparing the author's identified other-images of Coloureds to those of Blacks (5.5.1, C9), it becomes clear that his image of Blacks is much more positive. The reason could be that he grew up with Blacks, mostly Zulus, making this population group more familiar. On the other hand, the speaker has had much contact with Coloureds, since his move to Cape Town, mostly with those who tend to belong to the lower class, thus coming from a specific social milieu. They live mostly on the street, like the man he hired in the above story (CS4). Consequently, his knowledge of Coloureds is based on experiences with people of a specific social class, yet he applies it in a generalizing way to the whole group of Coloureds.

reflected in one of his statements: "I have had more dishonest dealings with Coloureds than I have had with Blacks." In the course of his varied work life in Cape Town, the author has met many Coloureds. His social situation and status are of interest in that he has undergone a process of deprivation. While up to the 1990s his entrepreneurial undertakings promised success and a future, his present career state points to a depreciated social status and even to the possibility of unemployment. Since the loss of his job at the end of apartheid, his standard of living has clearly declined. Accordingly, his societal and social status, his living situation and his social environment have changed. Because of his age and the socio-political circumstances, he now does not have the chance of employment in his former field of expertise. The author's statements about Coloureds have to be understood in light of his deteriorated social circumstances.

Looking at the interview as a whole, the author tries to illustrate in this "crime story" in an objective way what he later expresses as explicit subjective opinions. By confining himself to factual, descriptive language in the story, he intends to report the events in an objective, (unemotional) and suspenseful way. But during the subsequent two thirds of the interview, in response to the interviewer's inquiries following the "crime story," the author expresses his emotional tensions, which manifest themselves particularly in judgments of Coloureds. Here, his messages come across as self-revelations in sharp contrast to the relatively neutral elaborations of the first part of the interview.

In content, the topic and starting question in the story deal with a conflict between the author and a hired hand from the Coloured Community. This basic constellation is the core of the crime story. The topic could be: "No hope for Coloured criminals." The narrative unit is structured like a detective story with multicultural characters. In the introduction, the author describes the coincidental moment when a "Coloured man" approaches him, which introduces the main characters of the story: the "generous, White handyman," and the "poor, Coloured street boy," who is looking for a job. The first practical step in the employment arrangement is that the White man generously sees to it that the Coloured man's basic needs are met: "Now, he had been living in the street and so firstly I gave him some old clothes and a pillow and a blanket and I said I would be quite willing to give him...a night shelter." The status difference between the two main characters creates the tension, which then is unfolded in the drama. The main part of the drama introduces a third figure, the owner of a luxury apartment of White upper class standing. He wants his apartment to be renovated by the White handyman, who comes to him recommended by friends. The renovation work is almost finished. The author now zooms in on the course of events of a double theft. In a breach of trust, the Coloured man steals the key to the luxury apartment. The so far cooperating protagonists now become antagonists. The thief grabs as many prestigious objects as he can from the apartment and his employer's tools.

In the following, another character constellation comes to the fore: the White man from the upper class and the White man from the middle class. In harmonious cooperation, they perform a detective race to find the stolen property and the disappeared thief. In the course of further criminological events, other characters come to the scene: the neighborhood watch, the street boy's family of origin, and finally, as the highest institution for solving the case, the court.

In the end, the handyman makes a dramatic appeal to the thief, never to contact him again. This appeal peaks in the rhetorical question that marks the finale of the detective story: "What hope is there?"

Dramatically, this detective story has a complex structure. The exposition introduces the main characters and also establishes the plot: what will the cooperation between the middle class White man and the lower class, Coloured young man look like? The listener finds that the cooperation develops at first successfully– the work project is mostly completed – but that then the key disappears in a moment of inattentiveness of the White man. The drastic change consists in the fact that the leading characters suddenly become adversaries. Climax and *peripeteia* of the "drama" are the accomplished recovery of the property of the third figure, the White apartment owner, and the second figure, the White handyman. Various delaying mini-episodes point to two likely solutions: either the case is settled in an amicable way, outside of court, or ultimately in court. The narrator gives an account of the repeated, successful interventions of the communal neighborhood watch and the mother of the thief. But in the end, the court stuns us with its decision: The defendant is pardoned instead of receiving a long-term sentence. At first, this appears to be a positive result for the defendant. However, not the court has the last word, but the narrator of this short story. He can look ahead into the far future of the seemingly spared thief. He anticipates another type of justice awaiting the thief: the hopelessness of his existence ("What hope is there?")

With respect to some of his central linguistic means, it is striking that the word phrases and sentence part sequences run fluently without much subordination, following the so-called *paratactic* narrative style. He uses enlivening interjections only a few times, for example, to bridge the exposition and the escalating action (line 8ff): 'So, anyway, to cut a long story short, he worked for me, ach, for quite ten days and then after that....I paid him on a daily basis. Ahm, and then...." At some places, he interrupts his paratactic narrative flow by citation, symptomatic for his distant, reporting style (L 4): "Yes." This short "Yes" signals agreement. It is an assertive "Yes" that points to the cooperation of the leading characters. The second "break-in" of citation occurs in line 16: "No," equally short, followed by the author's explanatory remark: "I didn't need him on that Saturday (...) I didn't need his assistance." This "No" marks the change from assisting to distancing communication between the protagonists. While this examination of the portions of *oratio oblique* compared to the quotations could easily be continued with probably more interesting results, here it must suffice to simply point out the skilled narrative use of quotation in this detective story.

Next to the artful structure of this criminological "drama," the author also uses expert terminology, particularly special terms from the field of law, in the context of the trial at the end of the main part: "lenient," "released," "suspended sentence," "extenuate circumstances" and "rehabilitated." These findings suggest that the author wants to present a detective-like, legal situation, in which the inter-cultural aspect plays a minor role compared to the social status of the protagonist. The story can be categorized as a detective story, which plays a special role in the Anglo-American literary tradition and which also seems to be consistent with the author's cultural background and his personal interests, as he has mentioned in other conversations. We do not know whether the characters in this story are real people in real conflict situations or whether the author mainly delivers a poetic stylization of these characters. For the latter possibility speaks the rest of the intervie, in which the author openly and explicitly expresses his true attitude and feelings towards Coloureds, thereby casting an interpretive light on the story.

In summary, this short story deals partly with materialistic, partly with ideological-personal values. At the start, the author explains that, as an independent handyman, he employs people on a day's wage basis. Apparently, he understands work as a "survival value," consistent with Dzobo (see 1.4). In this case, his employee lives on the street, and the narrator offers him clothes, a pillow, a blanket and even the fee for a night at the homeless shelter. Also, in the following description of the apartment to be renovated, material objects stand the center of interest: "TV, M-net-decoder, CD-player" etc. In the end, it is the earning of "quick money" that gives away the thief since the narrator understands his value priorities. While, until now, the story includes only once the value of safety in the form of "security risk," since the perpetrator has continued access to the building, in the second part of the story, the immaterial values come to the fore. The author appears to appreciate the value of honesty since he describes with dismay that his employee lied several times. This observation of lying is now underlined by the description of the boy's family situation. The author emphasizes that not even his family stands behind him, because his behavior is so "bad." By showing how the boy has lost his family's trust, the author also shows the value of family connections. In the context of these values of honesty and family, the speaker reverts back to the importance of the material goods, such as his drill, the stolen goods, the money, and the above-mentioned gifts to the defendant. Only in the very end, the author comments on the boy as being "street smart" and "intelligent," who could "do something with his life," thus entering the world of positive, personal values of the young man, which unfortunately seem to be obscured by the immoral ones. It is striking that the narrator names here in his conclusion the value of "active life shaping," but at the same time denies the antagonist. these virtues. Since the young man has already committed a crime, he sees no hope for him. Thus *hope*, as an important Christian value, stands in the end of the story, but only in the form of abandoned hope. In the author's view, the boy's other value priorities prevent him from investing his positive qualities, such as "intelligence" and "smartness," in morally acceptable behavior.

This story, too, contains values that play a role in the visionary, national value discourses. Looking at the *balance concept of power, equality,* and *unity in diversity,* which are the corner stones of the Rainbow Nation concept, the following can be said for this conflict story:

While the listener in the beginning gets the impression that a spontaneously built, intercultural work team forms a unit – despite racial, cultural and social diversity - with the purpose to renovate a luxury apartment, it becomes increasingly clear that this work team actually is the opposite of a unit. Instead, it is divided by differences of social class, life styles and social milieus. Already at the start, there is a conspicuous social imbalance with respect to power and power distribution. The upper class employer, the middle class employee and the lower class day laborer work in the interest of the first on his apartment, which in itself implies a power imbalance between employer and employee. In addition, there is a social, economic, and educational imbalance between the three main characters, which actually make up the framework of the story and which constitute the plot to some extent. The rainbow concept, while applied on the surface since people of different socio-cultural and racial affiliations work together, does not come to bear in the sense of a fulfilled unity since the participants bring different interests and values into the situation, especially because of the unequal distribution of goods and resources. On one hand, this story deals with materialistic values, on the other hand with ideological values. In his working relationship with the Coloured assistant, personal values are important to the author, which he later finds missing in the employee. After the theft, he reveals the "bad" character of the young man. Here the author refers to values that consistently play a role in the national visions, such as *goodness of men* (Biko), and the religious-spiritual motivated *moral behavior,* and *moral attitudes* (Mandela) and the *moral character of a person* (Teffo/Roux), which the author cannot find in this young man. Prinsloo, too, names values such as *morality* in Ubuntu and assigns it to *personhood. Personhood* should be characterized by a *good moral personal behavior,* to which theft, of course, is the absolute opposite. The speaker criticizes the thief for his lack of moral behavior, thus indicating his sense of *justice.* Likewise, Mandela and Coetze demand *justice* for felonies and "immoral behavior," because they are damaging to society. In the Ubuntu-concept, justice is also combined with the value of *truth.* The narrator asks for honesty consistent with *truth.* He complains about the lies of the employee, who portrayed himself in court as having been cruelly exploited, instead of showing *gratitude* towards his employer for his generously help. Especially for Tutu, the Christian value of *gratitude* plays a prominent role in this story. The author repeatedly highlights his generous offering of material goods, such as clothes, and how important he finds the *fulfillment of material needs*, which Tutu demands for the whole society. With regard to the thief in this story, the value of the material is linked to the values of *giving, taking and sharing"* (Ubuntu) since on his flight from the security forces, he bargains with the foreman of the construction site – maybe a person of similar social class – and receives a hide-out in exchange for the tool *(reciprocity/*Ubuntu*)*. He shares his material goods to guarantee his *security* before the police. Again, the value of *human security*, which Mandela and Mbeki propagate, plays a role here – for the thief, who seeks a safe hide-out, and for the apartment owner and the middle class worker, who restore the security of the building by catching the thief. Marginally, the value of *family* comes into play. The thief argues that he has to work for his mother to save her from starvation, referring here to his *primary obligations* (Coetzee). Even if he is lying, he can expect understanding and more social acceptance of his actions when they are seen in the context his family's struggle for survival. However, his family, according to the author, has already thrown him out because of his previous "immoral" behavior and does not back him up. Thus, as already in CS1, CS2, and CS3, the family comes into the reader's view as valuable frame of reference. This time, the value of family membership is tied to the value of moral behavior.

In summary, it can be said that the author demands many values consistent with the national value discussion. Some he sees unfulfilled in the thief's behavior and actions; others he finds important and visionary.

Looking at the question which form of multiculturalism the author implicitly conveys through his daily experiences, the reader gets the impression that he describes aspects of both *critical* and *difference multiculturalism*. On one hand, he shows that he as a White man works together with a Coloured man, forming a working team, which basically creates a new work culture, individually, culturally and racially. Both men work together in line with *critical multiculturalism*. While it is extraordinary to the author that he as a White man employs a Coloured person, he describes the employee right at the beginning as "Coloured man," which shows that he spontaneously reduces him to his racial affiliation and separates himself from him.

Even if this short story does not make it absolutely clear, other parts of the interview show (see C9, 5.5.1) that his reality perception and construction contain features of *difference multiculturalism*. The speaker categorizes his surroundings in terms of group-specific characteristics, emphasizing separateness in that he presents differences as absolute facts, not as "differences-in-relation." It can be concluded that for the author both forms of multiculturalism exist, but that his everyday impressions and his reality constructions have to be assigned to *difference multiculturalism*.

5.6.5 The Twenty-First

The following two selections come from an interview (P19:27) with a White, Afrikaans speaking pastor of the Dutch Reformed Church in Cape Town.[223] The pastor lived and worked several years in a Coloured township. Since his appointment to his present, predominantly White congregation in Three Anchor Bay, he has promoted intercultural dialogue to open the church to members of other groups. This mainly happens through prayer circles, church choirs, and special church events.

He remembers two concrete conflict experiences involving the Coloured Community in his previous church, which – as he puts it – helped him to find access to certain cultural practices of this community, and simultaneously start a reflection process with respect to his understanding of self, others and culture:

> The Coloured people, for example, they, if they, if they...doing, at the 21, when one of the children get 21, you know, they have big party. That is actually bigger than a wedding or a funeral. And it's a very important for them. And that has been one of the conflict situation that I have been in. Because I think: "Ach, that is non-sense. 21 is just a birthday. That is not such a big event." And they have got such a big event in P.... all the times ...and Sunday morning, nobody is in church, because they left in the early mornings at the 21... ah...celebration...my council...my church council...so, I was standing there alone, because P. has got a 21 and the whole congregation, the whole community is at the birthday, everyone is invited. And that is not something that is common to our White people...we don't think like that about the 21, you know? So, and they give a lot of money out

---

[223] The reader can find further text excerpts by the same author are in R4, 5.4.2, WA2, 5.5.4, and CS6, 5.6.6.

for that occasion, it, it, it's ...one that I was involved was,...they haven't got the money, but everybody is giving money...the friends, giving money, the aunts are giving money, ...so that specific one was around 20000 Rand was the occasion, was the price, or was the cost of the occasion, you know? So, and...it was very funny for me. On the other side the church in P. was struggling, because they haven't got money...and they don't even think of the 20000 Rand that they give out and that was very strange to me....that Sunday morning I was preaching and I mentioned the 21, mentioned, ja: "I wonder if the Lord is...is...is going to announce that he has got a 21...if everybody in the community will come to his 21." And they were so furious. They actually made me to, to apologize in public for that, because that was, as they saw it, was insensitive and whatever. They said that they feel very strong about it.

And the other thing is, if it is a girl, the boy, they don't worry about it, but if it is a girl it must be that, the girl must be a virgin at that stage. Ah, of the 21. And she must wear White, she must display it to the community, because even if she is not a virgin at that moment she mustn't wear White, she must wear ...any other color. So, it is a play to the community. They are cheering, actually cheering about that. And that is the thing that ...we Whites don't understand, you know.(CS5)

This excerpt is striking because of the complexity of the topic. In the center of the conflict stands the tradition of Coloureds to celebrate the 21st birthday as a rite of passage, which is incompatible with the Christian tradition of Sunday worship. The first part of the topic deals with the description of the 21st birthday feast and is then extended to a comparison between traditions of Afrikaans, or Whites. The author inserts that this story is a conflict situation he himself experienced. The antithesis of the first part goes as follows: by playing down the value of the birthday party, he tries to build a cognitive consonance with the listener. He contrasts his own way of thinking by stating that the "21 celebration" is a huge event for Coloureds.

The speaker enters the story by immediately naming the participating population groups: "The Coloured people for example..." He describes the ritual and tells us that the feast is bigger than a wedding or funeral. With this depiction, he establishes right away a connection to himself and the interviewer, who both belong to the White, Christian community. For Christians, weddings and funerals are both huge festive events, which, until this day, take place in the framework of church and religion. Since the 21st birthday has, in the pastor's mind, no relationship to religious faith, the party tradition turns into a conflict experience for him. The interests and preferences of the parties are very different and incompatible. The pastor expects Sunday worship as usual, while the parishioners want the party at the same time. Their value priority clearly clashes with the pastor's: "Because I think: "Ach, that is non-sense. 21 is just a birthday. That is not such a big event." Coming from an Afrikaans background, where such a tradition does not exist, he cannot understand the importance of this rite of passage. Hence, initially his thoughts on the subject are quite ethnocentric.

In the second sub-topic, he talks about the consequences of their conflicting values. One Sunday morning he, the preacher, finds himself alone in the church, because the whole congregation, including his church council, attend a 21st birthday party. Even though, or maybe *because* he is the pastor, he is excluded from the feast and therefore, feels hurt. He underscores his deep consternation about the absence of even the church council with a clarifying *correctio:* "my council, my church council", framed by interjections and pauses. The narration peaks in a pronouncement: "I was standing there alone." The subsequent causal sentence intensifies this statement of loneliness: "..and the whole congregation, the whole community is at the birthday, everyone is invited." Here one can recognize that the *correctio* underlines his deep hurt. And yet, it appears, as if he wants to hide this personally important fact by way of *aposiopesis* since he does not say: "Everyone was invited - except me." We do not know the reasons why this congregation did not invite their pastor – whether it had to do with his position in the congregation, his racial or cultural affiliation, or simply personal reasons. Possibly, the hosts of the party knew that their pastor would disagree with their timing of the feast and simply wanted to circumvent an unpleasant conflict. But it is interesting that the author occupies a role that excludes him from the circle of party guests. In his story he emphasizes the cultural and racial factors that differentiate him from his parishioners. "And this is not something that is common to our White people...we don't think like that about the 21, you know?" Suddenly he no longer defines himself as the parish pastor, who stands abandoned in his church, but as a member of an ethnic group. He now bases his lack of appreciation for the importance of the celebration not on personal values, but on his belonging to a certain cultural group. Exactly at this point, he makes contact with the interviewer to confirm that she as a White person can understand him.

The third part of the topic deals with a money matter. The author is obviously very upset about the huge amounts of money that the parishioners spend on the 21st birthdays. The judgement burns on his tongue " So, and they give a lot of money out for that occasion, it, it, it's...one that I was involved was..." He begins to stutter - *iteratio verbi*- again with a concluding *aposiopesis,* the withholding of what he actually means; he swallows his judgment. But he is clearly irritated by the fact that the congregation has money for a party, but not for the church, whom he represents. His irritation becomes palpable in this antithetical wording: "It was very funny for me." Further, he comments: "they don't even think of the 20, 000 Rand that they give out and that was very strange to me." This perceived thoughtlessness in expenditures points to the self-evident readiness with which Coloureds invest their money on this party, and again, to their differing value priorities: the congregation prefers to spend money on their traditional feast and persons from their midst, rather than on their church.

The forth part sheds light on the author's response to the Sunday events. With the power of the word, he wants to make the congregation see their fault. In an analogy, he compares God with the birthday child, in order to put the people rhetorically under pressure: Would every parishioner come to God's birthday party? It is striking that the author with this analogy uses a scenic narrative style, concrete in his literal speech, which points to his emotional involvement and to the climax of the story: "I wonder if the Lord is...is...is going to announce that he has got a 21...if everybody in the community will come to his 21." The only citation in this excerpt is from the sermon (the pulpit speech) of the author, in which he indirectly compares himself with Christ, hinting that the Lord Jesus Christ would have been left just as lonely as he himself on that memorable Sunday morning. He lets them know that they have not acted in Christ's spirit. He makes God the moral authority, the judge over "correctness" and acceptability of cultural and religious practice. He now asks the congregation indirectly, but provocatively, to acknowledge God. Here the pastor's personal hurt about being excluded and not being informed shimmers through. He, the preacher of God's word, projects his own experience of being left out onto God. He asks the church to re-dedicate themselves to God.

This does not sit well with the congregation. The preacher's public apology makes up the fifth part of the topic, to which he refers also in CS6. Here, too, the author does not pass judgement on the reaction of the congregation, but simply points out their perceived feelings: "They were furious", and that they find the preacher "insensitive". Obviously, these strong feelings ("feel very strong") behind that vehement reaction cause him to cave in and apologize in front of the church. As the author demonstrates here, this public apology is culturally highly important in the Coloured Community, as it often is the case in Bantu groups. Public apologies are demanded instead of private ones. Pushed to the defensive, the author complies with the church's demand since he does not see another way to solve the conflict.

Finally, the sixth portion of the topic addresses a gender issue. The author introduces us to a remarkable custom: "And the other thing is..." In a reporting style, he conveys that a woman is expected to be still a virgin on her 21st birthday. She has to display this fact in public by wearing a White dress on her birthday, or another color, if she is not a virgin anymore. In the narrator's view, this is a highly valued rite in the Coloured Community. In an inserted subordinated sentence, he adds that a 21-year-old man does not have to demonstrate his "intactness" publicly. Hence, this important rite of passage is different for women and men. In wearing White, women are supposed to symbolize their "purity" and "intactness," representing certain moral values and attitudes, while sexual behavior before and after the 21st birthday is sanctioned for young men. The author tells us about the pleasure that the community derives from watching this public display ("play to the community") of generally accepted, gender specific values and norms: "They are cheering, actually cheering about that." He repeats "cheering" as if he cannot understand their excitement. He almost appears appalled and irritated about this unequal presentation of men and women. He concludes by saying: "And that is the thing...we Whites don't understand, you know?" It is interesting that the author, despite his social reality as a man, cannot understand this unequal public treatment of men and women. Equal rights for men and women appear to be a fundamental value to him, which he, as a Western-oriented man with European family background, has internalized to such a degree that he cannot accept such obviously unequal ritual. Pointing beyond the gender differences between himself and the interviewer, he now claims race as basis for his lack of understanding. Through a rhetorical, slightly suggestive question, he places the White interviewer on his side. She has no opportunity to respond since the answer is already a given.

The complexity of the main subject, the 21st birthday, is reflected in alternating narrative perspectives, and various narrative styles. While in the beginning the *auctorial* style dominates, the author interlocks inner monologues revealing his feelings about the 21st birthday tradition. In other parts, he comes into view as the I-narrator, like: "I was standing there alone." In commenting inserts, he reflects on differences in values between the racial groups. Finally, the short episode about money sounds very involved (see *aposiopesis*).

In this conflict story, the author highlights differences in value orientations between the White and Coloured Community. He confronts the (traditional) value of the 21st birthday, held by Coloureds, with the value of Sunday worship attendance, held by the church. Relevant in this context is also the value of *community* and the use of money. In addition, the author depicts the high value of public apology in the Coloured Community, which he, as a representative of the White Afrikaans society, finds irrelevant and irritating. As shown in the conflict examples CS3 and CS6, the tension between privacy and public is an issue of conflict in intercultural encounters. On one hand, there is the public apology, and, on the other hand, the public display of virginity. The author rejects both forms of public staging.

According to the speaker, Coloureds have a particular appreciation for the value of *community*. In the theoretical value discussions, too, the *community of brothers and sisters* (Biko), *brotherhood* (Mbeki) and the realization of *culture and community* (Coetzee), are essential values. This community develops as part of the *extended family concepts* (Ubuntu). The narrator portrays the Coloureds as having a strong *network of relationships (Tutu)*, strong value of mutual care *(concern for each other*/Biko*)*, of *solidarity and friendship (Biko)*, at least with respect to their in-group. In regard to the 21st birthday party, the speaker hits on values, such as *communication, cooperation and interaction* of the parishioners, which include the participation and *creative expression* of all community members. The author sees himself and the Coloured church members on opposite sides. To him, *God, religion* (/Mandela), and the rite of worship are highly important (*worship and God*/Biko), associated with *spirituality* (Mbeki), *(spiritual fulfillment* /Tutu), the subsequent *spiritual-religious experience,* and *African Humanism.* All these values in the realm of religion, spirituality and worship are of central importance to the pastor. Surely, they are also important to the parishioners, but given a choice between Sunday worship and traditional feast, their priority is very clear. In this situation, the author's reality construction as a pastor, is particularly determined by theological aspects, just as Teffo and Raux describe it *(reality of theological aspects).* When the speaker expresses his opinion about the Sunday morning event, the congregation is upset. Only his public apology, which costs him quite some energy, can reinstate *harmony, peace and anti-racism* (Tutu) between him and the pardoning congregation.

This conflict exemplifies an attempt by the pastor to realize the unity in diversity in the church as God's space. He recognizes the socio-cultural identities and ethnic diversities and tries to synthesize them in his church in the spirit of the "Rainbow Nation of God." [224] But he is not able to completely integrate this vision into his daily life because he comes up against his own limits of accepting the competing values. The priorities of parishioners and pastor do not lead to a unity between them, but rather to conflict-ridden differences. Granted that the speaker pursues the ideal-typical values of the *critical multiculturalism* and envisions a negotiation of differences of culture- related values and to clarify priorities, but in this particular situation he is not successful in initiating a dialogue. He comes only as far as realizing that his perspective is ethnocentric and that he has to come to grips with his limits to understand a phenomenon of a foreign culture. Even though he performs the public apology in order to solve the conflict, he continues to emphasize the difference between himself and the Coloureds, which he sees mostly as cultural. In some parts, it appears as if the author is inclined to "culturalize." He interprets all the described behaviors of the Coloureds and

---

[224] In his comments on the Rainbow Nation, the speaker calls it a miracle that the South Africans – despite great conflict potential and chances for intercultural misunderstanding – have come together in such a peaceful way. He sees the Rainbow Nation as a vision, which needs to be implemented through interactions and behaviors of the respective groups on the grassroots level (see R4, 5.4.2) (see R4, 5.4.2). But it becomes obvious that this implementation is difficult for the author, despite his high degree of reflection and his good intentions.

his   own   attitudes   before   the   cultural   background.
as White South African. His personal opinions and priorities, which are part of his
individual identity, his personality as pastor, as a male, as a Capetonian, as a Christian,
do not seem to matter here. Instead, he reduces all his personality aspects to his "White
culture," which he contrasts with the "Coloured culture." He views the differences as
fixed facts that Whites are unable to comprehend, instead of seeing them as relationship-
dependent variables of cultural relativity. Even though the author makes an effort to
reflect on and change his perceptions, *difference multiculturalism* dominates his
everyday perceptions.

5.6.6 The Choir

Next to the "Twenty-first," another story from the same interview (P19:27) comes
into view. Here, the speaker experiences another conflict with the Coloured Community,
which occurred in his present church. Again, he ends up apologizing publically, this
time before a choir:

The Choir of the P.[225] congregation was invited to this church, there was a service
here. That was the main part of this. It was actually like a musical. Like do certain
parts of the order, they will do it...the Benediction and they will sing it, you
know? So, it was a very big event and, ah …unfortunately…the driver (laughing)
got drunk the previous night and ...and (laughing) and they didn't show up
here…(laughing). So, it's a two hours drive from P. to Cape Town. And they
didn't show up. The service started at half past nine and at nine o'clock they
phoned me from P. and say: "We can't make it." And so, I was...I must conduct
the service and the main part of the service is the choir here...and...I haven't got a
sermon. So, it was a difficult …luckily…one of my guys, my organist is also a
singer and I just phoned the guy and...: "You must sing everything you can sing,
you must sing "I love changes" everything... then you must sing that, you know?
Or everything you can sing you must sing!.".. And, ah,...but after the service they

---

[225] P. Is a small village in the Western Cape, about two driving hours away from the church of the
pastor.

showed up...I think they felt guilty and they got another driver and they showed up and that was actually one of the other big conflict situations I was in and I was so furious and I said: "No, I can't do anything now. The service is over. All I can say to you is: "Go down to the beach and sing to the people over there!."" (laughing) I was rude....(laughing)...and they actually wrote me a letter, where they want me, ...they see me still like somebody who is ..ah...ah...not forget the past and, you know, and...those situation was immediately placed in: "You are White and we are Coloured." You know? And I spoke to the conductor and...the conductor and me we are very good friends, you know?...And...ahm, house friends...close friends...and I spoke to the conductor and she was also not very happy about my way of handling the situation and, and now, because I was so disappointed...the first thing that was coming out of my mouth was...when I saw them...was to say something that...that...let them feel the same way I feel. You know? And was wrong...I know, I was wrong and I apologized to her and she apologized to...we spoke about that a lot of times and...but they wrote me a letter, the choir, the chairman and he asked me to come to the choir and apologize. That is a very big thing for them. You must apologize in public. That's why...they want you to confess...they want you to confess...and....ahm....it must be publicly...it mustn't be private...because private isn't good enough. It is not...they want to feel good when you stand up before a lot of people and say that you are sorry, that you done this or that to them. That's why they always ask the White people in South Africa to do it publicly. And the White people they don't understand, because they think: "Well, we already said that we are sorry about Apartheid and most of us, the younger people didn't even know what was happening in South Africa. They.... they were just going on with the way their parents and their grandparents going on.... (CS6)

On a formal syntactical level, this text has two clearly structured sections of roughly the same length. In the first section, the author describes the irritating situation that an invited choir arrives with a two- hour delay – after the service.

The speaker mostly operates with paratactic phrases, whose flow is irregular and interrupted by numerous insertions and pauses: "So, it was a very big event and, ah,...unfortunately...the driver (laughing) got drunk the previous night and ...and (laughing) and they didn't show up here...(laughing)." To him, this invitation was a big event. He laughs when he talks about the choir having to cancel because of a drunken driver. The fact that the choir comes after all, but too late for the service, turns into one of the pastor's biggest conflict experiences. Furious, he sends them away: "All I can say to you is: "Go down to the beach and sing to the people over there!" (laughing).

The introductory part of this section is relaxed by the interviewee's five laughs. His laughing – "the analogue form of communication" (transl.), according to Watzlawick (2003:61f) – accompanies an almost comical short story about a choir, who entrusts a driver with the extremely important task to chauffeur them to a long- planned event, only to find him so drunk on that day that he cannot fulfil his task, thereby spoiling the whole service. The author laughs especially about his attempt to send the choir to the beach, and, finally, about his own state of mind. He is uncomfortable with his own "rude" behavior, his reprimanding of the choir since it is inconsistent with his social role as the pastor.

In the second section, he reflects on this situation before the background of his apartheid experiences. Here he leaves his humour behind and enters another level of perceiving and narrating by considering some questions in the ongoing interview situation. Especially the question of public confessions and apologies in the Coloured Community, as well as his coming to grips with apartheid time, point to the deep-seated dimension of the conflict. One gets the feeling that the ease and inner distance to the events are gone. Instead, the author's statements now explicitly focus on his disappointment and negative feelings. He receives a written reaction to his rude choice of words: "...and they actually wrote me a letter, where they want me, ...they see me still like somebody who is. ..ah...ah...not forget the past and, you know, and...those situation was immediately placed in: "You are White and we are Coloured. "You know?" This conflict, which until this moment could be considered an everyday occurrence, as it could happen anywhere in the world, now takes on a different character, which die author brings to light by using quotations. The choir members think the pastor cannot forget apartheid. In a letter they tell him their interpretation of his behavior. They believe that the pastor could only have treated them in that disrespectful way because they are Coloured and not regarded as equals. Thus, they perceive and interpret the situation according to categories and patterns from the past. In the author's view, the choir members are the ones imposing the "race conflict" component. The author himself seems to feel only angry about the choir's unreliability, unpunctuality and short-term cancellation.[226] In this case, we would be dealing with a value conflict concerning behavior in the area of time management, planning, and public accountability. While the pastor feels "dropped" by the choir, the choir members don't feel appreciated for the fact that they came at all. The pastor's angry and direct style of communication, which he himself calls "rude," makes them feel devalued and disrespected. They interpret this disrespect as an expression of racism, instead of looking at the possibility of culture-specific differences in dealing with such a conflict situations.

The collision of pastor and late choir takes on a historically orientated, collective component, which will characterize perceptions, expressions and behaviors from now on. Suddenly, the pastor feels guilty and finds himself in a defensive position (again). Now, he is not only burdened with the "guilt" of having been unkind and angry towards the Coloured choir, but also by the load of centuries of White colonialism and, especially, fifty years of Afrikaans apartheid. The roles here are clearly defined: the White pastor plays the guilty one, the perpetrator who has to apologize to the victims for his crime. From an etic perspective, this situation appears twisted. Wasn't it the choir who did not live up to their agreement because of a drunk driver? There is no mention of an apology by the choir for their failure to arrive on time, which is at the bottom of this conflict. On the contrary, the author seems to be so much caught in his thinking patterns of collective guilt and compensation that the thought of the choir needing to apologize *to him* does not even occur to him.

Further into the story, the pastor's closest confidante, whom he calls his "very good friend," comes into view. Not even she can understand his behavior. He expresses this in an especially pronounced *anacoluthon*.

---

[226] This interpretation seems justified since the speaker repeatedly emphasizes in different parts of the interview how important long- term planning and preparation of public presentations are to White Afrikaans speakers (see WA2, 5.5.4). Since he stands right before his public performance when he is informed of the choir cancellation, this should be reason enough to throw him off. It can be assumed that the pastor would have been equally furious if a White choir had cancelled with that kind of excuse. But it is hard to clarify in which way racial factors influenced his angry reaction.

> And I spoke to the conductor and...the conductor and me we are very good
> friends, you know?...And...ahm, house friends...close friends...and I spoke
> to the conductor and she was also not very happy about my way of handling
> the situation and, and, now, because I was so disappointed...the first thing
> that was coming out of my mouth was...when I saw them was to say
> something that...that...let them feel the same way I feel. You know?"

This laborious *anacoluthon* is accompanied by a *correctio,* "good friends, house friends, close friends." It has to be noted that this portion of speech is interrupted by eight pauses, which point to a constant oscillating between speaking and thinking, a cautiousness that might also indicate the author's desire to choose appropriate – that is, politically correct and primarily denotative – words in front of the interviewer. He explains that his own feeling of disappointment triggered in him the wish to disappoint the choir in return. He ends his explanation by addressing the interviewer ("you know?"), hoping that at least *she* might understand that his reaction to the disappointment was simply human and not tied to racism. But the choir's vehement response is ruled by the old apartheid schemes and points to a deeply rooted, collective inferiority complex. The choir, who in some way stages its own "inferior victim" role, demands the "culprit's" apology, and since their apartheid scheme tabs into its counterpart in the pastor, he now feels guilty and looses sight of the actual origin of the conflict.

The required apology is a deep-seated cultural feature. The speaker apologizes privately to his confidante, who acts as a spokesperson for the choir and whom he asks to pass his apology on to the others. But this private gesture is not accepted, and again - as before in the conflict story CS5 – he delivers a public apology, this time to the choir. The author now explains, through a change of perspective, why the public apology is so important to Coloureds:

> That's why...they want you to confess...they want you to confess...
> and...ahm...it must be publicly...it mustn't be private...because private
> isn't good enough. It is not...they want to feel good when you stand up
> before a lot of people and say that you are sorry, that you done this or that

to them. That's why they always ask the White people in South Africa to do it publicly." [227]

The religious term *confess*[228] is of central importance here. When a person confesses his/her sin, it happens in the context of assuming guilt [229] and responsibility. According to the author, the Coloureds — the use of third person singular leaves it open whether he means the choir members in particular, or the community of Coloureds in general — want to move the speaker to make a confession. At this point, he intentionally chooses a religiously loaded term to dramatize his feeling of standing before a high authority, a court, asking for pardon. Interestingly, the situation is mixed up. Actually, the pastor as the preacher of the gospel symbolizes and represents a higher authority, preaching and dispensing the forgiveness of sins. But here the pastor is in the role of the confessor, which probably means a loss of face to him in his cultural, professional and social position (see also 5.5.4, WA2). [230]

On one hand, the public apology is symbolically the key to the "freedom from guilt" and to a peaceful conflict resolution. On the other hand, it triggers intra-psychic conflicts in the narrator because of his social position. And yet, he complies with the demand. Even though it is probably hard for him, and even though he feels that a private apology is sufficient, he tries to understand the choir's thinking by switching to their perspective and emotional level. He assumes that the reason for them demanding the public apology is that they "want to feel good."

---

[227] This statement gives the impression that Coloureds aim particularly at Whites for public apologies. There is no hint that this kind of public apology is also practiced within their own group. Thus, the author seems to understand this event from a racial standpoint and as a consequence of apartheid.

[228] From a formal standpoint, the second part of the interview is also interesting in that word repetitions increase here, as: "I was wrong", apologize", confess." In the latter example, there is not only a word repetition, but also a sentence repetition, which is interrupted by self-reflective pauses. Through these repetitions and pauses, the author indirectly shows the depth of his remembered experience. Further redundancies occur in the use of the words "public" and "private", obviously because the public (versus private) nature of the confession ("I was wrong") is especially important. Amazingly, despite the apparently extremely unpleasant experiences and events, the author avoids – probably not lastly thanks to the many self-reflective pauses – denotative word usage.

[230] However, before experiencing this face loss himself, the pastor has already inflicted the same humiliation on the others by his impolite behavior. They demand his public apology as their culture-specific way of processing and solving a conflict. In the tradition of Bantu groups the public confession of guilt is the condition for the pardoning and reacceptance of the conflict partner into the community.

After looking at the Coloured perspective, the speaker looks at the in-group perspective of White South Africans, underlining the durability and current relevance of this issue by the *oratio directa:*

> And the White people they don't understand, because they think: "Well, we already said that we are sorry about Apartheid and most of us, the younger people didn't even know what was happening in South Africa." They... they were just going on with the way their parents and their grandparents going on.

Suddenly, while explaining White peoples' rejection of public apology, the speaker finds himself in a defensive position. In the center of this quotation stands the Whites' argument that they already apologized for apartheid, and that especially the young generation - to whom the speaker belongs – is innocent. Hence, the end of this conflict story is characterized by the author's self-justification and an appeal not to make the young South Africans responsible for the past.

For the listener, this end marks a last great change in the story. Our attention is now diverted from the pastor's behavior on that Sunday to the behavior of the White immigrants during the last centuries, which requires reparations and apologies on every level. In the last lines, the author, as pastor, virtually takes on the collective guilt for apartheid. At the same time, he unburdens and defends the young White generation for unconsciously taking over the ancestors' behavior forms and life styles. The generally presented status of the Whites as "culprits" he converts into that of "victims." They, too, are victims of apartheid and in need of "acquittal." The depth of the conflict reflected here requires a coming to terms with apartheid and especially reconciliation on an inter-personal and inter-group level as an integral part of societal transformation.

A comparison of the theoretical approaches in chapter 3 shows that the author here – as apparent already in CS5 and R4 - is torn between the ideal of *critical multiculturalism* and the everyday perception and translation of *difference multiculturalism.* He tries to bring the different population groups together through interactive meetings in the church to overcome the separating elements in worship in the spirit of the *rainbow people under God.* But temporarily he is disillusioned when his idea of a cooperative worship service is spoiled upon receiving the news of the drunken driver. The original conflict is compounded by the reconstruction of stereotypical roles, making it an extremely tense situation for all participants. By the end of this short story, there is a heaviness hanging over this whole narration, carrying the complexity of the socio-political situation. The listener, who understands the antagonist's entrapment in the thought-schemes of race and guilt, cannot help but sense the feeling of hopelessness, and of cognitive and emotional separateness. Hence, it becomes clear that neither example by this speaker finds the Rainbow Nation implemented on the level of everyday life. While acknowledging the cultural differences between the groups, he is not able to respect them in terms of "dignified ethnic identity" (More) of the Rainbow Nation concept. The main issue here, too, is the reconstruction of traditional patterns of behavior and interpretation, which tend to obstruct social encounters contrary to the spirit of the Rainbow Nation. As shown in the previous example, for the narrator his value constellation is centerd on God, church, and worship, similar to the leading South African representatives *(religion, worship, God /*Bike; *spirituality and God /*Mbeki*).* The *spiritual-religious dimension* is very important in that it seeks a cooperative construction of reality in the spirit of Ubuntu, and the *fulfilment of spiritual needs* (Tutu). Juxtaposed stands (as in CS5) again the community *of brothers and sisters* (Biko), distinguished by *brotherhood* (Mbeki), represented by the choir. The choir community also embodies the values of *music and songs*, which play a significant role in African communities (Biko). The ideal of *racial harmony* (Mandela) and *unity* requires *non-violent communication* from both sides in dealing with each other. These three values as expressions of *anti-racism* (Tutu) remain unfulfilled for the participants in these incidents. Apparently, both sides are lacking the ability of adequate *communication* and *mutual understanding,* even if the *cooperation* has already advanced to a certain degree.

We can conclude also for this last conflict example that some of the named values from the South African discourses represent ideals for people in everyday life. On one hand, they pick up values as desirable goals; on the other hand, they build on traditional values that have special meaning to their in-group and accordingly flow into their daily life as "living values." Individuals demonstrate a broad variety of values, which they prioritize depending on the kind of conflict and the group situation they encounter. In some situations, the fundamental, long-term value orientations predominate. *Spirituality* is such a core value for the pastor (CS5/CS6) since it has outstanding and behavior-guiding relevance in both stories.

5.6.7 Summary

In reviewing the results of the six conflict stories, we find agreements and divergences. Principally, the results of the linguistic analysis support and confirm the analysis of the content. With respect to content, the following points can be made:

Every conflict story is characterized by the assigning the participants to the familiar race categories, which are individually or collectively reproduced. The subject of race or racial affiliation plays an important role in these stories, in that it is a decisive factor in the perception and interpretation of the events and simultaneously the guiding factor for the current options of thinking, expression and behavior. An exception is the story CS2, in which the author declares the conflict with his mother over the dog as clearly and authentically rooted in culture, not in race. In every other story, the thinking in apartheid categories is part of the speaker's daily life. Despite their advanced consciousness, even these highly educated and thoughtful interview partners "regress" into apartheid conditioned thinking patterns in concrete conflict situation. Since the value of race affiliation is essentially determining social status (see CS1), it is often accompanied by feelings of inequality, inferiority or superiority (see CS1, CS3, CS6). The assignment of race categories even penetrates families. In CS1 the family is corroded by the previously race-dependent, hierarchical status assignments of individual family members. The same is true for the "mixed couple," where the construction of an "intact" family – independent from overlying race factors - seems to be important to the narrator (see CS1, CS3, CS4). Only in CS2, the conflict between mother and son can be resolved, because here the negotiation of cultural and individual schemes stands in the center – and not the reconstruction of social identities and categories.

Visible, in addition, is the value of a harmonious and mutually appreciating inter-human communication, i.e., non-violent communication as a means of conflict resolution. These are based in the notion of *conditio humana* (Coetzee) and the value of *being a human being* (see CS2), which again give way to the values of *sharing, mutual understanding, safety and security,* and the ability to adjust to certain situations. The value of *being human*, again, is linked to values such as close *friendship, close interpersonal relationships* (see CS3, CS6) and the value of *personhood*.

Another subject in these stories is conflicting norms of socially acceptable behavior in public (CS3, CS5, CS6). One instance deals with an inter-racial couple, the other with the issue of public versus private apology. Moreover, conflicts arise when choosing priorities between adherence to a sub-goup- specific tradition, and loyalty to the church. In CS4, the importance of *survival-* und *trans-survival-values* is emphasized since the focus here is the distribution of material goods.

The experienced conflict situations trigger different feelings, which reach from mourning and sadness (CS1), to irritation (CS2), fury and anger (CS3, CS4, CS5, CS6) to hopelessness (CS4).

Racial (CS1, CS3, CS6), and cultural (CS2, CS5) affiliation as well as the gender group (CS3) play an important role. In CS5, the significance of the conflict does not lie so much in the religious faith, but rather in the religious practice and is linked to the professional position of the pastor (CS5/CS6). In the conflict example CS4 the social class factor stands out.

It is not possible to say whether there are conflicting values and behaviors that manifest themselves particularly in one specific socio-cultural group. These stories have to be understood as individual constructions. And even though culture plays a role in each of them, the boundaries between individual and cultural influences and statements are flexible. Thus, it can be assumed that the attitude towards public performance (CS3, CS5, CS6) is a cultural phenomenon (CS2), and that the same is true for the treatment of animals and the use of communication styles (CS3, CS5). Yet, in CS4, the conflict seems to be driven by factors of social class.

In comparing the South African value discourses, the following points can be made: The postulated values in the national discourse – such as *familiy, solidarity, concern for each other, community of brothers und sisters* (Biko), *non-violent-communication, communication, moral attitudes* (Mandela), *family and network of relationships* (Tutu), *humanity of humankind, dignity, equality, spiritual self-fulfillment, religion, sharing and empathy* (Ubuntu), *justice, truth* (Coetzee) - are also presented as desirable in the data material. Conflicts arise mostly there, where these values, to the participants, are not visible in others' attitudes and behavior. Thus, values, such as *racial harmony* actually become more appealing, when they are seen as not prevalent in daily life.

Yet, it is also noticeable that some value orientations from the national discourses are already practiced on the daily life. For example, mother and son (CS2) have a relatively non-violent communication about the dog. In CS6, the Coloured choir represents a *community of brothers and sisters*, while the pastor from CS5 fights for his religion and *spiritual self-fulfillment.*.

Regarding the rainbow concept, we find that *diversity, unity* und *balance concept of power* are present as idealized values in the conflict stories, but not integrated in everyday cognition and behavior to the degree that they could overcome traditional value schemes of racial association and socio political in equality (e.g., CS3).

The six conflict stories pick up themes of the multi-culture debates. They contain descriptions of phenomena that tend to be interpreted in terms of *difference multiculturalism* (see CS1, CS3, CS4, CS5, CS6). The narrators experience separateness and differences (see CS3, CS5) of other group members, but hardly commonalities in daily life. Their attribution of cultural characteristics to other groups suggest the image of a homogeneous, monolithic culture. The positive side of cultural diversity – as ideal-typically represented in *critical multiculturalism*- is hardly visible. Likewise, the speakers have not fully internalized the transformation of social, cultural and institutional representations away from apartheid categories. If some of them question the constructs of race, gender and culture in their stories (see also CS1, I3), this is likely to be limited to people from the educational elite with corresponding abilities of reflection. Some stories give initially the impression (e.g., CS4) that the author's view is shaped by *critical multiculturalism* (for example, the description of the relaxed working climate between the White and the Coloured man). This impression changes during the course of the subsequent story, which integrates primarily separating statements reflecting *difference multiculturalism*.

James Mphahlele
Clause 4: "Freedom and Security of the Person."
350 x 570: Masonite Cut.
In: Images for Human Rights Portfolio.
© Artists for Human Rights Trust

5.7 Identity Conflicts

As shown in the previous chapter, the narrated conflict experiences are very diverse and comprise vastly different topic areas. Yet, the four following conflict stories center around one topic only: identity. They are about perceptions and definitions of the interviewees' own (see I2, I3, I4) and others' identity (I1). When constructing these identities, each of the interview partners faces special kinds of conflicts. What they all have in common is that their experiences stand in the context of the "Coloured Community." The speaker of I1 describes and analyzes the identity of Coloured men and women by focusing on the gender aspect, while the speaker of I2 and I3 talks about his identity conflict from the perspective of a Coloured person. The last author defines his own identity by distinguishing himself from the Coloured identity.

This chapter presents four interview excerpts, briefly summarizes them, and then analyzes and interprets them with respect to the following criteria:

- Value orientations and key terms in the context of the identity conflicts
- Social reality of the author
- If necessary, communication situation of interviewer and interviewee
- Evaluation with respect to the theoretical part of the work, such as
  - Theoretical approach of "post-modern identity" and its management (see 3.2).
  - South African value debate (see 3.4).
  - Aspects of the multiculturalism debate (see 3.1.2).

5.7.1 Coloured Gender Identity

The first identity story comes from a White man of British-Italian descent (P37: 46). The interview takes place in his office in a wealthy Cape Town district. He tells the following story in direct response to being asked about his conflict experiences. His background clearly shines through his narration: He works as a writer and volunteers at a church in his own part of town to promote communication between people of different socio-cultural and religious backgrounds. He prepares inter-religious worship services through music-projects. Because of his personal interest in other cultures and religions, the interviewee is active in the "Center for Spirituality," a meeting place for people from different cultures and religions with ongoing discussion circles. Also, he has studied conflict as part of his university studies. Accordingly, he is very reflective and analytical when describing his experienced conflict experience.

Ahm, what I found interesting is that within the Coloured area – and just now about some people want to be called Coloured and some don't want to be called Coloured – but within the Coloured area there is a lot of conflict around...the, the, the communities actually developing and who carries responsibilities actually for those communities. Who is the head of the community? Traditionally the male figure has come in or has, has, from the Western model, Western and somewhere African model, the male is the head of the community or the family particularly and, and collectively the community has, has selected male head figures. But because of the particular figures of the Coloured Community, they felt, they have historically felt not themselves belonging to either side. They have had enormous self-esteem issue problems, ahm...ahm...identity problems. And that has effected the males more than the females, the women. The men tend to be the ones who, who are, who stand up and give the identity. And they haven't known, they found it difficult to actually establish themselves and have a place that is meaningful and separate. And they need their identity, and they have actually remained on that responsibility and, and through abuse of alcohol and, and...sort of inappropriate behavior, dysfunctional behavior have relinquished that role. So, the women had to pick up that role and must establish who they are and what they need to do. So, within the church we found the women having to come in and take over. Ahm...and, and establish themselves and give directions. They have picked that up from...the predominantly White churches, because they have seen what is happening there. So, they are sort of...but with the lack of men, when men do come up...and a number of times we find men, ahm...capable of leadership and, and....men of quality, especially younger men who were coming in into their own. The women are criticizing and cut them down very effectively and very soon men leave and going elsewhere. So, the women almost with their criticism would destroy any...ah...upcoming leadership. Ah...I just to play the guitar for the music they have....leading the music is very much a cultural leadership position and...on a number of occasions I taught young men, 3 or 4 times, how to play the guitar. And they now soon started to play, they started to leave, but they were just pushed out of it through criticism, through...ah...very high expectations...ah...and through very high monitoring and it would slightly slip and they were gone. So, culturally there is a lot of conflict from the, the stereotypes of what is seen as adequate leadership and role models and what male and female identity structures look like. And the women feeling that the men have been inadequate have taken over. But in taking over to prevent that men coming into that position. And so there is a distortion and an ongoing conflict. Because at the moment there are a number of women who are leaving the church...socially. Not as pastors, because there is a White pastor, but in terms of the community, there are leaders, they come up and leave, come up and leave, come up and leave. I think they actually go and leave the church. They just go and do other things. And I think that happens quite a lot when....am I talking about the stuff you want to hear? Ahm...culturally I think where we are in terms of our civilization, ah...men, because women have become to a higher awareness of themselves...through the feminist movement and through a reaction of the years of parent abuse, being put down. They have come to a greater sense of awareness of themselves and about what they want and what they don't want. And men haven't done their same work. So, women are in the position where they are identifying problems and issues in men's behavior and identity structures and they are criticizing that. And the men, because they haven't done their own homework, are not able to counter and to stand against. And so the, sort of, syndrome of the inadequate male becomes stronger and stronger. And men are struggling with their identity and don't know how to be the "non-abusive-male." Strength is seen as dominating, in a domination. Ah...they don't know how to be the strong non-abusive-male. Strength is seen as a domination, in domineering. Abuse comes from that. So, 95% of, of social abuse happens in men to,... they don't know how else to be. But, because they feel belittled and losing their identity, they, their frustrations come out and, and abuse to try to regain, they don't know any other way. So, there is a strong difficulty in men and their own identity and that causing a lot of social conflict. But, it's not only, I mean, it's in Western culture generally. Most of the TV programs have the stupid man who is the father and who don't know what he is doing and there is a teenager who says: "Oh, come on Dad! Grow up and get a life!" (laughing). You know, it's, it's, it's a popular cartoon figure: a man who is an idiot. The man who tries to be sensitive doesn't know how to be a strong man, who is sensitive. So they try, they become feminine in their sensitivity and they follow a women's example and they don't know how to be a sensitive male in their own right. Those who are strong turn as I said to abuse and to overpowering with physical strength, and I think the horrendous rape statistics are signals to that that men are struggling with their own identity and don't know how to impose or how to, to...ah...ja, to assert that maleness." (I1)

The interview partner has observed that one conflict issue for people in the "Coloured area" is that of individual political responsibility and leadership. He specifies a value- and relationship-oriented conflict structure between men and women. While traditionally the "male figures"determined the distribution of power in the political and private spheres, social change brought enormous self-esteem problems for the "male head figures", which the author characterizes as "identity problems". While formerly men shaped the identity of the Coloured Community, today this is no longer the case. Instead, many men maneuver themselves out of identity-shaping positions through alcohol-abuse and "inappropriate" and "dysfunctional behavior". Women, on the other hand, have moved into leadership positions, replacing men, especially in the churches. The few men, who try to catch up, are often effectively curtailed in their activities by the women's criticism. The author provides an example from his own experience in the area of musical performance, showing how the "Coloured females" have pushed men out of their traditional roles. He guesses that this development is, on one hand, the lasting effect of the "feministic movement," and, on the other hand, the reaction to widespread abuse of women ("reaction...of parent abuse"). Both of these factors have produced a "high awareness" in modern, Coloured women, which empowers them to criticize "men's behaviors and identity structures". Men, on the other hand, have not developed constructive counter-strategies, because they have not done their "homework" and not taken charge of modifying and developing their own identities. Hence, they are at a loss at how to shape their new roles - strong and sensitive, but not abusive. They feel "belittled" by women, are frustrated and respond with abuse. Here the gender conflict gets a strongly social aspect. Finally, the author points out that this problem is reinforced by the portrayal of the stereotypical "stupid" man on television. He regards the high "rape-statistics" in South Africa as a symptom of the failed identity management of modern men.

Looking at the key terms and value orientations coming to bear in this conflict situation, it becomes clear from the outset that the author identifies the conflict-ridden value of "responsibility" as crucial. The current changes in the "communities" bring about a re-structuring of public offices, as well as power shifts in the institution of "family". Traditionally the "male figures" carried the responsibility in both areas. They were elected to public office by their community, which assured their "self-esteem" and (gender) identity. Being a male gave them the right to actively "stand up" for their positions and thus shape the community's identity. The author points out that their gender-specific identity was not co-defined by their skin color, but exclusively by their public leadership position. In their concurrent role as head of the household, men were in control of family and public life. Thus, the changes in the community have a more detrimental effect on men than on women. Even though men have maintained their internalized value of exercising public "responsibility", they have not been able to live up to them. Instead they abandon their traditional roles, turn to compensation in negative substitutes and destructive behaviors, and contribute to a growing identity loss in the Coloured community.

In the author's opinion, women have moved into this vacuum of power and responsibility. As if countering the males' failing sense of responsibility, they have taken over the former male roles by establishing themselves in society ("they must establish who they are") and providing leadership ("give directions"). By doing so, they are actively involved in the community's development. The author contrasts the very active role of women in their own identity development with the passivity of the men, which has resulted in an extremely unbalanced development. While the "male figures" increasingly lose their own traditional, positive identity formation, the women have gained a positive self- awareness ("sense of awareness of themselves"), and know what they want. The value implied here is that of feminine volition, the self-determination through one's own action- and behavior orientations. Another trait of the new feminine awareness is womens' analytical ability to identify, articulate and criticize the problems they see in the behavior of their male counterparts. These new capacities, which the women, according to the author, know how to use and see as a step forward, men might perceive as women's cognitive and intentional superiority, and thus as competition and threat Consequently, in churches men have often retreated from leadership positions because of womens' effective criticism of their inadequacies. Presumably, men experience this massive, collective criticism of women as destructive, as does the White author. The same happens in the area of "cultural leadership". While women hold young men to high musical standards and closely watch their performance ("high monitoring"), to men their criticism means something entirely different: They feel unwanted and pushed out of their traditional area of playing the musical instrument ("leading the music"). Thus, both sides handle the conflict issue of responsibility and "adequate leadership" in different ways. Women see males as inadequate, wanting to take over leadership positions; men feel "belittled," have low self-esteem, suffer loss of identity, which leads them to feelings of frustration and inferiority. This phenomenon of "male inferiority" faced with perceived "female superiority" represents a gender-role conflict that the author finds clearly unfortunate.

While men still hold on to their values of "strength" and "power", they unfortunately often fail to distinguish between strength and dominance. Strength to them means dominating with physical forces. The author regards the alarming rape statistics as an indicator for the dangerous consequence of this mistaken value-identification. At the same time, these statistics point to the severe identity crisis of men, who have great difficulty to analytically and affectively process these (value-) antagonisms. The author contrasts this male inability with the previously mentioned analytical and monitoring capabilities of women.

Occasionally it becomes evident that the author as a male tends to identify more with the side of the Coloured men than the side of the women. He shows this, for example, in his wording that men feel "pushed out" of their leading positions. On the other hand, he cannot understand that Coloured men retreat into alcohol and passivity, instead of actively striving to re-define their roles and identity. At the end of this interview excerpt, he expresses his wish for men to be strong and sensitive, presenting an ideal image of male identity and a positive value of "malenes" ("to be a sensitive

318

male in their own right"). After inserting his criticism of the Western television culture that currently portrays the strong man as violent, and the sensitive man as comical, he asks for a positive orientation of the "modern, Western man" that creates (new identities and) a new form of socially acceptable masculinity. This seems to be also important for the speaker's own identity development.

Obviously, we are dealing here with an overall significant historical change of values in the conception of gender roles, which the author sees particularly pronounced in the tension field between "Coloured males and females." Race comes into play here only in so far as the White narrator believes that this gender role conflict mainly occurs among Coloureds like amongst Whites, because Black South Africans still adhere to their traditional gender roles.[231] Unlike the male role-definitions, which lean on Western and African models, the women derive their recent concept of leadership from the change in the " South African" White churches, where women have been advancing into leadership positions for quite some time.

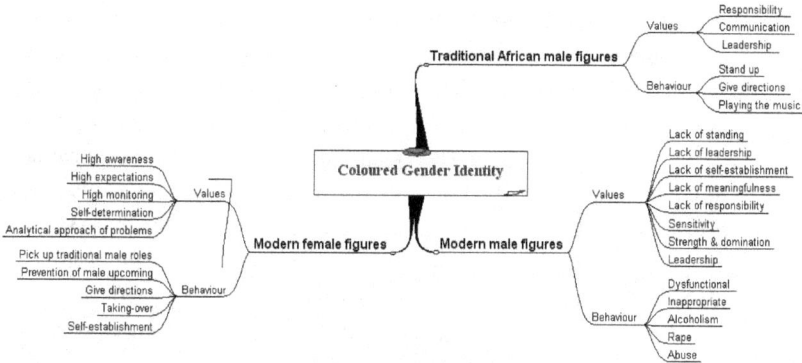

Graph 22: Coloured Gender Identity

---

[231] Similar is the inferiority complex of the Black businessman (see 5.7.4). In both cases, men demonstrate massive insecurities and irritations faced with a growing status of women in public positions.

In short, the author observes a change in the gender- specific traditional value orientations. Looking at his statements in the context of the political-ideological value discourses and the multiculturalism debate, the following can be said:

The listener gets the impression that in the Coloured Community a type of "difference multiculturalism" is growing. The gender groups are not cooperating in the face of social change, but rather define themselves over against the other and push forward in segregated ways. With respect to the ideological debates, the following value constellations play role for the author: Like Biko the author holds up the African value of music, but he also sees the value of *music, songs, rhythm* as important as part of the traditional male territory. Indirectly he describes values, such as "concern for each other" and "community of brothers and sisters" (Biko) as desirable, but missing among Coloured men and women. Also, the behavior he depicts contradicts the value of "problem solving through experiencing" (Biko), in that Coloured women value their own analytical abilities and problem-solve through the "analytical approach of problems." From our narrator's perspective, we cannot find such values as *non-violent communication, unity, equality* (Mandela) practiced between Coloured men and women. On the contrary, their style of communicating looks rather violent: women criticize men ruthlessly, and men turn to "abuse" and "rape." The often proclaimed *equality and unity*, especially advocated by Mbeki in the rainbow concept, is completely missing in the narrator's description. The women's struggle for equal rights in the public sphere has not led to unity of the genders, but to division instead. This takes its toll on families and social relationships, which Tutu claims as core values. The way women and men carry out their fight for equality and new roles have pushed the values of *harmony, peace and contentment* (Tutu) to the backseat. At best we can see them as desirable goals.

Hence, in the center of the conflict stands the re-definition of roles, of "role-rights" and of "community-rights," in line with Coetze. In question is here the clarification of "rights and duties," and the implicit acceptance of responsibilities. The "communal, social and cultural identity" (Coetzee) with respect to gender and (agreed upon) values goes through a process of regeneration, which, on one hand, orients itself at the "traditions and traditional thought styles," but, on the other hand, also at the current construction of "self- and collective understanding" of the gender groups. These values undergo societal and socio-cultural change, which is accelerated by women's new activities, consistent with some value orientations in Coetze's "social theory."

Regarding the theoretical assumptions on identity and identity-management (see 3.2), it is striking in this conflict story that the author finds the gender conflict particularly pronounced in the Coloured Community. He does not elaborate on self-images and how people re-invent themselves in the face of disintegrating traditional gender roles. All we hear is that men suffer a great loss of identity by abandoning their gender-specific identity aspects and not building on other aspects. He finds that the traditional gender definitions continue to dominate male identity, whereas identity is made up of multiple facets that need to be united. As seen in chapter 3.1, conflicts arise with the identity-shaping gender-role definitions, when the so-called "traditional" and "modern" definitions wrestle with each other on the intra-personal level, and - in the case of this story - when they simultaneously have to adjust to the gender role formations of women within the interplay of identity developments. In the course of societal change, new identity aspects form and need to be negotiated. At the same time, they construct new social trends, which can be perceived externally - as by our speaker- or inside the group.

5.7.2 Identity: Who am I?

After presenting an etic perspective on identity management and value transformation among Coloureds, the following shows an emic perspective. This excerpt (P22:30) comes from an interview with a priest, who feels himself belonging to the "Coloured Community." For a few months he has been working in an Anglican church in Woodstock, a Cape Town district populated predominantly by "Coloured working class." Typical for this area are a high unemployment rate and a relatively high potential of violence. Beside the numerous crimes committed by individuals, there are - like in other parts of town - organized gangs operating in drug traffic. Only a few months ago, a church staff member was shot right at the church entrance in the late afternoon.

The priest was transferred to this church by the bishop because his predecessor, a White colleague with a Ph.D., found the conditions in this part of town too difficult to handle and moved to a university congregation. In this excerpt, the clergy talks about his working conditions and about the issue of his identity. He begins addressing his actual conflict experience by talking about his White predecessor.

He has been here not two years and he lived in this house and after about three month he moved out, because of the social conditions in the area and...he was of a economic position, by words, his parents ...to buy a house in a suburb away from here, ah, and then after a while, I think after a year the Bishop moved him to a more middle class congregation related to the University and the argument used by the Bishop, communicating this to the politicians here, that this man has got a doctorate, is well educated and he should be used there. And that caused a lot of hurt, 'cause they liked him and they found in him a gentle person and ahm, they felt then rejected, because the question that arises ahm...are we not good enough? You know? Are we not educated enough? Are we not worthy of a pastor with a doctorate? Right? And, ahm...or really they had been complicated by his moving out of this area. Then people ask me questions...what about our safety? What about the safety of our children? How can you minister to us if you...take the option to leave while we have to remain and content with that? Now those are fair and unfair questions. For example the safety of this rectory. Ahm, if somebody comes to your door, if you are living in a neighbouring street, you know, at 10 o'clock at night or 9 o'clock at night: you don't have to open. But if somebody comes to knock at the pastors house...saying through the door that he wants bread...do I, do I not open? You know? So, we are more vulnerable and exposed because people have the legitimate right to come and knock at the door because of what we claim in terms of the Kingdom of God. Ahm...so, when I came, and I came here, there was a lot of resentment because I was black like them, you know? I was ahm...so I was worthy of them...in other words I shared their low, they ...they took me and they brought me down to their low self-esteem. So I can't be, there can't be anything special if the Bishop takes away an educated white man and brings a colored man in to meet the standards, so what is there about me? So, there was an antagonism. So those are the kind of conflicts, ahm...which is related to our past. Which is related to our socialization, which is related to our history, which is related to...how we answer the question to:...

"Who am I?" Because, if you are of mixed descent and without legacy: how do you answer that? So, ahm, before I go further is that any clear? Because I am talking and talking and...please interrupt me. Ja, well, so, I mean, that's the immediate conflict that I deal with." (I2)

The author reflects here on an experience that triggered a deep inner conflict in him: his predecessor ("he"), who worked in the congregation for two years, left the parsonage already after three months and moved to his own home in the suburbs, because he preferred the "social conditions" there. When the bishop eventually transferred this well-to-do White predecessor to a university congregation, he argued that this candidate with his "higher education" was better suited for a university than for a working class setting.

In the following three quarters of this excerpt, the pastor deals with his own and the congregation's hurt feelings. He raises the stinging question whether the church considers him inadequately or little educated since he was placed as a substitute into this "lower class" congregation.

He talks about his everyday situation in his role as a minister that makes him especially vulnerable. If he wants to be true to the gospel, even under difficult circumstances, he has to open his doors to people at all times, even in the middle of the night. He refers to his distress about having to share the "low self-esteem" of the "Coloured Community." His list of explanations for this painful "antagonism" peaks in the question of his identity: "Who am I?".

Looking at the conflicting value constellations in this excerpt, the following topics stand out:

1. Racial affiliation in relation to educational status and socio-cultural background
2. A sense of religious- ideological obligation ("Kingdom of God") to reside locally despite the threat to his personal safety
3. Feeling of inferiority and lack of self-esteem in the face of the authority's decision
4. Question of identity with respect to its conflicting aspects.

1. The author finds himself in a situation that he experiences as contradictory: His predecessor, a White, well educated man with a Ph.D. and a prospering economic position has obviously succeeded - in accordance with his educational and social prestige - to find a job in a university congregation. This he could achieve only with the endorsement of the bishop. Hence, for the White pastor an essential part of his identity is sanctioned: he returns to the place where he came from, namely to the university life, which is shaped by the educational and upper-class elite ("a congregation related to the university"). In contrast - and here the author's antagonism comes to the fore - the Coloured priest enters the abandoned congregation[232] without a doctor's title, that is, without "higher education." Apparently, the arrival of the Coloured priest has triggered a value conflict among the parishioners. To them the switch of priests is an insult. It shows them that they are not sufficiently valued and accepted. "And that caused a lot of hurt, 'cause they liked him and they found in him a gentle person and ahm, they felt then rejected, because the question that arises, ahm…are we not good enough?" The speaker describes the collective feeling of "hurt" effecting the parishioners when the White priest leaves. He offers another reason: they had developed a positive attachment to his collegue and had liked him as a person ("gentle person"). It is interesting that the speaker chooses the character term "gentle" to describe his predecessor and to indicate his acceptance by the parishioners, thereby completely ignoring racial, economic, social and educational factors. He is liked as a person ("personhood"). But the White minister does not reciprocate this acceptance by staying and sharing the same social conditions in solidarity, as they hoped. Instead, he uses the first opportunity to leave. The congregation, in turn, feels rejected. The value of mutual acceptance, of solidarity and "standing up for each other" in combination with the value of "person" has not come to bear in the relationship between congregation and pastor. The acceptance of the person beyond race, education, and economic status is only one-sided.

Furthermore, the phrase "gentle person" generates associations with *solidarity, reciprocity, giving and taking, empathy, mutual understanding, sharing,* as well

---

[232] One can assume that the speaker was socialized in a township, and comes from rather modest circumstances. This means that he probably had to work his way "up" to the position of a priest, which would reinforce his present antagonism: The White, highly educated, wealthy pastor from a well-off milieu can return to a church that befits his upbringing. The same is true for himself. After he has worked himself out of his working class milieu, he now - after his "fieldtrip" into the university life of the upper class - is re-planted in his original milieu: "to meet the standards."

communication, interaction and participation (see 3.4.1). When now the congregation associates the Ubuntu-values with Christian values, one can easily understand their disappointment about the pastor leaving them. He turns his back on them.

The author clearly describes the negative feelings of the parishioners caused by the priest's decision. Now, collectively the question of self-worth arises: "Are we not good enough?" Their hurt and sense of rejection are tied to the self-judgment as inferior. For the congregation, the value orientation of mutual acceptance and appreciation of "personhood" and the "collective consciousness," as represented in the Ubuntu concept, are not fulfilled. This collective outcry, the expressed feeling of inferiority, probably goes back partly to the apartheid ideology and its stratification of society in superior and inferior people. Hence, value levels mix with the collective heritage of the past, which until this day determines the status of a person.[233]

The author describes clearly and in great detail the feelings and needs of the congregation, not at least, because he - being himself a member of the Coloured Community and a succeeding pastor - can personally identify with them. He, too, feels deeply hurt and wrestles with his self-worth as a Coloured clergy. The question of self-worth is raised on different levels, first with respect to his superior. By supporting the white predecessor to leave the parish, the bishop exposes him to the insecurities and difficult social conditions of the district. Unlike his predecessor he does not have the chance to leave since he is lacking the influence, educational degree, money and affiliation with his predecessor's social group. Secondly, his self-worth is at stake with respect to the parishioners, who meet him with "resentment."

2. Another important key term for the local church, as well as for the Coloured priest is "safety," the desire to live and raise one's children in a peaceful environment. For both the priest and the parishioners the value of safety is important, but for the priest it is connected in an antagonistic way with his value of ministering to the people. His ministry is driven by the ethical imperative to be there with the people at all times,

---

[233] If the same happened in a German "working class" congregation, that a highly educated priest would be replaced by a less educated priest, the parishioners would certainly be effected, but it is very unlikely that they would suffer from the kind of inferiority feelings that are described here. These must be due to the South African history and its impact on personal, physical and mental attributions and feelings.

derived from the theological metaphor of the "Kingdom of God." It means his willingness to keep the parsonage's doors open, day and night, in order to assist people in need. The crucial value of "being available at all times" is part of his internalized professional ethos as a pastor, which outranks his value of his personal and family's safety. But it is the fact that he has been put into this dangerous situation to replace someone privileged that the author perceives it as an insult. It makes him less willing to fully embrace his task and lets him experience a flagrant antagonism of values instead. "So we are more vulnerable and exposed...." Because of his prominent position, the priest is even more vulnerable to dangers than his parishioners. While he is expected to be always accessible to them, they are not asked to keep their own doors open for others. For the priest, living according to the "Kingdom of God" ostensibly belongs to his highest personal values, which is also connected to his "spiritual self-fulfillment" and his job-specific "moral behavior," as also envisioned in Ubuntu. Thus, the eschatological metaphor of "Kingdom of God" spiritually resembles the idea of lived "humanity" and of "collective consciousness." But apparently the priest's idealized value-orientations are in conflict with his feeling that he has been thrown involuntarily into a working environment that endangers his life.

3. Finally, the author talks about his inner value-conflict, which he sees apparently related to his sense of vulnerability since he mentions it immediately following. On one hand, he does not feel fully appreciated by his boss, the bishop. The latter gave him a charge that he found too difficult to handle for a White person. On the other hand, the speaker does not feel supported and valued by his new congregation. He describes them as rather reserved towards him. The reasons for this cool reception he sees in his race: "...because I am Black like them, you know?" He believes that the parishioners cannot appreciate him because of him belonging to their own "less valued group" - in contrast to his White predecessor. He does not consider personality aspects or personal likes and dislikes as factors. Thus, it is possible that he uses racial aspects to cover up other possible reasons. Here, too, apartheid categories emerge, which in the priest's self-image guide the self-esteem of the Coloured Community and are transferred on him: "...I was worthy of them...in other words I shared their low, they...they took me and they brought me down to their low self-esteem." The speaker seems to have a hard

time to (re-) construct and maintain his self-worth aside from pre-conditioned and collectively reproduced apartheid concepts of race, value and identity. He falls back to an inferiority complex, the same that manifests itself collectively.

4. At the end of the reflective part, he remarks on the antagonism of the situation by referring to the frequent links between present conflicts and apartheid history. He points to the interrelationship between influential factors such as socialization, history and the question of one's own identity that becomes the key-question for him: "Who am I?"[234] In a constructivist fashion, the speaker now himself develops the basic question and reason for his present conflict: "Because when you are of mixed descent and without legacy: how do you answer that?" The author's awareness of being entangled in his own thinking structures emerges here. He himself has not overcome the socio-historical categories of "mixed" and "race," since they are tied up with old constructs of "missing legacy." This "legacy" can be interpreted in several ways: it could refer to the limited traditions of Coloureds in South Africa, going back only a few hundred years, in contrast to Blacks who can look back on many thousands of years of Black African traditions; or it could refer to the legacy of apartheid, which strengthened the middle position of Coloureds between Whites and Blacks, but was a position of little backbone and self-confidence. Finally he shows himself stuck with a dilemma: Even if he has already answered the question of his own identity for himself — as he impressively shows in I3 — the collectively reproduced identity-definitions through race and social ranking, catch up with him. The speaker takes this up with the remaining rhetorical question: "...how do you answer that?" He implies that he understands the attitude of the congregation, which is only too familiar to him. He lets us see the difficulty of overcoming historical constructions of reality and the great challenge of integrating visionary, new constructions of categories, perceptions and thought patterns.

---

[234] The same question another Coloured intellectual (see C1, 5.5.1, CS1, 5.6.1) poses to his father, respectively his family. The author's father from C1 responds in the conventional thinking structures of Black-White, Christian-Muslim. Like the priest here, the speaker then questions this way of thinking.

It remains unclear how he author wants to overcome his own socio-cultural and historical-ideological background and how he can raise the question of his own identity in the context of collective constructivism. [235]

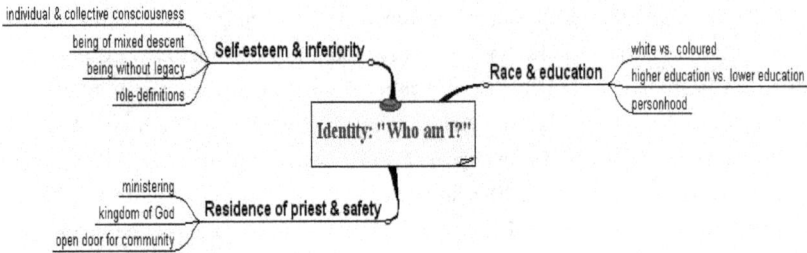

individual & collective consciousness
being of mixed descent
being without legacy
role-definitions

Self-esteem & inferiority

Race & education

white vs. coloured
higher education vs. lower education
personhood

Identity: "Who am I?"

ministering
kingdom of God
open door for community

Residence of priest & safety

Graph 23: Who am I?

Looking at this identity conflict in light of the South African value discourses, we can recognize outstanding values according to Mbeki, Tutu, Coetzee, Mandela and Biko. For the priest the desire for *humanity of humankind, equality & dignity* with respect to himself and his predecessor stands in the center. He wants to be appreciated as a person in his position by the bishop and his congregation and to be respected for his qualifications. What also comes into play is the continuously felt imbalance of power between the White predecessor with higher education and higher economic status. From the speaker's perspective there is no *balanced concept of power*. [236] Furthermore, he is neither connected to the bishop as his superior nor to his own congregation in *unity*, since both take their clue from the White predecessor and hardly support him as the successor. Other important values for him are *religion, spirituality, fulfillment of spiritual needs and God*, which are also claimed by Biko, Mbeki and Tutu as central. The values of *spirituality* and *religion* are of highest importance regarding the "Kingdom of God," even higher than the much addressed *safety,* and *human security* (Mandela/Mbeki), which is not guarantied in this city district. At the same time, it is

---

[235] The question of identity construction is meant as suggestion for a new orientation within the "Coloured Community." This he describes in chapter 5.7.3.

[236] This statement is consistent with the opinions in R1. Here, too, the speaker assumes a lack of balance of power in everyday life in the Rainbow Nation of South Africa.

clear that this fact brings about an inescapable dilemma since he needs the spiritual dimension for himself as a person, and the everyday safety for his family. In the Moment he cannot adhere to both values fully

It is also striking that, from the speaker's perspective, the Coloured Community associates inferiority feelings with Mbeki's favored values of "multicultural origin" und "identity of cultural diversity." Values like *cultural diversity*, which could be embraced especially by people of multicultural origin, are not necessarily perceived as positive and normative by Coloureds themselves. Instead, their "mixed descent" still induces feelings of inferiority and low self-esteem.[237] The political-ideological value-discourses are a constructivist-visionary attempt to change the existing value-concepts of "diversity" and "multicultural identity" and encourage their re-definition within the different socio-cultural groups. But it appears that in everyday life the form of *difference multiculturalism* prevails, which keeps different groups in their separate slots: The White man goes back to his White suburb; the Coloured priest is sent back to the Coloured inner city district. People continue to define themselves according to racial lines that separate them. The aspect of race and its associated self-worth encompasses their whole collective identity. As we will see in the next excerpt, the speaker had already left behind his previous socialization-bound identity definition over race. But now his new, multicultural identity form has trouble withstanding the collective constructions.

5.7.3 Multiple Identities

In a later part of the interview, the previous interviewee returns to the issue of his own identity and presents his definition. Highly reflective and self-confident, he describes his identity as a construct of multiple identities whose various aspects he has to accept and to balance. Through successful identity management (P22:30), he appears to have resolved for himself the identity conflict, which he finds typical for the Coloured Community:

---

[237] The same interview partner talks about this issue in the excerpt I3, in which he clarifies what multicultural descent means to him.

And, and, I am, I am comfortable with multiple identities. You know, I, I, I ahm...I am black, you know, it's a political identity that I shape my consciousness since about 1980 where Africans, Coloureds and Indians were common course ah... in the philosophy developed by Steve Biko. That you are...if you are oppressed, no matter the variation in the oppression under Apartheid, you're black, you know, and that's also, ah... leads me a bit what I call... way with other black people internationally. Ahm, people of the diaspora. So, there's a global identity that I share by the virtue of my blackness, ahm...that's a very profound thing to...to...to or via political identity. I'm, I'm African. That's the other aspect of my identity. Ahm...but I really celebrate "brownness." I, I, I celebrate "southerness". That puts me in touch with...Brazilians...ah...ach, just the, the, the...if you are north and we are south I celebrate that, that southern delight in laughter, joy of being and music and so forth. That's what we like. So, there's that very big global part of my identity, ahm...and I'm really comfortable with „colored". Ahm...that's also why...that's, that's the way I've been socialized, that's the community I've been at, that's a different, ah, part of me that I negotiate or that, that is emphasizing different parts...ah...when I meet my mother, ah...or when I meet my cousins...or this community, this community is a Coloured Community. Also shaped where I think, my little proverbs, my way of...you know, whatever I am. The way I cook and so forth. And there's a broader African identity that I inter-negotiate that is profound and ties me to a broader range of people, other people than I have been listening to. I've worked in Xhosa-speaking congregations, you know? Ah...for a significant part of my ministry. Ah, so that is also who I am. I don't walk away from that. And I just said that my blackness... and then there is the factor that I am a priest and then there is the factor that I'm my mother's son and, you know, all that things. Then I'm a father of children, I'm a married man, all those things come into play. Ahm...which I own and which one...the difficulty is that...people are not perhaps conscious that they can...people feel always that they must have one narrow ethnic identity that they must die for...I die for a, it's not worth it. I want to live for as so many people, because there are so many experiences that you are exposed to, that enriches you. And the conflict that you are seeking to identify is within the Coloured Community's inability amongst some to deal with that. Because if you claim your diversity you gotta, you gotta deal with that black woman. You know? You gotta deal with that black man who's in you blood, you gotta look at them and you must be able to eventually say: "I love myself and therefore I love you. And in loving you I love others who look like you. Others who are...." And so there is that equalizing of your identity, because in this diversity there can't be a hierarchy of privileged and of...ah, even to say: „Black is beautiful." can't be to say: „White is ugly." It has to affirm aspects of your identity but not to dispel other identities. You know?" (I3)

With the description of his own identity aspects, the author actually takes up the concluding question of I2, "Who am I?" Inherent in this question he sees great conflict potential since out of all the aspects making up someone's identity often only one is considered the main identity-shaping aspect. In detail he lists his own identity aspects - "blackness", "brownness", "southerness", "global identity" -, all of which need to be combined via constructive identity management. Then he explains his ties to his "African identity," and adds his different social roles: "I am a father of children, I am a married man...." The widespread phenomenon that people wish to narrow down their identity ("narrow ethnic identity") he finds to be a problem. He constructs his own identity by accepting his inner diversity. The challenge to him is to learn to love yourself and through this self-love also develop love for your neighbor. The author concludes by putting his identity concept in political terms: The need is for equality among the different identity aspects, to end the hierarchy of privileged and underprivileged. Accepting one aspect should not imply the rejection of the other: "...black is beautiful can't be to say: white is ugly."

Under close examination, his focus lies on his different identity aspects and their value orientation, which now need to be analyzed and interpreted. The speaker starts with his definition of identity that he associates with certain feelings: "And, and I am, I am comfortable with multiple identities." The listener gets immediately the impression that he has developed a positive self-esteem. But one can also sense his awareness that, in contrast, other Coloureds feel torn inside because of their own diversity.

When expounding his various identity aspects, he positively appreciates each aspect by outlining its special facets and value orientations. At first the author underscores his "black identity": "I am Black..." To him the historical-political identity of "blackness" comes first. Since the 1980's, the author regards Steve Biko as his idol and symbol of a "black humanity" (see 3.4.2) that revived solidarity among "Africans, Coloureds and Indians" under the common name "Black." He mentions the key slogan in this context, "I shape my consciousness", namely the active, responsible development of one's genuine black identity. To the speaker, "Black identity" is next to the historical-political also a political-philosophical, hence, collectively and individually shaped identity. Also, "Black identity" is not defined in racial, national, geographical or territorial terms, but in political terms. An individual is Black when understanding him/herself as "oppressed" and as part of the "diaspora." This expansion of his Black identity leads the author to acknowledge his "global identity" as another integral part.

He then describes the "African" aspect of his identity, which he explains as "broader African identity," or, further below, as "African identity." It connects him with people to whom he has no direct contact and whom he cannot "hear" directly.[238] The "broader African identity" appears to be his own construct, which helps him to integrate various, partially contradictory affinities. "Ah, so that is also who I am." He creates for himself a connection to all people in Africa without knowing them from "vis-à-vis situations" (Berger/Luckmann). This is consistent with Anderson's notion that nations and subgroups are thought constructs, which – independent from vis-à-vis contacts – shape identity. Yet, the speaker is not interested in establishing his nationality (see 3.1.1), but instead in constructing his own, trans-national identity aspect, that of his "African identity." Beyond all national identity constructs he discovers his "Pan-African identity." Identity-shaping for him were his experiences in working with Xhosa, his contact with a Bantu-speaking ethnic group that makes up one part of his identity. These experiences were essential for his self-awareness as "Black" and becoming conscious of his own ethnicity. The identification on both levels gave way to his own "broader African identity."

---

[238] This "broader African identity" has to be understood in terms of Pan-African identity and national African identity according to Anderson (3.3.1). The author feels connected with all people on his continent, even if he does not know them.

Like "Blackness" and "Africanness" he now presents "brownness" and "Southernness" are closely related. He appears to be especially passionate about these aspects of his identity since he uses the verb "celebrate" three times in this context. He feels spiritually connected with the people of the southern hemisphere, especially the Brasilians. He is at home with people who value laughter, who enjoy simply being alive and are connected through their love of music: "...if you are north and we are South I celebrate that, that Southern delight in laughter, joy of being and music and so forth." He contrasts these positively connoted qualities with the presumably different attitudes of the interviewer, who represents to him the northern hemisphere. This implies, on one hand, that the author has a positive auto-stereotype with respect to these identity aspects. His image of "northerners," on the other hand, comes across as negative, because he refers to them in distinction from his positive definition of "brownness" and "southernness." Probably the "error of leniency" plays an important role here: by creating a division of "northerners" and "southerners," the speaker might simply want to illustrate his self- and other-image aspects. But he might also prefer this categorization, in order not to appear regressing into the constructs of race, bemoaned in I2, and to meet his own need for new identity constructions. We can draw the conclusion that for the author the identity aspects of "brownness" und "southernness" are, in fact, the most important. At the very least he portrays them as such before the interviewer. The way he describes the southern culture (laughing, joy of being, music) is joyful. His emphasis on the differences between north and south and his clear distinction from the interviewer reminds of Biko's attitude of the "protection through emic perspective." By distinguishing himself from the interviewer, he clearly conveys his inside- perspective of "southernness," and his supposedly internalized joy-of-life value. At the same time, he stresses that it is impossible for the interviewer to share this attitude. Going even further in the interpretation, one could speculate that by his positive portrayal and distinction of the "southerners" from the "northerners" the author wants to compensate for an inferiority complex.

He now introduces another identity aspect with the same expression of satisfaction as the previous one ("I am comfortable..."): "And I am really comfortable with Coloured." Here he even adds "really" to underscore the positive feeling. Yet, in contrast to the celebratory description of "brownness" und "southernness," his positive appraisal of Coloured is rather restrained. He is comfortable with the label Coloured, but he does not celebrate it. He accepts this aspect because of the fact that his primary socialization took place among Coloureds and because their socio-cultural value orientations are the basis of his identity and personality. He also feels that this is his original family to which he belongs. From the social agencies of this community he internalized the cultural elements he appreciates, such as the special poetic language with its proverbs, and his style of cooking. Clearly he accepts the label Coloured for himself.[239] Knowing that one needs to accept the diverse inner structure of one's identity to become self-confident, he feels that the label "Coloured" stands for one of his many rich identity aspects. Therefore he can say without ambiguity "I am (really) comfortable."

Following the listing of his political-cultural identities, he now names his social, professional and family-related identity aspects: "I am a priest.", or, "I am my mother's son." Hence, his complete identity encompasses culturally and socially defined components. While each of his multiple identities is shaped by his own perspective, he also shows the counter design to his multiple identity: He finds that most people are neither aware ("unconscious") of their many identity aspects nor of their inherent values. They idealize their "narrow ethnic identity," as if it were their one and only identity, even to the point that they would sacrifice their lives for it. His term "narrow" points to the limitedness and danger of a purely ethnic orientation, whose end result often is conflict and death. This "narrow, ethnic identity" stands in contrast to the open, complex identity design that "enriches" and enlivens him and for which life is worth living. Instead of dying for one's ethnic group, he finds it worthwhile to "to live for so many people," to become rich in experiences.

Finally the author appeals to the people of the Coloured Community to come to grips with their diverse identity. They have to face the reality of their origins, their

---

[239] The discussion on the term "Colouredness" is very eventful and complex. Some people completely reject the label because it was constructed by colonialists and imperialist and later used by the apartheid government. Others cannot accept the generic term because the Coloured Community in itself is so diverse. Yet, others see the Coloured Community as a construct that has over time developed its own sub-groups and its own group-specific culture (see also Erasmus, 2001; Zygeye, 2001) and use "Coloured" as generic term for this diverse group.

"blood." His appeal peaks in a small homily, alluding to John, 13, 34: "I love myself and therefore I love you. And in loving you I love others who look like you. Others who are..." Loving one's own diversity allows people to respect other people of diverse identities as equal.

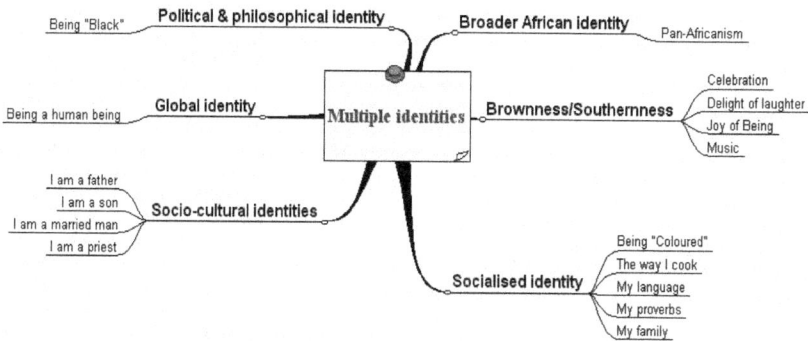

Graphic 24: Multiple Identities

In conclusion one can say that the author is highly aware of his identity aspects, whose different value orientations he can identify and appreciate. He takes up the values of the value discourses, as presented in chapter 3.4. He consciously chooses this uncommon, almost revolutionary, integrative approach.

With respect to his own identity, he actually pursues a type of *critical multiculturalism*, for he integrates all socio-cultural aspects of his identity and synthesizes them into a "multiple identity." As he constructs *critical multiculturalism* for his own identity, he attempts to carry it to the grassroots in the Coloured Community. He realizes the "unity in diversity" of the rainbow concept, first of all, by equally accepting all the aspects of his "patchwork identity," despite the contradictions between them. This he sees as a condition for accepting other people. He talks about his Black identity in the spirit of the "Black Consciousness Movement," which connects all people as "community of brothers and sisters" (Biko) and imparts their "concern for each other." In the aspect of his "broader African identity," he takes up on Mbeki's notion of a "Pan-African" nation. Integrating Mbeki's and Mandela's transnational aspirations, the author imagines a Pan-African connection with people whom he can meet in *brotherhood, equality* and *dignity*. Then he expands the Pan-African identity to the concept of "global identity," which creates a bond with all people on the basic level of *being a human being* and *humankind*, according to Mbeki's und Prinsloo's (Ubuntu) philosophical approaches. Knowingly or unknowingly he picks up the "nature of universals" (Teffo & Roux), which establish the global identity of being human. His socio-cultural identity is mostly family oriented ("married man, father, son"), underscoring the importance of family connections ("family and network of relationships"/Tutu). His original family-ties also inform his identity of "Colouredness", especially with respect to language and customs. Thus, again and again he derives his identity from the different communities of family and socio-cultural groups. In line with Coetze's social theory, he uncovers his "communal, social and cultural identities" - always mindful of his social ties to the different groups ("personhood and social relations/Teffo & Roux). His portrayal of his multiple identity is characterized by "anti-racism" (Tutu) and *inner harmony*, reflecting the different aspects of the *balanced concept of power* of the Rainbow Nation. The speaker's own diversity is made up of personal and collective concepts, such as his cultural perspective of "Colouredness," his political concept of "being Black," as well as his religious perspective of "being a priest." Consistent with Ubuntu, his social roles are an integral part of his self-concept. He claims all these aspects with passion and pride ("pride of self and own identity"/Ubuntu) wanting them to converse with each other.

The here outlined identity concept, which has overcome the *difference multiculturalism* of apartheid, seems to exemplify *critical multiculturalism* in one person. What makes it possible for the author to accept and live his personal diversity is his religious faith ("Rainbow Nation of God") and his Christian ethics of neighborly love and (self)-acceptance.

The excerpt I3 presents a contrast to excerpt I2. While I3 expresses the author's pride in his own diversity, in the conflict situation in I2 he actually describes the break-down of this self-confidence. After reading I2, we understand that his identity concept of acceptance and appreciation in I3 is merely an ideal. Looking at the actual conflict of the pastor in the congregation, it becomes clear that the integration of a positive "multiple identity" in daily life can be difficult. This is exactly the basic conflict in I2. The congregation does not share his concept of valued "multiple identity" and instead throws him back to old concepts and feelings. Thus, the author stands in an intra-personal dilemma between faith in his "multiple identity" and reconstruction of the reactionary concept of "Colouredness." Despite his resistance, it seems that the old concept with its accompanying low self-esteem gets a hold of his new "patchwork-identity-construct." Despite his high degree of self-reflection, the author appears incapable to solve the dilemma. Apparently it is his very knowledge of the connections that leads him to this trap. He watches helplessly as his "multiple identity" surrenders to the traditional identity constructions. Being an integral part of his socialization, they are so familiar to him that it is easy to resort to them. He is caught in the dilemma of wrestling with personal and societal realities, which have become the basic conflict of his current everyday life.

5.7.4 Self-Identity

The fourth and final identity conflict presented here is that of a Shona-speaking man, who was born in South Africa but mostly socialized in Zimbabwe (P2:52).[240] In the following excerpt, which is part of many recorded conversations, the author explicitly addresses his identity conflict. Because of language-difficulties and because of identifying with his torn apart family of origin the speaker does not associate himself with one particular group in Cape Town. He attempts to find his own identity definition: individualized, but also in sharp distinction from the Coloured Community.

There is the different kind of behaviors I have noticed amongst the races here in Cape Town. It's a pity that ah...ah...I'm only able to converse in English when I am here in Cape Town. Otherwise the other language I speak is Shona. Ah...I would have had a better picture if I was able to speak Afrikaans or Xhosa, which

---

[240] Other text excerpts of the same speaker can be found in W6, C12, CM3 (5.5) and in chapters 7.2 and 5.7.3, where the author describes his conflict experiences with his mother and with his White girlfriend in Cape Town. Both texts should be considered in addition to this identity conflict.

are the other two main languages apart from English here in Cape Town. But however I have noticed that there is a ...difference in the kinds of treatments...ah...one gets...when he speaks a certain language or he is unable to speak a certain language. Ah... according to my own observation I have noticed if one is non-white and he is unable to speak Afrikaans he is regarded as ...very lowly...I mean by the...majority of the people here or the dominant race here in Cape Town which is the so called Coloured people or mixture of...black and white. Not necessarily black and white but they are neither white nor black but a mixture. And they happened to be, I mean, ah...the majority here in Cape Town and the, the, the...their main language they use is Afrikaans. In actual fact that was the medium of instruction in schools before and it still is. Especially in the colored schools.

Okay, if I may clarify myself: my mother was colored and my father black from Zimbabwe. So, in actual fact my physical features they don't look typical black South African; neither do I, I mean, perfectly fit amongst the colored people. But now, I mean, I think, I've got, I resemble, or I've got, I've got a resemblance on both sides, but I don't fit on either of them. So, I mean, if I was to meet a colored person, he wouldn't really classify me as a black person, he would expect me to be able to speak Afrikaans. So, you see, in most cases they just start to speak, I mean, Afrikaans to me. The difficult part of it is, I can't answer back. And when I tell them, I mean, I can't speak Afrikaans, I'm sorry, but they may hear that I speak English fluently and very well, of which they do understand, but they have got ah...this complex, I don't know whether a superiority complex or an inferiority complex, which makes them not to want to communicate, I mean, in English. Which, I mean, is the language, I would have told them, I can only communicate in....Physically, one is able to see that their attitude has completely changed on their faces. You see, they become very unfriendly and they continue speaking in Afrikaans. And, all right, I would at times hear that they are trying to say that I'm putting on, that I'm trying to pretend not to be able to speak Afrikaans. But genuinely I can't. And after some time they would now switch to English: "So, all right, where do you come from, he? You're from Jo'burg, he?" And I would tell them: "No, I didn't grew up here, I grew up in Zimbabwe."

And...but anyway, to cut a long story short, generally they become very unfriendly if one is unable to speak Afrikaans, one they would have judged as someone who is supposed to be able to speak Afrikaans. You see? Or, what would happen with some of them, if I tell them I can't speak Afrikaans and they will try to, ah...try to speak a few words of Xhosa: "So, you speak Xhosa?" And, they don't say Xhosa (pronounced with click), they say Xhosa (pronounced without click). Ah...in my opinion not to say they can't actually say Xhosa (pronounced with click), but they try, like, as much as they can, to pronounce it in such a way to show that they can't speak it. To show that they can't speak it. Because, ah...it's a language which, I feel, they detest. You see? ... Okay, that is what I have experienced language-wise with the colored people here. (14)

The author offers here his observations of population groups and language affiliations. In his opinion, the manner in which people in Cape Town deal with each other or treat members of other groups largely depends on their language affiliation. "Non-Whites," who do not speak Afrikaans, are looked down upon. Then the author clarifies his own identity with respect to his family's diverse background and his own subsequent classification as both Coloured and Black. He describes a typical communication situation between him and a Coloured person and uses this example to discuss the predominant aspects of his own identity: language, socialization and physical features.

Looking at this text with respect to its core statements, two main points come into focus: On one hand, the author identifies himself over his language, his socialization outside the country and his physical features. On the other hand, he defines himself over against Coloureds, their language and certain behaviors, which he notices in his daily interactions and has come to resent. Of these key terms of his identity he uses language for the described situation. He immediately contrasts his knowledge of English and Shona with the predominant languages in the Western Cape, namely Afrikaans, the "mother tongue" of Coloureds, and Xhosa, the main Bantu language. His perception of people's behaviors and treatment of others is directly linked to their language affiliation and competence. In the intercultural context of his daily life, he experiences the high value and influence of language in that it is - still based on apartheid categories - a decisive indicator for one's social status. Even during the interview, the interviewee expresses his regret ("It's a pity...") that he can "only" speak English and Shona. He regards his lacking language competence as a personal deficit that deprives him of a broader understanding and of social acceptance: "If one is non-white and he is unable to speak Afrikaans he is regarded as very lowly." At this point, the second value component of identity comes into play: the "physical features" and especially skin color as one aspect of "race." What surfaces here is the speaker's sense of inferiority and his feeling to be regarded as inferior by Coloureds.[241] He conveys his image of Coloureds in a categorizing way: "...or mixture of...black and white. Not necessarily black and white, but they are neither white nor black, but a mixture." Even if he is not quite certain of their "color combination," he focuses his definition on skin color and language. Coloureds are a mixture of other groups, and - in the author's mind - seem to have no independent value of their own. He defines them as a "mixture between black and white." This characterization bears resemblance to the statement of the Coloured pastor in chapter 5.7.2, who finds that the Coloured congregation continues to feel as being of "mixed descent...without legacy" and constructs its self-image accordingly. This leads to the conclusion that both in-group (I2/I3) and out-group-members still define Coloureds in racial terms. It also becomes clear that the multicultural identity definition as described in I3 has not caught on with this interview partner, nor has it made its way into the mainstream of the Coloured Commuity.

Then the narrator elucidates how he defines himself: "If I may clarify myself...." The need to explain his own descent is predominant. He names his parents' origins and socio-cultural backgrounds: his mother Coloured from Cape Town, his father Black from Zimbabwe. He defines himself first over racial affiliation and geographic origin of his parents since these are easy-to-pinpoint facts. So he can satisfy his desire for clarity at least with respect to his parental lineage. About himself he says that he was socialized by Shona, thus naming a main culture- related aspect of his identity.[242] But as a result, he finds that he now cannot associate with one particular group in South

---

[241]The speaker also addresses his feelings and experiences of inferiority/superiority in the context of his relationships with *Coloureds* in other text excerpts: C12, CM3 (5.5.1/5.5.2) and chapter 5.6.3. Therefore it can be assumed that this is a leading issue in his identity concept.

[242] The identity aspects assigned to socialization play a prominent role with this, and also with the interview partner in I2 and I3. Here cultural, not racial aspects are important and fundamentally determine the inter-personal identity management.

Africa. He cannot be classified according to the prevalent (apartheid) categories because of his mixed biological parentage and because of his particular combination of language capabilities. He describes his physical characteristics which show "resemblance on both sides: "But now, I mean, I think.. I've got, I resemble, or I've got, I've got a resemblance on both sides, but I don't fit on either of them." The thought of resembling both sides seems to irritate him. He has difficulty finding the right words, indicated by his repeated *correctio*, which starts and stops his sentence seven times. It appears that he wishes to belong to one clearly definable socio-cultural group by fulfilling their language and "racial" norms so he could feel accepted. Instead, the bounderies of his identity aspects are fluctuating, and he cannot find clearly corresponding categories to assign himself to. Here, the narrator's inner conflict becomes evident. While he still begins his sentence by stating his similarities to both groups in a positive and accepting way, he ends with the rather troubled remark that he does not fit into either group.

In another informal conversation, the speaker talks about his time in Zimbabwe, his childhood, his youth and his young adulthood. He mentions that as a boy in the Shona community, he had a hard time being accepted as equal among his peers because of his physical characteristics: he was more light-skinned than the Shona. Thus, he experienced from early childhood the exclusion from the community because of exceptional physical features. If he had grown up in Cape Town with his mother, he would have been socialized by Coloureds and speak Afrikaans.

With an example he illustrates his difficulty in communicating with Coloureds. Often, they speak to him in Afrikaans so that he cannot respond accordingly. Also, they refuse to speak English because of their "inferiority or superiority complex." This negativity in his social encounters does not help him to fulfill his need for communication in a satisfying way. Often, his inability to speak Afrikaans — and this might in fact be a result of his other-image — is even interpreted as a gesture of arrogance. "And, all right, I would at times hear that they are trying to say that I'm putting on, that I'm trying to pretend not to be able to speak Afrikaans." His negative interpretation points to his pejorative attitude towards Coloureds,[243] which is also supported by his repeatedly expressed perception that Coloureds behave unfriendly towards him. He finds that they become unfriendly once their expectations with respect

---

[243] This assumption is confirmed in 5.6.2 and 5.6.3 and in C13 and CM3 (see 5.5.1/5.5.2).

to his group-affiliation are disappointed, which lets him conclude that Coloureds reject out-group members. Even when they address him in Xhosa, they show by the way they mispronounce "Xhosa" their personal disrespect towards Blacks.[244] His interpretation again points to his deep inner rejection of Coloureds (3.2). He cannot imagine a positive interpretation of their behavior towards him, one that does not include degradation of others. It is possible that the author in this relationship structure with Coloureds feels more drawn to the Shona-aspects of his identity. Or it could be that his own Coloured identity aspects, which were rejected by his Shona peers, now are rejected by himself and projected on the group of Coloureds. The author concludes this illustration of Coloured language attempts in Xhosa by claiming that language, physical features and socialization are closely related to certain behavior patterns.

Generally, the speaker often uses generalizing language elements. As already described in chapter 3.2, the author's self-image is much more differentiated than his image of Coloureds, whom he continues to depict in negative terms.

Regarding his social reality, it becomes obvious that it is difficult for him to establish long-term relationships with members of either group since as a person with fluctuating identity aspects and suspended group affiliation he experiences himself again and again as deficient, either with respect to his language, or his physical characteristics, or his social abilities, which are only partially consistent with group norms.

---

[244] He does not consider a positive interpretation, such as the possibility that Coloureds do not pronounce the clucking sounds because they are equally unable, or because they do not want to embarrass themselves with an incorrect pronunciation in front of someone whose mother tongue is Xhosa. Most of the White and Coloured interview partners made the effort to pronounce the clucking sounds. Some apologized that it was hard for them to use the sounds, but that they wanted to try anyway. Other White or Coloured interviewees who did not pronounce the sounds and were asked for the reason said they were unsure of the correct pronunciation. If one accepted the latter explanation as reason for avoiding the clucking sounds, it would be neither superiority nor general aversion, but only point to insecurity.

Coloured outgroup identity

Language — Afrikaans

Characteristics — Unfriendly / Negative attitude / Not communicating

Physical features — Mixture of black and white

Self-Identity

Language — English / Shona

Socialization

Self-identity

Physical features — Coloured (mother) / Black (father) / Mixture of black & coloured / Resemblances on both sides

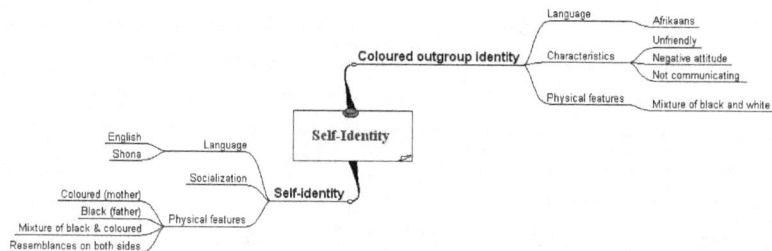

Graph 25: Self-Identitiy

His inner tension shows up in the speaker's current life style. He has only a very small circle of friends and acquaintances, who are mostly colleagues and customers, and: White. After many moves, the speaker now has settled in a part of Cape Town that is mainly populated by White middle class. Here he finds favorable conditions for his business and - as he often stresses - feels comfortable in the company of White people (see CS3, 5.6.3).[245] Not only is it obvious that he is not "White," which gives him the clarity of an unmistaken outsider status, but it also works to his advantage that Whites often appreciate the ability of Blacks to speak fluent English. He finds English as "world language" useful in his dealings with White conversation- and business partners. Then they are often impressed by his good second language skills and compliment him.

In the end, it is remarkable that for this interviewee other identity criteria, such as his being an entrepreneur or a politically interested person, do not come into play since he never names them.

In this identity conflict, too, there are visible agreements with the values from the political-ideological value discourses. In the center of the identity conflict stand elements of the Ubuntu concept. The author underscores repeatedly how important the *communication* with the Coloured Community is to him - be it in his business dealings

---

[245] Even though he often stresses how comfortable he feels with whites, at another place (see 5.6.3) the problem of such contacts shows up. As much as his sense of social status increases, so does also his irritation over his identity as a Black man.

or in everyday life. In the center stands *communication*, combined with *interaction* and *cooperation*, which he see as failed on the part of the Coloureds. But what we are seeing is an "assumed other-image" (see 3.2), to which the author relates his perception. His communication with Coloureds is not characterized - as according to Biko - by *solidarity* and a sense of *community of brothers and sisters*. Nor does he experience it as *non-violent communication*, something Mandela stands for. Instead, he perceives only affront, especially with respect to his language competence. His narrative is penetrated by divisions of "they" (Coloureds) und "I" (author himself), assigning the two sides different behaviors, attitudes, and language abilities. His perception of reality is one that is mostly characterized by *difference multiculturalism*. In his perceptions, elements of *critical multiculturalism* play no role with respect to his own multi-faceted personality and to his intercultural relationships. Tutu's multiculturalism, which lives through *peace, harmony and contentment* and eventually synthesizes diverse elements, is non-existent in this conflict story. Yet, what shimmers through is the author's desire for a change of communication towards *equality and dignity*. This appears to take a long time. There is hardly any *balanced concept of power* in place between the members of different groups, which would respect the different ethnic affiliations and promote *unity* and *communication*. The rainbow concept, which embraces multiculturalism and unity, does not exist in this identity conflict nor in the conflict narrative in CS3. Neither does the narrator display a sense of *racial harmony* (Mandela) or *anti-racism* (Tutu) since his perception reflects the segregating race-criteria of the past that also shape his constructions of reality. This is confirmed in the conflict situation in CS3 (see 5.6.3), but not in CS2. In both stories CS3 and CS2, the value of *origin, family* and *familial relationships* play an important role. Here he describes his own identity with the physical features of his parents, from which he derives his similarities to both "Blacks and Coloureds," and his sense of belonging. Hence, his family of origin is a decisive factor when it comes to defining his own identity - though under the impression of apartheid criteria.

Eventhough he talks about his different identity aspects, his image of his "multiple identity," which could eventually move beyond socially constructed norms and values, continues to be strongly determined by the norms and limits of socially constructed groups and identity assignments. The author remains stuck in social constructions without moving a step ahead and discover additional identity aspects. These could, along with Keupp, open him up to individual and social "creativity spaces" (transl.), prompting him to self-construct his identity, as the Coloured pastor in I3 actually prefers. However, both speakers the priest of I3 and the business man in I4 fall back into their identity dilemma. While the first knows about his possibilities to construct his identity reality for himself, he cannot fight the collective identity constructions and remains torn inside. Similarly, the business man feels that he and his identity aspects are lacking since he cannot see them fitting clearly into the pre-made group categories. Thus, he is left with a weak identity management without reflecting on the aspects of his "multiple reality" to take advantage of them and to reconstruct them.

5.7.5 Summary

While the text excerpt I1 deals with the topic of gender identity from the etic perspective of a White academically educated man, the Coloured pastor in I2 and I3 and the Black entrepreneur talk about their identity conflict from an emic perspective. In each case, the images of identity are connected with more or less differentiated and reflected self- and other-images. These inner images, the definition of their identity and the ways in which they approach it are strongly shaped by their respective social reality. Accordingly, the male intellectual in I1 describes and interprets his experiences analytically and only implicitly uses words with judgmental character. His view is strongly influenced by his male perceptions (I1). The Coloured pastor (I2/I3) presents his inner dilemma in an equally reflective and descriptive way – here from the perspective of a man who was previously classified as "Coloured." The response of the Black businessman, who unlike the other conversation partners does not have an academic background, proves less analytical and reflective and is more loaded with heavily judging and stereotyping statements about Coloureds. The speaker defines himself in strong distinction from his image of Coloureds.

Another topic that penetrates and partially dominates all the social realities in the four text passages is that of racial affiliation, which is linked to identity. I1 characterizes explicitly the group of Coloureds; I2 and I3 reveal the attempt of overcoming socially constructed race categories and the resulting identity dilemma, which make the author appear discouraged (I2). The entire excerpt I3 describes his endeavor to redefine and reconstruct his own identity to overcome the stratifying apartheid constructs on an intra-personal level. In contrast, the text I4 shows the hold that conventional thought patterns have on the businessman. He does not even contemplate breaking out of the historically defined, dominating identity categories of "Black" and "Coloured."

Closely related to the topic of identity and race are the aspects of gender (I1), education, security and societal recognition (I2), the affiliation with further identity-shaping sub-groups, such as socio-cultural groups (I3) or language groups (I4), as well as someone's socialization in the context of gender roles (I1), Coloured Community (I2)) or the origin of family members (I4). All these identity elements are characterized by race categories and accompanied by inferiority feelings. While I1 points to the inferiority feelings of Coloured men towards Coloured women, I2 expresses inferiority feelings of the Coloured priest towards the White priest with a doctorate, and I4 shows inferiority feelings of the speaker towards Coloureds since he does not fit the apartheid categories.

It becomes evident that the apartheid categories effect the construction of individual identities and their identity management to this day. Especially by listening to the description of the deeply rooted identity conflicts, even an outsider can sense the conflict potentials on the individual and intra-psychological level inherent in the new Rainbow Nation South Africa. It becomes also obvious that it won't be easy to overcome the established reality constructs. The societal counterparts to the inner "multiple identity," which are open for new reconstructive thinking and new "spaces of creativity," (see 3.2) have yet to be developed.

So far — and this is another result of this chapter — identity conflicts tend to display multiculturalism in the form of *difference multiculturalism*, as especially evident in I2 and I4. Yet, the excerpt I3 describes a type of *critical multiculturalism* in which all the multiple identity aspects and, applied to society as a whole, the multiple social aspects are integrated evenly, coexisting next to each other and intended to synthesize to a holistic identity, just like the unity in diversity of the Rainbow Nation should manifest itself in terms of "critical multiculturalism." However, this identity form remains still an ideal for the speaker (I3), who, being ahead of his time, is not yet able to realize it in his everyday life.

In view of the South African value discourses, the following points can be made: Mainly the pastor in I2 and I3 addresses the topic of the Rainbow Nation since the finishing line in his excerpt is a statement that can also be applied to the Rainbow Nation: accepting one part of one's identity cannot go hand in hand with the denial of another part. Also, the acceptance and integration of singular and multiple identity aspects has to first take place on the individual level before it happens on the societal level. The author pleads for a power balance between the sub-aspects and for "unity in diversity" on the intra - and interpersonal level.

The intellectual of I1 consistently refers to the values of the South African value discourses, which he does see neither promoted nor applied in the "Coloured gender conflict." He does not detect *non-violent communication*, as Mandela envisions it, or *equality and unity* of the genders, as Mbeki promotes it. The speaker describes exactly the opposite of *harmonic, peaceful family structures* (Tutu), namely a radical change from family values and an accompanying identity loss for men. His demands and values are consistent with Cotzee in his social theory: a new definition of *role-rights*, of individuals and groups, and a new *self- and collective understanding*. In I2 the Coloured pastor emphasizes the values of *humankind*, which plays such an outstanding role in Ubuntu, as well as *equality* und *dignity*, which run through Mbeki's and Mandela's speeches. He also incorporates values, such as *unity* (Tutu, Mandela) and the *balanced concept of power* of the Rainbow Nation concept. Clearly he points to the importance of spirituality, God and religion, which Biko emphasizes in his speeches. In I3 he especially names the acceptance of *multicultural origin*, which characterize Mbeki's speeches. On the basis of "being an African" he shows a Pan-African identity approach just like Mbeki.

In I3 again the Ubuntu values of *humankind* and *pride of self and own identity* come to the fore. To some degree he distinguishes, in line with Coetze, between *communal, social and cultural identities*. The value of *personhood* is tied to identity, as shown in the discourses on Ubuntu, or in Teffo's and Roux's writings, and seen as an integral part of social relationships. The Black businessman in I4 emphasizes especially the importance of *communication*, consistent with Ubuntu and Mandela's notion of *non-violent communication*. Thus, he misses in Coloureds an attitude of *solidarity* with Blacks, as propagated by Biko. In his interactions with Coloureds, he also misses a sense of *equality and dignity* (Mandela, Mbeki), which are supposed to manifest themselves in intercultural encounters. His conflict example does not display signs of *racial harmony* und *anti-racism* (Tutu).

With respect to integral values in these identity conflicts, we can conclude that the participants are aware and feel the importance of most of the values, such as *equality, dignity, humanity, "racial" harmony* and *peace*. It can be observed that they miss these values, respectively, their practical realization in the experienced conflict experiences. For example, the speaker in I4 desires a more pleasant communication. In part, it could be concluded that the value discourses emphasize especially those values that previously have not found much recognition in everyday life. Furthermore, the different population groups might interpret them in such different ways that they do not agree with each other's interpretations.

6. Results and Critical Reflection on the Study

Positioning itself within the segment of post-modern, urban- ethnological studies, this work explores conflict realities in the multicultural spaces of Cape Town. The selection of the samples (see 1.5) assures that the participants are open and ready to share their conflict experiences with the interviewer. It turns out that participants with whom the author can build longer lasting relationships, and with whom several formal and informal interviews can take place, tend to be much more personal and in-depth in their narration of conflict experiences. The growing trust in these more durable interview situations is then reflected in the communication structure: the initial one-sided narration is increasingly replaced by dialogue.

Since a large number of interviewees work at the front line of social-political change, the sample of the Western Cape represents two aspects of interest for this study: it functions as the external context of the examination, and, regarding content, it functions as point of reference for numerous conversation situations in post-apartheid South Africa. Western ethnologists might question the division of population groups into Coloureds, Blacks and Whites. However, it is remarkable that the overwhelming majority of interviewees themselves self-evidently uses these racial categories - whether critically or uncritically. Therefore, the continued use of racial terms is based on this reality.

Consistent with the research hypotheses, experiences from the apartheid-past determine especially "intercultural" conflict experiences. This shows up in the repeatedly surfacing themes of racial belonging, status, and feelings of inferiority/superiority. Yet, it has come as a surprise to the author, that ten years after apartheid the issue of race is of such penetrating importance in the construction of perceptions, identity and conscience in everyday conflicts. Remarkable here are the observed persistence of "external apartheid structures," and the intra-psychological manifestations of "internal apartheid structures" (see 2.2). Furthermore, the data material leads to the conclusion that the terminology and contents of race affiliation are continuously reconstructed and perpetuated. The case can be made that region-specific conflicts form especially in the context of the local population groups, their identity constructs, and their self/other-images like here especially between black and colored identity aspects.

Hence, it is possible that these patterns of racial assignments are continually passed on through individual and collective socialization.

It turns out to be a problem that the theoretical approaches of this work are only little compatible with each other. This makes it necessary to construct an all-encompassing link, so that the introduction of the research topic becomes transparent theoretically and methodologically. The main emphasis of the theoretical framework lies on contributions to conflict research and on the South African value discourses. The results from the theory discussion, leading up to the analysis, are then used to interpret the open or hidden value orientations in the interviews.

The methodological approach of this work is based on the recent discussions in the constructivist schools. The tool of the narrative interview proves to be useful in this investigation. This interview-form allows the interviewee to recall experienced conflicts freely, and express the layers of personal relevance.

When analyzing the content, the data reveal four prominent themes: the Rainbow Nation, self-and other-images, experienced conflict situations, and identity. The theme of Rainbow Nation consists of three aspects: First there is interpretation of the rainbow symbol as political or religious value. It turns out that the political interpretation predominates, which focuses mostly on the critical aspects of the symbol. In comparison, the religious interpretation points to cooperation and societal "unity in diversity." The second aspect consists of the visionary elements of the rainbow concept. Most of the interviewees' comments are in harmony with the visions of the theoretical discussions. Finally, the third aspect of the Rainbow Nation theme refers to the two transparent sides of multiculturalism. While there is evidence of the visionary power of the symbol when developed from the perspective of "critical multiculturalism," the interviewees show that their everyday life is determined by the elements of "difference multiculturalism." Yet, it needs to be considered that the sociological background of most interviewees represents upper middle class or the educational elite of the upper class.

With respect to self-and other-images, two aspects can be emphasized: one deals with the form of self-and other-images. They appear racial and religious, while the racial association predominates. The other aspect concerns the style of self-and other-images. Here it is striking that categorical statements on self-images occur more frequently than concrete-situational statements. On the other hand, categorical statements on other-images outnumber the corresponding concrete-situational ones many times.

The subsequent themes of "narrated conflict situations" and "identity conflicts" involve the analytical grasp of experienced daily conflict situations. While the narrated conflict experiences process problematic encounters, the second group of analyzed conversations tackles the perception of internal identity conflicts and also reflects critically on identity structures of other population groups. It is remarkable here that these narratives encircle the question of how the identity of Coloureds can be perceived and defined. The theme of identity gains an unexpected explosiveness since here the issue of inferiority/superiority and the negotiation of intra-psychological phenomena in the context of societal reality-constructions play a special role. Even if the concrete value orientations and key terms strongly overlap in the interviews, the "racial" orientations and definitions always superimpose on them. Despite the diversity of value orientations, the management of "survival values" unexpectedly is of little significance in these experienced conflicts. In the forefront, instead, stands the grappling with of "trans-survival-values." This is likely due to the fact that most participants belong to the middle and upper class, have secured the "survival values" for themselves and actively participate in the discussion on "trans-survival-values." This is true for identity conflicts as well as for conflicts in interpersonal encounters.

The content analysis of both themes with respect to the occurrences of aspects of "critical and difference multiculturalism" leads to the conclusion that here, too, the interviewees tend to be guided in their daily life by "difference multiculturalism," while principally envisioning aspects of "critical multiculturalism."

In the course of the investigation, specific social structures of communication have developed in the triangle of interviewer, interviewee and conversational setting. Consistent with Kerlinger's definition of the "error of leniency" in the relationship between interviewee and interviewer, there is much evidence (see, e.g., 5.4) that the interviewees occasionally employ the presumed opinions of the interviewer and insert them into the conversation. Just as expected, ethnic or socio-cultural affiliations are not the only relevant factors for the interviewees. Rather, we find a large array of value orientations in their conflict perceptions and constructions, derived from very complex social reality structures. Thus, the statements on values stand in the context of multiple identity-and reality aspects, which cannot be limited to the aspects of ethnic origin.

Choosing the title "exploratory study" for this work happened with great care. Therefore, at the end, some critical comments are appropriate. While this work initially was aimed at surveying and analyzing concrete conflict situations, some modifications were necessary because of the hermeneutically oriented work process. It turned out that the originally formulated expectation that the interviewees would simply share concrete conflict experiences was not met. Instead, they shared various kinds of conflict experiences that were not necessarily related to each other. With respect to the methodical procedure, the principle of "inter-subjective understanding" has proven to be helpful and relevant. The applied method of the "narrative interview," in retrospect, was very appropriate for this study and its goal. Nevertheless, there were weaknesses in some aspects of the methodical procedure:

The pre-definitions in selecting the target group were too vague. It would have made sense, for example, to isolate sub-groups based on career, social class or cultural background in order to make comparative and generalizing statements about sub-group-specific conflict settings and value orientations. Also, the number of conducted interviews and the size of the sample were too small to allow generalizing statements on culture-specific groups or members of certain ethnic groups, or even to highlight specific regional facets. Yet, the number of interviews was large enough to capture and portray a variety of attitudes, conflict experiences and value orientations.

The data material is insufficient for the initially intended in-depth analysis of value orientations. While it contains explicit value orientations, their statements are not formulated in relation to certain contexts of meaning. The interviewees use slogans like "equality" without clarifying what it means to them on a deeper level. A follow-up study could explore the behavior- and attitude-relevant value concepts and value constellations with each interviewee. This could happen in such a way that the interviewer explicitly highlights the value terms that the interviewees name during an interview and asks to clarify its meaning in the described situation, or even in the general context of the author's life experience. The gained insights then could be viewed in light of the interviewee's identity- and value management in interpersonal conflict experiences and his/her current social reality.

In retrospect, it might have been more productive and specific to conduct a series of extending interviews with a smaller number of interviewees, thus allowing a more in-depth look at the interviews by supplementing and comparing them. Also, the social and biographical reality with respect to different conflict experiences could then have been included more effectively. To some extent this happens in chapters 5.7.1/ 5.7.2 and 5.6.2/5.6.3, where the data material gathered in several meetings and shared everyday experiences produces a much more differentiated and precise interpretation. Some places in the data material show clearly how individual life processes strongly determine the perception and construction of conflict situations, self-and other-images and one's own identity. Here biographical facets of the person and his/her present social reality can be considered to a larger extent, so that the interpretation of the articulated value orientations gains different accents and can be more precisely related.

One longer period of field work would have benefited the building of trusting, intensive relationships aimed at developing a better understanding of the interviewee's etic perspective. This might also have given the opportunity to compare statements about conflicts and value orientations with the experienced everyday actions and behaviors and reveal more about the correlation of narrated and action-relevant value orientations. Nevertheless, during the two- till four- months field visits it was possible to build two lasting personal contacts over the last four years. They have proven especially fruitful for the contributions to this study.

In its present form this study provides a foundation for further research in the field of conflict studies value orientations and identity constructions.

Azaria Mbatha
Article 12: "Citizenship", 328x480,
In: Images for Human Rights Portfolio
© Artists for Human Rights Trust

7. Prospects

Visions and value discourses for a unified, peaceful community mark the beginning of post-apartheid South Africa's challenging path towards a new, multicultural nation driven by dynamic change.

At the end of this study, no more than humble prospects can be offered, based on the surveyed, analyzed and interpreted data of individual, everyday conflicts of people of different socio-cultural origin in Cape Town .

Remarkable is the unexpected high number of portrayed conflicts caused by self- and other-images, which went initially unnoticed in the data material. These constructs strongly effect perceptions, potential expressions, and interpretations of everyday situations and thus the conflict experience.

Striking is also is the thinking in "racial" categories reflected in the conflict narratives and the accompanying feelings of inferiority/superiority, which are to be interpreted as consequences of "inner apartheid" and intra- psychological identity conflicts. Here lies an interesting starting-point for subsequent studies: they would address identity constructions in the context of conflict experiences. Given the results of this study, special attention should be given to the identity conflicts of Coloured men and women in post-apartheid South Africa since they play an important role in the national construction. A suitable focal point of the research should be the investigation of value concepts of individual identity and intra-personal identity management. Starting with questions of individual identity, a connection to inter-personal relationship management should be made.

While in today's South Africa structures of "external apartheid" are being actively reformulated and are changing rapidly, it is necessary for the intra-psychological thinking structures and value orientations on the interpersonal level be re-constructed as well in order to overcome categorical, societal assignments from the past. This study wants to be a catalyst in this change by exposing different reality constructions of individuals as members if certain socio-cultural groups and their effects on experiences of daily conflict. The goal is to initiate a change of perspectives, as well as unmask prejudiced self-and other-images.

The presented data material, which has been evaluated from the perspective of an "outsider," offers an expanded view on individual experiences of this multicultural society. Hopefully, this invites the "insiders" to appreciate the vast possibilities of different reality constructs.

The results of this study are intended to stimulate discussions about methods of intercultural conflict management and training and encourage decisions on focal points in the intercultural processing of the past. Hopefully, the results can also impact the implementation of conflict-management programs in active NGO's and churches locally by motivating multiplicators in social work and churches to reflect on their daily work from a new perspective. Also, the results should motivate mediators, arbitrators and conflict managers to question the acquired cultural and emotional schemes of the conflicting parties and to clarify the existing value constellations in their practical conflict work. Accordingly, theoretical and practical areas of application are introduced in the following in order to develop systemic-perspective approaches in the dialogue between the presented results and the interested reader.

Churches and religion as spaces and phenomena of spiritual encounter will continue to play an important role in South Africa's national dialogue and at the grassroots. They function as platforms of non-violent communication for cross-cultural, meta-communicative processes and conflict resolutions. Here people can develop their individual personality in a safe environment, can contemplate their own identity and address their traumatic conflict experiences. Based on inter-human trust and faith in God, healing processes can be implemented, traumas and dreams processed, and training processes initiated.

The purposeful planning of intercultural training and conflict management programs in South Africa should come up with focal themes for each target group and devise corresponding culture-specific elements of training and conflict management. In a culture-appropriate way, they need to encourage self- and other-reflections and deal with aspects of multicultural realities.

In this context it is important to emphasize and deal with - through self-reflection - culture-specific, political, religious and/or class-specific identity elements. Through personality work around one's own identity and constructed self-images, the ties between rather negatively oriented self-image aspects and, e.g., inferiority thinking, can be positively re-formulated. At the same time, the reflection of narrated conflict experiences should break up the often stereotypical other-images. Here it might be helpful to start with language, looking at the verbal choices of names for one's own group and other groups with respect to descriptive, judgmental and interpretive statements. This break- down of verbal categorizations creates an awareness of the connection between one's own perceptions and the experienced, narrated situation, on one hand, and general assumptions of judgmental and interpretive character, on the other hand.

Next to the methods of self-and other-reflection, innovative training methods, such as "Culture-Assimilators", "Critical Incident-Techniques", "Case-Methods" (multi-perspective cases, open-case studies) and/or role plays and simulations should be utilized. Especially helpful is here the method of "culture-assimilation" in sensitizing trainees for culture-specific value-orientations and behaviors by illustrating concrete cases: The participants of different cultural groups read a concrete case description that ends with a question and is followed by alternative responses. Then they decide on one of the alternative answers and subsequently read several explanations for each answer. With this cognitive-interactive method culture-specific knowledge is passed on to the participants. The reading activity of the casework is followed by a series of discussions on these cases and their alternative responses and explanations from different cultural perspectives. The goal is to bring out the cultural commonalities and differences and to get a grasp on the value orientations behind the (conflict)-cases.

Beyond the cognitive and knowledge-oriented contents, it is important to look at the affective side of behavior- and action-oriented attitudes. This happens mostly through role-plays and simulation exercises that highlight the emotional behavior. Problematic experiences can then be processed in a safe, confidential environment. This should stimulate new interest in pursuing an authentic, intercultural dialogue even in everyday life.

The conflicts of values, structures, situations and relationships contained in the data material of this study can be viewed in the setting of inter-cultural mediation workshops. In grappling with the narrated conflict situations an emphasis should be placed on "non-violent communication," according to Marshall Rosenberg, and on uncovering the culture- and personality-related needs and feelings of the conflict parties. This procedure could be the first step in the de-escalation of conflict situations in that the participants gain new information about members of the involved groups. A successful outcome would be an empathetic behavior in (intercultural) conversations and relationships. The goal of "intercultural mediation" then is cooperative problem solving of the conflict partners. The broadened perspectives and cultural schemes gained through the training can make it possible to find "win-win"- solutions for the concrete conflict situation.

These new training possibilities could further soften identity definitions and their traditional rigid boundaries. Hence, the data of this study should support conflict trainers to effectively contribute to the process of reconciliation in the South African nation.

Bibliography

Agar, M.H. (1973):

Ripping and Running. A Formal Ethnography of Urban Heroin Addicts. Department of Anthropology, Hawaii. Seminar Press, New York.

Agar, M.H. (1980):

The Professional Stranger. An Informal Introduction to Ethnography. University of Houston, Texas. Academic Press, New York.

Agar, M.H. (1986):

Speaking of Ethnography. Qualitative Research Methods, Series 2. Sage Publications, London.

Aijmer, G. & Abbink, J. (2001):

Meanings of Violence. A Cross Cultural Perspective. Oxford.

Allport, G. (1954):

The Nature of Prejudice. Macmillian, New York.

Alsop, C.K. (2002):

Home and Away: Self-Reflexive Auto-/Ethnography. Forum Qualitative Sozialforschung. Online Journal, 3 (3). In: http://www.qualitative-research.net/fqs/fqs-eng.htm, December 2003.

Anderson, B. (1998):

Die Erfindung der Nation. Zur Karriere eines erfolgreichen Konzepts. Propyläen Taschenbuch. Aus dem Englischen "Imagined Communities" von Benedikt Burkhars und Christoph Münz. Erweiterete Ausgabe. Berlin: Ullstein.

Apple, M.W. (1993):

Series Editor's Introduction to Race, Identity, and Representation in Education. In: McCathy, C. & Crichlow, W. (eds.): Race, Identity, and Representation in Education. Routledge, New York, S. vii-ix.

Ashton, H. (1952):

The Basuto. International African Institute. Oxford University Press, London.

Atteslander, P. (1975):

Methoden der empirischen Sozialforschung. De Gruyter, Berlin.

Augsburger, D.W. (1992):

Conflict Mediation between Cultures. Pathways and Patterns. Westminster, John Knox Press, Louisville, Kentucky.

Avruch, K. (1998):

Culture and Conflict Resolution. United States Institute of Peace Press, Washington, D.C.

Balibar, E. (1990):

Paradoxes and Universality. In: Goldberg, D. T. (1990): Anatomy of Racism. University of Minnesota Press, Minneapolis, Oxford, S. 284ff.

Baumann, G. (1999):

The Multicultural Riddle. Rethinking National, Ethnic, and Religious Identities. Routledge, New York.

Bekker, S. (1993):

Ethnicity in Focus. The South African Case. Indicator South Africa. Center of Social and Development Studies at the University of Natal.

Bekker, S. et al (2000):

The Emergence of New Identities in the Western Cape. In: Politikon, (2000), 27(2), S. 221-237.

Berger, P.L. / Luckmann, T. (2000):

Die gesellschaftliche Konstruktion der Wirklichkeit. Eine Theorie der Wissenssoziologie. 17. Auflage. Fischer Verlag, Frankfurt a.M..

Berger, P.L. & Neuhaus, R. (1996):

To Empower People. The Role of Mediating Structures in Public Policy. American Enterprise Institute for Public Policy Research, Washington.

Bergmann, J.R. (2000):

Ethnomethodologie. In: Flick, U., v. Kardoff, E. und Steinke, I. (Hg.)(2000): Qualitative Forschung. Ein Handbuch. Rowohlts Enzyklopädie, Hamburg, S.118-135.

Besemer, C. (1995):

Mediation. Vermittlung in Konflikten. Stiftung Gewaltfreies Leben. Werkstatt für Gewaltfreie Aktion, Baden. Sechste Auflage.

Biko, S. (1984):

Some African Cultural Concepts. In: Coetzee, P.H. & Roux, A.P.J. (Hrsg.) (1998): Philosophy from Africa. A Text with Readings. International Thompson Publishing LTD, Johannesburg, S. 26-30.

Biko, S. (1984a):

The Definition of Black Consciousness. In: Coetzee, P.H. & Roux, A.P.J. (Hrsg.) (1998): Philosophy from Africa. A Text with Readings. International Thompson Publishing LTD, Johannesburg, S. 360-363.

Biko, S. (1987):

Steve Biko 1946-1977. I write what I like. A Selection of his Writings. Heinemann.

Bodley, J.H. (1983):

Der Weg der Zerstörung. Stammesvölker und die industrielle Revolution. München.

Bonacker, T. & Imbusch P. (1996):

Begriffe der Friedens- und Konfliktforschung: Konflikt, Gewalt, Krieg, Frieden. In: Imbusch, P. & Zoll, R. (Hrsg.)(1999): Friedens- und Konfliktforschung. Eine Einführung mit Quellen. 2. Auflage. Leske & Budrich, Opladen, S. 73-116.

Bond, M. (1998):

Social Psychology across Cultures. Prentice Hall Europe, Leicester.

Bourdieu, P. (1982):

Die feinen Unterschiede. Kritik der Gesellschaftlichen Urteilskraft, Frankfurt a.M..

Bourdieu, P. (1992):

Rede und Antwort. Suhrkamp Verlag, Frankfurt a. M..

Breutz, P.-L. (1975):

Die Südost-Bantu. In: Baumann, H. (Hrsg.)(1975): Die Völker Afrikas und ihre traditionellen Kulturen. Teil 1. Allgemeiner Teil und Südliches Afrika. Franz Steiner Verlag Gmbh, Wiesbaden, S. 409-455.

Broodryk, J. (1997a):

Ubuntu Management and Motivation. Johannesburg. Gauteng Department of Welfare Pretoria. Ubuntu School of Philosophy.

Broodryk, J. (1997b):

Ubuntu as a doctrine for the ordering of society. Unpublished doctoral dissertation. UNISA; Pretoria, South Africa.

Bryce, J. (1900):

Bilder aus Süd-Afrika. Verlag der Gebrüder Jänecke, Hannover.

Bude, H. (2000):

Die Kunst der Interpretation. In: Flick, U., v. Kardoff, E. und Steinke, I. (Hg.)(2000): Qualitative Forschung. Ein Handbuch. Rowohlts Enzyklopädie, Hamburg, S. 569-578.

Chanzan, N. et al (1999):

Politics and Society in Contemporary Africa. 3rd Edition. London.

Chidester, D. (1987):

Religious Studies as Political Practice. In: Journal of Theology for Southern Africa, 58, S. 4-17.

Chidester, D. (1992):

Religions of South Africa. Routledge, London and New York.

Chidester, D. (2000):

Mapping the Sacred in the Mother City. Religion and Urban Space in Cape Town, South Africa. In: Journal for the Study of Religion in Southern Africa, 13, 1 & 2, S. 5-41.

Coetzee, P.H. (1998):

Particularity in Morality and its Reaction to Community. In: Coetzee, P.H. & Roux, A.P.J. (Hrsg.) (1998): Philosophy from Africa. A Text with Readings. International Thompson Publ. LTD, Johannesburg, S. 275-291.

Coetzee, P.H. (Hrsg.)(1998):

Philosophy from Africa. A Text with Readings. International Thompson Publishing LTD, Johannesburg.

Eygelaar, C.S. (1998):

Food for Thought: Ubuntu-Sharing African Values. In: Milmed, September/October 1998, S. 4.

Comaroff, J.L. & Roberts, S. (1983):

Rules and Processes. The Cultural Logic of Dispute in an African Context. Chicago Press, London.

Comaroff, J. & Comaroff, J.L. (1993):

Introduction. In: Modernity and its Malcontents. Ritual and Power in Postcolonial Africa, S. xi-xxxvii. University of Chicago Press, Chicago.

Comaroff, J. & Stern, P. (1995):

Perspectives on Nationalism and War. Amsterdam.

Comaroff, J. & Comaroff, J.L. (1999):

"Occult economies and the violence of abstraction: notes from the South African postcolony."
In: American Ethnologist 26; S. 279-303.

Comaroff, J. & Comaroff, J.L. (2000):

Introduction. In: Comaroff, J. & Comaroff, J.L. (eds.) (2000): Civil Society and the Political
Imagination in Africa. Critical Perspectives, S.1-43.

Coulon, A. (1995):

Ethnomethodology. Qualitative Research Methods, Volume 36. University of Paris VIII. Sage
Publications. Thousand Oaks, London.

Craw, P. (1994):

Identity: Cultural, Transcultural, and Multicultural. In: Goldberg, D.T. (Hg.) (1994): Multiculturalism.
A Critical Reader. Cambridge, Blackwell. S. 371-387.

Dadder, R. (1987):

Interkulturelle Orientierung: Analyse ausgewählter interkultureller Orientierungsprogramme.
Saarbrücken.

Daily, J. (1991):

The Effects of Anger on Negotiations over Mengers and Aquisitions. In: Negotiation Journal, 1991,
7(1), S.31-29.

Darmstädter, T. & Mey, G. (1997):

Lieber nicht glücklich? Alternative Lesearten in der identitätstheoretischen Diskussion.
Forschungsbericht aus der Abteilung Psychologie im Institut für Sozialwissenschaften der Technischen
Universität Berlin, Nr. 97-2.

De Gruchy, J. (1995):

Christianity and Democracy. David Philip, Cape Town.

Delius, P. (1997):

A Lion Amongst the Cattle: Reconstruction and Resistance in Northern Transvaal. James Currey, Oxford.

Denzin, N.K. (1989):

Interpretive Interactionism. Sage Publications, Newbury Park.

Denzin, N.K. (2000):

Symbolischer Interaktionismus. In: Flick, U., v. Kardoff, E. und Steinke, I. (Hg.)(2000): Qualitative Forschung. Ein Handbuch. Rowohlts Enzyklopädie, Hamburg, S.118-135.

Department of Foreign Affairs (2001):

Department of Foreign Affairs, South Africa. Vision, Mission, Values. In: http://www.dfa.gov.za, Dec. 2003.

Devine, P. (1989):

Stereotypes and Prejudice. In: Journal of Personality and Social Psychology, 56, S. 5-18.

Duden (1990):

Das Fremdwörterbuch. 5., neu bearbeitete und erweiterte Auflage. Duden, Band 5. Dudenverlag, Mannheim.

Du Toit, F. (2001):

Proud to be White, Free to be African. In: Institute for Justice and Reconciliation, 9.7.2001, http://www.ijr.org.za/art_pgs/art22.html

Du Toit, F. (2002):

Distrust and fear stand in the way of reconciliation - report. In: Institute for Justice and Reconciliation, 12 August 2002, http://www.ijr.org.za/art_pgs/art43.html

Dzobo, N.K. (1975):

Values in Indigenous African Education. In: Brown, G.N. & Hiskett, M. (1975): Conflict and Harmony in Education in Tropical Africa. Allen and Unwin LTD, London, S. 76-90.

Ebr-Vally, R. (2001):

Diversity in the imagined *Umma*. In: Zegeye, A. (Hrsg..): Social Identities in the New South Africa. After Apartheid. Volume One. Social Identities South Africa Series, S. 269-300.

Efran, J., Lukens, M., Lukens, R. (1992):

Sprache, Struktur und Wandel. Dortmund.

Eibl-Eibesfeld, I. & Salter,F. G. (2000):

Intradoctrinability. Warefare and Ideology. Evolutionary Perspectives. Oxford, New York.

Eibl-Eibesfeld, I. & Salter,F. G. (2001):

Ethnic conflict and Indoctrination. Altruism and Identity in Evolutionary Perspectives. New York.

Ellis, C. & Bochner, A.P. (2000):

Autobiography, personal narrative, reflexivity: researcher as subject. In: Denzin, N.K. & Lincoln, Y.S. (Eds.): Handbook of Qualititiva Research. (2. Edition). Sage, Thousand Oaks, S. 733-768.

Ephirim-Donkor, A. (1997):

African Spirituality: on Becoming Ancestors. Trenton, N.J., Africa World P.: 1997.

Erasmus, Z. (2001):

Re-imagining coloured identities in post-Apartheid South Africa. In: Erasmus, Z. (Hrsg.)(2001): Coloured by History, Shaped by Place. New Perspectives on Coloured Identities in Cape Town. Social Identities South Africa Series. Kwela Books and SA History Online, Cape Town, S.13-28.

Erikson, E.H. (1953):

Wachstum und Krisen der gesunden Persönlichkeit. Klett Verlag, Stuttgart. (Beiheft zur Psyche, original 1950).

Fadiman, J. A. (1981):

An Oral History of Warfare. The Meru of Mt. Kenia. Akron.

Fisch, J. (1991):

Geschichte Südafrikas. München.

Fischer, H. (1992):

Feldforschung. In: Fischer, H. (Hg.)(1992): Ethnologie. Einführung und Überblick. Dritte Auflage.
Dietrich Reimar Verlag, Berlin, S. 79-99.

Ferguson, R.B. (1984):

Warefare, Culture & Environment. Studies in Anthropology. Orlando/Florida.

Fisher, G. (1998):

The Mindsets Factor in Ethnic Conflict. A Cross-Cultural Agenda. Intercultural Press, Yarmouth.

Flick, U. (2000):

Design und Prozeß Qualitativer Forschung. In: Flick, U., v. Kardoff, E. und Steinke, I. (Hg.) (2000):
Qualitative Forschung. Ein Handbuch. Rowohlts Enzyklopädie, Hamburg, S.13-29.

Flick, U., v. Kardoff, E. und Steinke, I. (Hg.)(2000):

Was ist Qualitative Forschung? Einleitung und Überblick. In: Flick, U., v. Kardoff, E. und Steinke, I.
(Hg.)(2000): Qualitative Forschung. Ein Handbuch. Rowohlts Enzyklopädie, Hamburg, S.13-29.

Flöel, C. & Haferburg, C. (2002):

Spatial Patterns of Religions in Greater Cape Town. In: Mitchell, G. & Mullen, E. (Ed.)(2002):
Religion and the Political Imagination in a Changing South Africa. Waxmann, New York, S. 207-220.

Flohr, A.K. (1994):

Fremdenfeindlichkeit. Biosoziale Grundlagen von Ethnozentrismus. Beiträge zur
sozialwissenschaftlichen Forschung, Band 124. Westdeutscher Verlag, Opladen.

Franchi, V. (2003):

Across or beyond the racialized divide? Current perspectives on "race", racism and "intercaultural"
relations in "post-apartheid" South Africa. In: Journal of Intercultural Relations, 27 (2003), S. 125-133.

Franchi, V. (2003a):

The racialization of affirmative action in organisation discourses: A case study of symbolic racism in post-apartheid South Africa. In: Journal of Intercultural Relations, 27 (2003), S. 157-188.

Franchi, V. & Swart, T.M. (2003):

From Apartheid to Affirmative Action: the use of "racial" markers in past, present and future articulations of identity among South African students. In: Journal of Intercultural Relations, 27 (2003), S. 209-237.

Frescura, F. (2001):

The Spatial Geography of Urban Apartheid. In: Zegeye, A. (Hrsg..): Social Identities in the New South Africa. After Apartheid. Volume One. Social Identities, South Africa Series, S. 99-126.

Friedrichs, J. (1990):

Methoden empirischer Sozialforschung. 14. Auflage, Westdeutscher Verlag, Obladen.

Fuchs, P. (1992):

Die Erreichbarkeit der Gesellschaft. Zur Konstruktion und Imagination gesellschaftlicher Einheit. Suhrkamp, Frankfurt a.M.

Furley, O. (Hg.)(1995):

Conflict in Africa. Tauris Academic Studies. I.B. Tauris Publishers, London, New York

Galtung, J. (1996):

Cultural peace: some characteristics. In: Unesco Publishing (Hg.): From a culture of violence to a culture of peace. Peace and conflict issues. Paris.

Gbadegesin, S. (1991):

Individuality, community, and the moral order. In: Coetzee, P.H. & Roux, A.P.J. (Hrsg.) (1998): Philosophy from Africa. A Text with Readings. International Thompson Publishing LTD, Johannesburg, S. 292-305.

Geertz, C. (1973):

Thick Description. Toward an Interpretative Theory of Culture. In: Geertz, C.: The Interpretation of Cultures. New York.

Geertz, C. (1979):

Deep Play. Notes on the Balinese Cockfight. In: Rabbinow & Sulivan: Interpretative Social Sciences. Berkley University Press.

Geertz, C (1987):

Dichte Beschreibung. Beiträge zum Verstehen kultureller Systeme. Suhrkamp, Frankfurt.

Gelfand, M. (1962):

Shona Religion. Juta & Co. Ltd., Wynberg, South Africa.

Geschiere, P. (1997):

The Modernity of Witchcraft: politics and the occult in postcolonial Africa. University Press of Virginia. Charlottesville, VA and London.

Glasl, F. (1990):

Konfliktmanagement. Verlag Paul Haupt, Bern/Stuttgart.

Glasl, F. (1997):

Konfliktmanagement. Ein Handbuch für Führungskräfte, Beraterinnen und Berater. 6. Auflage. Verlag Freies Geistesleben, Stuttgart.

Glasl, F. (2000):

Selbsthilfe in Konflikten. Konzepte, Übungen, Praktische Methoden. 2. Auflage. Verlag Freies Geistesleben, Stuttgart.

Gluckman, M. (1959):

Custom and Conflict in Africa. Basil Blackwell Oxford.

Gluckman, M. (1975):

Anthropology and Apartheid: The Work of South African Anthropologists. In: Meyer Fortes and Patterson (Hrsg): Studies in African Social Anthropology. Academic Press, London, S. 21-39.

Goldberg, D.T. (Hg.) (1994):

Introduction: Multicultural Conditions. In: Goldberg, D:T: (Hg.): Multiculturalism. A Critical Reader. Cambridge, Blackwell.

Goldin, I. (1983):

Coloured Identity and Coloured Politics in the Western Cape Region of South Africa. In: Vail, L. (Hrsg)(1983): The Creation of Tribalism in Southern Africa. University of California Press, Berkeley.

Goldin, I. (1987):

Making Race: the Politics and Economics of Coloured Identity in South Africa. Maskew Miller Longman, CT.

Grunebaum, H. & Robins, S. (2001):

Crossing the Colour(ed) Line: mediating the ambiguity of belonging and identity. In: Erasmus, Z. (Hrsg.)(2001): Coloured by History, Shaped by Place. New Perspectives on Coloured Identities in Cape Town. Social Identities South Africa Series. Kwela Books and SA History Online, Cape Town, S. 159-172.

Gudykunst, W. B. (Hg.)(1985):

Communication, Culture and Organisational Processes. Sage Publications, California.

Gudykunst, W.B. (1991):

Bridging Differences. Effective Intergroup Communication. Sage, Newbury Park.

Habermas, J. (1981):

Theorie des Kommunikativen Handelns. Band 1 und Band 2. Frankfurt/Main.

Habermas, J. (1984):

Vorstudien und Ergänzungen zur Theorie des kommunikativen Handelns. Frankfurt/Main.

Heitmeyer, W. (1997):

Einleitung: Sind individualisierte und ethnisch-kulturell vielfältige Gesellschaften noch integrierbar? In: Heitmeyer, W. (Hg.)(1997): Was hält die Gesellschaft zusammen? Frankfurt/Main.

Hemshorn de Sánchez, B. (2002):

Violence, Trauma and Ways of Healing in the Context of Transformative South Africa: A Gender Perspective on the Dynamic and Integrative Potentials of "Healing" in African Religion. In: Mitchell, G. & Mullen, E. (Ed.) (2002): Religion and the Political Imagination in a Changing South Africa. Waxmann, New York, S. 35-57.

Hermanns, H. (2000):

Interviewen als Tätigkeit. In: Flick, U., v. Kardoff, E. und Steinke, I. (Hg.)(2000): Qualitative Forschung. Ein Handbuch. Rowohlts Enzyklopädie, Hamburg, S.360-368.

Heuser, A. (2002):

Experiments in an Independent African Satyagraha: Gandhi, Shembe and the Roots of Passive Resistance in South Africa. In: Mitchell, G. & Mullen, E. (Ed.)(2002): Religion and the Political Imagination in a Changing South Africa. Waxmann, New York, S. 73-88.

Hirschberg, W. (1975):

Khoisan sprechende Völker Südafrikas. In: Baumann, H. (Hrsg.)(1975): Die Völker Afrikas und ihre traditionellen Kulturen. Teil 1. Allgemeiner Teil und Südliches Afrika. Franz Steiner, Wiesbaden, S. 383-408.

Honneth, A. (1994):

Kampf um Anerkennung. Zur moralischen Grammatik sozialer Konflikte. Frankfurt/Main.

Hornby, A.S. (1974):

Oxford Advanced Learner's Dictionary of Current English. New Edition. Oxford.

Horowitz, D. (2000):

Ethnic Groups in Conflict. Revised Version. Berkley.

Huber, O. (1995):

Beobachtung. In: Roth, E. (1995): Sozialwissenschaftliche Methoden. Lehr- und Handbuch für Forschung und Praxis. 4., durchgesehene Auflage. R. Oldenbourg Verlag München, S. 126-145.

Huntington, S.P. (1991):

The Third Wave. Democratisation in the Late Twentieth Century. Norman, London: Uni. of Oklahoma Press.

Huntington, S.P. (1997):

The Clash of Civilisations and the Remaking of World Order. Touchstone, New York.

Jeppie, S. (2001):

Re-classifications: Coloured, Malay, Muslim. In: Erasmus, Z. (Hrsg.)(2001): Coloured by History, Shaped by Place. New Perspectives on Coloured Identities in Cape Town. Social Identities South Africa Series. Kwela Books and SA History Online, Cape Town, S.80-96.

Johns, L. (2004):

Bosses Distorting Affirmative Action Act - Manuel. In: Cape Argus, Wednesday, April 7, 2004.

Johnson, A. (1995):

Conflict in South Africa. In: Furley, O. (Edt.) (1995): Conflict in Africa. Tauris Academic Studies. Tauris Publishers, London, New York, S. 46-71.

Johnson, J.C. (1990):

Selecting Ethnographic Informants. Qualitative Research Methods, Vol. 22. Sage, California.

Kerlinger, F.N. (1994):

Foundations of Behavioral Research. Educational and Psychological Inquiry. New York University. Holt, Rinehart and Winston, Inc.

Keupp, H. (1988):

Auf dem Weg zur Patchwork-Identität. Verhaltenstherapie & Psychosoziale Praxis. Mitteilungen der dgvt 4/88, S. 425-438.

Keupp, H. (1994):

Ambivalenzen postmoderner Identität. In: Ulrich Beck & Elisabeth Beck-Gersheim (Hrsg.): Riskante Freiheiten. Individualisierung in modernen Gesellschaften. Suhrkamp, Frankfurt a.M., S. 336-350.

Keupp, H. (1997):

Von der (Un-)Möglichkeit erwachsen zu werden - Jugend zwischen Multioptionalität und Identitätsdiffusion. Gemeindepsychologie-Rundbrief Nr. 1/97, S. 10-15.

Kirk, J. & Miller, M.L. (1980):

Reliability and Validity in Qualitative Research. Towards Theoretical Validity. In: Qualitative Research Methods, Fourth Edition, Series 1.

Körner, P. (2002):

The St. John's Apostolic Faith Mission and Politics: the Political Dimension of an Apostolic Indipendent Church. In: Mitchell, G. & Mullen, E. (eds.) (2002): Religion and the Political Imagination in a changing South Africa, Waxmann, New York, S. 133-151.

Kohler Riessman, C. (1993):

Narrative Analysis. In: Qualitative Research Methods, Volume 30. Sage Publications, California.

Kohnert, D. (2002):

Occult beliefs, globalization and the quest for development in African societies: the example of South Africa. In: Mitchell, G. & Mullen, E. (Ed.)(2002): Religion and the Political Imagination in a Changing South Africa. Waxmann, New York, S. 169-188.

Kohnert, D. (2003):

Witchcraft and transnational social spaces: witchcraft violence, reconciliation and development in South Africa's transition process. In: Journal of Modern African Studies, 41, 2 (2003), S. 1-29. Cambridge University Press

Kotzé, H.J. (1993):

Overlapping values of the South African elite: applying an adapted Wilson-Pattern C-Scale. In: South African Journal of Sociology, 1993, 24 (1).

Kotzé, H.J. (1997):

Culture, Ethnicity and Religion: South African Perceptions of Social Identity. In: Konrad-Adenauer-Stiftung (Hrsg.): Occasional Papers April 1997, Johannesburg.

Kowal, S. & O'Connell, D.C. (2000):

Zur Transkription von Gesprächen. In: Flick, U., v. Kardoff, E. und Steinke, I. (Hg.)(2000): Qualitative Forschung. Ein Handbuch. Rowohlts Enzyklopädie, Hamburg, S.437-447.

Kraus, W. (1996):

Das erzählte Selbst. Die narrative Konstruktion von Identität in der Spätmoderne. Centaurius, Pfaffenweiler.

Kroeber, A. & Kluckhohn, C. (1952):

Culture. A Critical Review of Concepts and Definitions. Cambridge, Mass.

Kromrey, H. (1998):

Empirische Sozialforschung. 8. Auflage. UTB, Leske und Budrich, Opladen.

Kuhn, H. (1999):

Konflikte systemisch und dynamisch lösen. In: Blätter der Wohlfahrtspflege, Stuttgart 146 (1999) 3/4, S. 55-57.

Kuper, L. (1981):

Genocide. Its political Use in the Twentieth Century. Harmondsworth.

Kuperus, T. (1999):

State, Civil Society and Apartheid in South Africa. An Examination of Dutch Reformed Church-State Relations. Macmillian, London.

Layes, G. (2003):

Interkulturelles Identitätsmanagement. In: Thomas, A., Kinast, E.-U., Schroll-Machl (2003): Handbuch interkultureller Kommunikation und Kooperation. Band 1: Grundlagen und Praxisfelder. V & R, Göttingen.

Lederach, J.P. (1988):

Of Nets, Nails and Problems: A Folk Vision of Conflict in Central America. Ph.D. diss., University of Colorado.

Lederach, J.P. (1989):

Director's Circle. In: Conciliation Quarterly, 8:3, Summer 1998, S. 12-14.

Lederach, J.P. (1995):

Preparing for Peace: Conflict Transformation Across Cultures. Syracuse Uni. Press, New York.

Lederach, J.P. (1996):

Preparing for Peace. Conflict Transformation Across Cultures. Paperback Ed.. Syracuse Uni. Press, New York.

Lewontin, R.C., Rose, S. und Kamin, L.J. (1988):

Die Gene sind es nicht. Biologie, Ideologie und menschliche Natur. Psychologie-Verlagsunion, München-Weinheim, 1988.

Lombard, K. (2002):

South African Schools: is the Rainbow Nation being overrun by racial storms? In: Institute for Justice and Reconciliation, 2 October 2002, http://www.ijr.org.za/art_pgs/art45.html

Lorenz, K. (1993):

Das sogenannte Böse. Zur Naturgeschichte der Aggression. München.

Louw, D.J. (2003):

Philosophy in Africa. Ubuntu: An African Assessment of the Religious Other. University of the North. http://www.bu.edu/wcp/Papers/Afri/AfriLouw.htm, 11.10.2003.

Lüders, C. (2000):

Beobachten im Feld und Ethnographie. In: Flick, U., v. Kardoff, E. und Steinke, I. (Hg.)(2000): Qualitative Forschung. Ein Handbuch. Rowohlts Enzyklopädie, Hamburg, S. 384-401.

Luhmann, N. (1987):
Soziale Systeme. Grundriß einer Allgemeinen Theorie. Frankfurt/M.

Lyotard, J.-F. (1987):
Der Widerstreit. München

Makgoba, M.W. (ed.) (1999)
African Renaissance. The New Struggle. Sandton, Cape Town, Maube Tafelberg.

Makulele, T.S. (1998):
Black Theology and the Reconciliation Discourse - Prospects. In: Journal of Black Theology in South Africa 12/1, S. 37-58.

Magubane, P. (1998):
Vanishing Cultures of South Africa. Changing Customs in a Changing World. Struik Publishers LTD, Cape Town.

Malherbe, J.G. & Kaphagawani (1998):
African Epistemology. In: Coetzee, P.H. & Roux, A.P.J. (Hrsg.) (1998): Philosophy from Africa. A Text with Readings. International Thompson Publishing LTD, Johannesburg, S. 205-216.

Malkki, L. H. (1997):
Purity and Exile: Violence, Memory and National Cosmology among Hutu Refugees in Tanzania. Chicago.

Mandela, N. (1964):
"I am prepared to die." Nelson Mandela's statement from the dock at the opening of the defence case in the Rivonia Trial Pretoria Surpreme Court, 20 April 1964. In: http://www.anc.org.za/ancdocs/history/rivonia.htm, 29.02.02.

Mandela, N. (1990):
Speech on Release from Prison 1990. In: Modern History Sourcebook: http://www.Mandela/1990MANDELA.htm, 05.02.02.

Mandela, N. (1994):

The Long Walk to Freedom. The Autobiography of Nelson Mandela. Abacus. London.

Mandela, N. (1999):

Africa. Nelson Mandela's Speech, Wednesday, June 16, 1999. In:
http://news.bbc.co.uk/hi/english/world/africa/newsid_370000/370736.stm, 29.02.02.

Mandela, N. (2000):

Ideas. Mandela. In: Monitor, Thursday, February 10, 2000. In:
http://www.csmonitor.com/durable/2000/02/10/fp15sl-csm.shtml

Marais, H. (2000):

Limits to Change: The Political Economy of Transformation. University of Cape Town Press, Cape Town.

Maringer, E. & Steinweg, R. (1997):

Konstruktive Haltungen und Verhaltensweisen in institutionalisierten Konflikten. Erfahrungen, Begriffe, Fähigkeiten. Berghof-Report Nr. 3, Berlin. Berghof Forschungszentrum für konstruktive Konfliktbearbeitung.

Martin, D.-C. (2001):

What's in the name "coloured"? In: Zegeye, A. (Hrsg..): Social identities in the New South Africa. After Apartheid. Volume One. Social Identities South Africa Series, S. 249-268.

Maslow, A. H. (1999):

Motivation und Persönlichkeit. Rowohlt Taschenbuch Verlag, Hamburg.

Matt, E. (2000):

Darstellung qualitativer Forschung. In: Flick, U., v. Kardoff, E. und Steinke, I. (Hg.)(2000): Qualitative Forschung. Ein Handbuch. Rowohlts Enzyklopädie, Hamburg, S. 578-587.

Mayer, C.-H. (2001):
Werteorientierungen an Sekundarschulen in Tanzania vor dem Hintergrund interkultureller und inner-afrikanischer Wertediskussionen. Ibidem-Verlag, Stuttgart.

Mayer, C.-H., Boness, C. & Thomas, A. (2003):
Beruflich in Kenia und Tansania. Trainingsprogramm für Manager, Fach- und Führungskräfte. Reihe Handlungskompetenz im Ausland. Vandenhoeck & Ruprecht, Göttingen.

Mayer, C.-H., Boness, C. & Thomas, A. (2004):
Beruflich in Südafrika. Trainingsprogramm für Manager, Fach- und Führungskräfte. Reihe Handlungskompetenz im Ausland. Vandenhoeck & Ruprecht, Göttingen.

Mayer, C.-H., Boness, C. (2004):
Interkulturelle Mediation und Konfliktbearbeitung. Bausteine deutsch-afrikanischer Wirklichkeiten. Waxmann. Münster.

Mayer, P. (1971):
Of Townsmen and Tribesmen. Conservatism and the Process of Urbanization in a South African City. Second Edition, Oxford University Press, Cape Town.

Mbeki, T. (1996):
"I am an African." African National Congress by the Constitutional Assembly of "The Republik of the Constitution Bill 1996", Cape Town, 8. May 1996. In: Mbeki, T. (1999): Serving the People: Four Speeches on the African Renaissance, S. 3-9.

Mbeki, T. (1999):
Serving the People. Four Speeches on the African Renaissance. Hrsg.: Embassy of the Republic of South Africa, Vienna, Austria.

Mbeki, T. (1999a):
35th Ordinary Session of the OAU Assembly of Heads of State and Government, Algiers, Algeria: 13 July 1999. In: Mbeki, T. (1999): Serving the People. Four Speeches on the African Renaissance, S. 11-19.

Mbeki, T. (1999b):

Launch of the African Renaissance Institute, Pretoria, 11. October 1999. In: Mbeki, T. (1999): Serving the People. Four Speeches on the African Renaissance, S. 21-29.

Mbeki, T. (1999c):

Opening of the Commonwealth Heads of State and Government Meeting, Durban, 12. November 1999. In: Mbeki, T. (1999): Serving the People. Four Speeches on the African Renaissance, S. 31-34.

Mbeki, T. (2001):

Unity in Action for Change. By the President, Mr. Thabo Mbeki, State of the Nation Address, 9. February 2001. National Assembly, Cape Town.

Mbigi, I. (1995):

Ubuntu: A rainbow celebration of cultural diversity. Ubuntu School of Philosophy. Pretoria.

Mbiti, J.S. (1990):

Afrikanische Religion und Weltanschauung. Berlin.

McLaren, P. (1994):

White Terror and Oppositional Agency: Towards a Critical Multiculturalism. In: Goldberg, D. T. (Hg.)(1994): Multiculturalism. A Critical Reader.Blackwell, Oxford, Cambridge, S. 45-75.

Merkens, H. (2000):

Auswahlverfahren, Sampling, Fallkonstruktion. In: Flick, U., v. Kardoff, E. und Steinke, I. (Hg.)(2000): Qualitative Forschung. Ein Handbuch. Rowohlts Enzyklopädie, Hamburg, S. 286-299.

Metzler-Literatur-Lexikon (1990):

Begriffe und Definitionen. Hrsg.: von Günther, Schweikle, I. (1990). J. B. Metzlersche Verlagsbuchhandlung, Stuttgart, S. 103.

Michler, W. (1995):

Afrika - Wege in die Zukunft. Ein Kontinent zwischen Bürgerkriegen und Demokratisierung. Horlemann, Aachen.

Milger, P. (1987):

Die Kreuzzüge - Krieg im Namen Gottes. München.

Mitchell, G. (2001):

The Invention of the South African Rainbow Nation. An analysis of religion and the politics of identity in diversity training programmes during the nineties. In: Laehnemann, J.(ed.) (2001): Peace Education from Faith Traditions, WCRP Peace Education Standing Commission, S. 25-29.

Mitchell, G. (2002):

Laying Claim to the South African Miracle: A Study of the Place of Religion amongst Competing Theories of Change. In: Mitchell, G. & Mullen, E. (Ed.)(2002): Religion and the Political Imagination in a Changing South Africa. Waxmann, New York, S. 9-35.

Mitchell, G. & Mullen, E. (Ed.)(2002):

Religion and the Political Imagination in a Changing South Africa. Waxmann, New York.

Moore, C.W. (1996):

The Mediation Process. Practical Strategies for Resolving Conflict. Second Edition. Jossey-Bass Publishers, San Francisco.

More, M.P. (1998):

Outlawing Racism in Philosophy: On Race and Philosophy. In: Coetzee, P.H. & Roux, A.P.J. (Hrsg.) (1998): Philosophy from Africa. A Text with Readings. International Thompson Pub. LTD, Johannesburg, S. 364-373.

Munzinger Archiv (1994):

Republik Südafrika. Politik, Wirtschaft, Soziales. Munzinger Archiv. Ravensburg.

Myers, S: & Filner, B . & IDI (1994):

Mediation across Cultures. A Handbook about Conflict and Culture. San Diego Mediation Center, Amherst Educational Publishing, San Diego.

Naudascher-Schlag, K. & Schillinger, H.R. (1994):

Von der Rassentrennung zur Regenbogennation. In: Zugehör, R. (1994): Kap der besseren Hoffnung? Horlemann, Bad Honnef.

Ndaba, W.J. (1994):

Ubuntu in Comparison to Western Philosophies. Ubuntu School of Philosophy, Pretoria.

Nyerere, J.K. (1997):

Africa Today and Tomorrow. Tanzania Printers Limited, Dar-es-Salaam.

Oruka, H.O. (1998):

Sage Philosophy. In: Coetzee, P.H. & Roux, A.P.J. (Hrsg.) (1998): Philosophy from Africa. A Text with Readings. International Thompson Publishing LTD, Johannesburg, S. 99-108.

Orywal, E., Rao, A. & Bollig, M. (1996):

Krieg und Kampf. Die Gewalt in unseren Köpfen. Berlin.

Owomeyela, O. (1996):

The African Difference: Discourse on Africanity and the Relativity of Cultures. University of Witwatersrand Press, Johannesburg.

Patterson, S. (1975):

Some Speculations on the Status and Role of the Free People of Colour in the Western Cape. In: Meyer Fortes and Patterson (Hrsg): Studies in African Social Anthropology. Academic Press, London, S. 161-205.

Prätorius, R. (1985):
Konflikttheorie. In: Nohlen, D. & Schulze, R.-O. (Hrsg.) (1985): Politikwissenschaft. Theorien, Methoden, Begriffe. München.

Prinsloo, E.D. (1995):
Ubuntu from a Eurocentric and Afrocentric perspective and ist influence on leadership. Ubuntu School of Philosophy. Pretoria.

Prinsloo, E.D. (1997):
The Ubuntu Concept of Caring. Ubuntu School of Philosophy. Pretoria.

Prinsloo, E.D. (1998):
Ubuntu Culture and Participatory Management. In: Coetzee, P.H. & Roux, A.P.J. (Hrsg.) (1998): Philosophy from Africa. A Text with Readings. International Thompson Publishing LTD, Johannesburg, S. 41-51.

Raum, O.F. (1980):
Das Weltbild der Xhosa (Südafrika). In: Raunig, W. (Hrsg.)(1980): Schwarz-Afrikaner. Lebensraum und Weltbild. Pinguin-Verlag, Innsbruck, S. 202-218.

Reed-Danahay, D.E. (1997):
Introduction. In: Reed-Danahay, D.E. (1997)(Eds.): Auto-/Ethnography. Rewriting the Self and the Social. Berg, New York, S. 1-17.

Ricci, I. (1980):
Mom's House, Dad's House. Collier Books, New York.

Ricoeur, P. (1979):
Der Text als Modell: hermeneutisches Verstehen. In: Bühl, W.L. (1979): Hermeneutisches Verstehen, München, S. 253-283.

Rosenthal, G. & Fischer-Rosenthal, W. (2000):

Analyse narrativ-biographischer Interviews. In: Flick, U., v. Kardoff, E. und Steinke, I. (Hg.)(2000): Qualitative Forschung. Ein Handbuch. Rowohlts Enzyklopädie, Hamburg, S. 456-468.

Schapera, I. (1934):

The Old Bantu Culture. In: Schapera, I. (1934) (Hrsg.): Western Civilization and the Natives of South Africa. Studies in Culture Contact. Routledge, London, S. 3-36.

Schütz, F. (1983):

Biographieforschung und narratives Interview. Neue Praxis 13, S. 283-293.

Schwartz, S.H. (1994):

Are there Universal Aspects in the Structure and Content of Human Values? In: Mayton, Lodges ad al (1994): Human Values and Social Sciences. Journal of Social Issues, Vol 50, No. 4, Winter 1994, S. 19-45.

Schwartz, T. (1992):

"Anthropology and Psychology: An Unrequited Relationship." In: Schwartz, T. et al (1992): New Directions in Psychological Anthropology. Cambridge Uni. Press, S. 324.

Senghor, L.S. (1961):

Négritude and African Socialism. In: Coetzee, P.H., Roux, A.P.J. (Eds) (1998): Philosophy from Africa. A Text with Readings: International Thompson Publ. LTD, Joburg, S. 438-448.

Senghor, L.S. (1963):

Negritude and African Socialism. In: St. Anthony's Papers (15), 1963, S. 9-22.

Shezi, S. (1995):

South Africa: The Transition and the Management of Collapse. In: Zartmann, I.W. (Edt) (1995): Collapsed States. The Disintegration and Restoration of Legitimate Authority. Bolder, London.

Shutte, A. (1993):

Philosophy for Africa. Rondebosch, South Africa. UCT Press.

Simmel, G. (1992):

Der Streit. In: Soziologie. Untersuchung über die Formen der Vergesellschaftung. Gesamtausgabe Band 2. Frankfurt/M.

Sindane, J. (1994):

Ubuntu and Nation building. Ubuntu School of Philosophy, Pretoria.

Sitas, A. (1998):

South Africa in the 1990's. The Logic of Fragmentation and Reconstruction. Transformation 36, S. 37-50.

South African Constitution (1997):

Preamble. Document Status. 7, February 1997.

South African Institute of Race Relations (Hg.)(2001):

South Africa Survey 2000/2001. Johannesburg.

Spradley, J.P. (1979):

The Ethnographic Interview. Holt, Rinehart and Winston, Inc., New York.

Spiegel, A. und Boonzaier, E. (1988):

Promoting Tradition: Images of the South African Past. In: Boonzaier, E. und Sharp, J. (edt): South African Keywords: The Uses and Abuses of Political Concepts, Cape Town, S. 40-67.

Statistisches Bundesamt (Hrsg.) (1995):

Länderbericht Südafrika 1994. Metzler Poeschel. Wiesbaden.

Steinke, I. (2000):

Gütekriterien qualitativer Forschung. In: Flick, U., v. Kardoff, E. und Steinke, I. (Hg.)(2000): Qualitative Forschung. Ein Handbuch. Rowohlts Enzyklopädie, Hamburg, S. 319-331.

Stellrecht, I. (1993):

Interpretative Ethnologie: Eine Orientierung. In: Schweizer/Schweizer/Kokot (ed.): Handbuch der Ethnologie, S. 29-78. Berlin.

Stephen, W. G. (1985):

Intergroup relations. In: Lindzey, G. & Aronson, E. (eds.): handbook of Social Psychology. 3rd edition, Vol. 2. Random House, New York.

Stiehm, J. (1994):

Diversity's Diversity. In: Goldberg, D.T. (Hg.)(1995): Multiculturalism. A Critical Reader. Blackwell, Cambridge.

Südafrikanische Botschaft (1997):

Das ist Südafrika. Teil 1. Bonn, Wien, Bern.

Südafrikanische Botschaft (1998):

Das ist Südafrika. Teil 2. Bonn, Wien, Bern.

Südafrikanische Botschaft (1999):

Das ist Südafrika. Teil 3. Bonn, Wien, Bern.

Tajfel, H. (1982):

Gruppenkonflikt und Vorurteil. Entstehung und Funktion sozialer Stereotypen. Bern.

Teffo, L.J. (1994a):

The Concept of Ubuntu as a Cohesive Moral Value. Ubuntu School of Philosophy. Pretoria.

Teffo, L.J. (1994b):

Towards a Conceptualization of Ubuntu. Ubuntu School of Philosophy. Pretoria.

Teffo, L.J. (1997):

An African Renaissance - could it be realized? Woord & daad 37 (361).

Teffo, L.J. & Roux, A.P.J. (1998):

Metaphysical Thinking in Africa. In: Coetzee, P.H. & Roux, A.P.J. (Hrsg.) (1998): Philosophy from Africa. A Text with Readings. International Thompson Publishing LTD, Johannesburg, S. 134-148.

Tempels, P. (1959):

Bantu Philosophy. E.T., Paris.

Tesch, R. (1990):

Qualitative research: Analysis types and software tools. Falmer, London.

Thommen, B. (1985):

Alltagspsychologie von Lehrern über verhaltensauffällige Schüler. Dissertation. Huber Verlag, Bern.

Thomas, A. (1996):

Psychologie interkulturellen Handelns. Hogrefe. Göttingen.

Trotha, T. von (1998):

Zur Ethnologie des Krieges. In: Hahn, H.P. & Splitter, G. (Hg.): Afrika und die Globalisierung. S. 405-413. München.

Turner, T. (1994):

Anthropology and Multiculturalism: What is Anthropology that Anthropologists Should be Mindful of? In: Goldberg, D. T. (Hg.)(1994): Multiculturalism. A Critical Reader. Blackwell, Oxford, Cambridge.

Tutu, D. (1976):

Brief an Premierminister John Voster vom 6. Mai 1976. In: Tutu, D. (1984): Gott segne Afrika. Texte und Predigten des Friedensnobelpreisträgers. Rowohlt, Reinbek.

Tutu, D. (1985):

The Question of South Africa. In: African Report, 30 (Januar-Februar 1985), S. 50-52. Original ein Statement vor dem UN-Sicherheitsrat, 23. Oktober 1984.

Tutu, D: (1995):

The Rainbow People of God. The Making of a Peaceful Revolution. London, Bantam Books.

Tutu, D. (1998):

Interview mit Bischof Desmond Tutu beim Weltwirtschaftsgipfel in Davos (1998). In:
http://www.agora/davos/tutu2.htm, 05.02.02.

Ury, W.L. (2000):

The Third Side. Why we fight and how we can stop. Penguin Group, New York.

Van der Merwe, W. E. (1996):

Philosophy and the multi-cultural context of (post) apartheid South Africa. In: Ethical perspectives 3:2,
S: 1-15.

Van Niekerk, A. (1994):

Ubuntu and Religion. Ubuntu School of Philosophy. Pretoria.

Van Niekerk, M. (1991):

Understanding Trends in "African Thinking"- A Critical Discussion. In: Coetzee, P.H. & Roux, A.P.J.
(Hrsg.) (1998): Philosophy from Africa. A Text with Readings. Intern. Thompson Pub. LTD,
Johannesburg, S. 52-85.

Van Warmelo, N.J. (1937):

Grouping and Ethnic History. In: Schapera, I. (1937)(Hrsg.): Bantu-speaking Tribes of South Africa.
An Ethnographical Survey. Routledge and Sons, LTD, S. 43-66.

Van Warmelo, N.J. (1975):

The Classification of Cultural Groups. In: Hammond-Tooke, W.D. (1975) (Hrsg.): The Bantu-speaking
Peoples of Southern Africa. Routledge & Kegan Paul, London, S. 56-84.

Vogt, R.W. (1997):

Die Gewalt besiegen. Visionen und Strategien zur Friedensmodellierung, Konfliktregulierung und Gewaltreduzierung. In: Meyer, B. (1997): Formen der Konfliktregulierung. Eine Einführung mit Quellen. Leske & Budrich, Opladen, S. 124-133.

Von Sicard, S. (1989):

Muslims and Apartheid: The Theory and Practice of Muslim Resistance to Apartheid. In: Journal Institute of Muslim Minority Affairs, Vol. 10:1, January 1989, S. 199-222.

Watzlawick, P., Beavin, J.H., Jackson, D.D. (1985):

Menschliche Kommunikation. 7. Auflage, Bern.

Watzlawick, P. (2001a):

Selbsterfüllende Prophezeiungen. In: Watzlawick, P. (Hrsg.)(2001): Die erfundene Wirklichkeit. Wie wir wissen, was wir zu wissen glauben. Beiträge zum Konstruktivismus. 13. Aufl.. Piper, München. S. 91-110.

Watzlawick, P. (2001b):

Bausteine ideologischer "Wirklichkeiten." In: Watzlawick, P. (Hrsg.)(2001): Die erfundene Wirklichkeit. Wie wir wissen, was wir zu wissen glauben. Beiträge zum Konstruktivismus. 13. Aufl., Piper, München, S. 192-228.

Watzlawick, P. (2001c):

Die Fliege und das Fliegenglas. In: Watzlawick, P. (Hrsg.)(2001): Die erfundene Wirklichkeit. Wie wir wissen, was wir zu wissen glauben. Beiträge zum Konstruktivismus. 13. Auflage. Piper Verlag, München, S. 229-235.

Watzlawick, P. et al (2003):

Menschliche Kommunikation. Formen, Störungen, Paradoxien. 10, unveränderte Auflage. Hans Huber, Bern.

Werner, O. & Schöpfle, G.M. (1987):

Systematic Fieldwork. Volume 2. Sage Publications, California.

Western, J. (1981):

Outcast Cape Town. London.

Wilson, M. (1962)

The Coherence of Groups. Paper read at the Social Sciences Research Conference. University of Natal, Durban.

Wilson, M. und Mafuje, A. (1963):

Langa. A Study of Social Groups in an African Township. Cape Town.

Winkelkotte, A.-K. (1996):

Handlungsspielräume, Überlebensspielräume. Magisterarbeit, Institut für Ethnologie, Universität Göttingen.

Wolff, S. (2000):

Cliffort Geertz. In: Flick, U., v. Kardoff, E. und Steinke, I. (Hg.)(2000): Qualitative Forschung. Ein Handbuch. Rowohlts Enzyklopädie, Hamburg; S. 84-96.

Wolff, S. (2000a):

Wege ins Feld und ihre Varianten. In: Flick, U., v. Kardoff, E. und Steinke, I. (Hg.)(2000): Qualitative Forschung. Ein Handbuch. Rowohlts Enzyklopädie, Hamburg; S. 334-349.

Whorf, B.L. (1976):

Sprache, Denken, Wirklichkeit. Beiträge zur Metalinguistik und Sprachphilosophie. Reinbek.

Zartmann, I.W. (Edt)(1995):

Collapsed States. The Disintegration and Restoration of Legitimate Authority. Bolder, London.

Appendix

Index of Tables and Graphs

Tables

1: Phasen der Explorationsstudie.

2: Prozentualer Anteil der Bevölkerungsgruppen in Südafrika und im Western Cape.

3: Religionszugehörigkeiten in Südafrika.

In: South African Institute of Race Relations (2001): South Africa Survey 2000/2001, Johannesburg.

4: Social Identities.

Kotzé, H.J. (1997): Culture, Ethnicity and Religion: South African Perceptions of Social Identity.

In: Konrad-Adenauer-Stiftung (Hrsg.): Occasional Papers April 1997, Johannesburg.

5: Vital Forces.

Teffo, L.J. & Roux, A.P.J. (1998): Metaphysical Thinking in Africa. In: Coetzee, P.H. & Roux, A.P.J. (Hrsg.) (1998): Philosophy from Africa. A Text with Readings. International Thompson Publ. LTD, Johannesburg.

6: Kriterien der sozialen Realität

7: Inhaltliche Textkriterien

8: CAF und CSF

9: Kriterien der Interviewpartner

10: Durchgeführte Interviews

11: Anzahl teilnehmender Organisationen

12: Teilnehmende Stadtteile

13: Selbstbilder von Coloureds

14: Fremdbilder von Coloureds

15: Fremdbilder von Coloureds

16: Fremdbilder von Coloured Muslims

17: Selbstbilder von Whites

18: Fremdbilder von Whites

19: Fremdbilder von Whites

20:: Selbstbilder von Afrikaanern

21: Fremdbilder von Afrikaanern

22: Selbstbilder von Jews

23: Selbstbilder von Blacks

24: Fremdbilder von Blacks

26: Fremdbilder von Foreigners

27: Textauszüge zu Selbst- und Fremdbildern

Graphs

1: Südafrika

In: Südafrika Karte. In: http://www.onlineholidays.de/pages/karte/mapsudafrika.html, 2003.

2: Die Provinzen Südafrikas.

In: Die Provinzen Südafrikas. In: http://www.estate-center.com/immo/suedafrika/lagecape.htm, 2003.

3: Religionszugehörigkeit und Bevölkerungsgruppenzugehörigkeit.

In: Flöel, C. & Haferburg, C. (2002): Spatial Patterns of Religions in Greater Cape Town. In: Mitchell, G. & Mullen, E. (Ed.)(2002): Religion and the Political Imagination in a Changing South Africa. Waxmann, New York.

4: Ethnische Gruppen im Western Cape.

In: Hirschberg, W. (1975): Khoisan sprechende Völker Südafrikas. In: Baumann, H. (Hrsg.)(1975): Die Völker Afrikas und ihre traditionellen Kulturen. Teil 1. Allgemeiner Teil und Südliches Afrika. Franz Steiner Verlag, Wiesbaden.

5: Gesellschaftliche Hauptzweige nach Baumann.

Baumann, G. (1999): The Multicultural Riddle. Rethinking National, Ethnic, and Religious Identities. Routledge, New York, S. 50.

6: More: Rainbow Nation

7: Prinsloo: Ubuntu

8: Biko: Black Consciousness Movement

9: Mandela: A Peaceful Nation

10: Mbeki: African Renaissance

11: Tutu: Reconciliation

12: Coetzee: Social Theory

13: Teffo & Roux: Metaphysics

14: Stadtteile Kapstadts

In: Stadtteile Kapstadts. http://www.portfiliocollection.com, 2003

15: R13 Rainbownation

16: R1 Rainbownation

17: R16 Rainbownation

Index of Abbreviations

AIC	African Independent Churches
ATR	African Traditional Religion
a.m.	Above mentioned
CWD	Catholic Welfare and Development
Etc.	et cetera
ch.	Chapter
L.	Line
NGO	Non-Governmental-Organisation
NGK	Nederduitse Gereformeerde Kerk
RSA	Republic of South Africa
P.	Page
SACC	South Africa Council of Churches
Transl.	Translated by the translator
UCT	University of Cape Town
UWC	University of Western Cape
YMCA	Young Men Christian Association
vs.	Versus

Index of Interviews

Excerpt	Code of Interview
Rainbownation (Kap 5.4)	
R13	P29:37
R1	P22:30
R16	P39:48
R4	P19:27
R6	P11:17
R7	P5:11
R8	P18:26
Self- and Other Image (Kap. 5.5)	
C1	P36:45
C9	P25:33
C12	P2:52
CM3	P2:52
CM4	P9:14
W3	P7:13
W4	P8:15
W6	P2:52
W7	P16:24
W9	P5:11
WA1	P17:25
WA2	P19:27
WA4	P7:13
J1	P34:41
J2	P63:p4
B1	P41:50
B2	P28:36
B4	P30:38
B8	P32:3
B9	P7:13
B12	P8:15
F1	P1:22
F3	P28:36
Narratives (Kap. 5.6)	
CS1	P36:45
CS2	P2:52
CS3	P2:52
CS4	P25:33
CS5	P19:27
CS6	P19:27
Identity(Kap. 5.7)	
I1	P37:46
I2	P22:30
I3	P22:30

Nr.	Sex	Origin	Profession	Organisation	Community
P32:3	m.	White, English	Reverend	Methodist Church	Sea Point
P44:9	m.	White, English	Director & Programme Manager	Institut for Justice and Reconciliation	Rondebosch
P4:10	m.	White, English	Pastoral assistant	Anglican Church	Sea Point
P5:11	m.	Coloured	Priest	Catholic Church	City Bowl
P6:12	m. m.	White, English Black, Xhosa	Programme Manager Social worker	Catholic Welfare & Development	Elsies River
P7:13	m. w.	White, English White, English	Priest Lecturer	Full Gospel Church	Three Anchor Bay
P9:14	m.	White, English	Priest	Catholic Church	Kraaifontain
P8:15	m.	White, English	Priest	Catholic Church	Langa
P10:1 6	w.	Black, Xhosa	Domestic worker	Catholic Church	Langa
P11:1 7	m.	Black, Xhosa	Governm. Administrator	Catholic Church	Langa
P12:1 8	w. w.	Coloured Coloured	Domestic worker Domestic worker	Anglican Church	Sea Point
P13:1 9	w. m.	Coloured Coloured	Domestic worker Social worker	Catholic Welfare & Development	Elsies River
P14:2 0	m.	Coloured	Priest	Catholic Church	Belgravia
P3:21	m.	White, Afrikaans	Minister	Lutheran Church	City Bowl
P1:22	w.	White, Afrikaans	Secretary	Duch Reformed Church	Three Anchor Bay
P15:2 3	w.	White, English	Senior Lecturer	UWC	Bellville
P16:2 4	m.	Black , Xhosa	Coordinator	Catholic Church	Kayelitsha
P17:2 5	m.	Coloured	Priest	Anglican Church	Bo-kaap
P18:2 6	m.	Black, Tswana	Senior Lecturer	Lutheran Church	City Bowl
P19:2 7	m.	White, Afrikaans	Minister	Dutch Reformed Church	Three Anchor Bay
P20:2 8	w.	White, English	Teacher	United Congrega-tional Presbyterian Church	Rondebosch
P21:2 9	m.	White, English	Programme-Coordinator	Community Peace Programme	Observatory
P22:3 0	m.	Coloured	Priest	Anglican Rectory	Woodstock
P23:3 1	w.	Coloured	Nurse	Seven Day Adventists	Three Anchor Bay
P24:3	w.	Coloured	Domestic worker	YMCA	Observatory

2	w.	Coloured	Domestic worker		
	w.	White, English	Secretary		
	m.	White, English	Director		
P25:3 3	m.	White, English		Catholic Church	Sea Point
P26:3 4	m.	White, English	Coordinator	Quaker Peace Center	Mowbray
P27:3 5	m.	Coloured	Community worker	Quaker Peace Center	Mannenburg
P28:3 6	w.	Coloured	Field worker	United Congregational Presbyterian Church	Rondebosch
P29:3 7	m.	White, English	Director	UCT	Rondebosch
P30:3 8	w. m.	Coloured White, English	Domestic worker	Dutch Reformed Church	Three Anchor Bay
P31:3 9	m.	White, Afrikaans	Director	University of Stellenbosch	Stellenbosch
P33:4 0	w.	Coloured	Domestic worker	Durch Reformed Church	Three Anchor Bay
P34:4 1	w.	White, English	Educator	Jewish community	Sea Point
P35:4 3	m.	Coloured	Policy Programme	Center of Conflict Resolution	Rondebosch
P36:4 5	m.	Coloured	Musician	United Congregational Presbyterian Church	Rondebosch
P37:4 6	m.	White, English	Sociologist, Academic	Center for Spirituality	Hout Bay
P38:4 7	m.	Coloured	Consultant, Mediator	Mediation & Transformation Practise	Kuils River
P39:4 8	m.	Coloured	Trustee	Institut for Healing of Memories	Sybrand Park
P40:4 9	w.	Coloured	Librarian, senior position	Center for Spirituality	Claremont
P41:5 0	m.	Black, Xhosa	Social worker, NGO	Institut for Healing of Memories	Sybrand Park
P43:5 1	m.	White, English	Director	Interfaith Initiative	University Estate
P2:52	m.	Black, Shona	Interior Designer/ Enterprineur	End Time Message, Christian Fellowship	Kenilworth

ibidem-Verlag

Melchiorstr. 15

D-70439 Stuttgart

info@ibidem-verlag.de

www.ibidem-verlag.de
www.edition-noema.de
www.autorenbetreuung.de

www.ingramcontent.com/pod-product-compliance
Lightning Source LLC
Chambersburg PA
CBHW060134280326
41932CB00012B/1519